D0642364

Global Leadership

Global Leadership, Second Edition, provides an important overview of a key emerging area within business and management. It is essential reading for students of leadership, organizational theory, strategic management, human resource management, and for anyone working and managing in the global arena.

Mark E. Mendenhall holds the J. Burton Frierson Chair of Excellence in Business Leadership in the College of Business Administration at the University of Tennessee, Chattanooga.

Joyce S. Osland is the Lucas Endowed Professor of Global Leadership at San José State University's College of Business in San José, California (Silicon Valley).

Allan Bird is Darla and Frederick Brodsky Trustee Professor in Global Business, Northeastern University, and Visiting Professor, Rikkyo University.

Gary R. Oddou is a professor of international management and directs the Global Business Management program at California State University, San Marcos.

Martha L. Maznevski is Professor of Organizational Behavior and International Management at the Institute for Management Development (IMD), and the Master of Business Administration Program Director.

Michael J. Stevens is Department Chair and Professor of Management at Weber State University.

Günter K. Stahl is Professor of International Management at WU Vienna and Adjunct Professor of Organizational Behavior at INSEAD.

Routledge Global Human Resource Management Series
Edited by Randall S. Schuler, Susan E. Jackson, Paul Sparrow and Michael Poole

Routledge Global Human Resource Management is an important new series that examines human resources in its global context. The series is organized into three strands: Content and issues in global human resource management (HRM); specific HR functions in a global context; and comparative HRM. Authored by some of the world's leading authorities on HRM, each book in the series aims to give readers comprehensive, in-depth, and accessible texts that combine essential theory and best practice. Topics covered include cross-border alliances; global leadership; global legal systems; HRM in Asia, Africa, and the Americas; industrial relations; and global staffing.

Managing Human Resources in Cross-border Alliances
Randall S. Schuler, Susan E. Jackson, and Yadong Luo

Managing Human Resources in Africa
Edited by Ken N. Kamoche, Yaw A. Debrah, Frank M. Horwitz, and Gerry Nkombo Muuka

Globalizing Human Resource Management
Paul Sparrow, Chris Brewster, and Hilary Harris

Managing Human Resources in Asia-Pacific
Edited by Pawan S. Budhwar

International Human Resource Management (Second Edition)
Policy and Practice for the Global Enterprise
Dennis R. Briscoe and Randall S. Schuler

Managing Human Resources in Latin America
An Agenda for International Leaders
Edited by Marta M. Elvira and Anabella Davila

Global Staffing
Edited by Hugh Scullion and David G. Collings

Managing Human Resources in Europe
A Thematic Approach
Edited by Henrik Holt Larsen and Wolfgang Mayrhofer

Managing Human Resources in the Middle-East
Edited by Pawan S. Budhwar and Kamel Mellahi

Managing Global Legal Systems
International Employment Regulation and Competitive Advantage
Gary W. Florkowski

Global Industrial Relations
Edited by Michael J. Morley, Patrick Gunnigle, and David G. Collings

Global Leadership
Research, Practice, Development
Mark E. Mendenhall, Joyce S. Osland, Allan Bird, Gary R. Oddou, Martha L. Maznevski, Michael J. Stevens, and Günter K. Stahl

Global Compensation
Foundations and Perspectives
Edited by Luis Gomez-Mejia and Steve Werner

Global Performance Management
Edited by Arup Varma, Pawan S. Budhwar, and Angelo DeNisi

Managing Human Resources in Central and Eastern Europe
Edited by Michael J. Morley, Noreen Heraty, and Snejina Michailova

Forthcoming:

Global Careers
Edited by Michael Dickmann and Yehuda Baruch

Global Leadership (Second Edition)
Research, Practice, and Development
Mark E. Mendenhall, Joyce S. Osland, Allan Bird, Gary R. Oddou, Martha L. Maznevski, Michael J. Stevens, and Günter K. Stahl

Manager-Subordinate Trust
A Global Perspective
Edited by Pablor Cardona and Michael J. Morley

Global Leadership

Research, Practice, and Development

2nd Edition

Mark E. Mendenhall, Joyce S. Osland, Allan Bird,
Gary R. Oddou, Martha L. Maznevski, Michael J. Stevens,
and Günter K. Stahl

Routledge
Taylor & Francis Group

NEW YORK AND LONDON

First published 2013
by Routledge
711 Third Avenue, New York, NY 10017

Simultaneously published in the UK
by Routledge
2 Park Square, Milton Park, Abingdon, Oxon OX14 4RN

Routledge is an imprint of the Taylor & Francis Group, an informa business

Library of Congress Cataloging in Publication Data
Global leadership : research, practice, and development / Mark E.
Mendenhall ... [et al.]. – 2nd ed.
    p. cm.
Includes bibliographical references and index.
1. Leadership. 2. Executives – Training of. 3. International business enterprises – Personnel management. I. Mendenhall, Mark E., 1956–
HD57.7.G6527 2012
658.4′092–dc23   2012010533

ISBN: 978-0-415-80885-9 (hbk)
ISBN: 978-0-415-80886-6 (pbk)
ISBN: 978-0-203-13801-4 (ebk)

Typeset in Times New Roman
by HWA Text and Data Management, London

Contents

Preface

In 1990 C.K. Prahalad, in his article, "Globalization: The Intellectual and Managerial Challenges," presciently wrote that leaders would exist in

> ...a world where variety, complex interaction patterns among various subunits, host governments, and customers, pressures for change and stability, and the need to re-assert individual identity in a complex web of organizational relationships are the norm. This world is one beset with ambiguity and stress. Facts, emotions, anxieties, power and dependence, competition and collaboration, individual and team efforts are all present . . . Managers have to deal with these often conflicting demands simultaneously.
>
> (p. 30)

The reality that Prahalad foresaw has long since arrived; globalization and its demands have shifted the skill set necessary to lead in the 21st century. Headhunters are desperately trying to find executives with the right mix of skills, but they are rare and difficult to find. But what are the skills that global leaders should possess in order to be successful, and what exactly is global leadership? Companies are grappling with these issues, and social scientists are hurriedly working to produce empirically sound insights to guide the selection, training, and ongoing development of global leaders.

The combined factors of the leadership demands of globalization on firms, firms' responses to those demands, and social scientists' efforts to investigate global leadership spawned a sub-field in international management and international human resource management: global leadership. This field began to come into existence in the mid-1980s, but took hold firmly in the 1990s. Today, numerous scholars are actively investigating the dimensions of global leadership. Our hope is that this book will enable students, practitioners, and scholars to have ready access to the knowledge that the field has generated thus far, and will aid in the systematic investigation of the phenomenon in the future. This second edition includes new studies and practices that have emerged since the publication of the first edition in 2008. We plan to revise the book every four years so that each new edition can serve as a valuable resource to scholars and managers who desire to gain an in-depth understanding of what is known in the field at the current time.

Each chapter from the first edition has been updated to reflect research that has been published since 2008. Additionally, due to the increase in scholarship in the field, three new chapters have been included in this edition (Chapters 4, 11, and 12 – see below).

Chapter 1, "Leadership and the Birth of Global Leadership," traces the heritage of scholarship from which the field of global leadership was built. It is important to review the roots of global leadership because the field of global leadership has inherited some of the same challenges that exist in the general field of leadership as well. Chapter 1 also explains why global leadership is conceptually different from general leadership and provides a definitional framework for the rest of the book.

In Chapter 2, "The Multidisciplinary Roots of Global Leadership," Joyce Osland emphasizes that in addition to the general field of leadership the field of global leadership also owes a debt of gratitude to other fields of study that focus on bridging cultures, communicating and being effective across cultures, working overseas, and managing and leading people from other nations. The contributions of the fields of intercultural communication competence, expatriation, global management, and comparative leadership upon the global leadership literature are reviewed in this chapter. Chapter 3 then discusses and reviews the primary studies and models of global leadership that currently exist in the field.

Chapter 4 integrates the current research on global leadership competencies and attempts to map its content domain while Chapter 5 reviews the extant process models that have been developed to describe the process of global leadership development, as some scholars have approached the conceptualization of global leadership from a process rather than a content model-building perspective.

Chapter 6 reviews the assessment tools and methods that scholars have used to measure global leadership competencies. Current tools that are used are reviewed, as well as other assessment tools that exist and could be applied fruitfully to the study of global leadership competencies.

Chapter 7 focuses on principles derived from empirical research that are critical to successfully leading global teams. In Chapter 8, the focus shifts to the outcomes of global leadership development: knowledge creation and knowledge transfer. In this chapter, the concept that global leaders act as repositories of knowledge, and thus become key components of a firm's human capital is delineated. Also, recent research conducted in the area of the transfer of global skills is addressed.

By all accounts in the general leadership literature, one important aspect of leadership is to initiate change. A key function of global leaders is to lead global change efforts. In Chapter 9 the universal aspects of managing change as well as the factors that seem particularly important in global change efforts are discussed and, since innovation and change go hand in hand, how global leaders can promote and lead innovation is addressed.

Chapter 10 broaches the critical human resource management issue of how to best go about training and developing global leaders. "Best practice" global leadership development practices are reviewed and critiqued, and this is followed by a discussion of the implications of the research findings in the field for the design of global leadership development programs.

Chapter 11 addresses an emerging research stream in the field of global leadership: "Responsible Global Leadership." The authors address the ethical and corporate responsibility dimension of global leadership, and the emerging research findings related to it. Chapter 12 is devoted to looking to the future of the field, its research gaps, and the areas of the field that require more attention from scholars and managers.

We hope that you enjoy this new edition and find it useful in your work. Please feel free to contact any of the authors with your feedback or queries.

Acknowledgments

We would like to express our deep gratitude for the indefatigable patience and professionalism of our editor, John Szilagyi. His belief and vision of the importance of publishing a second edition of the book has been the polar star by which we navigated as we steered our work to its completion.

We express our appreciation also to Sara Werden and Manjula Raman for their expertise and wisdom in shepherding this project to its final publication.

We also would like to thank the generous support of the following institutions for their support of this project:

The Dixie Group
The J. Burton Frierson Chair of Excellence in Business Leadership
The Donald and Sally Lucas Family Foundation and the Global Leadership
     Advancement Center at San José State University
The Darla and Frederick Brodsky Trustee Professorship in Global Business at
     Northeastern University
IMD
The International Organizations Network (ION)

Finally, and most importantly, we would like to thank our families for supporting and sustaining us not just in our work on this project, but in every aspect of our lives.

Allan: Diane, Kyle and Corie and Olivia, Allyson and John, Jared, and Cami
Gary: Kara, Christian, and Luc
Günter: Dorit and Hannah
Joyce: Asbjorn, Ellie and Katrina, Jessica, Joe, Zoe and Lucy, Michael, Anna,
     Jacob, and Gavin
Mark: Janet, Anthony, Nicole, Alexis, Zachary and Bryan, Clarisse, Thomas, and
     William.
Martha: Brian, Andrea, Katie, and Julianna
Michael: Mary Ellen and their munchkins

Contributors

Allan Bird
Darla and Frederick Brodsky Trustee Professor in Global Business
Northeastern University

Celia Chui
HEC Lausanne and the Institute for Management Development

Thomas Maak
Professor in the Department of People Management and Organisation
ESADE

Martha L. Maznevski
Professor of Organizational Behavior and International Management, and Master
of Business Administration Program Director
IMD

Mark E. Mendenhall
J. Burton Frierson Chair of Excellence in Business Leadership
University of Tennessee, Chattanooga

Gary R. Oddou
Professor of International Management
California State University, San Marcos

Joyce S. Osland

Lucas Endowed Professor of Global Leadership and Executive Director, Global Leadership Advancement Center

San José State University

Nicola M. Pless

Associate Professor in the Department of Social Sciences

ESADE

B. Sebastian Reiche

Assistant Professor of Managing People in Organizations

IESE Business School

Günter K. Stahl

Professor of International Management at WU Vienna and

Adjunct Professor of Organizational Behavior at INSEAD

Michael J. Stevens

Department Chair and Professor of Management

Weber State University

1 Leadership and the Birth of Global Leadership

MARK E. MENDENHALL

> Leadership is one of the most observed and least understood phenomena on earth.
>
> (James MacGregor Burns 1978: 2)

The purpose of this book is to introduce you to research that has focused on leaders and leadership in the context of global business and globalization. However, before a proper introduction to the field of global leadership can be undertaken, it will first be necessary to review the field from which the discipline of global leadership evolved: leadership.

It was not until the beginning of the twentieth century, when scholars began applying the scientific method to social processes, that the study of leadership became widespread both in academe and in the business world (Yukl 2006: 2). Before this time period, leadership had been studied mostly via historical analysis, within military studies, and through biography (Bass 1990; Yukl 2006). The vast majority of empirical work in the 1930s–1970s was undertaken by North American and British scholars (Bass 1990), and the context of their study of leadership was primarily domestic in nature; that is, from the early part of the twentieth century through the 1970s the vast majority of social scientific studies of leadership, and concomitant theoretical developments in the field, were firmly housed in Anglo–North American contexts. In the 1980s, European and Japanese social scientists began making contributions to the study of leadership in English language academic journals, which extended the reach of the influence of their findings among scholars globally (Bass 1990: xiv). By 1990 Bass would note that there were over 7,500 scholarly studies of leadership extant. The output of research studies on leadership in the twenty-first century has not diminished (Day and Antonakis 2011: 3).

The empirical findings within the leadership field are complex, paradoxical, intriguing, and, at times, problematic. Various scholars have undertaken reviews and categorizations of the plethora of empirical studies that exist in the field. We have chosen to use the categorizations of the field by Bass (1990) and Yukl (2006) due to the comprehensive nature of their work and the scope of the studies that they covered in their reviews of the field.

Approaches to the Study of Leadership

Scholars are not all cut from the same cloth, thus they embark on the study of leadership from different perspectives and purposes when they ascertain what type of overall research approach they will use in their investigations of leadership. From these differing vantage points of the study of leadership have come varying approaches to the study of the phenomenon. These varying approaches can be categorized in a variety of ways (Day and Antonakis 2011); however, we will primarily rely on Yukl's 2006 work to provide an overview of the field. In his review of the leadership literature domain, he subsumed the complexity of these approaches into five general types: 1) the trait approach, 2) the behavior approach, 3) the situational approach, 4) the power-influence approach, and 5) the integrative approach.

The Trait Approach

Early studies of leadership from the 1900s through the 1940s focused primarily on the discovery of key traits that separated leaders from their peers. The assumption was that internal traits, motives, personality characteristics, skills, and values of leaders were critical to leader emergence, and would predict who would and would not emerge as leaders (Day and Antonakis 2011). Numerous studies have been carried out using this approach, and after reviewing their findings, Bass noted that it was "reasonable to conclude that personality traits differentiate leaders from followers, successful from unsuccessful leaders, and high-level from low-level leaders" (1990: 86). The following traits were correlative to leadership emergence and managerial success (Bass 1990: 87):

- strong drive for responsibility and completion of tasks

- vigor and persistence in the pursuit of goals

- venturesomeness and originality in problem solving

- drive to exercise initiative in social situations

- self-confidence and a sense of personal identity

- willingness to accept the consequences of his or her decisions and actions

- readiness to absorb interpersonal stress

- willingness to tolerate frustration and delay

- ability to influence other people's behavior

- capacity to structure social interaction systems to the purpose at hand.

While these general findings correlated with leadership behavior, they were insufficient for predictive purposes; in other words, while some traits tended to correlate with leadership, they did not predict leadership behavior strongly enough to make them useful to real-world organizations. For example, an individual may score high in all or most of these traits, yet may not wind up emerging as a leader in the workplace or some other social situation. Thus, traits may be necessary but insufficient in and of themselves, for leader emergence and effective leadership. Scholars realized that while traits play a role in leadership, other variables are also at play that likely influence the enactment of effective leadership (Yukl 2006: 182–183). Bass concluded that "who emerges as a leader and who is successful and effective is due to traits of consequence in the situation, some is due to situational effects, and some is due to the interaction of traits and situation" (1990: 87). For more in-depth treatment of the trait approach please see the reviews of Judge et al. (2002) and Zaccaro (2007).

The Behavior Approach

In partial reaction to the general failure of the trait approach as a singular method for understanding leadership dynamics, many scholars began instead to focus on the study of actual leadership behavior versus the internal mechanisms within a person that might cause leadership behavior (Bass 1990: 511). The focus of these scholars was to better understand what managers and leaders actually *do* while on the job and to ascertain which of these behaviors reflect effective versus ineffective leadership. This approach began in the 1950s and elicited hundreds of studies, and the pioneering research that emerged especially from Ohio State University and the University of Michigan during the decade of the 1950s had a significant impact on the field (Bass 1990: 511; Yukl 2006).

The Ohio State studies found the repertoire of managers' behaviors can be linked to one of two core dimensions: 1) "initiating structure" (task-oriented), or 2) "consideration" (people-oriented). More specifically, initiating structure "shows the extent to which a leader initiates activity in the group, organizes it, and defines the way work is to be done" (Bass 1990: 512). It involves the maintenance of performance standards, meeting deadlines, decision making regarding job assignments, establishment of communication and work organization, etc. Consideration "describes the extent to which a leader exhibits concern for the welfare of the other members of the group" (Bass 1990: 511). It involves expressing appreciation for performance, focusing on workers' job satisfaction, paying attention to self-esteem levels of workers, making workers feel at ease, listening and acting on subordinates' suggestions, etc. (Bass 1990: 511).

Scholars found that there is no one specific configuration or balance of these two dimensions that predict leadership effectiveness across social and work situations. For example, initiating structure becomes more critical to effective leadership when there is less structure within the group (Bass 1990). Additionally, interactions between these two factors (initiating structure and consideration) influence effective leadership; for example, "the initiation of structure by the leader (if structure is low) improves the subordinates' performance, which, in turn, increases the leader's subsequent consideration and reduces the leader's initiation of structure" (Bass 1990: 543). The studies carried out at the University of Michigan produced similar findings to those conducted at Ohio State University (Yukl 2006).

In short, while many insights were gained regarding understanding what constituted effective leadership, again, these insights did not engender a significant increase in the ability to predict who would emerge as leaders among their peers (Yukl 2006: 51–54) due to the complex nature of how initiating structure and consideration dynamically related to each other and with various types of different work and social situations (Bass 1990).

The Situational Approach

The decades of the 1960s and 1970s saw an increase in scholars who were interested in how the situation (the context, environment) influenced leadership effectiveness. This was in partial reaction to the results of the trait and behavioral approaches which revealed that the situation or context likely has an influence on effective leadership in addition to trait and behavioral tendencies. The aim of scholars using this approach has been to ascertain what contextual intervening variables exist that influence leadership outcomes. For example, in some types of organizational settings, a specific trait in a person may assist them in being an effective leader while that same trait may, in a completely different context, be a detriment to effective leadership outcomes. For example, would the traits and qualities that made the brusque World War II general George Patton a highly effective leader cause him to also be an effective president of a Parent–Teacher Association in a modern neighborhood school district?

Theories developed from this approach are sometimes called "contingency theories" and they focus on delineating the relationships between person, situation, and leadership outcomes. Among others, the most prominent contingency theories developed during this time period were the Fred Fiedler's *Least Preferred Coworker (LPC) Model*; the *Path-Goal Theory of Leadership* of Robert House; Paul Hersey and Kenneth Blanchard's *Situational Leadership Theory*; Kerr and Jermier's *Substitutes for Leadership Theory*; and the decision-making model of leadership of Victor Vroom, Phillip Yetton, and Arthur Jago. While compelling in nature, in general these theories' predictive power turned out to be less than adequate when empirically tested (Yukl 2006: 215–239). Yukl has observed that "most contingency theories are stated so ambiguously that it is difficult to derive specific, testable propositions" from them, and that the empirical studies that have tested them have not been especially rigorous in their methodological designs (Yukl 2006: 230). Despite the unresolved questions that surround these theories, they have provided the field with an important perspective: that the situations that leaders find themselves in do matter, and do influence leadership outcomes. Elements of situation or context that influence leadership outcome includes "the make up of the subordinates and the organizational constraints, tasks, goals, and functions in the situation" (Bass 1990: 510). Despite these contributions to the field, few scholars now focus exclusively on studying leadership using this approach. Citing Gardner et al. (2010), Day and Antonakis (2011) report that

> Only about 1% of the articles published in the last decade in *Leadership Quarterly* focused on contingency theories. A contributing factor to this waning interest may be that parts of this literature have led to the development of broader contextual approaches to leadership.
>
> (p. 9)

The Power-influence Approach

Some scholars have always been interested in studying leadership through the lens of the concept of power and authority; that is, they focus on the influence processes that flow from leaders to subordinates, and view leadership as primarily a phenomenon of influence. Yukl observes that

> This research seeks to explain leadership effectiveness in terms of the amount and type of power possessed by a leader and how power is exercised. Power is viewed as important not only for influencing subordinates, but also for influencing peers, superiors, and people outside the organization, such as clients and suppliers.
>
> (Yukl 2006: 14)

This approach is quite common by scholars who employ an historical analysis approach to the study of leadership. Common areas of study within this approach are the difference between power and authority, the outcomes of influence attempts (particularly, commitment, compliance, or resistance), the nature of influence processes, typologies of power, how power is acquired and lost, and the cataloguing of influence tactics (Yukl 2006: 146–177). The studies extant in this sub-field exhibit a wide variety of scope in terms of approach and thus render even a summary review problematic; however, to provide a glimpse into their nature, we will share Yukl's overview of research on influence tactics and Bass's overview of sources of power.

Yukl notes that scholars have delineated eleven separate influence tactics that managers and subordinates use to exert power: rational persuasion, inspirational appeals, consultation, collaboration, apprising, ingratiation, exchange, personal appeals, coalition tactics, legitimating tactics, and pressure (Yukl 2002: 167). These tactics, their directional usage, how they are used in differing sequences and combinations, and their likely effectiveness have been investigated. Though this research has provided much clarity regarding how influence is used in organizations, there is still much to be learned about the complexity in which these tactics are combined, deployed, and shifted due to a multitude of contingency factors. Yukl (2002: 169–170) concluded that

> Most researchers treat each influence attempt as an isolated episode, rather than as part of a sequence of reciprocal influence processes that occur in an evolving relationship between the parties. As a result, we still have only a very limited understanding of influence processes in organizations and the implications for effective leadership.

French and Raven (1959) delineated five types or sources of power (expert, referent, reward, coercive, and legitimate), and their model became a foundation for many subsequent studies that focused on power and its relationship to leadership (Bass 1990: 231). Bass states that each of these five bases or sources of power can be summarized as follows (1990: 231–232):

- Expert power is based on B's perception of A's competence.

- Referent power is based on B's identification with or liking for A.

- Reward power depends on A's ability to provide rewards for B.

- Coercive power is based on B's perception that A can provide penalties for not complying with A.

- Legitimate power is based on the internalization of common norms or values.

While the above model seems straightforward, it turns out that the enactment of power between leaders and subordinates is complex and sometimes counterintuitive. For example, power of leaders can be diluted or counteracted by subordinates who possess high levels of self-confidence, self-esteem, and high levels of knowledge and competence regarding the task they are assigned to carry out (Bass 1990: 251). Thus, power is not a unidirectional, top-down force that flows from manager to subordinate. Bass (1990: 251) concluded that "the concept of power leaves unexplained much of what is involved in the leadership role," and that power "is not synonymous with leadership."

In the 1980s and 1990s some scholars focused on a particular mode by which power can be deployed by leaders, and this came to be known by varying names, such as: *transformational leadership, visionary leadership*, and *charismatic leadership*. Bass (1985) was a major contributor to this sub-field of leadership, and he argued that "previous paradigms of leadership were mainly transactional; that is, they were focused on the mutual satisfaction of transactional (i.e. social exchange) obligations" and held that another conception of leadership was required to account for situations where "idealized and inspiring leader behaviors induced followers to transcend their interests for that of the greater good" (Day and Antonakis 2011: 11). The importance of the concepts of vision, mission, charisma, and the ability to communicate lofty ideals to followers flows from this approach to the study of leadership.

The Integrative Approach

Yukl (2006: 15) terms the usage of the above four approaches, in any combination within a single research study, as the integrative approach to the study of leadership. Over the past ten years more scholars have begun to turn to this approach to the study of leadership, but it is still the exception in the field (Yukl 2002: 13). Many scholars in the field are turning to this approach as a possible catalyst for new insights and discoveries in leadership. Day and Antonakis (2011) summarize this position well in the following statement:

> It appears that our accumulated knowledge is such that we can begin to construct hybrid theories of leadership, or even hybrid-integrative perspectives, … including not only psychological and contextual variables but biological ones as well…It is only through efforts to consolidate findings that leadership research will go to the next level where we may finally be able to construct and test more general theories of leadership…Now leadership researchers need to begin to conceptualize ways in which many of the diverse findings can be united and otherwise synthesized and integrated.
>
> (pp. 13–14)

We also include within the integrative approach the recent application of nonlinear dynamics and system theory to the study of leadership. These approaches attempt to study leadership as a holistic phenomenon, assuming mutually causal relationships between all the relevant variables at play (Wheatley 2006). This approach is problematic, as measuring such complexity in real time is virtually impossible, even with the increased capability of present computer processing and software capabilities. However, attempting to get at the complexity by using different approaches in the same study has been viewed increasingly by some scholars as the best overall way to study leadership and management processes (Wheatley 2006).

Leadership Theories

Within each approach to the study of leadership described above, scholars developed different types of theories to guide their study of leadership. These theoretical developments, as you will soon see, have had an impact on how global leadership has been studied as well. There are three categorizations of leadership theories made by Yukl (2006: 18–19): 1) leader versus follower-centered theories, 2) descriptive versus prescriptive theories, and 3) universal versus contingency theories.

Leader versus Follower-centered Theories

As the terminology of this categorization suggests, some scholars have focused mostly on developing theories that describe and delineate behaviors associated with leaders as opposed to their followers. This tendency was quite common in studies associated with the trait, behavior, and power-influence approaches discussed above. The tendency to focus almost solely on the leader as the center of theory building has been strong in the field, and even those working from a contingency approach have featured leader more so than follower dimensions in their research (Yukl 2006: 18).

The tendency to focus on the leader as the primary element of leadership predated the social scientific study of leadership; historians, biographers, theologians, and military academies have taken this approach for centuries (Bass 1990: 37). This perspective of leadership in the social sciences has been dubbed, "The Great-Man Theory" of leadership, and any theory that purports to focus mainly on the leader to the exclusion or downgrading of other variables that are part of the leadership process is often termed a "Great-Man" theory (Bass 1990).

Scholars have attempted to remedy this imbalance by studying the role of followers' perceptions, attitudes, and decision making towards leaders. The emergence of Vertical Dyad Theory (Dansereau et al. 1975) and Leader-Member Exchange Theory (Graen and Uhl-Bien 1995) reflected attempts to delineate the quality and nature of the relationships with leaders and their followers. These and other scholars' research has been labeled the "Relational School of Leadership" by Day and Antonakis (2011) in their review of the field. Also, the 1980s and 1990s saw an influx of studies on the nature of charisma and leadership, with a focus on the part of some scholars on the role of followers' perceptions in charismatic leadership. They focused on studying characteristics in leaders' behaviors that triggered attributions of leadership in the minds of followers. These studies provided important insights into why followers decide to follow or ignore the influence attempts by people who sought to be leaders.

Descriptive versus Prescriptive Theories

A descriptive theory attempts to "explain leadership processes, describe the typical activities of leaders and explain why certain behaviors occur in particular situations" (Yukl 2006: 18). That is, descriptive theories are most concerned with mapping the behavioral terrain and tendencies within a given phenomenon in the hope that an in-depth understanding of the outward behavior of the phenomenon will yield insight for scholars and practitioners alike. Descriptive theories are particularly common within the behavior approach to the study of leadership (Yukl 2006: 18).

Alternatively, Yukl notes that "prescriptive theories specify what leaders must do to become effective, and they identify any necessary conditions for using a particular type of behavior effectively" (2006: 18). Prescriptive theories try to get beneath why effective behaviors are triggered so that insight can be gained regarding what leads to effective leadership. Sometimes, leadership theorists combine aspects of both the descriptive and prescriptive approaches in their theory-building efforts.

Universal versus Contingency Theories

Universal theories are constructed to apply to leadership issues in and across all contexts, and can be either prescriptive or descriptive in nature; for example, "a descriptive universal theory may describe typical functions performed to some extent by all types of leaders, whereas a prescriptive universal theory may specify functions all leaders must perform to be effective" (Yukl 2006: 19). Contingency theories set forth the various conditions that can intervene in leadership attempts that can influence their success or failure and map the relationships between the variables at play in such situations. Thus, from the contingency perspective, the future success of any leadership act is contingent upon the degree to which that act is congruent with the external conditions that are necessary in order for it to have its desired effect.

Contingency theories can be either prescriptive or descriptive as well; "a descriptive contingency theory may explain how leader behavior typically varies from one situation to another, whereas a prescriptive contingency theory may specify the most effective behavior in each type of situation" (Yukl 2006: 19).

Unresolved Problems in the Field of Leadership

The extant empirical and theoretical studies on leadership, while shedding much light on leadership, have also yielded challenges that have not yet been resolved by scholars working in the field. Because these challenges affect how global leadership is both studied and applied, it is necessary to review these issues before introducing you to the domain of global leadership.

Problems of Definition

In his review of the leadership literature, Rost (1993: 7) found that 60 percent of the studies from 1910 to 1990 contained no clear statement of definition for the phenomenon they investigated, *leadership*. The scholars simply assumed that others shared their assumptions and concept of leadership. Those scholars who did wrestle with how to best define leadership for research purposes have not reached consistent agreement as to how to best define the phenomenon (Bass 1990; Rost 1993; Yukl 2006).

To study a concept like leadership scientifically, it is important to narrow one's definition of the phenomenon under study so as to be able to have a target that is manageable in terms of measurement. Broad definitions of a phenomenon require powerful, costly, complex, and sophisticated measurement instruments due to the necessity of having to simultaneously measure a myriad of variables that systemically interact within the phenomenon. Because it is both expensive and extremely difficult to create tools to accomplish both comprehensive and rigorous measurement of a phenomenon as complex as leadership, social scientists focused on more narrow aspects of leadership to study rather than the entire phenomenon itself in their research designs. This enabled their studies to be more rigorous in nature and more practical from a logistical and financial standpoint. This approach, however, has produced some unfortunate side effects for the field.

Because social scientists have dissected leadership into its component sub-processes in order to enhance the methodological rigor of their research designs, their definitions of these component sub-processes have often simply been labeled as *leadership* when in reality their definitions reflect only parts of what constitutes leadership. As Yukl (2006) points out, social scientists have indeed tended to define leadership in terms of the portion of it that interested them as a target for their research studies, and thus "leadership has been defined in terms of traits, behaviors, influence, interaction patterns, role relationships, and occupation of an administrative position" (Yukl 2006: 2) instead of in holistic ways. This has led to a plethora of definitions of the phenomenon of leadership and of differing conceptualizations of the nature of leadership (Yukl 2006).

As early as 1959 Warren Bennis observed that social scientists were acting much like the proverbial blind men who each touched a different part of an elephant and then declared that the elephant was either like a wall (girth), spear (tusk), snake (trunk), tree (leg), fan (ear), or rope (tail):

> Always, it seems, the concept of leadership eludes us or turns up in another form to taunt us again with its slipperiness and complexity. So we have invented an endless proliferation of terms to deal with it…and still the concept is not sufficiently defined.
>
> (p. 259)

Ralph Stogdill in his 1974 review of the leadership literature stated that "there are almost as many definitions of leadership as there are persons who have attempted to define the concept" (p. 259). The situation hasn't changed today, over thirty years since Stogdill's observation (Bass 1990; Rost 1993; Yukl 2006). Day and Antonakis (2011) concluded in their review that "…leadership is often easy to identify in practice but it is difficult to define precisely. Given the complex nature of leadership, a specific and widely accepted definition of leadership does not exist and might never be found" (p. 5).

An example of how lack of agreement over definition can cause confusion is the "leadership versus management" dichotomy. There is some disagreement in the field as to whether *leadership* is qualitatively different from the concept and practice of *management*. Warren Bennis (1989) illustrates the argument of one camp that holds that the two concepts are inherently different, and that the differences are reflected in the behavior of leaders and managers when he contends:

> The leader innovates; the manager administrates.
> The leader inspires; the manager controls.
> The leader sees the long term; the manager sees the short term.
> The leader asks "what?" and "why?" – the manager asks "how?" and "when?"

Most scholars agree that leadership and management are different processes but that dimensions of both are shared or overlap somewhat, and to be an effective leader one must possess skills necessary to be both a good leader and a good manager (Day and Antonakis 2011: 5; Yukl 2006: 6–7). Management is seen as resulting from a strong focus on meeting objectives, goals, and targets via the deployment of traditional administrative practices and techniques while leadership involves attaining goals via "purpose-driven action" that flows from shared vision, and transformation and intrinsic motivation of followers (Day and Antonakis 2011: 5). However, attempts at differentiating or integrating the roles, process, and relationships inherent in leadership and management systems have proven to be complex and unsuccessful and remains as an important challenge in the field (Yukl 2006: 7).

Rost (1993: 6) argues that though the definitional problem in the field is bad enough, the attitude of many scholars continues to exacerbate the situation. He argues that many scholars do not see anything wrong at all with the multiplicity of definitions of leadership that exist, and that they simply "accept definitional ambiguity and confusion as something that behavioral and social scientists have to put up with and work around." This definitional permissiveness and ambiguity, it can be argued, has created a hodgepodge of empirical findings that do not make sense when compared against each other (Argyris 1979; Hosking and Morley 1988; Rost 1993). In other words, "the concept of leadership does not add up because leadership scholars and practitioners have no definition of leadership to hold on to" (Rost 1993: 8). The moral of the ancient Indian parable of the *Blind Men and the Elephant*, (please see Figure 1.1) it seems, can also be credibly applied to modern leadership scholars as well (Saxe 1878: 150–152).

It was six men of Indostan,
To learning much inclined,
Who went to see the Elephant
(Though all of them were blind),
That each by observation
Might satisfy his mind.

The First approach'd the
    Elephant,
And happening to fall
Against his broad and sturdy
    side,
At once began to bawl:
"God bless me! but the Elephant
Is very like a wall!"

The Second, feeling of the tusk,
Cried, – "Ho! What have we here
So very round and smooth and
    sharp?
To me 'tis mighty clear,
This wonder of an Elephant
Is very like a spear!"

The Third approached the
    animal,
And happening to take
The squirming trunk within his
    hands,
Thus boldly up and spake:
"I see,"– quoth he – "the
    Elephant
Is very like a snake!"

The Fourth reached out an eager
    hand,
And felt about the knee:
"What most this wondrous beast
    is like
Is mighty plain,"– quoth he –
"'Tis clear enough the Elephant
Is very like a tree!"

The Fifth, who chanced to touch
    the ear,
Said – "E'en the blindest man
Can tell what this resembles
    most;
Deny the fact who can,
This marvel of an Elephant
Is very like a fan!"

The Sixth no sooner had begun
About the beast to grope,
Then, seizing on the swinging
    tail
That fell within his scope,
"I see," quoth he "the Elephant
Is very like a rope!"

And so these men of Indostan
Disputed loud and long,
Each in his own opinion
Exceeding stiff and strong,
Though each was partly in the
    right
And all were in the wrong!

Moral,
So, oft in theologic wars
The disputants, I ween
Rail on in utter ignorance
Of what each other mean;
And prate about an Elephant
Not one of them has seen!

Figure 1.1 The Blind Men and the Elephant

Source: Saxe (1878)

Problems of Balkanization

John Godfrey Saxe's classic poem (Figure 1.1) applies not only to the methodological dissection of the phenomenon of leadership and the resultant problems of definition that this has caused, but to another contributing problem in the field as well: lack of multidisciplinary thinking (Rost 1993). Leaders and leadership have been a prime focus of the research of many social scientists throughout the nineteenth, twentieth, and twenty-first centuries, and the fields in which leadership has been studied are wide ranging: anthropology, the arts, business, education, history, international relations, law, military, political science, psychology, religion, and sociology (Yukl 2006: 1–2). Rost (1993: 1) notes that:

> These one-discipline scholars are easily recognized because they almost always put an adjective in front of the word leadership, such as business leadership, educational leadership, or political leadership; and they strongly hold the assumption that leadership as practiced in the particular profession they are studying is different from leadership as practiced in other professions.

Because leadership is studied by a variety of disciplines, each with its own preferred paradigms, worldview, and methodology, the opportunity for a broader understanding of the phenomenon exists. Unfortunately, natural bridging mechanisms do not exist between these disciplines that would allow for the dissemination and integration of scholars' findings. Interdisciplinary research is rare in academe, because it requires the learning of an entirely new scholarly paradigm, and such an endeavor is not only formidable from an intellectual standpoint, it is pragmatically troublesome as well. Time, effort, energy, and money that can be spent within a known research stream have to be shifted to the personal education of the scholar. Few scholars have the luxury to retrain themselves in new ways of thinking and researching, and thus the "elephant" of leadership winds up being carved up and scrutinized from many disciplines with only minor forays of attempted integration.

While there is a trend toward multidisciplinary approaches to the study of leadership by some scholars, the lion's share of leadership research is still conducted within unitary disciplines (Rost 1993). This lack of integration between academic disciplines is not unique to the field of leadership, but nevertheless, the comparative paucity of multidisciplinary work in the field has no doubt restricted the development of more complex and robust models of leadership.

The Problem of Zeitgeist

In addition to the natural tendency for scholars to falsely delimit a phenomenon in order to enhance methodological rigor, Drath (1998) argued that there is another dynamic at play that influences how leadership is studied. How scholars study leadership (*i.e. which part of the elephant they choose to focus on*) often reflects the popular views, cultural mindset, and innovative ideas regarding what constitutes *good* or *ideal* leadership during the time period in which the studies take place.

Drath (1998) contends that the influence of a given Zeitgeist on the construct of leadership causes leadership to be an evolving concept, and that leadership development methods follow the preferred ideational notion regarding leadership of a given time period. A summary of his conceptualization of the conceptual evolution of the idea of leadership is given in Figure 1.2. If one accepts Drath's

	Ancient	*Traditional*	*Modern*	*Future*
Idea of leadership	Domination	Influence	Common goals	Reciprocal relations
Action of leadership	Commanding followers	Motivating followers	Creating inner commitment	Mutual meaning making
Focus of leadership development	Power of the leader	Interpersonal skills of the leader	Self-knowledge of the leader	Interactions of the group

Figure 1.2 Evolving Views of the Construct of Leadership

perspective, leadership is an evolving phenomenon that is difficult to pin down through definition because society's view of it changes over time. It is a "complex and layered construction that has built up over the course of history... This layered meaning makes it complex and hard to define, but it also makes it a versatile, useful tool that can be employed in a variety of forms" (Drath 1998: 409).

Defining Leader Effectiveness

Another problem regarding leadership involves how effective leadership outcomes are measured. How does one know if someone is an effective leader? Is it based on the achievement of their vision for the organization or group that they lead? If so, Gandhi would necessarily be assessed as not being an effective leader because he was not able to create a united India. Most people would hesitate to state categorically that Gandhi was not an effective leader, so if the obtaining of the ultimate purpose of the leader is not a good criterion for measuring effective leadership outcomes, what is?

Traditionally social scientists have measured leader effectiveness using a wide variety of outcome variables (Yukl 2006: 9–10), some of which are: net profits, profit margin, sales increases, market share, return on investment, return on assets, productivity, attitudes of followers, commitment, absenteeism, voluntary turnover, grievances, complaints, and job transfer requests. Note that not all the variables listed are commonly included in any one empirical study, but rather reflect the range of variables that have commonly been used by leadership scholars.

If managers are able to increase sales and market share in their divisions, yet have fairly high levels of voluntary turnover, grievances, and complaints, are they effective leaders? And if they have low levels of voluntary turnover, grievances, and complaints, yet have declining sales and low market share, are they effective leaders? Again, the aspect of leadership effectiveness that is most salient to the researcher often drives how leadership is defined, and the interpretation of the subsequent empirical findings.

Willingness to Follow versus Gaining Compliance

Some definitions of leadership rely heavily on the notion that leaders must be able to influence other people to do tasks that are necessary to be done for the survival of the group or organization. This has led to another bifurcation among scholars, however: "Do leaders have to elicit a willingness to follow them from subordinates in order to be an effective leader or is it enough to be able to gain compliance from subordinates?"

How one answers this question has significant implications in terms of what variables one selects to use in a research study and how one even evaluates who is a leader and who is not. In a company, how a human resources (HR) manager answers this question elicits marked differences in the design and implementation of leadership development programs.

Conclusion

Based upon scholars' assumptions and biases regarding how they view leadership, research methodologies are constructed and studies are carried out. It is no wonder then that research support for traditional leadership theories is mixed, at best (Yukl 2006).

It would be incorrect to infer from the discussion thus far, however, that there is complete theoretical or empirical confusion in the field of leadership. Social scientists have done a credible job of delineating in detail many sub-processes and components of the leadership phenomenon, and much valuable information has been learned and applied to good measure by managers and organizations from the extant empirical and theoretical literature. We will now begin to introduce how the heritage of the field of leadership has influenced the development of the study and understanding of global leadership.

Global Leadership: Where Did it Come From?

The emergence of international business as a separate field of study in the 1950s and 1960s (Toyne and Nigh 1997) opened the view of some scholars working in that area to consider how leadership operated in other cultures and the attendant implications of these cross-cultural leadership differences for international businesspeople working in multinational corporations. However, these types of studies constituted a minority of the studies conducted in the international business field; the prevailing areas of study focused on macro-level issues that related to "the firm's relationship with its external environment" (Boyacigiller and Adler 1997: 398).

In the 1960s some scholars studying business management began to look at the challenges associated with managing human resources in multinational corporations (MNCs), and this led to a more sophisticated understanding of the nature of national cultures and their effects upon how MNC subsidiaries should be managed on a country-by-country basis. This rubric of research was termed "comparative management," due to the focus of studying how indigenous cultures differed across dimensions of leadership, motivation, decision making, etc. These scholars also did pioneering work in extending anthropological frameworks of culture to the study of business practices (Redding 1997; Schollhammer 1969).

The 1970s saw an increase in the number of studies done on expatriate managers and their challenges associated with managing subordinates from national cultures different from one's own, in contexts outside of one's country of birth (Mendenhall and Oddou 1985). Studies of expatriate managers increased significantly in the late 1980s and throughout the 1990s, raising awareness and insight regarding the role that culture plays as a contingent variable in cross-cultural managerial and leadership effectiveness (Thomas and Lazarova 2006). Much of this research was driven in the background by the advent of globalization as a new reality in international business. Attendant with the rise of globalization in the 1990s was the prospect that the

> traditional distinction between domestic and multinational companies had started to become blurred. International competition was no longer the preserve of industrial giants…Statistics from the 1960s show that only 6 percent of the U.S. economy was exposed to international competition. By the late 1980s, the corresponding figure was over 70 percent and climbing fast.
>
> (Evans et al. 2002: 25)

In the mid 1980s, Gunnar Hedlund observed the following, presaging the current reality of global business:

> A radical view concerning globality is that we are witnessing the disappearance of the international dimension of business. For commercial and practical purposes, nations do not exist and the relevant business arena becomes something like a big unified "home market."
>
> (1986: 18)

Responding to Hedlund's prescient view above, Evans et al. (2002: 25) observed: "By the early 1990s, this was no longer a radical proposition." The management challenges that continually spawned out of globalization increased the need on the part of MNCs to develop executives who could manage and lead from a global perspective (Mendenhall et al. 2003). Suddenly, leadership was deemed to be more complex and challenging than it once was due to the onslaught of the processes of globalization. Various scholars' surveys of the HR concerns of MNCs in the past ten years have elicited almost identical findings: that developing global leadership and business competence in leaders is a high priority for most firms (Gregersen et al. 1998; Mendenhall et al. 2003; Suutari 2002). In other words, firms have begun to realize that people are the key to global success. Perhaps the concern can be summarized usefully with the following statement (Black, et al. 1999b: 1–2):

> People formulate and implement strategy…The strategy of a company is a function of its strategy makers. For example, whether they recognize or miss global threats or opportunities is a function of their experience and perspective. How they structure an organization for global reach and results depends on how they see the world of organizations, markets, competitors.

There is no doubt that executives face complex challenges of leadership because of the evolving globalized context in which they work, but what is it about the global context that is so challenging? "The term 'global' encompasses more than simple *geographic reach* in terms of business operations. It also includes the notion of *cultural reach* in terms of people and *intellectual reach* in the development of a global mindset" and global skills (Osland et al. 2006).

Lane et al. (2004) argued that globalization is a term that has been used to attempt to describe what is in reality "increased complexity." They argue that there are four dimensions of complexity in the global context that together in a systemic, ongoing "combining" cause a plethora of business challenges that often are unforeseen and inherently unpredictable to executives. The first dimension, multiplicity, reflects the geometric increase in the number and type of issues that global leaders must deal with compared to domestic leaders: "Globalization is not just about 'more;' it's about "more and different." Multiplicity reflects the necessity of global leaders having to deal with more and different competitors, customers, governments, stakeholders, and non-governmental organizations (NGOs), in addition to multiplicity on all aspects along the value chain. Additionally, organizations must choose from an almost infinite variety of permutations of models of organizing and conducting business in their worldwide operations (Lane et al. 2004).

The second aspect of the complexity inherent in globalization is the notion of interdependence. Lane et al. (2004) note that, "with fast and easy movement of capital, information, and people, distributed units are no longer isolated." Interdependencies generate complexity in that global leaders must be able to attend to, and manage, more complex systems of human and technological interaction compared to domestic leaders. The increase of interdependencies in economies, along all aspects of the value chain, mergers and acquisitions, alliances, joint ventures, virtual teamwork, etc., all create a higher bar for leaders in terms of performance and skill set acquisition.

Ambiguity is the third element of global complexity. Lack of information clarity, unclear cause and effect relationships, and equivocality regarding information (where multiple interpretations of the same facts are possible) exists in domestic work settings, but is increased in global work settings. Additionally, cross-cultural differences in norms in the interpretation of both qualitative and quantitative information add to the challenge of managing across borders (Lane et al. 2004).

These three elements of globalization, in operation together, cause a multiplier effect that continually produces dynamic complexity in the global business realm.

And, "as if multiplicity, interdependence, and ambiguity were not enough on their own, the whole system is always in motion, always changing. And it seems to be changing at a faster rate all the time" (Lane et al. 2004: 17). Flux, the ever-changing meta-context in which dynamic complexity takes place, is an environment of nonlinear, ongoing shifting in terms of system dynamics, values, organizational structure, industry trends, and socio-political stability.

The responses to the challenges of the complexity of globalization on the part of industry were swift: "We need executives who can handle this complexity and we need them fast." Global leadership development programs were established and training quickly ensued. These programs were normally generated internally within companies, often with the assistance of external consultants, and were not based on empirical findings of the actual dimensions of global leadership but rather on what seemed to make sense to the designers (Von Glinow 2001).

Von Glinow (2001) noted that in the 1990s some global firms designed programs around what they traditionally viewed as the three to five core skills they associated with global executive competence while other firms developed programs that addressed upwards of thirty or more skills that they felt were important in the development of global leaders. This hodgepodge approach led to poor results, further exacerbating the problems that firms faced: developing executives who could lead globally. When firms turned to academe for help, there was no response except: "We are not really sure what the dimensions of global leadership are that should act as anchors and as guides for your training curricula." Scholars began to respond to these business needs and a field was born (Mendenhall 2006).

The field of global leadership thus began with a small cadre of scholars who were: 1) determined to map the phenomenon in order to assist firms in their global leadership development efforts, and 2) eager to explore the empirical and theoretical dimensions of leadership as it applied to globalization. The field of global leadership is in its nascence, yet it has built a base of research that can offer useful direction to organizations who struggle with developing an executive cadre that is truly global in mindset and in leader-related competencies. The need for global leaders in firms has not changed; what has changed is that compared to the 1990s there is now more research from which to base global leadership development programs upon. The purpose of this book is to share this research and to draw conclusions from it relating to organizational practice. Before we embark on that journey, however, we must first address one more critical question: "What is the difference between global leadership and 'regular' or 'traditional' leadership?"

Global Leadership versus Traditional Leadership

Some executives and managers wonder what is so special about the notion of global leadership—is it not simply sound leadership principles applied to the global context? And if so, does it really make much sense to carve out an entirely different term when a better one, *leadership*, exists? In a way, it is a similar argument to the one heretofore discussed: what is the real difference between leadership and management? In this case, the permutation is: "Are not global leadership and traditional leadership in essence the same concept?"

Some scholars working in the area of global leadership concede the point that while most—if not all—competencies associated with leadership from the traditional/domestic leadership literature are necessary to lead globally, the global context places such high demands on the deployment of those competencies, that for all intents and purposes, the skill level and deployment demands render the phenomenon to be so different in degree that it makes sense to address it as being different in kind to traditional leadership.

Specifically, the global context significantly increases for leaders the valence, intensity, and complexity of key contextual dimensions that also exist for those leading in a domestic context. In can be argued that global leadership

> …differs from domestic leadership in *degree* in terms of issues related to connectedness, boundary spanning, complexity, ethical challenges, dealing with tensions and paradoxes, pattern recognition, and building learning environments, teams, and community and leading large-scale change efforts—across diverse cultures.
>
> (Osland and Bird 2006: 123)

Additionally, it can be argued that global leadership differs from domestic leadership in *kind* due to the nature of the outcomes the global context potentially can produce in people who must live and work in it. Living and working constantly in a global context, and experiencing the ongoing intensity of the dimensions of complexity discussed by Lane and his colleagues, can trigger a transformational experience within managers (Osland 1995). These powerful transformational or crucible experiences (Bennis and Thomas 2002; Osland 1995) have been found to produce new mental models in the individual—new worldviews, mindsets, perceptual acumen, and perspectives that simply do not exist within people who have not gone through such a series of experiences in a global context. It is this transformational process that can only occur within someone working globally that leads many scholars to infer that global leadership significantly differs in degree—or perhaps even kind—from traditional leadership to warrant studying it as a separate phenomenon (Osland et al. 2006).

As we move now to a more in-depth treatment of the theories, models, and findings in the field of global leadership, it is important to pause and consider what we, the authors, mean when we will use the term global leaders/leadership. Just as in the traditional leadership literature, there is no agreed upon definition of global leadership in the field. For the purposes of this book, we will use the following broad definition when we refer to global leaders/leadership:

Global leaders are individuals who effect significant positive change in organizations by building communities through the development of trust and the arrangement of organizational structures and processes in a context involving multiple cross-boundary stakeholders, multiple sources of external cross-boundary authority, and multiple cultures under conditions of temporal, geographical, and cultural complexity.

2 The Multidisciplinary Roots of Global Leadership

JOYCE S. OSLAND

So the journey is over and I am back again where I started, richer by much experience and poorer by many exploded convictions, many perished certainties. For convictions and certainties are too often the concomitants of ignorance ... Those who like to feel they are always right and who attach a high importance to their own opinions should stay at home. When one is traveling, convictions are mislaid as easily as spectacles; but unlike spectacles, they are not easily replaced.

(Aldous Huxley 1926)

The field of leadership, reviewed in the previous chapter, is not the sole contributor to understanding global leadership. The differences in degree and kind between domestic and global leadership are also rooted in global leadership's multidisciplinary evolution. There are numerous fields that global leaders would benefit from studying, such as international affairs, economics, anthropology, and cross-cultural psychology, to name just a few. However, the field of global leadership has drawn heavily from four fields of study in particular that address communicating and being effective across cultures (intercultural communication competence), working overseas (expatriation), managing around the world (global management), and leading people from other nations (comparative leadership). We will briefly cover the highlights of these fields that relate to global leadership and identify their contributions to the study of global leadership.

Intercultural Communication Competence

Living in a diverse world—or leading a diverse work force—is more than a mental construct, a memorized list of cultural differences, or a willingness to be tolerant. It's about examining how well we function at the margins and interfaces of life, where divergent ways of being and believing meet and collide.

(Kemper 2003)

Given the context in which they work, global leaders have to function well at the margins where cultures and divergent perspectives collide. Intercultural communication competence (for reviews, see Dinges and Baldwin 1996 and Deardorff 2006) has much to contribute to any field that crosses cultural boundaries. It is especially important, however, for global leaders as they attempt to understand and motivate followers, partners, and stakeholders, transmit their vision, and receive feedback from others. As you can imagine, the ability to engage in active listening and accurately interpret communications are especially crucial for global leaders working with people of diverse cultural backgrounds.

Intercultural communication competence has been defined as "the ability to effectively and appropriately execute communication behaviors that negotiate each other's cultural identity or identities in a culturally diverse environment" (Chen and Starosta 1999: 28). Appropriateness means taking cultural expectations and the feelings of the other person into consideration and behaving consistently in accordance with those expectations. Intercultural communication competence comprises knowledge, skills, attitudes, and awareness (Fantini 2000). It includes knowledge that is culture-specific (pertaining to a particular country), culture-general (pertaining to all foreign cultures), and context-specific (e.g. a business setting). Individuals who are competent also possess a good understanding of their own culture.

Intercultural communication competence involves the ability to establish interpersonal relationships, communicate effectively, manage psychological stress, adjust to different cultures, deal with different society systems and understand others (Hammer et al. 1978; Wiseman and Abe 1984; Paige 1993). According to Gudykunst (1994) the most important intercultural skills are: mindfulness, cognitive flexibility, behavioral flexibility, tolerance of ambiguity, and cross-cultural empathy. Cognitive flexibility can be defined as "the ability to understand, consider, and weigh multiple frameworks, or schemas" (Endicott et al. 2003: 415). Behavioral flexibility refers to a willingness to adopt and use different styles appropriately. Tolerance of ambiguity is "the way people process information about ambiguous situations and stimuli when confronted with an array of unfamiliar, complex, or incongruent clues" (Furnham and Ribchester 1995: 179). People with a low tolerance find ambiguity stressful, attempt to avoid it, and react prematurely to remove the ambiguity. Those with a high tolerance find ambiguity interesting and challenging in a positive way. Empathy is defined as "the ability to experience some aspect of reality differently from what is 'given' by one's own culture" (Bennett 1993: 53). Mindfulness is defined as the process of thinking in new categories, being open to new information, and recognizing multiple perspectives. Being mindful means switching from automatic communication routines to paying attention simultaneously to the internal assumptions, cognitions, and emotions of both oneself and the other person (Thich 1991). Thus, a related skill is the ability to see things through the eyes and mind of others, which is known as perspective taking (Tye 1990). Although we may refer to some of these skills using different terminology, all of them have been identified in the global leadership research as important competencies.

Paige (1993) built on these ideas to create the following description of intercultural communication competence, which includes the ability to do the job in question (technical skills) and acknowledges contextual variations (situational factors):

- knowledge of the target culture

- personal qualities (i.e. flexibility, tolerance of ambiguity, sense of humor, openness)

- behavioral skills (communicative competence)

- self-awareness (one's values and beliefs)

- technical skills (e.g. the ability to accomplish tasks)

- situational factors (e.g. clarity of expectations, psychological pressure).

"There is no prescriptive set of characteristics that guarantees competence in all intercultural relationships and situations" because competence also depends on the "characteristics of the association" between the communicators and on the situation itself (Lustig and Koester 2003: 65). Not every relationship or every situation requires the same skill set. For example, some people function as cultural mentors who make themselves available to explain what is going on to foreigners working in their country (Osland 1995). Their motivation often comes from having first-hand experience of the difficulties of crossing cultures and knowing which aspects of their culture puzzle foreigners. It is possible to ask such cultural mentors more direct questions about their culture, with less fear of giving offense, than with more parochial people from the same culture. Thus, in the context of interacting with a cultural mentor, there may be less need for mindfulness and behavioral flexibility and a greater sense of freedom to "be oneself."

Several caveats concerning intercultural competence may initially seem counterintuitive (Bennett and Salonen 2007). First, foreign language fluency does not guarantee intercultural competence (Hammer 2007). It can be an advantage, however, where locals appreciate those who make the effort to learn their language. But fluency does not automatically translate into intercultural competence. For example, French-speaking European expatriates in Burkina Faso shared that language with many locals. This was not the case for other expatriate nationalities who bumbled around in broken French or one of the local dialects. However, the Africans treated expatriates differently, based not on their language fluency, but on their intercultural competence—whether they were respectful and took the time to observe local greeting rituals and build relationships. Second, cultural knowledge does not equal intercultural competence (Bennett 2009). A person may know intellectually that a relationship focus is more important than a task focus in certain cultures without having the actual ability to connect with others and build relationships. Similarly, individuals can be experts on Indian culture and even spend their life researching Indian leadership without being able to effectively lead Indians. Cultural knowledge is crucial; to apply it, however, means we have to be able to close the knowing–doing gap. Third, simply living in a foreign country does not guarantee intercultural competence (Hammer 2007).

"Learning from experience requires more than being in the vicinity of events when they occur; learning emerges from the ability to construe those events and reconstrue them in transformative ways" (Bennett and Salonen, 2007: 1). Our last caveat is not counterintuitive to anyone who has ever tried to change human behavior. According to a multidisciplinary review of international research (Mendenhall, Stahl, Ehnert, Oddou, Osland and Kühlmann 2004), intercultural training is more likely to result in knowledge acquisition than in changing attitudes, behavior, adjustment or performance. To summarize, intercultural competence, like global leadership, does not develop easily or quickly without transformational experiences, careful design, and a strong motivation for personal development in this area.

Some scholars view intercultural communication competence as a process that begins with an ethnocentric view that is eventually transformed into intercultural communication competence (e.g. Hoopes 1979; Bennett 1993; Pedersen 1994; Fennes and Hapgood 1997). Fennes and Hapgood (1997) argue that this process includes: overcoming ethnocentrism, acquiring the ability to empathize with others; and acquiring the ability to both communicate and cooperate across cultural boundaries. The capacity to expand and adapt one's frame of reference and match the behaviors of others is implicit in this process (Fennes and Hapgood 1997). The basic tools used to understand the cultural communication patterns are (Bennett 2009):

- communication styles (e.g. low- versus high- context, emotionally restrained versus emotionally expressive, direct versus indirect, linear versus circular, self-effacing versus self-aggrandizing) (Ting-Toomey 1999; Saphiere et al. 2005)

- nonverbal communication (e.g. use of time, touching, gestures, facial expressions, voice pitch, eye contact (Knapp and Hall 2005; Ting-Toomey 1999)

- value orientations (e.g. collectivistic versus individualistic, particularistic versus individualistic, status, high- versus low- power distance) (Kluckhohn and Strodtbeck 1961; Fiske 1992; Schwartz 1994; Trompenaars and Hampden-Turner 1993; Hofstede 2001; House et al. 2004)

- interaction rituals (e.g. turn-taking in conversation, greetings and farewells) (Tannen 1994; Ting-Toomey 1999)

- conflict styles (e.g. controlling, direct, collaborative, avoiding) (Ting-Toomey and Oetzel 2001; Hammer 2005)

- cognitive styles (e.g. holistic versus analytical logic, objective versus subjective ways of knowing, dialectic versus integrative thinking patterns, doubting game versus believing game thinking patterns) (Elbow 1973; Riding and Rayner 2000; Hayashi and Jolley 2002; Nisbett 2003).

Given the extent of intercultural communication in which global leaders engage, competence in this area is a necessity. To global leadership, the field of intercultural communication competence contributes many valuable lessons, in particular, the importance of:

- learning the expectations and communication practices of other cultures

- practicing mindfulness, empathy, perspective taking, and suspended judgment (which are all foundations for a global mindset)

- accepting that our way of viewing the world is unique to ourselves or our culture and learning to understand and value other views

- adapting to other cultures

- building relationships, handling stress, and switching communication styles as appropriate

- acknowledging that different competencies and skills are required in different contexts and situations.

Expatriation

Expatriates are employees who have been sent by their employers to reside and work outside of their home country to a related unit in a foreign country on temporary assignment, usually for a term(s) that lasts more than six months and less than five years (Aycan and Kanungo 1997). The word 'expatriate' is used to refer to business people, diplomats, employees of international non-profit organizations, military personnel, and missionaries among others. "Self-initiated expatriate" or "foreign worker" are newer terms that refer to an individual who relocates voluntarily to a foreign country on his or her own initiative (independently of any employer and without organizational assistance) and is hired under a local, host-country contract (Inkson et al. 1997; Crowley-Henry 2007). International students are not technically categorized as expatriates because they lack an employer, but they share the experience of learning to adapt and function in another culture.

Previously expatriates were sent by organizations in industrialized countries. Today's expatriates flow in bilateral and multilateral directions, depending on the demand and supply of expatriates (Collings et al. 2007). For example, given the shift in economic power, emerging market economies such as China and India are using their new wealth to acquire firms elsewhere. Therefore, they are sending out more expatriates to Western countries (Tung and Varma 2008). Globalization has also caused more "brain circulation" as people study and work in a foreign country and eventually move back home, with the option, however, of returning to their adopted country (Tung and Varma 2008).

Just as immersion in a foreign country is the most efficient and effective way to learn its language, an expatriate assignment is commonly viewed as the best way to develop global leaders. When asked to name the most powerful experience in their lives for developing global leadership capabilities, 80 percent of those surveyed responded that it was living and working abroad (Gregersen et al. 1998). This belief in the crucial role of international assignments in developing global leaders prompted renewed interest in the nature of the expatriate experience, selection, adjustment, transformation, and effectiveness.

The Expatriate Experience

The intrinsic nature of an overseas assignment makes it a valuable opportunity for personal growth (Mendenhall and Oddou 1985; Osland 1995). In addition to supplementary, more important, and broader work responsibilities, expatriates generally have more independence and potential impact on operations than they do in a domestic job (Oddou and Mendenhall 1988). The challenging nature of the experience leads many people to question their mental models and develop new ones, which contributes to a global mindset. For better or worse, expatriates are upended by concurrent changes in cultures, job context, and social support—a Petri dish for stress, accelerated learning, paradoxes, and personal transformation (Osland 1995).

Paradoxes and contradictions are an inherent part of the cross-cultural experience. Paradox can be defined as "a situation involving the presence of contradictory, mutually exclusive elements that operate equally at the same time" (Quinn and Cameron 1988). Examples of expatriate paradoxes are "seeing as valid the general stereotype about the culture but also realizing that many host-country nationals do not fit that stereotype," "as a result of being abroad a long time, feeling at ease anywhere but belonging nowhere," and "possessing a great deal of power as a result of your role but downplaying it in order to gain necessary input and cooperation" (Osland 1995). Expatriates deal with these and other paradoxes by trying to understand the "foreign" side of the paradox, determining their role in the specific situation and whether they have an ethical right to take action, weighing the contingencies, discerning critical factors for success or effectiveness, picking their battles, accepting what they cannot change, and learning from the experience so they could apply it to the next paradox (Osland 2001). Wrestling with paradox helps develop cognitive complexity, the ability to manage uncertainty, and behavioral flexibility—all aspects of global leadership. The link between expatriation and global leadership development will be delineated more fully in Chapter 10.

Expatriate Selection

Despite uncertain results, some firms continue to select expatriates solely on their technical competence, past performance in a domestic setting, or their willingness to go abroad (Mendenhall et al. 2002; Graf 2004; Anderson 2005; Tye and Chen 2005). While technical skills are necessary, organizational and technical knowledge do not ensure expatriate success (Tung 1981; Varma et al. 2001). Willingness to undertake an international assignment is a crucial component, since "no amount of training can prepare a reluctant candidate to do well abroad" (Tung and Varma 2008: 369). However, willingness to go is merely a threshold requirement rather than a guarantee of success. Past performance in a domestic setting is not a good predictor of excellent performance overseas (Miller 1973; Black et al. 1999a). The strengths of many North American high-potentials actually translate into liabilities in the global context (Ruben 1989). The characteristics that get U.S. high-potentials noticed—"propensity for risk-taking, a passion or commitment to seeing the organization succeed, courage to go against the grain, and a keen mind" (Spreitzer et al. 1997: 25)—are usually found in hard-driving, self-motivated, assertive, and outwardly passionate and self-confident individuals (Mendenhall 2001a). These qualities are not universally valued and may in fact lead to failure in other countries. The same findings may apply to high-potential employees of other nationalities.

After reviewing the literature, Kealey (2003) proposed that the "model cross-cultural collaborator" possesses three categories of non-technical skills: 1) adaptation skills (e.g. flexibility, stress tolerance), 2) cross-cultural skills (e.g. realism, cultural sensitivity), and 3) partnership skills (e.g. openness to others, professional commitment). Recent research has utilized the revised NEO Personality Inventory (NEO PI-R), Five-Factor Model of personality (Costa and McCrae 1992) to judge whether particular personality traits correlate with expatriate outcomes such as adjustment, effectiveness, and likelihood of completing their assignment. The results indicate that expatriates who are emotionally stable, outgoing and agreeable, open to experience (Shaffer et al. 2006), flexible and not ethnocentric appear to function better than other expatriates (Caligiuri 2000; Caligiuri and Di Santo 2001). This research also indicated that selection practices should identify people who are motivated to attain assigned task goals and interact with others in the workplace and who show cultural flexibility (Shaffer et al. 2006; cf. Black et al. 1999b). Cultural flexibility is the ability to substitute activities enjoyed in one's native country with existing, and usually distinct activities, in the host country (e.g. baseball instead of cricket or vice versa). A meta-analysis of thirty studies identified these predictors of expatriate job performance: cultural sensitivity, local language ability, and four of the Big Five personality traits—extroversion, emotional stability, agreeableness and conscientiousness (Mol et al. 2005). Surprisingly, openness was not a predictor. Some variables were not measured in enough studies to provide conclusive evidence, but they seem promising: cultural flexibility, selection board ratings, tolerance for ambiguity, ego strength, peer nominations, task leadership, people leadership, social adaptability, and interpersonal interest (Mol et al. 2005). Cultural sensitivity, which was highly correlated with expatriate job performance, will be addressed in Chapter 6 using its more recent connotation—cultural intelligence.

Table 2.1 Individual Determinants of Expatriate Adjustment and Related Global Leadership Competencies

Expatriate Adjustment Determinants	Related Global Leadership Competencies
Self-efficacy	Personal literacy, optimistic
Resilience	Resilience, resourceful, energetic
Behavioral flexibility	Flexibility
Curiosity	Inquisitiveness, cultural interest
Extroversion	*No correlate*
Broad category width	Savvy
Flexible attributions	Cognitive complexity
Open-mindedness	Open-mindedness
High tolerance for ambiguity	Duality, cognitive complexity
Empathy/respect for others	Cultural sensitivity, social literacy
Nonverbal communications	Social literacy
Relationship skills	Social literacy, building partnerships
Willingness to communicate	Social literacy, constructive dialogue

Researchers have identified the individual and external characteristics that correlate significantly to expatriate adjustment, which can also be viewed as selection criteria. The individual determinants are shown in Table 2.1. This exhibit also indicates the global leadership competencies identified in empirical research that appear to be conceptually similar to expatriate adjustment determinants. All the expatriate adjustment determinants, with the exception of extroversion, relate to a subset of global leadership competencies. This provides evidence of similarity between these two fields and explains why expatriation is included in discussions of global leadership and its development. The overview of the global leadership literature in the next chapter indicates, however, that global leadership is more extensive and broader in scope than expatriate adjustment.

Expatriate Transformation

The developmental models of expatriate adjustment are more accurately called transformational models. Peter Adler (1975) developed a five-stage model comprised of 1) contact with the other culture, 2) disintegration, 3) reintegration, 4) autonomy, and 5) independence. Pedersen described the transformation that occurs during culture shock as "a series of degeneration and regeneration events or crises in a nonregular and erratic movement of change" that is both conscious and unconscious as the person tries to be more successful in the other culture (Pedersen 1995: 4). Osland (1995) uses the framework of the hero's journey, with its stages of separation and departure, initiation, and return as a metaphor for expatriate transformation.

There are many reports, both anecdotal and empirical, of ways that expatriates change as a result of an international assignment. According to Osland (1995), they reported four types of changes in an American sample: positive changes in self, changed attitudes, improved work skills, and increased knowledge. The *positive changes in self* were increased tolerance, patience, confidence, respectfulness, maturity, open-mindedness, competitiveness, adaptability, independence, and sensitivity, and decreased impulsiveness. The *changed attitudes* concerned a broader perspective on the world, greater appreciation of cultural differences, increased realization of how fortunate they were, different attitudes toward work, and a feeling that life is more interesting now than before. These attitudes are indications of greater cognitive complexity. The *improved work skills* they mentioned referred to improved interpersonal and communication skills, especially better listening skills, improved management style, a better understanding of power, the ability to do higher-quality work, and broadened exposure to business. The *increased knowledge* they reported comprised a wide array of topics related to both global business and foreign countries. These findings confirm the original research by Oddou and Mendenhall (1991: 30), in which 135 expatriates were surveyed to discover the "value added" of their assignments: increased global perspective of their firm's business operations; greater planning ability; increased ability to communicate with people of diverse backgrounds; better able to conceptualize and comprehend business trends and events due to their exposure to contrasting cultural, political and economic work systems; and better motivators as a result of working with culturally diverse personnel overseas. These changes have much in common with the global leadership competencies discussed in Chapter 3: business savvy, continuous learning, ability to manage uncertainty, cognitive complexity, behavioral flexibility, and cross-cultural skills. The particular ways they change and the degree to which expatriates are transformed varies according to the individual expatriate and the type of adventure he or she sought overseas (Osland 1995) or the type of assignment they hold (Zaccaro et al. 2006).

Repatriates, however, showed agreement in their description of the transformation process itself—a process of letting go and taking on (Osland 1995) that is summarized in Table 2.2. Many forms of transformation involve a death ("letting go") and rebirth ("taking on"). During their sojourn, expatriates let go of cultural certainty and take on the internationalized perceptions of the other culture. They learn how other countries perceive their country, perhaps in ways that are not always favorable; and they learn that other countries have advantages their own does not. Thus, they begin to see their country's flaws and develop a more cognitively complex, realistic view of it, rather than the implicit faith and pride they had previously. One expatriate reflected, "I still love my country, but I certainly have a better understanding about why other countries don't think as highly of us."

Expatriates let go of their unquestioned acceptance of basic assumptions and take on the internationalized values of the other culture. Rather than taking their own cultural values for granted, contact with the other culture leads them to question

Table 2.2 The Expatriate Transformation Process

Letting Go	Taking On
Cultural certainty	Internalized perceptions of the other culture
Unquestioned acceptance of basic assumptions	Internalized values of the other culture
Personal frames of reference	New or broader schemas so that differences are accepted without a need to compare
Unexamined life	Constructed life
Accustomed role or status	Role assigned by the other culture or one's job
Social reinforcement knowledge	Accepting and learning the other culture's norms and behaviors
Accustomed habits and activities	Substituting functional equivalents
Known routines	Addiction to novelty and learning

Source: Reprinted with the author's permission from J. Osland (1995) *The Adventure of Working Abroad: Hero Tales from the Global Frontier* (San Francisco, CA: Jossey-Bass), p. 141.

the validity of their assumptions. At the same time, they may adopt, consciously or unconsciously, the values of the other culture, a natural part of the acculturation process (Berry 1983). According to one expatriate, "I started to look at the world like the Colombians do and learned to not worry about things I cannot control." At the same time expatriates may be shedding some of their peripheral values; however, their core values (e.g. patriotism, religious values) become even stronger. As an expatriate reported, "I became more American while I was there. Even though I accepted the way things are there, it made me realize how American I really am."

Expatriates let go of their personal frames of reference and take on new or broader schemas so that differences are accepted without the need to compare them to a cultural frame of reference. In the beginning of a sojourn, people naturally make comparisons between what they observe and what they know from home, their frame of reference. Over time, that frame is expanded to include the new culture, and eventually well-adapted expatriates feel no need for comparisons with home-country standards. Instead, they develop new schemas to organize their perceptions. "I used to make negative comparisons between the employees here and my subordinates at home; eventually, I just began to appreciate the locals for who they are and stopped making any comparisons at all. They both have strengths and weaknesses."

Expatriates let go of an unexamined life to take on a constructed life that they themselves put together piece by conscious piece. The surprises, changes, and contrasts (Louis 1980a) trigger introspection and an examination of their life in many expatriates. In some cases, it is difficult to replicate the life they had prior to expatriation. Thus, expatriates, and spouses in particular, are compelled to create a new life for themselves after carefully considering what to include. As an expatriate noted, "My wife had nothing. I mean, she woke up and had no structure to her day. She really had to construct her life, and fortunately [she] did it."

Expatriates let go of their accustomed role or status and take on the role assigned by the other culture or by their job. Being a manager in a high-power distance, authoritarian culture entails a higher status position than being a manager in a low-power, egalitarian culture. Regardless of their position, they are a stranger in a foreign land and may be stereotyped in negative ways for their inability to speak the language or for their nationality. Thus, they have to learn to handle the roles assigned to them and still maintain their own sense of identity.

Expatriates let go of the social reinforcement knowledge from their own culture and take on the other culture's norms and behaviors. Beginning at a young age, people learn how to behave appropriately or to obtain desired reactions in their own culture. Some of that knowledge becomes irrelevant in another culture, and expatriates have to give up some of their own cultural scripts to adopt those of the other culture. This involves both acceptance and learning. As one expatriate commented, "I know how to get things done in my own culture, but they [tactics] don't work here and I had to figure out new tactics, whether I wanted to or not."

Expatriates let go of accustomed habits and activities to take on substitutes that are functionally equivalent. This is similar to the cultural flexibility mentioned above. It is not always possible to engage in the same activities and hobbies found at home so many expatriates take on replacements that serve the same function. Rather than bemoan the loss of her symphony choir at home, one expatriate simply learned whatever instrument would allow her to continue playing music with others in each foreign country.

Finally, expatriates let go of their known routines and take on novelty and learning. The comfort and security of one's own culture is replaced by the uncertainty and surprises of the other culture. Well-acculturated expatriates learn to value this novelty and are energized by the endless opportunities to learn. "As one expatriate described it, living abroad is like returning to childhood when every day brings novel adventures and something new" (Osland 2001: 151). Osland (2001) identified the impetus behind expatriate transformation as their desire to become acculturated, to fit into another culture, and to be effective at work, which leads us to the next topic, expatriate effectiveness.

Expatriate Effectiveness

Neither companies nor scholars have been completely clear or in agreement on what constitutes expatriate effectiveness (Harrison et al. 2004; Shaffer et al. 2006). "Corporations have defined it as accomplishment of assignment objectives, attrition rates or increased revenues, but few have systems in place to track these outcomes and attribute them to individual assignees" (Shaffer et al. 2006). Scholars have measured effectiveness in terms of adjustment (Black 1988; Black et al. 1991), the strength of their plans or decisions to go home early without completing their assignment (withdrawal cognitions) (Black and Gregersen 1990; Naumann 1992; Takeuchi et al. 2002), and job performance (Arthur and Bennett 1997). The core aspects of job performance for expatriates are fulfilling specific task requirements and developing and maintaining relationships with host country nationals (Harrison and Shaffer 2005: 1455). Similarly high-involvement leadership, which was defined as emphasizing both task and consideration for people, was more effective outside the United States than within the United States (Stroh et al. 2005). While these two facets—task and relationship—are especially important for expatriate effectiveness, there is, however, much more uncertainty about what tactics are needed to achieve work goals and develop social relationships with strangers in an unfamiliar culture. Intercultural competence was identified as a key factor for Australian expatriates working in Asia (Lloyd et al. 2004).

Results of Expatriation

Caligiuri and Di Santo (2001) studied what companies hoped to accomplish via expatriation. They asked several focus groups consisting of a total of thirty-six global HR managers and fourteen line managers in a global business unit this question: "What is your organization hoping to develop in employees sent on global assignments?" Content analysis on the answers yielded eight developmental goals of global competence, which were subsequently categorized as knowledge, ability, or personality-related. In addition to reducing ethnocentrism, the other goals involved increasing:

- the ability to transact business in another country

- the ability to change leadership style based on the situation

- knowledge of the company's worldwide business structure

- knowledge of international business issues

- the network of professional contacts worldwide

- openness

- flexibility

The researchers then surveyed three groups in three different firms as to how they rated themselves on the eight categories. Group members were all current or former participants in the firms' global leadership development program: 1) "prepatriates" who were selected for the programs but who hadn't yet been sent abroad, 2) expatriates who were currently abroad, and 3) repatriates who had returned home after an international assignment.

The results indicate three findings. First, some personality traits, like flexibility and level of ethnocentrism, did not change as a result of a global assignment. No significant differences were revealed in these two traits, which is not surprising since personality traits tend to be stable, enduring patterns of how individuals feel, think, and behave over time (Buss 1989; Costa and McCrae 1992). Because most global leadership models include personality traits, this finding highlights the importance of careful selection procedures. Second, knowledge can be developed as a result of global assignments, which was indicated by higher scores in reported knowledge of professional contacts worldwide and the company's worldwide business structure. Third, global assignments can sensitize individuals to the challenges of working abroad and increase their humility. Surprisingly, prepatriate scores were significantly higher than those of expatriates or repatriates for openness, ability to transact business in another country, ability to change leadership style, and knowledge of international business issues. Presumably, an international experience made expatriates and repatriates aware of what they do not know (Caligiuri and Di Santo 2001). To use the conscious competence learning model (Howell and Fleishman 1982), prepatriates might be categorized as "unconscious incompetence" whereas the expatriates and repatriates may well have advanced to "conscious incompetence." This underscores the learning and cognitive change that takes place in global assignments.

The study of expatriation makes numerous contributions to the field of global leadership, including its findings on antecedents, selection, adjustment, effectiveness, expatriate transformation, and the inherent paradoxes that lead to development of a global mindset.

Global Management

While traditional expatriate managers concentrate on a single foreign country and their relationship with headquarters, global managers are responsible for understanding and operating in the worldwide business environment (Adler and Bartholomew 1992: 53). One definition of a global manager is "someone who is assigned to a position with a cross-border responsibility, who needs to understand business from a worldwide rather than from a countrywide perspective, needs to balance potentially contradictory demands in the global environment and who must be able to work with multiple cultures simultaneously rather than with one culture at a time" (Cappellen and Janssens 2005: 348). The study of global managers shares some similarity and overlap with the study of global leadership. Indeed, a major criticism directed at some of the early research on global leadership was that these roles and terms were used interchangeably (Osland et al. 2006). While acknowledging that global leaders both lead *and* manage, our definition of global leadership stipulates in addition that "global leaders are individuals who effect significant positive change in organizations." This requirement is based on Kotter's (1990a; 1990b) classic study of the difference between leaders and managers, which concluded that leaders, unlike managers, are change agents. There is no evidence to date that this distinction between domestic leaders and managers does not hold true in the global context. Some global managers may also be global leaders if they are change agents and build a global community with a unified purpose, but not all global managers are automatically global leaders. Titles alone do not guarantee leadership behavior. Nevertheless, there are interesting global manager research findings that hold lessons for global leadership.

As with global leadership, the literature on global managers comprises both empirical research and the expert opinion of people who work in the area. The global manager descriptions in this paragraph fall into the latter category. Weeks (1992) described the successful international manager as someone with knowledge of the business, high degrees of tolerance and flexibility, and the ability to work with people; these characteristics appear on our list in Table 2.1 for both expatriate adjustment determinants and global leadership competencies. Given the transnational structure they deemed necessary for global organizations, Bartlett and Ghoshal (1989) contended that effective global managers require the cognitive complexity to hold the matrix of a multistructured entity in their mind and be capable of reorganizing form to follow function as dictated by changing business demands. Adler and Bartholomew (1992) recommended that global managers be "cultural synergizers" while Bartlett, Doz and Hedlund (1990) referred to them as "cross fertilizers" or "cross-pollinators." All these authors arrived at their conclusions after taking a serious look at globalization and what it meant for organizations and then extrapolating, relying on inductive reasoning, what kind of managers were needed.

In contrast, the research that follows is empirical in nature. We can get some sense of who global managers are from a study of Finnish global managers with more than one expatriate assignment (Suutari and Taka 2004). Their most typical career anchors (Schein 1996) were "managerial competence" and "pure challenge." They also included "internationalism" as one of their top career anchors, which underscores how important it is to them to work in global jobs in global settings— and how difficult it may be for them to return to purely domestic work. Cappellen and Janssens (2008; 2010) analyzed the narratives of forty-five global managers to learn about the characteristics of their work and the competencies they acquired.

Two key questions regarding global managers are "What do they actually do and is that different from domestic managers?" To answer the first question, scholars began by looking at the roles performed by domestic managers and Mintzberg's (1973) observation of managers as they went about their daily work. He explicated these managerial roles: monitor, spokesperson, leader, liaison, decision maker, innovator, and negotiator. Mintzberg noted, however, that not all managers perform the same roles in the same manner because there are four sets of variables that determine how they do their work: environment (differences in milieu, industry, and organization), job (difference in job level and function), person (differences in manager personality and style characteristics), and situation (differences in temporal and contextual features).

Not all scholars accept a universal theory of management or Mintzberg's managerial roles. Some research indicates that roles vary depending on national culture and the level of industrialization (Lubatkin et al. 1997a; 1997b). An environmental difference noted in a study of Central American managers seemed to necessitate an additional managerial role. Observations of managers confirmed that they performed the roles identified by Mintzberg, but they also carried out a protector role with the government (Osland, 1991). This role involved keeping close tabs on potential governmental actions that would impact their business, trying to ward off detrimental legislation or regulations, and trying to craft special arrangements that would protect their firm from damage or risk even if the government did take action. Lobbyists and government liaisons might be more likely to perform this role in larger countries, but the social networks of the Central American managers allowed them to have advance knowledge and to influence government actions in a way that was deemed different from the traditional liaison role.

A research team at the Center for Creative Leadership found significant differences in how domestic and global managers perform their roles (Dalton et al. 2002). They surveyed 211 managers of various nationalities who worked at four organizations (two Swiss, one Swedish and one U.S.). Based on Mintzberg's work and their research data, they developed and used seven managerial roles in their research, which appear in Table 2.3.The sample contained both global and domestic managers, and the researchers tested a variety of factors related to managerial effectiveness (e.g. personality) and surveyed their bosses about their effectiveness. The findings indicated both similarity and difference between global and domestic managers; the research team attributed the differences to the complexity of the global environment.

Table 2.3 Global Managerial Roles

Informational Roles	
1. Monitor	Scan environments, monitor units, probe and seek information, act as corporate nerve center of incoming information
2. Spokesperson	Communicate and disseminate information with multiple levels of the internal and extra-organizational system, advocate and represent the organization
Interpersonal Roles	
3. Leader	Motivate, coach, build teams, maintain corporate climate and culture, and supervise the work of others
4. Liaison	Network, coordinate, link entities, and span organizational boundaries
Action Roles	
5. Decision maker	Take action, troubleshoot, make decisions, and use power to get things done
6. Innovator	Try new approaches, seize opportunities, generate new ideas, and promote a vision
7. Negotiator	Make deals, translate strategy into action, negotiate contracts, manage conflict, and confront others

Source: Printed with permission from the Center for Creative Leadership.

The patterns of traits, role skills, and capabilities global managers need to be effective are similar to that of domestic managers. The bosses of global managers say emotional stability, skill in the roles of leader and decision maker, and the ability to cope with stress are key components to managerial effectiveness regardless of the job's global complexity. In addition, bosses look to conscientiousness, skill in the role of negotiator and innovator, business knowledge, international business knowledge, cultural adaptability, and the ability to take the perspective of others as significant to the effectiveness of global managers.

(Leslie et al. 2002: 63)

Emotional stability, decision maker and negotiator roles, and the ability to learn played a more significant role with global managers than they did with domestic managers. Surprisingly, previous international exposure and work did not contribute to the global managers' effectiveness, and the cosmopolitan managers were not viewed as trusted or well liked by their peers and other colleagues, according to their bosses' perceptions (Leslie et al. 2002). As one would expect, the selection criteria utilized in this study did not stipulate leadership roles or abilities. While future research may discover that their findings also apply to global leaders, we cannot make this assumption a priori.

The shared platform between domestic and global jobs plus the additional demands placed on global managers was confirmed in another study that interviewed fifty-five chief executive officers (CEOs) from various industries in fifteen countries (McBer 1995). Participants described critical incidents that were content analyzed to identify the factors that predicted effectiveness in global managers. Three of the competencies they identified were deemed universal and thus shared by both global and domestic managers: sharpening the focus, building commitment, and driving for success. However, they also identified three competencies that varied depending on the cultural context: business relationships, the role of action, and the style of authority.

The research of Spreitzer et al. (1997) was guided by their belief that critical skills for managers are learned from experience. Therefore, the ability to learn should be a selection criterion when companies hire or promote international managers. They developed an instrument for early identification of international executives, called Prospector, that included two categories of behaviors and competencies for international managers (expatriates or executives in an international job). The learning-oriented behaviors are: uses feedback, seeks feedback, cross-culturally adventurous, seeks opportunities to learn, is open to criticism, and is flexible. The competencies are: sensitive to cultural differences, acts with integrity, committed to success, has broad business knowledge, brings out the best in people, is insightful, has the courage to take a stand, and takes risks. International managers were more likely to be described as effective if they were cross-culturally adventurous and insightful, sought opportunities to learn, and were open to criticism (Spreitzer et al. 1997).

The Corporate Leadership Council (2000) surveyed some of its corporate members on issues relating to developing and retaining future global leaders. They identified the six global management skills in highest demand, some of which are focused on specific tasks. This list includes: intercultural adaptability, ability to develop individuals across diverse cultures, global strategic thinking, global team building, ability to start up business in new markets, and ability to interact with local political interests.

A comparison of global manager and global leader competencies will no doubt show areas of overlap since many of the competencies mentioned in this section appear in Table 2.1. The key lessons from the study of global managers are the significant differences between domestic and global managers in terms of how they perform their roles and the findings on characteristics related to perceived effectiveness.

Comparative Leadership

The field of comparative leadership studies the differences and similarities in the indigenous leadership styles of different countries or regions. Leadership schemas and behaviors, as well as perceptions of what constitutes effective leadership vary from one culture to another. Comparative leadership studies often measure the different styles in the leadership continuum mentioned in Chapter 1 across cultures or rely on cultural value dimensions (Parsons and Shils 1951; Kluckhohn and Strodtbeck 1961; Hofstede 1980b; Hall and Hall 1990; Fiske 1992; Trompenaars and Hampden-Turner 1993; Schwartz 1994) to identify or distinguish national or regional leadership styles and practices. The word 'leader' has different connotations in different languages. For example, the term conjures the positive image of a heroic figure in Anglo-Saxon countries but brings to mind the negative image of dictators in countries like Germany and Spain (Den Hartog and Dickson 2004). In The Netherlands, the term for the equivalent of followers or subordinates (*medewerkes*) translates as "coworkers," and is reflective of its more egalitarian culture (Dickson et al. 2009).

Researchers discovered national differences in leadership characteristics, such as leader status, goals, role, communication, influence, decision making, and perceived effectiveness. For example, cultures characterized by large power distance tend to have autocratic leaders and followers who are less likely to challenge or disagree with them (Adsit et al. 1997). Therefore, participative management techniques imported from low power distance cultures may not be appropriate (Newman and Nollen 1996). In a study of a Russian factory, participative management actually decreased rather than increased productivity (Welsh et al. 1993). Participative leadership is still not culturally endorsed in Russia as much as in other countries (House et al. 2004). Asking for advice and input may be interpreted as incompetence or weakness in cultures in which leaders are supposed to be omnipotent experts. In collectivist cultures, followers are more likely to identify with leaders' goals and the group or organization's shared vision (Earley and Gibson 1998; Triandis 1995). Thus, they are more likely to exhibit a higher degree of loyalty than people from individualistic cultures who tend to place more value on personal goals and self-interest. For recent reviews on leadership from a cross-cultural perspective, see Gelfand et al. (2007), Aycan (2008), and Dickson et al. (2009).

Culture is not the only source of differences in national or regional leadership patterns. A country's unique history, geography, economic development, technological status, and institutions all influence leadership patterns. Behrens (2009), for instance, takes a multidisciplinary view (economics, history, literature) to describe management and leadership in Argentina, Brazil, and the United States. Cheung and Chan (2005) used a similar approach to explain the foundations of eminent Hong Kong Chinese CEOs.

Many comparative leadership studies measure well-established frameworks of leadership styles across cultures. Despite documented national differences in leadership, research findings also point out commonalities. A large comparative study that examined how managers from various countries handle routine work events found both cultural differences and similarities (Smith and Peterson 1988). Bass (1997) found another similarity in comparative leadership studies— laissez faire leaders are perceived as ineffective by their subordinates. Aspects of charismatic and transformational leadership—motivational, encouraging, communicative, trustworthy, dynamic, positive, confidence building—are universally preferred (Den Hartog et al. 1999).

The most extensive comparative leadership contribution to date comes from Project GLOBE(House et al. 2004). A 180-member multinational research team studied the relationship among leadership, societal values, and organizational culture. They obtained data on indigenous leadership from over 15,000 middle managers in sixty-two countries who worked in the telecommunications, food, and banking industries in their own countries. The researchers developed a new cultural framework, composed of nine dimensions: performance orientation, assertiveness, future orientation, human orientation, institutional collectivism, in-group collectivism, gender egalitarianism, power distance, and uncertainty avoidance (Javidan and House 2001). Subsequently, the managers' responses on these dimensions were used to categorize the sixty-two countries into ten culture clusters. These clusters reported different "culturally endorsed implicit leadership theories": charismatic/value-based, team-oriented, participative, humane-oriented, autonomous, and self-protective. Thus, the cultural dimensions were shown to influence expectations of leaders.

Project GLOBE also found that different countries have both similar and different views on leadership. As shown in Table. 2.4, they identified a list of leader attributes that are universally acceptable, universally unacceptable, and culturally contingent (i.e. they work in some cultures but not in others)

Table 2.4 Project GLOBE Leadership Traits

Universally Acceptable Traits	Universally Unacceptable Traits	Culturally Contingent Traits
Decisive	Ruthless	Enthusiastic
Informed	Egocentric	Self-sacrificial
Honest	Asocial	Risk-taking
Dynamic	Non-explicit	Sincere
Administratively skilled	Irritable	Ambitious
Coordinator	Non-cooperative	Sensitive
Just	Loner	Self-effacing
Team builder	Dictatorial	Compassionate
Effective bargainer		Unique
Dependable		Willful
Win–win problem solver		
Plans ahead		
Intelligent		
Excellence-oriented		

Source: Based on Den Hartog et al. (1999).

(Den Hartog et al. 1999). Similar business conditions and practices, technology, more well-educated employees, and the presence of multinational enterprises may be responsible for at least partial convergence on leadership views. The selection criteria for Project GLOBE did not include evidence of global leadership roles or skills, since this was not their focus. Future research could test whether or not these universal attributes are also characteristic of effective global leaders. Based on their findings about cultural differences and diverse leadership profiles, GLOBE researchers argue that global leaders require a global mindset, tolerance of ambiguity, and cultural adaptability and flexibility (Javidan et al. 2006).

The major contribution of comparative management to the field of global leadership is the understanding that national leadership styles have certain aspects in common as well as many differences rooted in culture or a country's unique history. Therefore, when global leaders have followers from different cultures, they have to be prepared to switch styles based on the situation and the people involved (Gill and Booth 2003).

Thanks to the groundwork laid in the fields of intercultural communication competence, expatriation, global management, and comparative leadership, the nascent field of global leadership has strong supportive roots. Our next chapter details the growth of global leadership as a field of study in its own right.

3 An Overview of the Global Leadership Literature

JOYCE S. OSLAND

> Your life is your message. Leadership by example is not only the most pervasive but also the most enduring form of leadership. And because the world is becoming more interconnected, standards of leadership have an impact that extends around the globe. Now, as never before, a higher standard of leadership will serve us all.
>
> (Nair 1994)

History is graced with leaders who fit most people's definition of global leaders—political leaders like Mahatma Gandhi, military leaders like Alexander the Great, and spiritual leaders like Mother Theresa—whose impact and followers extended far beyond the borders of their own country. Such famous figures often capture the imagination and loyalty of a broad audience due to the confluence of their unique vision and its relevance to the environmental context. Difficult times demand constructive leaders just as surely as destructive leaders create difficult times. Today's global leaders, however, are not necessarily famous; there are more and more of them performing less visible leadership roles in an increasingly complex, ambiguous, multicultural environment. Business CEOs with a reputation as change agents on a global scale are perhaps the first group that comes to mind for business students and practitioners, but people who integrate acquired companies into large transnational firms, who command coalition forces in the military, who run global non-profit organizations, and who lead multinational political organizations are all examples of current global leaders. Our definition of global leadership does not restrict global leaders to an organization's upper echelon; anyone who leads global change efforts in the public, private, and non-profit sector is a global leader.

Businesses that are extending their reach globally, taking products global, and employing a global workforce all have need of global leaders. Figuring out what global leadership looks like and how it can be developed was the impetus for much of the literature we will review in this chapter.

Discussions of global leadership begin by distinguishing how their role differs from that of domestic leaders (Osland et al. 2012a), international leaders, and global managers (see Chapter 2). Early definitions of global leadership borrowed and extrapolated traditional, domestic leadership definitions (Yeung and Ready 1995), but scholars quickly recognized that global leadership was far more complex than domestic leadership due to the pressures and dynamics of global competition (Weber et al. 1998) that broadened the scope of the leader's work. Adler clarified the issue when she wrote,

> Global leaders, unlike domestic leaders, address people worldwide. Global leadership theory, unlike its domestic counterpart, is concerned with the interaction of people and ideas among cultures, rather than with either the efficacy of particular leadership styles within the leader's home country or with the comparison of leadership approaches among leaders from various countries—each of whose domain is limited to issues and people within their own cultural environment. A fundamental distinction is that global leadership is neither domestic nor multidomestic.
>
> (Adler 2001: 77)

Global Leadership Literature Review—Early Literature

As with the topic of global managers in Chapter 2, prescriptions about global leaders come from a variety of sources, primarily expert opinion and empirical research. Our chronology of the literature begins with the earliest publications in the 1990s, which consisted of extrapolations from the domestic leadership literature, interviews, focus groups, or observations from the authors' consulting or training experiences (Lobel 1990; Kets de Vries and Mead 1992; Tichy et al. 1992; Rhinesmith 1993; Moran and Riesenberger 1994; Brake 1997).

Lobel briefly reviewed early research on the managerial competencies for global leadership and noted that these relational characteristics were frequently repeated: "flexibility, curiosity and openness to other ways of living and speaking, and nonjudgmental acceptance of cultural differences" (1990: 40).

Tichy and his colleagues wrote about "true globalists," as they called them, who have 1) a global mindset; 2) a set of global leadership skills and behaviors; 3) energy, skills, and talent for global networking; 4) the ability to build effective teams; and 5) global change agent skills (Tichy et al. 1992). They believe, as we do, that the best global leadership systems develop people and the organization simultaneously. Training and developing future leaders without also carrying out organization development (OD) activities to enable the organization to function globally and take advantage of these leaders makes their potential effectiveness a greater gamble.

Kets de Vries and Mead (1992) developed a list of leadership qualities that included: envisioning, strong operational codes, environmental sense-making, ability to instill values, inspiring, empowering, building and maintaining organizational networks, interpersonal skills, pattern recognition and cognitive complexity, and hardiness. Moran and Riesenberger (1994) held a focus group with international managers who suggested several competencies that were categorized as attitudes, interaction, cultural understanding, and leadership.

Rhinesmith, a consultant, authored an insightful book, *A Manager's Guide to Globalization* (1993; 1996), based on his work with multinational corporations. He identified twenty-four competencies that he categorized as 1) Strategy and Structure; 2) Corporate Culture; and 3) People. Subsequently, Rhinesmith (2003) created a simpler model centered on global mindset, which he describes as fundamentally "making decisions with increasing reference points." In this model, global mindset has two components. The first is intellectual intelligence (which he relates to cognitive complexity). Intellectual intelligence entails both business acumen and paradox management (which is similar to the previous discussion on expatriate paradoxes). Its second component is global emotional intelligence (which he relates to cosmopolitanism). Global emotional intelligence is comprised of cultural self-awareness, cultural adjustment, cross-cultural understanding, and cross-cultural effectiveness. Thus, global emotional intelligence involves both self-management and cultural acumen. Intellectual and global emotional intelligence are the basis for the global behavioral skills that make up the global manager's leadership style, as seen in the model found in Figure 3.1.

Rhinesmith believes that the paradoxes of global business are never fully resolved and put to rest. There will always be global–local tensions, for example, that must be continually balanced and managed. He suggests five steps for managing paradoxes: 1) identify the competing forces of the paradox (e.g. individual versus team; stability versus change; centralization versus decentralization; work versus family); 2) create a paradox management grid to show the positive and negative forces of the competing forces; 3) optimize, rather than maximize, your

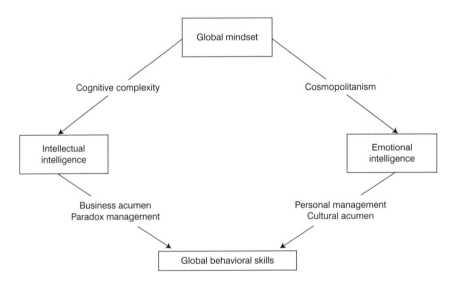

Figure 3.1 Rhinesmith's Basic Components of a Global Mindset

Source: S. Rhinesmith. (2003) "Basic components of a global mindset." In M. Goldsmith et al. (eds) *The Many Facets of Leadership* (Upper Saddle River, NJ: Financial Times/Prentice Hall), p. 218.

primary responsibilities by seeking win–win solutions; 4) include contradictions in your thinking by meeting with stakeholders likely to have opposing views; and 5) create paradox alarm metrics that sound when negative reactions build up (Rhinesmith 2003).

Brake wrote a perceptive book, *The Global Leader: Critical Factors for Creating the World Class Organization* (1997), based on the global business literature and interviews with practitioners at leading firms. To think about the universal leadership process, Brake was guided by the image of Shiva, the Hindu deity who weaves together seemingly contradictory qualities and is sometimes portrayed with six faces that symbolize his many facets. Shiva has a third eye that enables him to see inward. "Shiva performs the Dance of Life within a ring of fire. He is not consumed by the fire, but appears to draw on the energy of the fire for his own vitality" (Brake 1997: 31). He sees global leaders as working in the center of a ring of fire that is global competition. They can either embrace the fire's energy to generate higher levels of performance or perish in the fire. The global leadership process that leads to higher performance consists of three steps (Brake 1997: 31–32):

1   Framing the global competitive challenges as opportunities.

2   Generating personal and organizational energy.

3   Transforming energy into world-class performance.

Brake notes that global leaders sometimes have to unlearn what previously made their firm successful. He developed the Global Leadership Triad (Brake 1997), which consists of three sets of competencies, shown in Figure 3.2. Most of the individual competencies have been discussed previously in this chapter or their meaning is obvious; definitions are provided below only for the exceptions, where Brake's meaning may vary from the readers'.

Business Acumen. Business acumen is "the ability to pursue and apply appropriate professional knowledge and skills to achieve optimal results of the company's global stakeholders" (Brake 1997: 45). In this category, depth of knowledge refers to "demonstrating the willingness and an ability to switch perspectives between local and global/functional and cross-functional needs and opportunities" (Brake 1997: 45). In today's language, this would be called global mindset. The stakeholder orientation balances the needs of both internal (e.g. functional areas) and external groups (e.g. customers, communities). Total organizational astuteness "demonstrates insights into 'how the business works' above and beyond his or her immediate area and seeks to use this knowledge to get things done within and among organizational units" (Brake 1997: 47–48). Brake's description of this competency illustrates some of the deep organizational knowledge required in global careers:

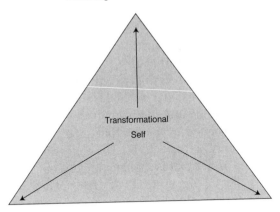

Relationship Management
- Change Agentry
- Community Building
- Conflict Management and Negotiation
- Cross-Cultural Communication
- Influencing

Transformational
Self

Business Acumen
- Depth of Field
- Entrepreneurial Spirit
- Professional Expertise
- Stakeholder Orientation
- Total Organization Astuteness

Personal Effectiveness
- Accountability
- Curiosity and Learning
- Improvisation
- Maturity
- Thinking Agility

Figure 3.2 Brake's Global Leadership Triad

Source: Reprinted with permission from T. Brake (1997) *The Global Leader: Critical Factors for Creating the World Class Organization* (Chicago, IL: Irwin Professional Publishing), p. 44.

1 Draws on a range of information-gathering skills to build a realistic profile of the global organization.

2 Creates or utilizes multiple internal networks for sourcing business intelligence, expertise, global best practices, and resources and for promoting coordination, and so forth.

3 Recognizes key organizational constituencies and decision makers and relies on political savvy to create alliances and foster collaboration to realize global goals.

4 Recognizes the assumptions and mental models entrenched in the organizational culture and articulates them when they need to be reviewed and questioned for change to take place.

5 Understands and fosters the continuous review of key organizational processes, systems, standard operation procedures, working methods, and so forth.

6　Demonstrates a good sense of timing in putting forward new ideas and proposals.

7　Analyzes key global trends and forecasts how they will impact organizational strategy, structure, and systems.

Relationship Management. Relationship management is "the ability to build and influence collaborative relationships in a complex and diverse global network to direct energy toward the achievement of business strategies" (Brake 1997: 48). In this category, change agentry is both the openness to new ways of doing things and the ability to motivate others to identify and implement desired changes (Brake 1997: 48). Community building is the willingness and ability to partner with others in interdependent relationships to accomplish business goals (Brake 1997: 49).

Personal Effectiveness. Personal effectiveness is "the ability to attain increasing levels of maturity to perform at peak levels under the strenuous conditions of working in a global enterprise" (Brake 1997: 52). Brake's definition of maturity includes a sense of humor, self-confidence, resilience, the ability to deal with crises and setbacks and recover quickly from mistakes.

At the center of the triad is the concept of the Transformational Self, "a philosophy of possibility and personal engagement with the world – that is, a drive toward meaning and purpose through activity strengthened by reflections, personal mind management, and openness to change" (Brake 1997: 44). This is central to both domestic and global leadership in his view.

Kanter (1997) argued that global business leaders should be cosmopolitans who can integrate and cross-fertilize knowledge and manage dispersed centers of expertise, influence and production. In addition to creating new communication routes, they need to move capital, ideas, and people to whatever world location they are needed. Dalton (1998: 386) wrote that global leaders should possess 1) a high level of cognitive complexity to gather and understand contradictory information from multiple sources and to make effective decisions; 2) excellent interpersonal skills that would buy them time to figure out how to behave in a particular situation and country; 3) the ability to learn from experience; and 4) advanced moral reasoning to understand ethical dilemmas.

Petrick and his colleagues (1999) contended that two global leadership skills result in the corporation's reputational capital, an intangible resource for sustainable competitive advantage. The first skill is behavioral flexibility, which is defined as the ability to balance four competing values and performance criteria: 1) profitability and productivity; 2) continuity and efficiency; 3) commitment and morale; and 4) adaptability and innovation (Denison et al. 1995). The second skill is stewardship of sustainable development, which involves acting as a responsible steward of human and natural resources and promoting, concurrently, economic, social, biological, and ecological development (Petrick et al. 1999: 61). By exercising these two skills, global leaders increase their firm's reputational capital, which is a component of social capital. Social capital, rooted in trust and common norms, reduces transaction costs among cooperative partners and accelerates global prosperity (Coleman 1988; Petrick et al. 1999).

Other types of capital are also important for global leaders. In a conceptual article, Harvey and Novicevic argue that global assignments (i.e. expatriation and inpatriation) contribute to the development of four types of global leader capital (2004: 1177):

- Human capital—the skills and competencies that leaders need to have based on expert and referent power in their organization.

- Cultural capital—acceptance and social inclusiveness due to having tacit knowledge of how the organization operates.

- Social capital—the standing and concurrent ability to draw on standing to accomplish tasks in an organization.

- Political capital—the ability to use power or authority and gain the support of constituents in a socially effective way.

A global leader's political capital is crucial because it can be used to decrease the level of conflict among foreign subsidiaries and ensure that diverse views are represented. Politically skilled leaders also generate more support and acquiescence (Harvey and Novicevic 2004).

Based on Asian-Pacific experience, a practitioner article describes global leadership capability as a "behavioral blend of cross-cultural competence combined with leadership skills" (Carey et al. 2004: 13). The authors' proposed core capability attributes and performance attributes appear below (Carey et al. 2004: 16).

1 Inclusion—demonstrates vision that is inclusive and decision-making that is collaborative.

2 Credibility—cultivates and inspires trust in a culturally diverse workforce, remaining consistent to their values.

3 Synergy—motivates and empowers diverse individuals, results in synergistic organizations.

4 Flexibility—adapts to global complexity and change.

5 Compassion—demonstrates empathy and sensitivity to diversity (different genders, cultures, races, and nationalities).

Numerous case studies and interviews provide anecdotal descriptions of global leaders (Taylor 1991; McFarland et al. 1993; Maruca 1994; McKibben 1997; Marquardt and Berger 2000; Emerson 2001; Green et al. 2003; Bingham et al. 2000; Millikin and Fu 2005; Nohria 2009). For example, in an interview John Pepper, former CEO of P&G, came up with his own list of global leader competencies: dealing with uncertainty; knowing customers; balancing tensions between global efficiency and local responsiveness; and appreciating diversity (Bingham et al. 2000). The seven *Advances in Global Leadership* volumes (Mobley et al. 1999; Mobley and McCall 2001; Mobley and Dorfman 2003; Mobley and Weldon 2006; Mobley et al. 2009; 2011; 2012) are a source of current thinking, findings, and implications for future research. Gill (2012), a political scientist, published an edited volume on the global crises and the crisis in global leadership. It is an analytical and normative treatise that questions current thinking on global crisis, leadership, democracy, justice, and sustainability in the emerging world order. Global leadership books written primarily for business practitioners include Nirenberg (2002), Brown (2007), Cohen (2007), Hames (2007), Wibbeke (2009), and Gundling et al. (2011). For published reviews of the global leadership literature, see Hollenbeck (2001), Suutari (2002), Jokinen (2005), Mendenhall and colleagues (2008), Osland (2008, first edition of this book), Osland et al. (2009), and Osland et al. (2006; 2012b).

Global Leadership Literature Review—Empirical Studies

Most empirical work on global leadership has attempted to answer these two questions: "What capabilities do global leaders need to acquire in order to be effective?" and "How can managers most effectively develop these characteristics?" The complete list of extant empirical studies on global leadership is described in Table 3.1 and in the following sections. With few exceptions, the methodologies most commonly utilized to study global leadership are surveys and/ or interviews.

Holistic Core Competence

One of the most insightful early studies was carried out by Wills and Barham (1994). After interviewing sixty successful senior executives from nine global firms, they argued that international executives operate from a deep holistic core competence composed of three integrated parts: cognitive complexity, emotional energy, and psychological maturity. Cognitive complexity and the ability to understand other viewpoints were demonstrated by cultural empathy, active listening, and a sense of humility. Emotional energy was manifested by emotional self-awareness, emotional resilience, risk acceptance, and the emotional support of their family. This support served as a coping mechanism as well as a source of emotional energy that could be applied at work. Finally, psychological maturity

Table 3.1 A Chronological List of Empirical Research on Global Leadership

Authors	Description	Method	Findings
Yeung and Ready (1995)	Identifies leadership capabilities in a cross-national study	Surveys of 1,200 managers from ten major global corporations and eight countries	Capabilities: articulate vision, values, strategy; catalyst for strategic and cultural change; empower others; results and customer orientation
Adler (1997)	Describes women global leaders in politics and business	Archival data and interviews with women global leaders from sixty countries	Their number is increasing and they come from diverse backgrounds; are not selected by women-friendly countries or companies; use broad-based power rather than hierarchical power; are lateral transfers; symbolize change and unity; and leverage their increased visibility
Black et al. (1999a)	Identifies capabilities of effective global leaders and how to develop them	Interviews of 130 senior line and HR executives in fifty companies in Europe, North America and Asia and nominated global leaders	Capabilities: inquisitive, character, duality, savvy. Development occurs via training, transfer, travel, and multicultural teams
Kets de Vries with Florent-Treacy (1999)	Describes excellent global leadership	Case studies involving interviews with three global leaders (CEOs)	Identifies best practices in leadership, structure, strategy, corporate culture
Rosen et al. (2000)	Identifies leadership universals	Interviews with seventy-five CEOs from twenty-eight countries; 1058 surveys with CEOs, presidents, managing directors or chairmen; studies of national culture	Leadership universals: personal, social, business, and cultural literacies, many of which are paradoxical in nature
McCall and Hollenbeck (2002)	To identify how to select and develop global executives and understand how they derail	Interviews with 101 executives from thirty-six countries and sixteen global firms nominated as successful global executives	Competencies: open-minded and flexible; culture interest and sensitivity; able to deal with complexity; resilient, resourceful, optimistic, energetic; honesty and integrity; stable personal life; value-added technical or business skills
Goldsmith et al. (2003)	To identify global leadership dimensions needed in the future	Thought leader panels; focus groups with twenty-eight CEOs, focus/dialogue groups with at least 207 current or future leaders; interviews with 202 high potential next generation leaders; seventy-three surveys from forum group members	Fifteen dimensions: integrity, personal mastery, constructive dialogue, shared vision, empowerment, developing people, building partnerships, sharing leadership, thinking globally, appreciating diversity, technologically savvy, customer satisfaction, anticipating opportunities, leading change, and maintaining competitive advantage
Bikson et al. (2003)	Examines impact of globalization on HR needs, global leadership competencies, and policies and practices needed to produce sufficient global leaders	Structured interviews with 135 U.S. HR and senior managers in public, for-profit, and non-profit sectors. Unstructured interviews with twenty-four experts	Insufficient future global leaders who have the required integrated skill repertoire: substantive depth in organization's primary business; managerial ability (especially teamwork and interpersonal skills); strategic international understanding; and cross-cultural experience.
Kets de Vries et al. (2004)	Describes the development of 360-degree feedback instrument, GlobeInvent	Based on semi-structured interviews with a number of senior executives	Twelve dimensions/psychodynamic properties: envisioning, empowering, energizing, designing, rewarding, team-building, outside orientation, global mindset, tenacity, emotional intelligence, life balance, resilience to stress

Source: Adapted and updated from J. Osland, A. Bird, M. E. Mendenhall, and A. Osland (2006) "Developing global leadership capabilities and global mindset: A review." In G.K. Stahl and I. Björkman (eds) Handbook of Research in International Human Resource Management (Cheltenham, UK: Edward Elgar Publishing), pp. 205–206.

implies the presence of a strong value system that gives their lives meaning. Wills and Barham (1994) identified the following three values as central features of the psychological maturity found in international managers: curiosity to learn, living in the 'here and now' by taking full advantage of the present, and personal morality. Wills and Barham did not refer to their interviewees as leaders or global leaders since the latter term was not in use when they completed this work. Since the subjects were selected by their organization's human resource managers as highly successful and because they managed across a number of countries simultaneously, it is likely that many, if not all, of their subjects would fit today's definition of global leaders.

Eight Nation Competency Study

Yeung and Ready (1995) produced the first quantitative study, using a sample of 1,200 managers from eight nations in ten major corporations (who were not necessarily global leaders themselves). The participants were presented with a list of competencies and asked to select those items that fit their description of global leaders. The capabilities on which they agreed were:

- articulate a tangible vision, values, strategy

- be a catalyst for strategic change

- be a catalyst for cultural change

- empower others

- results orientation

- customer orientation.

This list describes a transformational leadership style and a strong performance orientation.

Women Global Leaders

Adler (1997; 2001) noted that most leadership research has studied men. Previously, she disproved the myth that women expatriates could not succeed as well as men on overseas assignments and identified areas where they performed better than men (Adler 1994). Next, she studied senior women global leaders in politics and business from sixty countries using archival data and interviews (Adler 1997). The numbers of women presidents and prime ministers increased rapidly from zero in the 1950s to twenty-one in the 1990s.

By contrast, research from other sources shows that the numbers for women leaders in business merely inch up annually, and there is little hope that this will change quickly. There are less female CEOs in publicly held corporations; most female CEOs have founded their own firm or taken over family businesses. There are only eighteen female CEOs, 3 percent, in *Fortune 500* companies (Catalyst 2012). The number of female board members is highest in Scandinavia: Norway, 40.1 percent; Sweden, 27.3 percent; and Finland, 24.5 percent (Catalyst, 2011). Norway was the first country to set a quota of 40 percent females on their boards (*La Tribune* 2006). Other European countries (Spain, France, The Netherlands, Iceland, Italy, and Belgium) also have some type of quota in place (CWDI 2011). However, percentages still range widely in Europe. Women hold 16.1 percent of board seats in the United States, 15.8 percent in South Africa, 8.5 percent in China, 5.3 percent in India, and 0.9 percent in Japan (Catalyst 2011).

Adler (2001) argues for the feminization of global leadership due to the rapid increase in women political leaders and because traits and qualities generally associated with women have been linked to global leadership. For example, some research has found that women have a more participative, interactional, and relational leadership style (Fondas 1997) said to be more suited to a global setting (Hampden-Turner 1994). Adler's findings on women global leaders were (2001: 90–96):

1 *They come from diverse backgrounds*. Their route to leadership shows no predictable pattern.

2 *They were* not *selected solely by women-friendly countries or companies.*

3 *Their selection symbolizes hope, change, and unity*. Their position as outsiders and selection against the odds implies the possibility of societal or organizational change. Violeta Chamorro of Nicaragua and Corazon Aquino of the Philippines were voted president after their husbands were assassinated. They symbolized the desire for national unity.

4 *They are driven by vision, not by hierarchical status*. For instance, Dame Anita Roddick, founder and former CEO of The Body Shop, was not driven to be a CEO but to practice corporate idealism as far back as the early 90s:

   Leaders in the business world should aspire to be true planetary citizens. They have global responsibilities since their decisions affect not just the world of business, but world problems of poverty, national security and the environment. Many, sad to say, [have] duck[ed] these responsibilities, because their vision is material rather than moral.

   (Roddick 1991: 226)

5 *They use broad-based popular support rather than traditional, hierarchical party, or structural support*. Women political leaders gained support directly

from the people while female entrepreneurs gained support directly from the marketplace.

6 *Their path to power is through lateral transfers rather than the traditional path up the hierarchy.*

7 *They leverage the increased visibility they receive as women or "the first woman."* They receive more media attention than men, which they can use as a platform.

Although many of the women studied received a great deal of media attention, their intended circle of influence did not extend beyond their country or company. Not all of them were known as global change agents. But recognizing who they are, the reality of their proportional numbers, and understanding their path to power enriches our general understanding of global leadership. Adler's work is also a good reminder to scholars to ensure that their global leadership samples include gender diversity.

The Global Explorer Model

Black et al. (1999a) took a qualitative, exploratory approach to determine what capabilities global leaders needed to acquire and how managers could most effectively develop them. They interviewed over 130 senior line and HR executives in fifty companies in Europe, North America, and Asia and then interviewed forty nominated global leaders from these firms. The result was the Global Explorer Model, which consists of these global characteristics:

- Inquisitiveness—a love of learning, being intrigued by diversity.

- Embrace Duality—uncertainty is viewed as invigorating and a natural part of global business.

- Exhibit Character—the ability to connect emotionally with people of different backgrounds and cultures; consistently demonstrate personal integrity in a world full of ethical conflicts.

- Demonstrate Savvy—business savvy and organizational savvy.

Inquisitiveness is the centerpiece of the Global Explorer Model because of its fundamental importance. Whenever John Pepper of P&G went to a new country, he visited five local families to see how they cleaned their houses, washed their clothes, and took care of their children's hygiene before going to the office (Black 2006: 184). Pepper was curious about how the local people performed the tasks related to P&G's products. Black (2006) devised a list of recommendations for distinguishing between the inquisitive and the non-inquisitive.

- *Inquisitive people seek out the new rather than the comfortable.* Inquisitive people gather information about the foreign country and business before going on trips. Once there, they take advantage of the opportunity to learn about the country, to make contacts, and to experience the novelty of a foreign culture rather than cocooning themselves in a four-star hotel and eating the same food found at home.

- *Inquisitive people act as travelers rather than tourists.* Unlike tourists who unquestioningly accept their own civilization, travelers constantly compare and contrast the new things and ways of doing things with what they already know. If the new way is superior, they are willing to adopt it. Kraft Foods adopted the local distribution system for ice cream in China, even though it seemed less efficient at first glance. Given the storage capacity of small stores and the narrow crowded streets, bicycles equipped with dry ice were a better solution than Kraft's usual large refrigerated trucks (Black 2006).

- *Inquisitive people question rather than confirm.* When confronted with different ways of doing business, inquisitive people are quick to ask questions that lead to new understandings rather than assuming that they already understand. Rather than simply trying to confirm what they already believe, inquisitive people are sincere about seeking new information.

Inquisitiveness is an aspect of global mindset as is *Embracing Duality*. Similar to the paradoxes inherent in the expatriate experience (Osland 1995), global leaders also deal with the simultaneous existence of two contradictory conditions rooted in the global versus local tensions. For example, the corporate vice president of HR for International Flowers and Fragrances (IFF), Eric Campbell, said,

> The best local and global leaders in our company are curious enough to pay attention to the extremely subtle nuances of any locale – whether in New York or Jakarta – as well as smart enough to notice consumer similarities around the world.
>
> (Black 2006: 191).

One can spot those who embrace duality if they:

- *embrace rather than avoid ambiguity.* Ambiguity is an inherent aspect of global business. There are no easy answers to reap from the past when today's global leaders have to unravel and resolve novel, complex, rapidly changing situations. Some people complain and blame others when things are not clear and structured, while others see opportunity and challenge in ambiguity. As Black (2006: 192) concludes, "When faced with high ambiguity, high-potential global leaders have fun; low-potential leaders have anxiety attacks."

- *act rather than freeze in the face of ambiguity.* Instead of waiting for enough information and analysis to act, people who embrace duality are willing to move forward in ambiguous situations. Businesses that wait for 100 percent certainty generally find themselves beaten by the competition. For instance, high-tech companies that wait to roll out fully debugged products can lose out to companies that have already moved on to next generation technology.

The bedrock of *Exhibiting Character* is integrity (Morrison 2006). "The global leader with integrity exhibits this quality by demonstrating a strong and consistent commitment to both personal and company standards" (Morrison 2006: 166). Morrison identified four distinguishing characteristics of global leaders with high ethical standards (2006: 175–177):

- They like and are interested in people (can connect emotionally, trustworthy).

- They constantly probe ethical issues.

- They are committed to the company's standards and apply them wherever they are.

- They know when to "hang tough" and when to be flexible on ethical issues.

According to the Global Explorer research, the recommended ways to develop these competencies are: training, international transfers in particular, travel and multicultural teams (Black et al. 1999a). The Global Explorer Model is parsimonious and easily grasped. The researchers used an exploratory qualitative approach, which is highly appropriate for a new field of study. They interviewed an impressive number of participants and took care to select them from numerous companies from three continents to avoid a culturally or organizationally biased view. Although not everyone in their sample was identified as an actual global leader, their results are in line with those of other global scholars.

The New Global Leaders

Kets de Vries, a psychiatrist, began his empirical work on global leaders with Florent-Treacy by doing case studies of three global leaders who were acknowledged as highly successful global CEOs: Richard Branson at Virgin, Percy Barnevik at ABB, and David Simon at British Petroleum (Kets de Vries with Florent-Treacy 1999). They had several leadership characteristics in common. Although their communication styles were different, all three had a simple, compelling vision that they expressed with enthusiasm and self-confidence. They were accessible to followers and possessed enough empathy to allow them to "recognize and contain followers' anxieties" during the change process (Kets De Vries with Florent-Treacy 1999: 156). The three CEOs gained power by sharing it, sharing information, and empowering employees. Furthermore, they surrounded themselves with colleagues who made up for their own weaknesses. The CEOs devoted energy to developing an organizational culture characterized by shared values, open communication, challenge, commitment, autonomy, innovation and learning, good corporate citizenship, and rewards for excellence. Finally, the three global leaders put in place sophisticated information technology (IT) systems and decentralized, flat, networked structures that minimized bureaucracy. The result was adaptability and a strong customer-orientation.

> These three leaders have focused on process: constructing the kind of high-performance learning organization that encourages individual contribution. They put a high value on their roles as guardian of culture and teacher. As Barnevik has said, "Ninety percent of leadership is process; only 10 percent is strategy. Of that 10 percent, 2 percent is analysis and 8 percent is having the guts to make tough decisions."
>
> (Kets de Vries wth Florent-Treacy 1999: 166–167)

Perhaps for this reason, Kets de Vries and Florent-Treacy (2002) describe global leadership as a combination and expansion of both leader and manager roles. Kets de Vries continued using a clinical orientation, based on psychoanalysis, cognitive psychology, and family systems theory, to puzzle out the dynamics between leaders and followers and the "inner theatre" of global leaders (Kets de Vries et al. 2004). He interviewed CEOs who participated in a leadership program at INSEAD, entitled "The Challenge of Leadership: Developing Your Emotional Intelligence" and other INSEAD participants and students (Kets de Vries and Florent-Treacy 2002; Kets de Vries et al. 2004). This convenience sample appears to be based on the assumption that all global managers and those with the title of CEOs are, by definition, global leaders.

Five professors performed content analysis on the CEO interview transcripts, which yielded twelve dimensions of global leadership, shown in Box 3.1. Global leaders perform two roles at the same time: charismatic and architectural. The charismatic role includes "envisioning, empowering and energizing," originally identified by Tichy and DeVanna (1986) as the role of transformational leaders attempting to make fundamental organizational change. In the charismatic role, global leaders direct, inspire, and motivate followers. In the architectural role they implement processes to improve the organizational design and appropriately control and reward employee behavior (Kets de Vries and Florent-Treacy 2002).

Kets De Vries' psychoanalytical background led him to this prescription for healthy leadership—self-awareness, a well-rounded and balanced personal life, and the ability to suffer fools and laugh at oneself (Coutu 2004: 66). His dimensions of global leadership include the need to pay attention to work, career, life and health stress issues, and balance life's pressures appropriately.

Box 3.1 The Global Leadership Life Inventory Dimensions

1 Articulating a compelling vision, mission and strategy with a multi-country, multi-environment, multi-function and multi-gender perspective that connects employees, shareholders, suppliers and customers on a global scale

2 Giving workers at all levels a voice by empowering them through the sharing of information and the delegation of decisions to the people most competent to execute them.

3 Energizing and motivating employees to actualize the organization's specific vision of the future.

4 Creating the proper organizational design and control systems to make the guiding vision a reality, and using those systems to align the behavior of the employees with the organization's values and goals.

5 Setting up the appropriate reward structures and giving constructive feedback to encourage the kind of behavior that is expected from employees.

6 Creating team players and focusing on team effectiveness by instilling a cooperative atmosphere, building collaborative interaction, and encouraging constructive conflict.

7 Making employees aware of their outside constituencies, emphasizing particularly the need to respond to the requirements of customers, suppliers, shareholders and other interest groups, such as local communities affected by the organization.

8 Inculcating a global mentality in the ranks—that is, instilling values that act as a sort of glue between the regional and/or national cultures represented in the organization.

9 Encouraging tenacity and courage in employees by setting a personal example in taking reasonable risks.

10 Fostering trust in the organization by creating, primarily through example, an emotionally intelligent workforce whose members know themselves and know how to deal respectfully and understandingly with others.

11 Articulating and modelling the need for life balance for the long-term welfare of employees.

12 Paying attention to work, career, life and health stress issues, and balancing appropriately the various kinds of pressures that life brings.

Source: Reprinted with permission from M.F.R. Kets de Vries, P. Vrignaud, and E. Florent-Treacy (2004) "The global leadership life inventory: Development and psychometric properties of a 360-degree feedback instrument." *International Journal of Human Resource Management*, (15) 3: 475–492.

Global Literacies

Rosen, a psychologist and consultant, and his research team—Digh, Singer, and Phillips (2000)—interviewed seventy-five CEOs of major companies from twenty-eight countries and surveyed 1058 respondents from eighteen countries, including CEOs, presidents, managing directors, and chairmen. The purpose of their research was to

> 1) define the characteristics most common to successful global leaders and their companies; 2) identify the leadership factors most likely to predict global success in the twenty-first century, and 3) identify the unique national contributions to leadership around the world.
>
> (Rosen et al. 2000: 377)

They concluded that the most successful business leaders demonstrate four universal leadership qualities called global literacies.

Personal literacy has to do with understanding and valuing oneself. In addition to self-awareness, leaders should be open, honest, and committed to learning and principles. Social literacy involves "challenging and engaging others" and hinges on the ability to form collaborative relationships and networks. Business literacy pertains to focusing and mobilizing the organization. Finally, cultural literacy involves understanding and leveraging cultural differences (Rosen et al. 2000: 50). Many of the components of each literacy have somewhat contradictory titles; for example, confident humility and reflective decisiveness. This was done purposely to reflect the cognitive complexity required of global leaders as they balance the complexity and tensions of today's world. These terms reflect the need to move beyond "either–or" thinking more common in Western thought patterns to "both–and" thinking that is more characteristic of Asian thought patterns (Nisbett 2003).

Rosen has a comprehensive view of global leaders. "Traditionally, we have asked if we have global customers or services; but in the 21st century, all markets are global and everyone needs to survive in a global marketplace. Therefore, we are all global leaders" (Rosen in Thaler-Carter 2000: 82). To transform into a global company, Rosen argues that we need leaders who are capable of seeing the world's challenges and opportunities, thinking with an international mindset, acting with fresh, global-centric leadership behaviors, and mobilizing a world-class team and company (Rosen et al. 2000).

Competencies of the Global Executive

Although McCall and Hollenbeck (2002) titled their book, *Developing Global Executives: The Lessons of International Experience*, their study focused on global leaders. In fact, theirs is the only study to date whose selection criteria specifically included effectiveness. They interviewed 101 executives (ninety-two men and nine women) who were nominated by their companies because they were considered to be extremely successful global executives. This sample came from thirty-six countries and worked for sixteen global companies.

McCall and Hollenbeck report that there is no agreement on a universal set of global competencies because global jobs are very diverse—"there is no universal global job" (McCall and Hollenbeck 2002). They found many different paths to global leadership (McCall and Hollenbeck 2002: 200). Only half of these executives had backgrounds that could explain their interest in global work. Some were attracted by the travel or adventure; others simply fell into global work and went overseas at the behest of the company rather than their own initiative. McCall and Hollenbeck noted that it is easier to derail in a global career than a domestic one because there are more hazards and traps.

They identified a set of seven global executive competencies that allow people to work successfully across cultures (McCall and Hollenbeck 2002: 35):

- being open-minded and flexible in thought and tactics

- possessing cultural interest and sensitivity

- having the ability to deal with complexity

- being resilient, resourceful, optimistic, and energetic

- operating from a state of honesty and integrity

- having a stable personal life

- possessing value-added technical or business skills.

Global Leadership—The Next Generation

A team of consultants and executive coaches—Goldsmith, Greenberg, Robertson, and Hu-Chan (2003)—was sponsored by the Accenture Institute of Strategic Change to research the next generation of leaders. Arguing that today's leadership skills will not be sufficient for the future due to the changing nature of global business, they sought the opinion of both current and prospective leaders. They gathered information from future leaders from around the world in several ways—focus groups with twenty-eight CEOs, various focus groups/dialogue forums with current and future global leaders, seventy-three surveys, and over 200 interviews with high-potential leaders nominated by 120 international organizations (for-profit, governmental, multilateral, and non-profit). More than 60 percent of the interview sample was under the age of forty; more than 33 percent were still in their 20s. They began their research efforts by convening a group of thought leaders, renowned experts on domestic leadership of the future rather than specialists in comparative or global leadership. Their bibliography does not include the global leadership literature, further proof that their jumping-off point was domestic leadership. This project is more practitioner-oriented and provides extensive practical advice for skill development; it is less rigorous from an academic standpoint than some of the other global leadership literature. Nevertheless, the findings are interesting and provide a slightly different perspective on global leadership.

Goldsmith and his colleagues identified fifteen dimensions of global leadership, found in Box 3.2. They note that many aspects of leadership are universal and unlikely to change; thus, ten of their dimensions are also found in domestic leadership and were also important in the past. They predict that the five dimensions shown below, however, will be especially important in the future:

1   thinking globally

2   appreciating cultural diversity

3   developing technological savvy

4   building partnerships and alliances

5   sharing leadership.

They place special emphasis on the last factor, shared leadership.

> Because no individual is likely to embody all of the needed and critical capabilities, and because the very nature of business organization—merged, allianced, out-sourced, and virtual—is beginning to dictate it, shared leadership is expected to gain pre-eminence as the operating model of the future. In the future, there will be fewer "all-knowing" CEOs; instead, leadership will be widely shared in executive teams. New demands for collective responsibility and accountability for results will emerge, as will new competencies for sharing leadership. The sheer number of alliances and networks means that more than one person will lead these structures.
> (Goldsmith et al. 2003: xxxii)

According to their survey results, the most important competencies for the future, in descending order of importance, are: builds effective alliances with other organizations; genuinely listens to others; creates and communicates a clear organization vision; is a role model for living the organization's values; unites organization into an effective team; makes decisions that reflect global considerations; views business from the ultimate customer perspective; clearly identifies priorities and focuses on a vital few; builds effective partnerships across the company; and consistently treats people with respect and dignity (Goldsmith et al. 2003: 321).

Box 3.2 Next Generation Dimensions of Global Leadership

1   Demonstrating integrity—demonstrates honest, ethical behavior
     in all interactions, ensures high standards for ethical behavior are
     practiced throughout the organization, avoids political and self-serving
     behavior, courageously stands up for beliefs, role model for living the
     organization's values.

2   Encouraging constructive dialogue—asks for feedback on what
     they can improve, genuinely listens to others, accepts constructive
     feedback, tries to understand the other person's frame of reference,
     encourages others to challenge the status quo.

3   Creating a shared vision—creates and communicates a clear vision,
     effectively involves people in decision-making, inspires people to
     commit to the vision, develops an effective strategy to achieve the
     vision, and clearly identifies priorities.

4   Developing people—treats people with respect and dignity, asks
     people what they need to do their work better, provides the training
     people need, provides effective coaching and developmental feedback
     in a timely manner, and recognizes achievements.

5   Building partnerships—treats coworkers as partners rather than
     competitors, unites organization into an effective team, builds
     partnerships across the company, and discourages destructive
     comments about other people or groups.

6   Sharing leadership—willingly shares leadership with business
     partners, defers to those with more expertise, seeks win–win, joint
     outcomes, and keeps the focus on superordinate goals and the greater
     good.

7   Empowering people—builds people's confidence, takes risks in letting
     others make decisions, provides freedom needed to do their job well,
     and trusts others to do their work, thereby avoiding micromanagement.

8   Thinking globally—adaptability, gains necessary global experience,
     understands impact of globalization and helps others understand it,
     decisions include global considerations.

9   Appreciating diversity—sees difference and diverse opinions as
     an advantage and helps others to perceive this, expands cultural
     knowledge, effectively motivates people from other cultures.

continued ...

Box 3.2 continued

10 Developing technological savvy—acquires necessary technological knowledge, recruits people with technological expertise, manages use of technology to increase productivity.

11 Ensuring customer satisfaction—inspires others to achieve high levels of customer satisfaction, views business processes from ultimate customer perspective, regularly solicits customer input, consistently delivers on customer commitments, and understands competitive options available to customers.

12 Maintaining a competitive advantage—communicates a positive, can-do sense of urgency toward getting the job done, holds others accountable for results, eliminates waste and unneeded cost, provides products and services that create a clear competitive advantage, and achieve results leading to long-term shareholder value.

13 Leading change—sees change as an opportunity, not a problem, challenges the system when needed, thrives in ambiguous situations, encourages creativity and innovation, effectively translates creative ideas into business results.

14 Achieving personal mastery—self-awareness, emotional intelligence, self-confidence, invests in personal development, involves others to complement personal weaknesses.

15 Anticipating opportunities—invests in learning about future trends, anticipates future opportunities, inspires a focus on future opportunities and not simply on present objectives, develops ideas to meet changing environmental needs.

Source: Adapted from M. Goldsmith, C. Greenberg, A. Robertson, and M. Hu-Chan (2003) *Global Leadership: The Next Generation* (Upper Saddle River, NJ: Prentice-Hall), pp. 329–333.

The Rand Study—New Challenges for International Leadership

A Rand study set out to answer a series of questions, including the impact of globalization trends on major public and private sector organizations and the kinds of competencies needed in professionals working in international organizations (Bikson et al. 2003). The remaining questions centered on the global talent pipeline, its future prospects, and practical methods for improving the development of global leadership capabilities. Structured interviews were done with 135 human resource managers and senior managers of seventy-five public, for-profit, and non-profit organizations. An expert panel was nominated to deal with the development policies, which will be discussed in Chapter 10.

The results pointed to some differences in the competencies valued by different sectors (e.g. substantive domain knowledge, foreign language proficiency, and competitiveness and drive). However, the participants agreed on an integrated repertoire of skills that include (Bikson et al. 2003):

- *Substantive depth (professional or technical knowledge) related to the organization's primary business processes.* Depth is needed for sound decision making about risks and opportunities and to gain the respect and trust of followers.

- *Managerial ability, with an emphasis on teamwork and interpersonal skills.* These skills are necessary for working with various partners and because decision making at all hierarchical levels has become more collaborative.

- *Strategic international understanding.* The leader's strategic vision for the organization is based on an understanding of both the global context and local operational realities.

- *Cross-cultural experience.* Academic instruction and language acquisition are no substitutes for real work experience in another culture.

A global leadership shortfall is predicted for the for-profit, non-profit, and especially public sectors because they have not developed enough future leaders (Bikson et al. 2003). Problems in the global talent pipeline have been signaled elsewhere (Charan et al. 2001; Mercer Delta 2006; Logan 2008); McKinsey and Company (1998) sounded the alarm about the War for Talent after completing a year-long study of over seventy firms. Fred Hassan, Chairman and CEO of Schering-Plough, reflected on the difficulties of changing company mindsets during the Pharmacia–Upjohn merger,

> My experience with that change process convinced me that identifying and developing people with global attitudes requires personal involvement from the top. The CEO has to see himself as the chief developer of talent, no matter how large the company.
>
> (Green et al. 2003: 41)

Developing the Global Leader of Tomorrow

The Developing the Global Leader of Tomorrow research was conducted by a consortium of business schools; the lead author was Gitsham (2008) who had thirteen other supporting authors. Surveys were administered to 194 CEOs and senior executives, and interviews were conducted with thirty-three HR, sustainability, and other thought leaders at firms that participate in the United Nations (UN) Global Compact. The results identified changes in the external environment and the necessity to respond with capabilities and culture as well as policies and systems. Three clusters of knowledge and skills were identified in the areas of context, complexity, and connectedness. The context cluster included the ability to scan the environment, understand the risks and opportunities of environmental and social trends, and take them into consideration when responding. The complexity cluster refers to leading under conditions of ambiguity and complexity, which involves flexibility and being responsive to change, finding creative solutions to problems, learning from mistakes, balancing both short- and long-term considerations, understanding the interdependency of their actions, and making ethical decisions. The connectedness cluster includes the ability to understand the actors in the wider political landscape and build relationships with external partners and engage in stakeholder dialogue. Unfortunately, the participants reported a performance gap: 76 percent think it is important that their own organization develop these competencies, but only 7 percent believe their organizations are currently doing this effectively. Sixty-two percent think it is important that both business schools and professional associations should develop them, but a similarly limited percentage believe they are doing so effectively (8 percent for business schools and 5 percent for professional associations).

Predictors of Global Leader Effectiveness

Despite all the different approaches to global leadership competencies, few studies have focused on effectiveness or included supervisor ratings of effectiveness. Caligiuri and Tarique carried out a program of research that addressed the relationship among effectiveness, job tasks, antecedents, competencies, and developmental activities.

While the majority of global leader scholars directly asked participants to identify competencies or how global leadership should be developed, Caligiuri (2006) used a job analytic approach. She did a job analysis first and then worked backwards to determine the knowledge, skills, ability, and other personal characteristics (KSAOs) that might lead to effective performance in those tasks. International human resources professionals from European and North American firms participated in surveys and focus groups to identify ten global work activities that are both common among and unique to global leaders. Global leaders:

1   work with colleagues from other countries

2   interact with external clients from other countries

3   interact with internal clients from other countries

4   often speak another language (other than their mother tongue) at work

5   supervise employees who are of different nationalities

6   develop a strategic business plan on a worldwide basis

7   manage a budget on a worldwide basis

8   negotiate in other countries or with people from other countries

9   manage foreign suppliers or vendors

10 manage risk on a worldwide basis for their unit.

Next, Caligiuri and Tarique (2009) surveyed a sample of 256 nominated global leaders (91 percent male) from seventeen countries in a UK firm. They defined global leaders as "high level professionals such as executives, vice presidents, directors, and managers who are in jobs with some global leadership activities such as global integration responsibilities" (Caligiuri and Tarique 2009: 336). Their findings indicate that global leadership effectiveness was predicted by high-contact leadership development activities, moderated by the personality characteristic of extraversion. High-contact activities included structured rotational leadership development programs, short-term expatriate assignments, long-term (greater than one year) expatriate assignments, global meetings in other countries, membership on global teams, and mentoring by people from other countries. In contrast, low-contact activities comprised formal university coursework, cross-cultural training programs, psychological assessments, assessment centers for leadership development, diversity training programs, and language training programs. Effectiveness was measured by self-report data that employed a five-point Likert scale (1=not at all effective, 5=very effective) for each of the ten task items identified in the previous paragraph. An acknowledged limitation of this study was single source data— the absence of performance ratings from a source other than the participants.

This limitation was rectified in the final stage of their study, which also included performance effectiveness data from the participants' immediate supervisors (Caligiuri and Tarique 2011). A sample of 420 global leaders or international executives was matched with 221 supervisors in three large multinational conglomerates. The former group was identified by human resource personnel as "global leaders" who were engaged in global work. The global leader sample included participants from forty-one countries, 64 percent from the United States, and almost one-quarter female. Findings indicated that the combined effect of three personality characteristics (extraversion, openness to experience, and conscientiousness) and cultural experiences (both organization-initiated experiences and prior non-work experiences) predicted dynamic cross-cultural competencies (tolerance of ambiguity, cultural flexibility, and reduced ethnocentrism). These competencies in turn predicted supervisor ratings of global leader effectiveness, which means they function as mediators between developmental experiences and personality characteristics as they relate to global leader effectiveness. Organization-initiated cross-cultural experiences included these specific high-contact activities: long-term expatriate assignments, membership on a global team, mentoring by a person from another culture, and meetings in various international locations. Non-work cross-cultural experiences included family diversity, international vacation travel, international volunteer work, and study abroad.

The practical lessons for companies are that not everyone benefits equally from cross-cultural developmental experiences and not all experiences are equal. Organizations should assess employees to determine which ones have the requisite personality traits that lead to cross-cultural competencies. They should also ensure that experiences are high contact in nature, which means they should provide trainees with opportunities to learn and practice appropriate behaviors and have a considerable amount of interpersonal contact.

Moro Bueno and Tubbs (2004) interviewed twenty-six international leaders from various countries to discover the competencies of effective global leaders. The most frequent responses were: communication skills, motivation to learn, flexibility, open-mindedness, respect for others, and sensitivity.

Expert Cognition in Global Leaders

Another team of scholars (Osland et al. 2007) set out to identify what expertise in global leaders looks like. Their findings contribute to a greater understanding about the process of global leadership. Relying on the expert cognition literature, they began with a conceptual argument that global leaders are experts who develop a specific expertise required by the unique challenges of leading in a global context (Osland and Bird 2006). Because experts have more on their cognitive "radar screens" and have more effective and appropriate behaviors to draw upon, the researchers assumed there might be more to learn from this population than from average or ineffective global leaders. In a qualitative exploratory study, participants who had successfully carried out a global change were nominated by HR personnel, other global leaders, and consultants (Osland et al. 2007; Osland 2010; Osland et al. 2012a). Subsequently, they were vetted by the research team to ensure they met the selection criteria: 1) a global focus in their work (as opposed to a single-country or regional focus); 2) documented success as a global change agent; 3) at least ten years of experience as a leader in their field to qualify as an expert; and 4) demonstrated intercultural competence. These criteria winnowed out all but the very best candidates in organizations.

Utilizing cognitive task analysis (CTA), a methodology designed to distinguish between experts and novices, they employed structured interviews that combine critical incidents and hierarchical task analysis. Methodological guidelines indicate that conducting CTA with three to five experts is sufficient for identifying expert cognitive perspectives and processes because experts share the same domain expertise (Crandall et al. 2006). However, the researchers took a more conservative approach and increased their sample to twenty participants. The final set of twenty global leaders included American, Indian, French, and German participants; all but one participant was male.

Participants were prompted to relate a story concerning the implementation of a significant and successful global change initiative that a novice could not have accomplished. Content analysis revealed that these global leaders described their work context as precarious and ambiguous, involving huge challenges and many multiplicities to manage (Osland et al. 2012a). Many of them were sailing in uncharted waters, charged with missions no one had accomplished before. They dealt with the resulting ambiguity by choosing the right team members, relying on a learned problem-solving process, and trusting the team and their own capability to figure things out along the way—even if they had no clear sense of what the exact outcome would look like. They described their approaches to work in terms of: problem solving, strategic thinking, boundary spanning and stakeholder management, and global skills. These global leaders interacted with their environment via multiple forms of sense making (Osland et al. 2009; 2010), as shown in a case study of a typical global leader who successfully resolved a challenging complex problem for a high-tech company. A closer look at the work context of global leaders illustrated its influence on their expertise development and provided useful distinctions between domestic and global leaders (Osland et al. 2012a).

Global Leadership Competency Frameworks and Models

Everyone agrees that more global leaders are needed; there is less consensus on what global leaders do and the competencies they should possess. The various lists of competencies contain no surprises, but they are overlapping and separated at times only by semantic differences (Jokinen 2005). There is growing consensus that global leadership consists of core characteristics, context-specific abilities, and universal leadership skills. There is less agreement on which competencies fit into these categories. This section describes efforts by scholars to create frameworks for global leadership competencies.

The Multidimensional Construct of Global Leadership

Mendenhall and Osland's (2002) review of the empirical and non-empirical literature yielded fifty-six global leadership competencies, a list too large to be useful. Noting that there were numerous areas of overlap across the various lists, they concluded that global leadership is a multidimensional construct with at least six core categories of competencies: 1) cross-cultural relationship skills, 2) traits and values, 3) cognitive orientation, 4) global business expertise, 5) global organizing expertise, and 6) visioning. Their categorization of the global leadership competencies appears in Figure 3.3.

Global Leadership Dimensions

with attendant competencies

Relationship Skills

Close Personal Relationships

CC Communication Skills

"Emotionally Connect" Ability

Inspire, Motivate Others

Conflict Management

Negotiation Expertise

Empowering Others

Managing CC Ethical Issues

Organizing Expertise

Team Building

Community Building

Organizational Networking

Creating Learning Systems

Strong Operational Codes

Global Networking

Strong Customer Orientation

Traits

Curiosity/Inquistiveness

Continual Learner

Learning Orientation

Accountability

Integrity/Courage

Commitment

Hardiness

Maturity

Results-Orientation

Cognitive

Environmental Sensemaking

Global Mindset

Thinking Agility

Improvisation

Pattern Recognition

Cognitive Complexity

Cosmopolitanism

Managing Uncertainty

Local vs. Global Paradoxes

Business Expertise

Global Business Savvy

Global Organizational Savvy

Business Acumen

Total Organizational Astuteness

Stakeholder Orientation

Results-Orientation

Vision

Articulating a tangible vision and strategy

Envisioning

Entrepreneurial Spirit

Catalyst for Cultural Change

Change Agentry

Catalyst for Strategic Change

Empowering, Inspiring

Figure 3.3 Mendenhall and Osland's Literature Review Results: The Six Dimensions of Global Leadership and their Competencies

Source: M. Mendenhall and J. Osland (2002) "Mapping the terrain of the global leadership construct." Paper presented at the Academy of International Business, San Juan, Puerto Rico, June 29.

Integrated Framework of Global Leadership

After reviewing the expatriate and global leadership literature, Jokinen (2005) proposed an integrated theoretical framework of global leadership that includes three types or layers of competencies: a fundamental core, mental characteristics, and behavioural skills, shown in Table 3.2. She argues that the fundamental core of global leadership consists of self-awareness, engagement in personal transformation, and inquisitiveness. These characteristics set the stage for the development of other competencies; thus, they are not end-state competencies but indicators of the potential for global leadership. The second layer in her framework consists of mental characteristics that affect the way people approach issues and thereafter guide their actions. The desired mental characteristics consist of: optimism, self-regulation, motivation to work in an international environment, social judgment skills, empathy, cognitive skills, and the acceptance of complexity and its contradictions. The last layer is behavioural and concerns tangible skills and knowledge that lead to concrete actions and results. It includes social skills, networking skills, and knowledge. Jokinen notes that these competencies are continuums. She recommends, therefore, that "the emphasis shift from identifying specific lists of competencies to defining and measuring their ideal level in individuals" (Jokinen 2005: 212).

Table 3.2 Jokinen's Integrated Framework of Global Leadership

Layers of Competencies	Competencies
Behavioral Skills	Social skills, networking skills, and knowledge
Mental Characteristics	Optimism, self-regulation, motivation to work in an international environment, social judgment skills, empathy, cognitive skills, and the acceptance of complexity and its contradictions
Fundamental Core	Self-awareness, engagement in personal transformation, and inquisitiveness

Source: Table created based on the research findings reported in T. Jokinen (2005) "Global leadership competencies: A review and discussion." *Journal of European Industrial Training*, 29(2/3): 199–216.

The Pyramid Model of Global Leadership

The Pyramid Model was developed originally via a modified Delphi technique with a team of international management scholars who were members of the International Organizations Network (ION). They identified the key competencies of global managers (Bird and Osland 2004). The model, shown in Figure 3.4, was subsequently expanded and adapted for global leaders by Osland for this book, based on a review of the recent global leadership literature. The model takes the form of a pyramid to reflect the assumption that global leaders have certain threshold knowledge and traits that serve as a base for higher-level competencies. The five-level model suggests a progression that is cumulative, advancing from bottom to top. Level 1, the foundation, is comprised of *global knowledge*, which will be discussed more fully in Chapter 9. Let's look at an example of an Indian manager-turned-entrepreneur who capitalized on the knowledge acquired in years of international work with a large high-tech firm. He saw the promise in a new invention to monitor people under anesthesia. Rather than locating all operations in one country, he took advantage of his extensive personal network: mathematicians in Switzerland, research and development (R&D) engineers and manufacturers in India, and sales people in the Silicon Valley. His lengthy experience working with different cultures made it possible to convince people to join him in this venture. Due to his familiarity with technology and new products, all the IT and accounting functions were handled on the web. His experience with marketing led him to develop a marketing plan that focused only on countries with either "lots of money" or "lots of people." Thus, his reliance on various types of global knowledge made it possible for him to successfully run a worldwide company with a very small number of people.

Level 2 consists of four specific *threshold traits*: integrity, humility, inquisitiveness, and resilience. These are relatively stable personality traits that are difficult for some people to learn; therefore, they are recommended as selection criteria based on the research findings for expatriates and international managers. Look at the similarities, for example, between these traits and the characteristics included in the competencies Wills and Barham (1994) discovered in global leaders: sense of humility, emotional self-awareness and resilience, psychological maturity, curiosity to learn, and personal morality.

Figure 3.4 The Pyramid Model of Global Leadership

Source: Adapted from A. Bird and J. Osland (2004) "Global competencies: An introduction." In H. Lane et al. (eds) *Handbook of Global Management* (Oxford: Blackwell), pp. 57–80.

Without integrity, global leaders cannot earn the respect they need from people within and without their organization to be effective. In cross-cultural settings where pressure to adapt or fit in is combined with incomplete and inaccurate understandings, integrity prevents leaders from errors in judgment that can come back to haunt them and their companies. Research has identified honesty and integrity as critical success factors for global leaders (Black et al. 1999a; Morrison 2001; McCall and Hollenbeck 2002).

Integrity also helps global leaders change the minds of their diverse followers. Gardner (2006) argued that leaders in general need three intelligences: 1) linguistically gifted to be good storytellers; 2) interpersonal intelligence to understand, motivate, listen, and respond to people's needs; and 3) existential intelligence that allows them to pose fundamental questions that eventually lead to their vision. Leaders also need instinct and integrity, in part because they are in the business of changing minds, which is even more challenging when those minds have been differentially programmed by culture and historical background. Leaders of diverse populations (i.e. global leaders) have two tools: the stories they tell and the lives that they lead. There must be resonance between the two—a leader's story has to be embodied in his or her personal life for the story to be credible. Gandhi changed the prevailing mindset that revolution is possible only through war when he successfully led India's peaceful protest against British colonization. His story was simple: we want to be treated as equal fellow human beings, not make war or shed blood. The story was backed up, however, by "an integrated program of prayer, fasting, and facing one's opponents without weapons" (Gardner 2006: 85). Gandhi himself led a simple, ascetic life in keeping with his story. "When all is said and done, the most important ingredient for a story to embody is truth; and the most important trait for a leader to have is integrity" (Gardner 2006: 112). Gandhi, a well-respected global leader, is also known for his humility, another threshold trait.

Without humility, managers are not open to learning from other cultures or organizations and are not willing to be taught by others. Humility is the opposite of arrogance and ethnocentrism, which can lead people to assume that they already know all the answers. Carlos Ghosn is the first non-Japanese chairman and CEO of Nissan; he also holds the same positions at Renault. He stated,

> Well, I think I am a practical person. I know I may fail at any moment. In my opinion, it was extremely helpful to be practical [at Nissan], not to be arrogant, and to realize that I could fail at any moment.
>
> (Millikin and Fu 2005: 121)

The desire to have new experiences and to learn from them is called inquisitiveness, which is described in detail in the previous section on the Global Explorer Model. The final trait is resilience, which refers to the optimism and persistence needed to keep moving forward despite adversity and the hardiness necessary to deal with the stresses inherent in global work. The concept of hardiness comes to us from the literature on stress and Big Five personality research. Within the Big Five, hardiness is usually referred to as emotional stability, a factor found to relate to expatriate effectiveness (Mendenhall and Oddou 1985) and performance (Caligiuri 2000). McCall and Hollenbeck (2002) refer to this as "resilience." Meyer and Kelly (1992) call it "emotional resilience" and characterize it in this fashion:

> The emotionally resilient person has the ability to deal with stressful feelings in a constructive way and to "bounce back" from them. Emotionally resilient people ... have confidence in their ability to cope with ambiguity ... and have a positive sense of humor and self-regard.

We can see a link to emotional intelligence in this description. While it is possible for people to increase their resilience and emotional intelligence, it is simpler and a safer bet for organizations to select potential global leaders who already possess this trait.

Level 3 is composed of *attitudes and orientations*, the global mindset that influences the way global leaders perceive and interpret the world. While there is still no generally accepted definition of the global mindset construct, the most extensive effort to map this domain was contributed by Levy and her colleagues who argue that global mindset is composed of two factors that we have previously mentioned in passing: cognitive complexity and cosmopolitanism (Levy et al. 2007). Cognitive complexity refers to a knowledge structure composed of differentiation (the number of dimensions or constructs an individual uses to describe a particular domain, such as globalization or leadership) and integration (the links or relationships the individual sees among the differentiated constructs) (Bartunek et al. 1983). The more cognitively complex people are, the more dimensions and relationships they perceive; in other words, highly complex people have more differentiated and integrated domains. Higher levels of cognitive complexity correlate with the ability to hold competing interpretations (Bartunek et al. 1983), balance contradictions, ambiguities, and trade-offs (Tetlock 1983), and deal with dualities or paradoxes (Evans et al. 2002; Levy et al. 2007).

Cosmopolitanism is the polar opposite of parochialism, and this construct contains two aspects related to global mindset.

> First is an orientation toward the outside and the external environment, rather than a focus on the inside, the local or the parochial. A second key aspect is the characteristic of openness, which represents not only being interested in others but willing to engage and be open to exploring the alternative systems of meanings held by outsiders and to learn from them.
> (Levy et al. 2007; Beechler and Javidan 2007)

Global mindset makes it possible for leaders to see beyond the narrow confines of their own culture.

Knowledge, personality traits, and attitudes become valuable only when they are translated into action. Thus, level 4 focuses on the *interpersonal skills* that global leaders need to cross cultures: mindful communication, creating and building trust, and the ability to work in multicultural teams. In the expert global leader study (Osland et al. 2007), these skills were key components in their stories of critical leadership challenges. Fred Hassan, Chairman and CEO of Schering-Plough, argued that doing well in business is about "getting to the hearts of people—that's something you don't learn in business school. Can you teach someone to engender trust? That separates leaders from managers" (Simons 2003).

The top of the pyramid, level 5, contains *system skills*, which are really meta-skills that encapsulate many other skills required for global work. They all require global knowledge, global mindset, cross-cultural expertise, and the ability to both adapt to cultural differences and leverage them for competitive advantage. The central focus at this level is the ability to influence people and the systems in which they work, both inside and outside the organization.

The boundary spanning aspect refers to the ability to communicate and serve as a liaison with different functional areas, businesses, and external organizations and indirect stakeholders. Boundary spanning roles include: representative, gatekeeper, advice broker, and trust broker (Friedman and Polodny 1992). Global leaders deal with a wide variety of stakeholders such as industry consortia, government agencies, regulators, suppliers, NGOs, the media, and business partners.

Global leaders have to build a community inside their far-flung organizations to provide all members with a sense of membership. When J.T. Wang became President of Acer Inc. in Taiwan, he followed these guiding principles: the principle of one company, the policy of one brand, and the spirit of one team (Shih et al. 2006). Building a community seems to be a precursor to global change efforts (Osland 2004). Sometimes, these communities are composed not only of employees but also of stakeholders and organizations within and beyond the industry.

Leading change on a global level is another meta-skill found at this level. It begins with environmental scanning and understanding the complexity one's organization faces and developing a new vision; subsequently, global leaders are catalysts for learning and change. They devote a good deal of their time to changing the mindset of their followers and to pushing strategic change. This topic will be discussed in greater depth in Chapter 9.

Another competency is called architecting, which refers to organizational design and alignment. It involves ensuring that all the various building blocks of the organization—strategy, structure, employee selection, training, retention, organizational culture, managerial style, systems such as planning, budgeting, and control and information systems, communication processes, financial reporting and accountability, performance metrics, and so forth—are coordinated and integrated to the optimal degree. Integration and coordination are enduring challenges for global firms seeking to align global strategies with local business processes and needs and to grow by acquiring foreign firms. Furthermore, the changes global leaders want to make result in the need to realign and redesign the organizational components so they complement rather than block the change.

Nestlé was once a cautionary example of poor integration. At one point in its history, it had five different email systems and twenty versions of accounting and planning software. Because each Nestlé America factory had a different code for vanilla, they paid over twenty different prices for the exact same vanilla—to the same vendor (Busco, Frigo, Giovannoni, Riccaboni, and Scapens 2006)!

It is a fairly simple matter to design processes that resolve problems like Nestlé's, which the company did. The more difficult challenge is to change the mindset of employees so that they themselves are willing and able to forecast and fix problems at work. Architecting also includes the human side of business—the social architecture that builds motivated employees, healthy workplaces, and effective organizational cultures. As Warren Bennis commented, "The key to competitive advantage in the 1990s and beyond will be the capacity of leaders to create the social architecture that generates intellectual capital" (1997: 87). Global leaders are responsible, in the final analysis, for the design and function of the global organization itself.

The influence process is a universal aspect of leadership; in the global leadership context, however, it involves understanding how to influence multiple stakeholders effectively, across cultural and organizational boundaries. Before a misadventure with financial derivatives forced it to merge with another Brazilian company and operate under another name, Aracruz Celulose S.A. was the world's largest pulp producer. The firm won numerous best practices awards for sustainability and human resources. Its internal operations were widely admired. Despite these accolades, the firm also had to deal with external stakeholders who pressured the firm. As part of the landless movement in Brazil, indigenous groups, who claimed that the company bought their traditional lands, invaded and damaged Aracruz property. The company maintained that the Indians never lived on the land in question and turned to the judicial system to resolve the lengthy controversy. The indigenous people had a government agency on their side advocating for them. Aracruz was also compelled to take into consideration the environmental activists who criticized the company for its monoculture of eucalyptus trees, water use, and the bleaching process that produces white paper. The Brazilian Indians and environmentalists were supported by European activists who convinced the Swedish royal family to disinvest in Aracruz. Activists also petitioned, unsuccessfully, the Norwegian parliament and Norway's Petroleum Fund to take similar steps. Aracruz had attempted to come to agreements with some of the external stakeholders in the past, but the agreements with the indigenous people kept unraveling. Their situation highlights the difficulty of finding lasting solutions to ambiguous, complex societal problems that involve multiple stakeholders (Osland and Osland 2007).

Making ethical decisions is the ability to make decisions and take actions that conform to a high ethical standard. This involves the capacity to see things from a larger perspective and to use systems thinking and consider the implications of individual and organizational actions for all parties who might be affected. Decision making tends to violate ethical standards when it loses sight of the larger system and, instead, focuses on the narrow concerns or interests of individuals, organizations, or industries.

The graphic representation of the Pyramid Model does not accurately reflect the dynamic nature of global leadership process that occurs when leaders interact with the environment. The model's contribution, however, is the identification of different building blocks of global leadership and the simplification of a complex array of competencies. It was designed to be used in conjunction with the Effectiveness Cycle (Bird and Osland 2004), which does take a process approach.

The Effectiveness Cycle

The Effectiveness Cycle (Bird and Osland 2004: 59–61), which describes what effective global managers do at the most basic level, consists of three stages:

- Stage 1: Perceive, analyze, and diagnose to decode the situation— this involves matching characteristics of the current situation to past experiences, scanning for relevant cues or their absence, framing the situation in terms of experience and expectation, and setting plausible goals for the outcome.

- Stage 2: Accurately identify effective managerial action—given the situation and the desired outcome, which nuanced actions would be the most effective? This judgment relies on global knowledge, experience, contingency factors, and the ability to imagine and predict the results of various responses.

- Stage 3: Possess the behavioral repertoire and flexibility to act appropriately given the situation—in this stage, the emphasis moves from cognition to behavior.

Effectiveness is predicated on both cognitive and behavioral knowledge and skills developed over time. The model assumes that people first think and then act. However, global leaders used cognitive and behavior skills and knowledge simultaneously or iteratively in descriptions of their problem-solving and decision-making processes and methods for dealing with extreme uncertainty in challenging global leadership incidents (Osland et al. 2007).

Beechler and Javidan (2007) also adopted the effectiveness cycle (Bird and Osland 2004) to describe a global leader's response to the environment in their proposed model of global mindset and global leadership. The centerpiece of this model is global mindset. Leaders with a global mindset possess: 1) global intellectual capital (knowledge of the global industry, knowledge of global value networks, knowledge of the global organization, cognitive complexity, and cultural acumen); 2) psychological capital (positive psychological profile, cosmopolitanism, and passion for cross-cultural and cross-national encounters); and 3) social capital (structural, relational, and cognitive social capital). The ability to influence people from different sociocultural systems is the outcome of global mindset and the behavioral repertoire reflected in the Effectiveness Cycle. Their descriptions of the components of global mindset include many of the behavioral global leadership competencies. The distinction between global leadership, and global mindset and the cognitive–behavioral competencies are issues that researchers in this field have yet to resolve.

Content Domain of Intercultural Competence in Global Leadership

Bird et al. (2010) conducted a review of the global leadership and expatriate literature to develop a comprehensive delineation of the content domain of the intercultural competence required for effective global leadership. The domain consists of *perception management, relationship management* and *self-management*. Perception management includes how people cognitively approach cultural differences (nonjudgmentalness, inquisitiveness, tolerance of ambiguity, cosmopolitanism, and category inclusiveness). Relationship management refers to people's orientation to the importance of relationships (relationship interest, interpersonal engagement, emotional sensitivity, self-awareness, and social flexibility). Self-management considers their identity and ability to manage their emotions and stress effectively in light of the challenges inherent in working across cultures (optimism, self-confidence, self-identity, emotional resilience, non-stress tendency, stress management, and interest flexibility). Sixteen of these seventeen competencies, as measured by the Global Competencies Inventory (GCI) described in Chapter 6, can be used to enhance global leadership selection and personal development.

The framework and the GCI measure were shown to have predictive validity in a study of Japanese expatriates (Furuya et al. 2009). Higher levels of these global competencies had a positive influence on these global leadership-related variables: global business acumen, interpersonal skills, and systems management skills. They were also associated with higher levels of competency transfer and job performance. Structural equation modeling identified linkages from organizational support, intercultural personality characteristics, self-adjustment, and repatriation policies to outcomes of global competency learning and transfer, which in turn lead to heightened job motivation and performance. Organizational support and higher pre-assignment scores in intercultural personality characteristics were associated with increases in individual learning and the subsequent transfer of global competencies upon repatriation. Self-adjustment, organizational support, and supportive repatriate HR policies are positively related to global management competency transfer. This transfer is also associated with higher job motivation and work performance.

Construct Definition of Global Leadership

As you have no doubt observed throughout this review, different researchers define global leadership in very different ways. Some samples contain expatriates and global managers rather than global leaders, according to the definition we set out in Chapter 1. This makes it difficult to compare and consolidate findings and prevents the field from progressing. Mendenhall, Reiche, Bird and Osland (2012) tackled this problem of construct definition with respect to the word "global" in global leadership. After reviewing the literature, they argued that global has three dimensions: contextual, relational, and spatial-temporal. The contextual dimension refers to the level of *complexity* inherent in an international leader's responsibilities, which determines whether or not they merit being called a global leader. The relational dimension refers to *flow*, which relates to the boundary spanning aspect of their work. The degree of flow can be assessed by measuring the richness (frequency, volume, and scope of information flow) and quantity (number of channels required to perform the requisite boundary spanning in the role). The spatial-temporal dimension is termed *presence*. It refers to the degree to which an individual has to physically move across geographical, cultural, and national boundaries rather than communicate across them using virtual technologies. These three dimensions can be employed to select samples and to distinguish among global managers, domestic leaders, and global leaders. In the same vein, the authors contributed a definition of global leadership that might serve as a reference point for other scholars:

> An individual who inspires a group of people to willingly pursue a positive vision in an effectively organized fashion while fostering individual and collective growth in a context characterized by significant levels of complexity, flow, and presence.

What Do We Know and Still Need to Know about Global Leadership?

This section summarizes the progress the field has made and the research work that still remains. As with most young fields of study, the quality and focus of the research varies. Some of the reviewed literature and research did not undergo a peer review process and is therefore more difficult to judge in terms of rigor. Despite valuable contributions to date, not all findings are definitive. For example, there is no consensus on the construct definition of global leadership, although one has now been proposed to jumpstart the discussion (Mendenhall, Reiche, Bird and Osland 2012). In some research, the onus of defining global leadership was left to interviewees ("What characteristics do global leaders have?" "Who would you nominate as global leaders?"). In other studies, the definition was merely assumed ("all global managers or CEOs are global leaders"). Several studies asked global managers or HR managers for their opinion about global leader capability without clarifying whether respondents were themselves global leaders. As a result, conceptual confusion persists, as do questions about whether there is a significant difference between global managers versus global leaders, or between global versus domestic leaders. In both sample selection and writing, the terms "global leader" and "global manager" are frequently used interchangeably, which is puzzling given the significant distinctions between managers and leaders in the leadership literature

(Kotter, 1990a; 1990b). Mendenhall and his colleagues' (2012) attempt to define what "global" means is one step towards resolving this confusion.

Several studies employed exploratory designs, which is appropriate in a nascent field of study. No one, however, has replicated Mintzberg's (1973) landmark observation of managerial behavior with global leaders by following them around as they do their work. Data collection to date is limited to opinion about global leaders or self-reports. There are no studies of their actual behavior. Only self-report measures and interviews have been employed.

The global leadership research has, for the most part, taken a *content* approach and focused on identifying competencies. The list of fifty-six global leadership competencies, which has no doubt increased, contained in the literature is a list too large to be useful (Mendenhall and Osland 2002). Many of the models of global leadership contain overlapping concepts in non-exclusive categories. The good news is that many of these competencies have been identified over and over, in various types of research. Cognitive complexity, behavioral flexibility, intercultural competence, learning ability, and integrity, for example, surface repeatedly. The question of what it is, in terms of competencies at least, seems to have achieved a reasonable level of consensus. We also know that global leadership is a multidimensional construct, even though those competencies are categorized differently. And we have a better understanding of the construct domain of the intercultural competence dimension of global leadership (Bird et al. 2010).

Competency research, while very useful, is never the complete answer. It fails to explicate the process that global leaders utilize or to identify the contingencies that influence their behavior in specific contexts. Nor does it distinguish between essential and nonessential competencies. Are these competencies crucial at all times or important only in certain situations? Leadership requirements can vary by level, culture, and situation, as well as by functions and operating units, so competency lists might not apply across the board (Conger and Ready 2004a: 45; see also Conger and Ready 2004b).

The competency approach also fails to answer the conundrum of exemplary global leaders who succeed despite glaring weaknesses. In reality, few leaders live up to the idealized view of leadership that competency lists portray (Conger and Ready, 2004a). No one was found to possess all the attributes identified in a study of the top twenty-five business leaders of our time (Pandya and Shell 2005). Instead, leaders possess some combination of competencies; which ones and in what levels create different acceptable profiles of global leaders? McCall and Hollenbeck (2002) noted that complex, high-level executive jobs are accomplished in various ways by executives with multiple forms of talent. Therefore, we would expect that global leaders can be effective without acquiring all competencies, but there is no research to prove or disprove this hypothesis. Furthermore, the rise and fall of certain well-known global business leaders and the instances of domestic leaders who rise to the challenge of a one-time global leadership role may indicate that global leadership can be manifested in both episodic and long-term behavior.

Wills and Barham (1994) conceived of behavioral competencies and skills as merely the outside layers of what characterizes successful global leaders. To focus solely on behavioral competencies would be misleading if they are correct that global leaders operate from a deeper holistic core competence composed of cognitive complexity, emotional energy, and psychological maturity. Kets de Vries and Florent-Treacy (2002) also take a more holistic view of global leaders.

Yet another concern is that the unique nature of leadership and what motivates it may have nothing at all to do with competencies. As Margaret Wheatley stated,

> I think we start in the wrong place if we ask, "What are the traits that I have to acquire?" The place to start is, "What are the things I care about that I'm willing to step forward to figure out how to be a leader?"
>
> (Madsen and Hammond 2005: 75)

The passion to make a difference and the willingness to allow others to participate in creating it is more likely to result in leadership success than simply acquiring and checking off a list of competencies.

Scholars have focused more on what global leaders are like than on what they actually do. However, we now have a slightly better, if still incomplete, understanding on this topic. Caligiuri (2006) identified ten tasks resulting from a job analysis (e.g. works with colleagues from other countries, negotiates in other countries or with people from other countries, manages worldwide budget). These tasks are situational or contextual, that is, people who find themselves in global jobs could be expected to perform these objective tasks, which provides a useful task domain. However, job analysis never describes the complexity of how people carry out these tasks effectively, and, in the global leadership field, it does not resolve the global manager versus global leader question. Being assigned those tasks does not necessarily make a person a leader. Kets de Vries et al.'s (2004) list of twelve global leader tasks focuses more on the leadership actions that influence employees (e.g. "inculcating a global mentality in the ranks – instilling values that act as a sort of glue between the regional and/or national cultures represented in the organization"), the organization (e.g. "creating the proper organizational design and control systems to make the guiding vision a reality, and using those systems to align the behavior of the employees with the organization's values and goals"), and self-management (e.g. "articulating and modeling the importance of the need for life balance for the long-term welfare of employees"). Finally, we have the expert cognition study (Osland, et al. 2007; Osland 2010; Osland et al. 2012a) with stories describing how expert global leaders view their context and their work and how they use sense making to interact with their environment and the people in it (Osland et al. 2009). These studies bring us closer toward explicating process models of global leadership, but more descriptive research is needed, both for clear understanding and, subsequently, to guide training and development.

Understanding the antecedents and predictors of global leadership effectiveness has always been hampered by the limited number of studies that have used samples of nominated effective global leaders (Wills and Barham 1994; McCall and Hollenbeck 2002; Osland et al. 2007; Osland et al. 2012a). Black et al. (1999a) had a partial sample of nominated global leaders. Work by Furuya and his colleagues (2009) and Caligiuri and Tarique (2009; 2011) provide direction for needed future research on effectiveness.

Adler (1997; 2001) noted that most leadership research has studied men. Over a decade later, this is still true. While this might be an artefact of lower numbers of business women in high-level positions in general or the industries that have been studied (e.g. high technology), it is still problematic.

While the research is advancing, global leadership is still an emerging field, reminiscent of the first stages of domestic leadership research that also began by examining traits and subsequently evolved more complex theories. There are still many gaps to fill. In particular, the field needs more consensus on the definition and parameters of the global leadership construct, in part so that sample selection criteria show greater consistency. Mendenhall and Osland (2002) argue for more exploratory empirical research, with multiple paradigmatic approaches, on the multidimensional global leadership construct—cross-cultural relationship skills, traits and values, cognitive orientation, global business expertise, global organizing expertise, and visioning. We have limited agreement and knowledge about the antecedents and outcomes of global leadership. Systematic analyses of factors that promote or impede global leadership effectiveness and development is needed. The determination of measures for global leadership effectiveness and performance is another foundational task. Models from exploratory research should be tested or developed to yield models or theories amenable to the generation of propositions and hypotheses that, in turn, can be empirically tested (Mendenhall 1999). Empirical research should be conducted on how the various global leadership competencies influence one another, or assume greater or less importance due to context, task, or cultural distance and under what conditions they develop and can be deployed (Mendenhall 2001a). More longitudinal research on global leadership developmental process and development best practices would be helpful. To avoid a Western and male bias, future research should include globally diverse subjects and settings.

Several studies have pointed out the importance of a diverse family background and international exposure and cultural contact during childhood (e.g. Kets de Vries and Florent-Treacy 2002; McCall and Hollenbeck 2002; Caligiuri 2004). However, Osland and her colleagues (2007) found that not all expert global leaders developed in this fashion. What is the impact of childhood, family background, and early international experiences, and is this a requirement in all profiles of global leaders? Given the importance of the motivation to learn in developing the necessary global leadership skills and knowledge, future research could describe more fully the role played by motivation to learn and learning (Jokinen 2005). Finally, the ability to measure the level of global leadership capacity in both individuals and organizations would be very useful.

4 Mapping the Content Domain of Global Leadership Competencies

ALLAN BIRD

Studies of newly emerging phenomena often transition through several phases. The first is characterized by wonder-tinged curiosity accompanied by an effort to find labels and names to describe a phenomenon. When myriad observers are exploring simultaneously, they are likely to come up with different names or focus on different aspects of the phenomena, assigning unique descriptors. Transition to the next phase occurs when the observers become "groundskeepers" and set about pruning the labels and ordering the descriptions. But the newly formed garden doesn't flourish until borders are established and distinctions are made among plants.

From the early 1990s forward, a growing number of scholars have studied global leaders and attempted to delineate the competencies that are critical to their success. Reviews of this literature (Bird and Osland 2004; Jokinen 2005; Mendenhall 2001a; Mendenhall and Osland 2002; Osland 2008; Osland et al. 2012a) found that social scientists have delineated over 160 competencies that influence global leadership effectiveness; however, many of these competencies overlap conceptually and are often separated only by semantic differences (Jokinen 2005; Osland 2008).

Unfortunately, further progress in delineating the relationships among various competencies within the global leadership competency literature will be difficult without first bringing some order to the global leadership garden. Building on the strong foundation provided in Chapter 3, in this chapter we offer an organizing framework. To avoid unnecessary duplication, we will refer primarily to models, competencies, and research addressed previously, referring the reader to Chapter 3 for more detailed discussion of the specific models and competencies.

A decade previously, Mendenhall and Osland (2002) documented this trend of proliferation when they identified fifty-six different competencies. Since then, there has been a nearly three-fold explosion in competencies. Their initial efforts at cultivating and ordering the garden of global leadership consisted of grouping the many dimensions into six broad categories, reflecting the type of competency—traits and values, cognitive orientation and so forth (see Table 4.1).

Table 4.1 The Terrain of Global Leadership Constructs

Cross-cultural Relationship Skills	Traits and Values	Cognitive Orientation	Global Business Expertise	Global Organizing Expertise	Visioning
Building relationships	Inquisitiveness and curiosity	Environmental scanning	Global business savvy	Team building	Articulating a tangible vision and strategy
Cross-cultural communication skills	Continual learner	Global mindset	Global organizational savvy	Continuity building	Envisioning
Ability to emotionally connect	Accountability	Thinking agility	Business acumen	Organizational networking	Entrepreneurial spirit
Inspire, motivate others	Integrity	Improvisation	Stakeholder orientation	Creating learning systems	Catalyst for cultural change
Conflict management	Courage	Pattern recognition	External orientation	Architecting and designing	Catalyst for strategic change
Negotiation expertise	Commitment	Cognitive complexity	Results orientation	Global networking	
Empowering others	Hardiness	Cosmopolitanism		Strong customer orientation	
Managing cross-cultural ethical issues	Maturity	Managing uncertainty		Business literacy	
Social literacy	Results-orientation	Local versus global paradoxes		Change agentry	
Cultural literacy	Personal literacy	Behavioral flexibility			
	Tenacity				
	Emotional intelligence				

Source: Adapted from M. Mendenhall and J. Osland (2002) "Mapping the Terrain of the Global Leadership Construct." Paper presented at the Academy of International Business, San Juan, Puerto Rico, June 29.

Table 4.2 Jokinen's Synthesis of Global Leader Competencies

Layers of Competencies	Competencies
Behavioral Skills	Social skills Networking skills Knowledge
Mental Characteristics	Optimism Self-regulation Motivation to work in an international environment Social judgment skills Empathy Cognitive skills Acceptance of complexity and its contradictions
Fundamental Core	Self-awareness Engagement in personal transformation Inquisitiveness

Source: T. Jokinen (2005) "Global leadership competencies: A review and discussion." *Journal of European Industrial Training*, 29(2/3): 199–216.

Consideration of the six categories raises several questions about the organizing structure. For example, the six categories are not of the same qualitative type or, conversely, conceptually overlap. Skills are qualitatively different from values. Some types of expertise may overlap with certain types of cognitive orientation, the latter of which may be a consequence of expertise or vice versa.

Three years after the Mendenhall and Osland effort, Jokinen (2005) sought to order the field by reviewing the literature and synthesizing competencies into three broad "layers," as presented in Table 4.2. The *Fundamental Core* consisted of those predispositional personality competencies that provided a foundation on which other competencies could stand. *Mental Characteristics* constituted those attitudes, cognitive skills, and processes that aided information processing and mental functioning. Finally, *Behavioral Skills* encompassed that broad set of competencies that supported effective action. A careful consideration of the layers suggests some categorical ambiguity, e.g. knowledge is not behavior. Similarly, *Optimism*, though included in the *Mental Characteristics* layer, is usually understood to be a personality characteristic and so more likely fits into the *Fundamental Core* range. A broader critique of the Jokinen conceptualization is that it is overly focused on within-person and interpersonal competencies, leaving business and organizational capabilities largely unaddressed.

In the ensuing years since Jokinen's integrating and synthesizing effort the field has expanded further, with researchers proposing new competencies and suggesting new organizing frameworks. In the following section we review these efforts—both theoretical and empirical—and propose a general organizing scheme.

Organizing the Global Leader Competencies

To comprehend the proliferation of identified global leader competencies we reviewed theoretical and empirical studies published from 1993 to 2012. The first serious work on global leadership incorporating an organizing framework and competencies was Rhinesmith's 1993 volume. The most recent publication, predicated on empirical work, was that of Gundling et al. (2011). Over this nineteen-year time period, sixteen refereed journal articles, book chapters or volumes presented a total of 160 separate competencies associated with global leadership. The list of publications and their attendant competencies are shown in Table 4.3.

Although Rhinesmith (1993) and Yeung and Ready (1995) preceded it by several years, Brake's (1997) volume is the first to suggest a set of competencies and a clearly defined organizing framework. Brake proposed three groupings of competencies—*Business Acumen, Relationship Management*, and *Personal Effectiveness*. Subsequently, several others have suggested groupings that seem to follow a similar pattern. For example, Rosen and associates (2000) identify four "literacies"; however, their set of sixteen competencies can largely be grouped into the three categories that Brake roughly defines. Similarly, Bird and Osland (2004; 2008) propose what they call a global leadership pyramid, with four levels, but again the groupings that emerge can easily be sorted into a three-category set. Other works, e.g. Kets de Vries and Florent-Treacy (1999), McCall and Hollenbeck (2002), Goldsmith and associates (2003), or Gitsham (2009), don't identify "umbrella" labels to order group competencies. Nevertheless, each of these, as well, lend themselves to a grouping roughly consistent with Brake's formulation. To that end, we propose three categories of competencies—*Business and Organizational Savvy, Managing People and Relationships*, and *Managing Self*. We discuss each of the three as well as the specific competencies that fall within their purview in subsequent sections.

Before moving on, however, it is worthwhile to point out several other conclusions that can be drawn from the list of competencies presented in Table 4.3. First, scanning the columns and rows, it is apparent that global leadership competencies span a range of qualitatively different types. There are *predispositional characteristics of personality* (e.g. inquisitiveness, optimism, conscientiousness, extraversion); *attitudinal orientations* (e.g. cosmopolitanism; appreciating cultural diversity; results orientation); *cognitive capabilities* (e.g. cognitive complexity, intellectual intelligence, embrace duality); *motivational inclinations* (e.g. motivation to learn; tenacity); *knowledge bases* (value-added technical and business skills, global knowledge, business acumen); and *behavioral skills* (building partnerships and alliances, cross-cultural communication, boundary spanning). In other words, (and as noted in Chapter 3) the range of competencies identified is extensive and wide-ranging in type. Global leadership is a multifaceted phenomenon and the competencies associated with performing at a high level are multifaceted as well.

Table 4.3 Competency Distribution Across the Three Primary Categories of Global Leadership Competency

Authors	Business and Organizational Acumen	Managing People and Relationships	Managing Self
Rhinesmith, (1993)	Intellectual intelligence Business acumen	Emotional intelligence Cultural acumen	Cognitive complexity Cosmopolitanism Personal management
Wills and Barham (1994)			Cognitive complexity Emotional energy Psychological maturity
Yeung and Ready (1995)	Articulate a tangible vision Catalyst for strategic change Catalyst for cultural change Results orientation Customer orientation	Being able to empower others	
Brake (1997)	**Business acumen** • Depth of field • Entrepreneurial spirit • Stakeholder orientation • Total organizational acumen **Relationship management** • Change agentry • Community building	**Relationship management** • Community building • Cross-cultural communication • Influencing	**Personal effectiveness** • Accounting • Curiosity and learning • Maturity • Thinking agility
Black et al. (1999a)	Demonstrate savvy		Inquisitiveness Exhibit character Embrace duality
Kets de Vries and Florent-Treacy (1999)	Visioning Designing and aligning Outside orientation	Energizing Team building Rewarding and feedback Emotional intelligence	Global mindset Tenacity Life balance Resilience to stress
Rosen et al. (2000)	**Business literacy** • Chaos navigator • Business geographer • Historical futurist • Leadership liberator • Economic integrator **Cultural literacy** • Inquisitive internationalist • Global capitalist	**Social literacy** • Pragmatic trust • Urgent listening • Constructive impatience • Connective teaching • Collaborative individualism • Cultural literacy • Proud ancestor • Respectful modernizer • Culture bridger	**Personal literacy** • Aggressive insight • Confident humility • Authentic flexibility • Reflective decisiveness • Realistic optimism
McCall and Hollenbeck (2002)	Able to deal with complexity Value-added technical and business skills	Cultural interest and sensitivity	Open-minded and flexible in thought and tactics Resilient, resourceful, optimistic and energetic Honesty and integrity Stable personal life
Goldsmith et al. (2003)	Developing technical savvy Building partnerships and alliances	Appreciating cultural diversity Sharing leadership	Thinking globally
Bikson et al. (2003)	Substantive depth related to the organization's primary business processes Strategic international understanding	Managerial ability, with an emphasis on teamwork and interpersonal skills Cross-cultural understanding	

Authors	Business and Organizational Acumen	Managing People and Relationships	Managing Self
Moro Bueno and Tubbs (2004)		Communication skills Respect for others Sensitivity	Motivation to learn Flexibility Open-mindedness
Bird and Osland (2004)	**System skills** Influence stakeholders • Lead change • Span boundaries • Build community • Architecting Global knowledge	**Interpersonal skills** • Mindful communication • Create and build trust • Multicultural teaming	**Threshold traits** • Integrity • Humility • Inquisitiveness • Resilience **Attitudes and orientations** • Global mindset • Cognitive complexity • Cosmopolitanism • System skills Make ethical decisions
Osland et al. (2007)	Strategic thinking Oscillation between detail and big picture Boundary spanning Stakeholder management	Skilled "people reading" Creating and relying on trust	Tolerance of ambiguity Inquisitiveness Creative problem solving
Gitsham (2008)	**Context** • Environmental scanning • Understand environmental risks and social trends **Complexity** • Responsive to change • Finding creative solutions • Balancing short- and long-term considerations • Understanding interdependence	**Connectedness** • Understand actors • Build relationships	**Complexity** • Flexibility • Learn from mistakes
Caligiuri (2006); Caligiuri and Tarique (2009)	Interact with external clients from other countries Interact with internal clients from other countries Develop a strategic business plan on a worldwide basis Manage a budget on a worldwide basis Manage foreign suppliers or vendors Manage risk on a worldwide basis	Work with colleagues from other countries Often speak another language Supervise employees of different nationalities Negotiate in other countries or with people from other countries Extraversion	Openness to experience Conscientiousness
Bird et al. (2010)		Relationship Management Relationship Interest Interpersonal Engagement Emotional Sensitivity Self Awareness Social Flexibility	**Perception Management** • Nonjudgmentalness • Inquisitiveness • Tolerance of Ambiguity • Cosmopolitanism • Interest Flexibility **Self-management** • Optimism • Self-confidence • Self-identity • Emotional Resilience • Non-stress Tendency • Stress Management

continued …

Table 4.3 continued

Authors	Business and Organizational Acumen	Managing People and Relationships	Managing Self
Gundling et al. (2011)	Frame Shifting Expand Ownership Adapt and Add Value Third Way Solutions	Cultural Self-awareness Results Through Relationships Develop Future Leaders Influence Across Boundaries	Inviting the Unexpected Core Values and Flexibility

Major reviews of global leadership competencies focused on organizing the field

Authors	Business and Organizational Acumen	Managing People and Relationships	Managing Self
Mendenhall and Osland (2002)	**Vision** • Articulating a tangible vision and strategy • Envisioning • Entrepreneurial Spirit • Catalyst for Cultural Change • Change Agentry • Catalyst for Strategic Change • Empowering, Inspiring **Business Expertise** • Global Business Savvy • Global Organizational Savvy • Business Acumen • Total Organizational Astuteness • Stakeholder Orientation • Results Orientation **Organizing Expertise** • Community Building • Creating Learning Systems • Strong Operational Codes • Strong Customer Orientation	**Relationship Skills** • Close Personal Relationships • Cross-cultural Communication Skills • "Emotionally Connect" Ability • Inspire, Motivate Others • Managing Cross-cultural Ethical Issues **Organizing Expertise** • Team building • Organizational Networking • Global Networking	**Traits** • Curiosity/Inquisitiveness • Continual Learner • Learning Orientation • Accountability • Integrity/Courage • Commitment • Hardiness • Maturity • Results Orientation **Cognitive** • Environmental Sense Making • Global Mindset • Thinking Agility • Improvisation • Pattern Recognition • Cognitive Complexity • Cosmopolitanism • Managing Uncertainty • Local versus Global Paradox
Jokinen (2005)	**Behavioral Skills** • Knowledge	**Behavioral Skills** • Social skills • Networking skills **Mental Characteristics** • Social judgment skills • Empathy	**Mental Characteristics** • Optimism • Self-regulation • Motivation to work in an international environment • Cognitive skills • Acceptance of complexity and contradictions **Fundamental Core** • Self-awareness • Engagement in personal transformation • Inquisitiveness

Boldfaced items refer to "umbrella" competency categories that encompass two or more sub-dimensions. In some instances, an umbrella category may contain sub-dimensions that apply to more than columns.

Competencies are distributed roughly equally across the three categories—55 of the 160 competencies fall into the *Business and Organizational Acumen* grouping, with 47 and 58 competencies in the *Managing People and Relationships*, and *Managing Self* groups, respectively. Despite fairly even distribution across categories, there is considerable variation among scholars with regard to focus. Wills and Barham (1994), for example, focus on only competencies related to managing self, while Yeung and Ready (1995) concentrate primarily on business and organizational savvy, to the exclusion of competencies involving the management of self. In some cases this focus appears to be intentional. Bird and associates (2010) explicitly center their attention on interpersonal and self competencies, noting that their exclusion of business or organizational competencies is conscious and reflects a focus on a subset of global leader competencies associated with intercultural effectiveness.

Missing from Table 4.3 is an acknowledgement that many studies delineate relationships among the competencies that cannot be displayed in a table format. The formulation by Black et al. (1999a) is typical of this approach. In their particular case, they lay out the linkages between their four competencies, detailing how each links to and reinforces the others. Though this aspect of the various competency frameworks was addressed in Chapter 3, it is important not to ignore this element when considering Table 4.3.

Lastly, the bottom section of Table 4.3 incorporates the Mendenhall and Osland (2002) and Jokinen (2005) conceptualizations, showing how their synthesized competencies would fit into the current format.

Competencies of Business and Organizational Acumen

One group of global leadership competencies relates to a practical understanding of business and organizational realities and how to get things done efficiently and effectively. They reflect global leadership on a larger scale, "at a distance," and are directed toward the entire organization or to a global unit or initiative within the organization. Business and organizational acumen appears to entail five composite competencies: *Vision and Strategic Thinking, Business Savvy, Organizational Savvy, Managing Communities*, and *Leading Change*. Each of these competencies encompasses a variety of more specific skills, abilities, knowledge bases, or orientations. They are presented in Table 4.4 in order of frequency of dimensions cited, i.e. of the fifty-five competencies in this category, the largest number entailed capacity related to *Vision and Strategic Thinking*, the second largest number related to *Business Savvy* and so forth. The table also notes instances where a given dimension was cited by more than a single study, e.g. build community, under *Managing Communities*. Of the five competencies, the first three account for roughly 80 percent of all dimensions cited. The remaining two, *Leading Change* and *Organizational Savvy*, accounted for about 10 percent each.

Table 4.4 Business and Organizational Acumen Competencies

Vision and Strategic Thinking	Business Savvy	Managing Communities
Intellectual intelligence	Business acumen	Customer orientation
Articulate a tangible vision	Results orientation	Stakeholder orientation
Depth of field	Entrepreneurial spirit	Building partnerships and
Visioning	Demonstrate savvy	alliances
Chaos navigator	Business geographer	Influence stakeholders
Historical futurist	Economic integrator	Build community (2)
Able to deal with complexity	Global capitalist	Stakeholder management
Strategic international	Value-added technical and	Interact with external clients
understanding	business skills	from other countries
Strategic thinking	Developing technical savvy	Interact with internal clients
Oscillation between detail and	Substantive depth related to	from other countries
big picture	the organization's primary	Manage foreign suppliers or
Environmental scanning	business processes	vendors
Understand environmental	Finding creative solutions	Expand ownership
risks and social trends	Manage risk on a worldwide	Outside orientation
Balancing short- and long-term	basis	Boundary spanning (2)
considerations	Adapt and add value	
Understanding interdependence	Third way solutions	
Develop a strategic business		
plan on a worldwide basis		
Frame shifting		
Responsive to change		

Organizational Savvy	Leading Change
Total organizational acumen	Catalyst for strategic change
Designing and aligning	Catalyst for cultural change
Architecting	Lead change
Manage a budget on a	Change agentry
worldwide basis	

(#) indicates multiple references for the designated competency.

Careful analysis of the specific dimensions cited and their origins suggests that scholars who focused on this specific aspect of global leadership competency were more likely to differentiate a broader number of dimensions. For example, Yeung and Ready (1995) concentrated almost exclusively on competencies in this group. In doing so, they identified three dimensions—*articulate a tangible vision, catalyst for strategic change*, and *catalyst for cultural change*—that might be better thought of as being tightly integrated. After articulating a tangible vision, a global leader must then be able to act as a catalyst for strategic and cultural change. Moreover, of the three remaining dimensions they focus on, two fit into other competencies in this grouping—results orientation into *Business Savvy* and customer orientation into *Managing Communities.* In a similar vein, Bird and Osland (2004) differentiate among three different dimensions within the *Managing Communities* competency—span boundaries, influence stakeholders, and build community.

Vision and Strategic Thinking

This encompasses three primary capabilities. The first is the ability to comprehend the complexity of the environment and think about it in strategic ways. Dimensions such as intellectual intelligence, depth of field, oscillation between detail and big picture, balancing short and long term, or understanding interdependence characterize varying aspects of the ability to think strategically. The second capability entails activities related to developing and articulating a global vision for the organization or business unit. The third capability constitutes aspects of skills enabling global leaders to develop a strategic plan and implement it.

Business Savvy

Business savvy may be characterized as primarily a knowledge-based competency, entailing as it does practical understanding and wisdom. It can be broken down into two types of knowledge and a general orientation or attitude toward finding efficient solutions to add value. General business savvy may link to strategic thinking in the *Vision and Strategic Thinking* competency, but appears to reflect a broader, practical-oriented knowledge. A second type of knowledge is technically oriented or grounded in the operational processes of the organization. These two types of knowledge complement the third dimension, which is a value-added orientation that combines an entrepreneurial spirit with a focus on creative solutions.

Managing Communities

The third dominant competency centers on the ability of global leaders to attend to the broader network of relationships in which a firm is embedded. The nature of the global economy in the twenty-first century is that firms find it necessary to collaborate or, at a minimum, cooperate with a wide variety of actors, from buyers to suppliers to competitors to shareholders to non-governmental entities and interest groups. This requires boundary-spanning skills, one of the most distinctive competencies differentiating global leaders from their domestic counterparts (Osland, Bird and Oddou 2012a). In addition to the ability to span boundaries, global leaders must also be able to influence stakeholders, the second dimension in *Managing Communities*. Finally, boundary spanning and influencing stakeholders, while having value in their own right, work primarily in the service of the third dimension, which is the ability to forge a firm and a disparate set of stakeholders into a viable community in order to accomplish strategic objectives.

Organizational Savvy

This is the fourth competency and addresses the ability of global leaders to design organizational structures and processes in ways that facilitate global effectiveness. Two of the four dimensions focus on design issues. The remaining two are focused on functioning effectively within the organization.

Leading Change

The final competency may represent a set of capabilities that enable global leaders to implement change. It may be appropriate to view the other four competencies as instrumental in that they support this capability. The primary thrust of global leadership is to bring about change (Osland et al. 2006; Mendenhall et al. 2012).

Competencies of Managing People and Relationships

The second group of global leadership competencies is directed toward people and relationships. They represent leadership at "close quarters," i.e. leadership of those with whom one interacts directly, often in person. More broadly, they are focused on managing people and interpersonal relationships. Table 4.3 identifies forty-seven competency dimensions that fall into this group. We identify five composite competencies: *Cross-cultural Communication, Interpersonal Skills, Valuing People, Empowering Others*, and *Teaming Skills*. The competencies and their dimensions are presented in Table 4.5. Of the five competencies, the first three account for roughly 70 percent of all dimensions cited.

With one exception, all of the studies cited in Table 4.3 incorporate one or more dimensions covered by this group of competencies. The two most frequently cited competencies, *Cross-cultural Communication* and *Interpersonal Skills* would appear to have large overlap. Nevertheless, numerous studies (c.f. Bird et al. 2010; Caligiuri and Tarique 2009; Rosen et al. 2000) make distinctions between the two types of competencies. The distinction appears to be between the more general interpersonal skills, including sensitivity to relationships, emotional sensitivity and so forth, and those specifically related to communicating across cultures.

We discuss each of the five competencies below. Though presented in Table 4.5 in order of the number of dimensions ascribed to them, they are discussed in a sequence that reflects their relative importance and their relationship to one another.

Table 4.5 Managing People and Relationships Competencies

Cross-cultural Communication	Interpersonal Skills	Valuing People
Cross-cultural communication	Emotional intelligence	Skilled people reading
Culture bridger	Influencing	Understand actors
Cultural interest and sensitivity	Urgent listening	Cultural acumen
Appreciating cultural diversity	Relationship interest	Respectful modernizer
Cross-cultural understanding	Interpersonal engagement	Respect for others
Communication skills	Emotional sensitivity	Pragmatic trust
Mindful communication	Self-awareness	Create and build trust
Work with colleagues from other countries	Social flexibility	Creating and relying on trust
Often speak another language	Collaborative individualism	
Supervise employees of different nationalities	Sensitivity	
Negotiate in other countries or with people from other countries	Build relationships	
Cultural self-awareness	Results through relationships	
	Extraversion	

Empowering Others	Teaming Skills
Being able to empower others	Team building
Energizing	Managerial ability, with an emphasis on teamwork and interpersonal skills
Rewarding and feedback	Multicultural teaming
Connective teaching	
Sharing leadership	
Develop future leaders	

Valuing People

Although the third most prevalent competency, *Valuing People* also appears to be foundational in that all other competencies can be viewed as predicated on it. It encompasses three distinctive dimensions that have at their core a recognition of the value of people as individuals. The first is a respect for people and their differences. This respect either leads to or is derived from a deep understanding of people as individuals and an ability to comprehend people—their emotions, intentions and motivations. The third dimension of *Valuing People* is an orientation toward and an ability to create and maintain trusting relationships.

Interpersonal Skills

These represent the primary competency within the grouping, and include a range of predispositional, attitudinal, cognitive, motivational, and behavioral dimensions. For example, extraversion and relationship interest are usually considered to be predispositional (Bird et al. 2010), while interpersonal engagement and emotional sensitivity are more often viewed as attitudinal and cognitive, respectively. Social flexibility and building relationships are best classified as behavioral skills. The competency can be broken into two broad dimensions: emotional intelligence and relationship management skills. The former includes such abilities as sensitivity, interpersonal engagement, and self-awareness. The latter includes dimensions related to behaviors that involve managing relationships, e.g. influencing, urgent listening, and using relationships to achieve results.

Cross-cultural Communication

The third competency is concentrated on communicating across cultural differences. Cross-cultural communication usually entails a high level of mindfulness, i.e. a conscious awareness of contextual, cultural, and individual differences and the way in which these differences influence how messages are encoded, transmitted, received, and interpreted, as well as the reciprocal feedback process. There appear to be two components for this competency. General cultural awareness can be divided into awareness of cultural differences of others and awareness of one's own cultural influences. The second component relates to specific cognitive and behavioral skills in an intercultural context. These include the ability to speak the other person's language, skills at negotiating across cultures, and the ability to contextualize general communication skills in culturally appropriate ways.

Empowering Others

This is the fourth competency and addresses the ability of global leaders to energize direct reports, colleagues, and superiors by increasing their sense of personal self-efficacy. This may entail coaching skills, understanding how to delegate authority in culturally appropriate ways, the ability to instruct others or, more broadly, to aid in their personal and professional development.

Teaming Skills

The final competency relates to the ability to work effectively in multicultural and global virtual teams. This includes the ability to lead teams as well as to take a subordinate role and work as a value contributor to the teams' effort.

Competencies of Managing Self

The final group of global leadership competencies are directed inward to the predispositional, cognitive, and attitudinal processes in the mind of the global leader or involve aspects of personal management. Leading in a global context is personally challenging and requires a special mix of capabilities for managing oneself. Of the three groupings, the *Managing Self* category drew the most dimensions at fifty-eight. There was also wider agreement across studies with

Table 4.6 Managing Self Competencies

Resilience	Character	Inquisitiveness
Resilience to stress	Integrity (2)	Inquisitiveness (4)
Resilient, resourceful,	Accounting	Curiosity and learning
optimistic and energetic	Maturity	Aggressive insight
Resilience	Exhibit character	Open-mindedness
Emotional resilience	Honesty	Openness to experience
Non-stress tendency	Conscientiousness	Inviting the unexpected
Stress management	Self-identity	Nonjudgmentalness
Realistic optimism	Core values and flexibility	Confident humility
Optimism	Make ethical decisions	Motivation to learn
Self-confidence	Tenacity	Humility
Personal management		Learn from mistakes
Life balance		
Stable personal life		

Flexibility	Global Mindset	
Thinking agility	Global mindset (2)	
Authentic flexibility	Cosmopolitanism (3)	
Open-minded and flexible in	Cognitive complexity (2)	
thought and tactics	Thinking globally	
Flexibility (2)		
Interest flexibility		
Tolerance of ambiguity (2)		
Embrace duality		

#) indicates multiple references for the designated competency.

regard to specific dimensions. Labels such as "resilience," "inquisitiveness," and "flexibility" received multiple citations. *Global Mindset*, the least referenced composite competency (see Table 4.6), nevertheless had multiple references to a limited number of descriptive labels. Unlike the first two categories, where three of five competencies garnered upward of 70 percent of the dimensions, in this category the distribution across the five categories was relatively even. *Inquisitiveness* had the most with fourteen dimensions. *Global Mindset* had the least with eight; however, this was roughly double the number of the least referenced competencies in the other two categories.

Despite the attention directed to this set of competencies, it is also worth noting that of the sixteen studies cited in Table 4.3, two (Yeung and Ready 1995; Bikson et al. 2003) do not identify any dimensions falling into this category.

Resilience

This refers to a set of dimensions that relate to a global leader's ability to cope with the highly stressful challenges of leading across multiple time zones, large distances, myriad cultures, and widely varying national international political and regulatory systems. This competency is comprised of two broad dimensions. The first relates to a set of predispositional and attitudinal capabilities. The predispositional facets of this dimension include non-stress tendency, optimism and resilience, which are also referred to as hardiness or low neuroticism (Costa and McCrae 1992). Attitudinal facets include self-confidence and resourcefulness. The second dimension is primarily behavioral and it involves the pursuit and management of activities and lifestyle choices—exercise, meditation, hobbies, proper rest, dietary habits, etc.—that reduce stress and facilitate recovery from stressful activities. More broadly considered, this dimension incorporates a life balance between work, social interest, and the maintenance of personal physical, psychological, social, and spiritual well-being.

Character

Character can be defined as an admixture of integrity, maturity, and conscientiousness. Black et al. (1999a) place a strong emphasis on character, describing it as one of four critical elements. Similarly, Bird and Osland (2004) identify it as one of four "threshold traits" that provides a foundation for other global leader competencies. McCall and Hollenbeck (2002) frame integrity as a core honesty. A second facet of character is maturity, which entails a sense of self-awareness and clarity around personal values as well as a measured sense of one's place in the world. Related to this is a notion of accountability, being responsible for one's actions. Bird and associates (2010) call this facet *Self-identity*, which they define as an awareness of one's personal values and the way they impact one's interactions with others. Gundling, Hogan and Cvitkovich (2011) label this *core values and flexibility*. The third facet of character can be described as *persistence*. Kets de Vries and Florent-Treacy (1999) call this *tenacity*, a commitment to persevering through difficult times. It is closely related to the predispositional quality of *conscientiousness* that is part of the Big Five set of personality characteristics (Caligiuri and Tarique 2009).

Inquisitiveness

The most cited competency in this group, inquisitiveness refers to an innate curiosity, an openness to learning, and humility. Black et al. (1999a) view *inquisitiveness* as the most essential personal quality of global leaders, considering it an animating force that undergirds other competencies. A second facet of this competency is *openness*, which is broadly framed as being open to new ideas, new experiences, and new people. Moro Bueno and Tubbs (2004) label it *open-mindedness*, and identify a related facet of willingness to learn. The third facet is *humility*, which can be described as not letting pride or self-consciousness interfere with learning. Rosen and associates (2000) refer to it as *confident humility*, not feeling threatened by the need to learn and open to being taught by others. Bird and Osland (2004) define *humility* as a passive counterpart to *inquisitiveness*. As opposed to actively seeking out and exploring novelty and difference, *humility* entails allowing oneself to be taught by others.

Global Mindset

This is a cognitive competency that reflects a combination of perspective, attitude, and knowledge. It can be broken down into two facets. The first is *cognitive complexity*, specifically a highly contextualized, multifaceted, multilayered approach to the environment. The cognitively complex global leader starts from an assumption that any situation is characterized by myriad interdependencies and that relationships involve complex, dynamical properties. The second facet of global mindset is *cosmopolitanism*, an interest in and knowledge of the world—nations, social and political institutions, cultures, and people, etc. (Levy et al. 2007).

Flexibility

The final competency involves willingness to adapt and adjust to varied situations. It incorporates a cognitive component, *intellectual flexibility*, which Black et al. (1999a) refer to as *embracing duality*, and it parallels and supports the *cognitive complexity* facet of global mindset. Bird and associates (2010) focus on *tolerance of ambiguity*, a construct established more broadly in psychology; however, their specific strain of *tolerance of ambiguity* is specific to the intercultural context common to global leadership. Flexibility also incorporates a behavioral component, *behavioral flexibility,* which entails a willingness to adapt or adjust one's behaviors to fit differing circumstances or situational demands (Bird et al. 2010).

Concluding Thoughts

After cultivating, weeding, sorting, and organizing the global leadership competency garden, we have pruned the original list of 160 competencies down to 15 and ordered them in three broad categories. Each of the fifteen competencies reflects a complex, multifaceted construct. For example, *Inquisitiveness* includes facets related to *curiosity, openness to experience*, and *humility*. The final ordering is presented in Table 4.7. Though the table may give an impression of simplicity—three groups of five competencies each—the multifaceted aspect of each competency encompasses significant complexity. Moreover, the various facets of a given competency span predispositional, attitudinal, cognitive, behavioral, and knowledge aspects. As shall be seen in the subsequent chapters addressing how to assess and develop global leadership capabilities, the variety of competency aspects creates significant challenges.

Recently Mendenhall and associates (2012) sought to clarify the definition of global leadership. Their stated intent was to bring definitional clarity to the study of global leadership. By reviewing previous definitions and explicitly addressing

Table 4.7 A Framework of Nested Global Leadership Competencies

Business and Organizational Acumen	Managing People and Relationships	Managing Self
Vision and strategic thinking	Valuing people	Inquisitiveness
Leading change	Cross-cultural communication	Global mindset
Business savvy	Interpersonal skills	Flexibility
Organizational savvy	Teaming skills	Character
Managing communities	Empowering others	Resilience

areas of disagreement or confusion, they sought to avoid the fragmentation that has afflicted other areas of inquiry. They also hoped to facilitate a more focused and disciplined approach to theoretical and empirical work on global leadership. This chapter has sought a similar aim, the facilitation of the development of a common body of knowledge on global leadership by stemming the proliferation of competency dimensions. Doing so increases the likelihood that the interpretation of empirical results will be less problematic and the accumulation and integration of findings will be more easily achieved.

It is questionable whether any field of inquiry can move forward if it persists in accommodating an ever-increasing array of constructs, many of which have largely overlapping construct domains. The nature of rigorous inquiry holds that there is always the possibility that new theory and new empirical findings may lead to a reformulation of existing organizing frames, an extension or elaboration of current constructs, or even the development of new ones. It is also the case that as a field matures, consolidation enhances research progress. In short, it is easier to grow a well-trimmed garden.

Process Models of Global Leadership Development

JOYCE S. OSLAND AND ALLAN BIRD

> If we want to understand leadership, we need to look at our own experiences. I believe that we carry within us enough experience to form our own simple, coherent approach to being a good leader. Creating and clarifying our own leadership approaches will help us (one by one and in our own ways) truly make a difference.
>
> (Margaret Wheatley, cited in Madsen and Hammond 2005)

> The next CEO of GE will not be like me. I spent my entire career in the U.S. The next head of General Electric will be somebody who spent time in Bombay, in Hong Kong, in Buenos Aires. We have to send our best and brightest overseas and make sure they have the training that will allow them to be the global leaders who will make GE flourish in the future.
>
> (Jack Welch, former CEO of GE, cited in Black and Gregersen 1999)

Now that we have a better idea of what global leaders are like, the natural follow-on questions are "How did they get that way?" and "How can we develop prospective global leaders?" Carlos Ghosn, award-winning Chairman, CEO, and President of Nissan and Renault, is one of the most famous global leaders in the business world. A look at his background shows that he was born in Brazil and educated in France. Ghosn worked in the United States for seven years as head of Michelin and spent three years with Renault in France before becoming President and CEO of Nissan. One of the few non-Japanese CEOs of Japanese companies, Ghosn is so popular that bento box lunches are named after him on some restaurant menus. He is given credit for Nissan's leadership in the electric car market as well as Nissan's successful turnaround effort and cross-border alliance with Renault.

Although cultural differences crippled other cross-border automotive alliances, such as Daimler-Chrysler, Ghosn sees them as opportunities.

> When you have taken the time to understand [that people don't think or act the same way] ... and when you are really motivated and mobilized by a very strong objective, then the cultural differences can become seeds for innovation as opposed to seeds for dissention.
>
> (Emerson 2001: 6)

He believes that in order to call yourself "international": "you have to go to countries that have a totally different way of thinking, a totally different way of organization, and a totally different way of life" (Emerson 2001: 7). Ghosn had an international experience early in life when he studied abroad, has lived in four continents, and clearly appreciates cultural differences. In this respect, his background is similar to many other global leaders.

Kets de Vries and Florent-Treacy (2002) identify the foundation for developing global leadership in their research sample as:

- family background that involved *intercultural experiences* (mixed-culture marriages, bilingual parents, exposure to other cultures);

- *early education* involving international schools, summer camps, and travel;

- *later education* that included exchange programs, languages, and international MBA programs; and

- *spouse and children* who are supportive, adventurous, adaptable, and mobile.

However, this may also reflect the type of background that was typical in their research sample at INSEAD, a highly diverse graduate business school in France. Osland and her colleagues (Osland et al. 2007) found that not all of their expert global leaders had international backgrounds. They were, however, highly intelligent, quick learners who had been transformed by exposure to significant non-cultural differences at some point and, as a result, developed cognitive and social flexibility.

To complement the individual personal development that lays a foundation for global leadership development, organizations provide professional development in the form of training, transfer, teamwork, and travel. These same four development activities, especially transfer, were suggested as the most effective ways to develop global leadership in other research (Black et al. 1999a). Transfer, more commonly referred to as international assignments, varies in terms of the type of development that is sought. Zaccaro et al. (2006) identify three types of experience-based developmental job assignments. "Stamping-in" experiences involve work assignments where the individual is given tasks that require them to apply recently acquired skills or knowledge so as to reinforce and internalize what was previously learned. By contrast, action-learning assignments place managers in the position of working on real-time problems of importance to the company and requiring more than just applying learning. The final type identified by Zaccaro and associates are "stretch" assignments that move people out of their comfort zones and require them to approach the task differently—to work with challenging problems in unusual circumstances with significant uncertainty and risk. By and large, many international assignments are seen as fitting the latter type. Nevertheless, it is useful to recognize that all three types play a role in the developmental process. We will discuss the organizational role in development more directly in Chapter 10. In this chapter, our focus is *how* global leaders develop.

While the global leadership literature provides numerous recommendations concerning global leadership development, few of these recommendations are based on empirical research (for a review of the literature on global leader development, see Suutari 2002). The exceptions included interviews with global managers and leaders asking for either recommendations or personal accounts concerning global leadership development (Black et al. 1999a; Kets de Vries and Florent-Treacy 2002; McCall and Hollenback 2002) and the sole longitudinal study of global leaders (Graen and Hui 1999). In a longitudinal study, the eventual career progress of Japanese global leaders (Graen and Hui 1999: 17–18) was predicted by three behaviors that occurred in the first three years of their career: 1) building effective working relationships characterized by trust, respect, and obligation with immediate supervisors; 2) networking derived from their contacts at prestigious universities; and 3) doing more than was expected in the face of difficult and ambiguous performance expectations. The last element, "difficult and ambiguous performance expectations," is an example of the challenging experiences that constitute a common element in all models of global leadership development (Kets de Vries and Florent-Treacy 2002; McCall and Hollenbeck 2002; Osland et al. 2006). As Mary Catherine Bateson wrote in *Peripheral Visions: Learning along the Way*: "Insight, I believe, refers to that depth of understanding that comes by setting experiences, yours and mine, familiar and exotic, new and old, side by side, learning by letting them speak to one another" (Bateson 1994:14).

We will look at three models of global leadership development in the following sections.

The Chattanooga Model of Global Leadership Development

In 2001, a team of scholars[1] spent two days at the Frierson Leadership Institute at the University of Tennessee, Chattanooga, reviewing their collective experience and wisdom as scholars and consultants in the area of global leadership. What emerged from that intensive effort was a framework for developing global leadership talent that came to be known as the Chattanooga Model. It was a process model of global leadership based on the assumption that global leadership development in an individual was a nonlinear, emergent process that is moderated by a variety of key variables, across time (see Figure 5.1)

To understand how the process works, let's begin in the lower left-hand corner of the model by focusing on the potential global leader. This model assumes that a manager enters a global/cross-cultural context, probably through an expatriate assignment, and is immersed in that environment over an extended period of time. Entering managers bring with them certain basic, core stable personality traits, including fairly immutable competencies (ambition, desire to lead, sociability,

---

1   The team consisted of Allan Bird, Nakiye Boyacigiller, Paula Caligiuri, Mark Mendenhall, Edward Miller, Joyce Osland, Guenter Stahl, and Mary Ann Von Glinow.

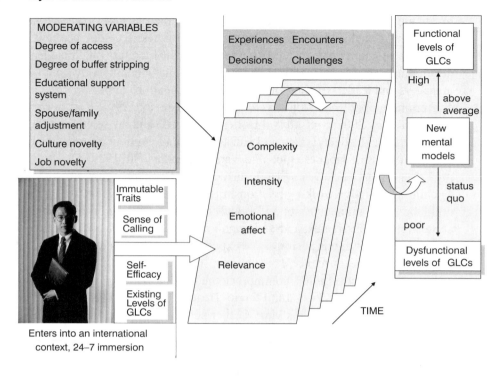

Figure 5.1 The Chattanooga Model of Global Leadership Development

openness, agreeableness, emotional stability, etc.) and cognitive processes (attribution flexibility, cognitive complexity, tolerance for ambiguity, etc.). The degree to which managers perceive a sense of calling with respect to global work or perceive themselves as global citizens and view the assignment as something that fits "who they really are" can influence both their attitude towards the hardships they may encounter and whether they will be more likely to develop leadership capabilities as opposed to simply engaging in bureaucratic behaviors in the international assignment. Managers also enter this context with existing levels of self-efficacy that are brought to bear on various aspects of living and working globally. Finally, managers enter the global context armed with varying existing levels of global leadership competencies.

Thus, each manager enters the global context with a unique configuration of individual variables, bringing that configuration to bear upon the multitude of daily experiences he or she encounters in the new milieu. The "folders" or "pages" in the center of Figure 5.1 are representative of single experiences, interactions, and challenges the individual passes through over time. The recursive arrow in the model indicates that a current experience can cause, through its effect on memory, a revision or revisiting of past experiences. The development process is not based on a sequence of independent experiences; rather, each experience is tied to past experiences and constitutes a sense-making process of learning and acquiring global leadership capability. Bennis and Thomas (2002: 14) refer to this process as constituting "crucible" situations "characterized by the confluence of powerful intellectual, social, economic, or political forces" that severely test one's patience and one's beliefs, and that produce a transformation in managers, leaving them deeply different relative to who they were prior to the crucible experience.

The specific nature of various global/cross-cultural crucible experiences is critical to the development of global leadership. The transformative potential of each experience can be understood in terms of four elements. Experiences with higher levels of each one possess greater transformational potential.

Complexity embodies the degree to which the experience involves situations or issues that are multilayered or multifaceted, i.e. can be understood in multiple ways or involve competing perspectives. For example, conducting a performance appraisal in an acquired language with a direct report in another country is more complex than conducting the same performance appraisal in one's native language in one's home country with an employee who shares one's cultural background. In addition to mastering elements of multiple cultures, the necessity of conveying and receiving nuanced meaning accurately further increases complexity. More complex experiences have more transformative potential because there is a larger volume of information—different layers, multiple explanations—available for processing. Also, the processing of that information can be addressed from multiple perspectives.

Intensity involves the degree to which the experience requires concentrated attention or effort. For example, engaging in high-level international negotiations with a short deadline has a higher degree of intensity than fact-gathering. More intense situations compel more attention. More intense experiences have more transformative potential because the higher level of attention increases the prospect for absorbing more information, particularly more context-specific information. Higher levels of context-specific information provide increased probabilities for improved cue identification and subsequent explanation.

Emotional affect addresses the extent to which emotion is present or stimulated by the experience. For instance, overseas experiences and sophisticated simulations can elicit strong affect such as frustration, stress, or the elation that comes from mastering a difficult challenge. More affective experiences have more transformative potential because experiences with a strong affective element are recalled more vividly and are available for recall over a longer duration. Hence they are more accessible for subsequent reflection. Also, as a trigger event, strong emotion may stimulate autonomic responses that, in themselves, have transformative potential.

Relevance is the extent to which the experience is perceived as relevant to an objective or value important to the individual. More relevant experiences possess more transformative potential because they are likely to elicit higher levels of attention and information gathering, are more easily placed in an existing schema, and more likely to elicit sense-making behavior given greater motivation to learn and understand the experience. As with the other elements, more relevant experiences are more likely to be recalled for reflection purposes.

Relevance is distinct from the other three in that it is separable from the experience itself in a way that the other three are not. Objectives and values may change over time, leading to a reassessment of the significance or triviality of the experience or elements within the experience. For example, an interaction with someone may seem trivial in the moment and then afterward become significant when it is learned that the person is important, e.g. the president of a potential client company.

The transformational potency of experiences can be diluted or even cancelled out by a series of moderators that are found in the upper box on the left side of Figure 5.1. In some cases, the experiences are buffered by organizational policies or by the individuals themselves; in others, the experiences are simply not novel or challenging enough to trigger transformation. Experiences are buffered when the degree of access to transformative experiences is constrained by companies or the individual managers. For instance, if company policy is to provide expatriates with chauffeurs, translator/assistants, and housing in expatriate enclaves, their managers may live in a bubble that separates them from the foreign culture and limits contact with its citizens. There are numerous examples of expatriates who socialize only with their compatriots and enroll their children in international schools, which buffers them from transformative experiences. The final two moderators relate to the degree of challenge in such experiences, which is couched here in terms of cultural novelty and job novelty. This assumes that a greater degree of novelty or difference will necessitate the adaptation and growth that develops global leaders. In sum, each of the variables in this section moderates the transformative role or strength of potential experiences and therefore either enhances or detracts from global leadership development.

The critical factor in the global leadership development of any manager is access to high-level challenges. Consistent access to the right sorts of challenges may produce, in some cases, solid global leadership competency development over time, which brings us to the outcomes on the right side of the model. Success, however, is not guaranteed, and access may also lead to failure. Managers may be given the right kind of experiences but find they are unable to handle them or learn from them because the challenges are overwhelming. Although the goal of challenging experiences is to help managers develop new mental leadership models, there is the possibility that the newly developed models are actually dysfunctional, reflecting a learning of the wrong lessons. For example, stereotypical thinking, misattributions, and inaccurate cause-and-effect links are frequent examples of learning the wrong lessons and developing inaccurate mental models. Though these mental models appear at the end of the process in Figure 5.1, such models are being created over and over again, in response to each experience the individual has; thus, the developing framework is malleable, but with the potential to harden into a dysfunctional systemic framework if experiences are not handled effectively over time.

In summary, the Chattanooga model perceives the global leadership development process as emergent in nature and dynamic in process. If a manager's immutable personality traits, access to powerful challenges, etc., are consistent with what is required to work and learn in the global context, a functional global leadership process will ensue, and the manager will develop global leadership competencies. It is important to recognize, however, that other outcomes ranging from "status quo" to "dysfunctional" can result. At any point in time, a manager's developmental trajectory can rise or fall, moderated by the unique constellation of forces that impinge upon any given experience.

The Global Leadership Expertise Development Model (GLED)

The GLED model expands upon the Chattanooga model but focuses primarily on the development of expertise in global leaders. The argument that global leadership development is a process of personal transformation is a recurrent theme. Presuming this thesis is cogent, it is likely that global leadership development is not a linear progression that simply adds to an existing portfolio of leadership competencies, but rather a nonlinear process whereby deep-seated change in competencies, expertise, and worldview through experiential learning occur over time (Osland et al. 2006). As with the previous model, this one relies on transformative crucible experiences that test a person's mettle and beliefs. Traditional training cannot in and of itself be the primary tool through which GL expertise and competencies are inculcated within individuals. Organizations need to ensure that prospective global leaders are exposed to transformational experiences in their developmental process.

Based on the research literature and the presumption that GL development is an emergent phenomenon, we offer the following process model, referred to as the GLED model (see Figure 5.2) to illustrate GL expertise development. This model is an extension of the Chattanooga Model in Figure 5.1.

The left side of the GLED model contains four categories of *antecedents*: individual characteristics, cultural exposure, global education, and project/job novelty. The individual characteristics category comprises the content domain of intercultural competence for global leaders (Bird, Mendenhall, Stevens and Oddou 2010). The other three categories also contain variables related to one or more aspects of GL development or expertise (Black et al. 1999a; Kets de Vries and Florent-Treacy 2002; McCall and Hollenbeck 2002; Caligiuri 2004; Yamazaki and Kayes 2004).

Four dependent variables—cognitive processes (expert decision making), global knowledge (facts related to the global environment and work domain),

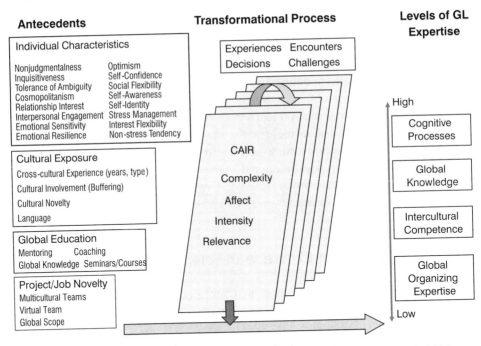

Figure 5.2 A Model of Global Leadership Expertise Development (Osland et al. 2006; Osland & Bird 2008)

intercultural competence (ability to work effectively across cultures), and global organizing expertise (systems thinking and architecture necessary to create and maintain effective global organizations)—combine to determine the *level of GL expertise*. These categories are based on Mendenhall and Osland's (2002) categorization of GL competencies. GL expertise is conceptualized as a continuum. Domestic leaders or novice global leaders may manifest some degree of GL expertise as a result of their work or experience with other nationalities. Similarly, not all global leaders will be fully expert. As Dreyfus and Dreyfus (1986) note, there are several stages in the developmental journey from novice to expert. Higher measures of the antecedents are predicted to correlate with higher measures of GL expertise.

The relationship between the antecedents and outcome measures is mediated by the *transformational process*, which consists of experiences, interpersonal encounters, decisions, and challenges that relate to GL expertise. Not all cross-cultural experiences develop GL expertise, so transformational experiences differ from those found in the cultural exposure category. Furthermore, not all global or cultural experiences have the same impact (McCall and Hollenbeck 2002; Osland et al. 2006). The transformational process, as in the Chattanooga Model, refers to a series of crucible experiences with varying degrees of complexity, emotional affect, intensity, and developmental relevance. Experiences with higher levels of each of these four elements possess greater transformational potential that, in turn, will result in developing a higher level of GL expertise.

Kohonen (2005) proposes an identity construction perspective in global leader development that is consistent with the Chattanooga and GLED models. She posits that the transformation described in these models represent occasions for professional and career identity construction. Coping and competency-development experiences associated with these international assignments give rise to a re-evaluation of one's identity. This may be particularly true with regard to global leader competencies such as global mindset.

A longitudinal examination of GL development would presumably reveal that dynamic individual characteristics increase as a result of transformational experiences and that current experience can cause, through memory, an updating or reliving of past experiences. Thus, GL development over time is more spiral-like and recursive than Figure 5.2 suggests (Osland et al. 2006). The GL development process is not based on independent experiences; rather, each experience is tied to past, multiple experiences and constitutes a sense-making process of learning and acquiring global leadership expertise (Osland et al. 2006).

Both the Chattanooga model and the GLED model are conceptual in nature and have yet to be fully validated, though recent empirical work on several fronts points to their validity. For example, Caligiuri and Tarique (2011) found that personal predispositions of openness to experience and extraversion related positively to tolerance of ambiguity and cultural flexibility and negatively to ethnocentrism. Additionally, emotional stability was also related to lower levels of ethnocentrism. They also found that high-contact experiences, particularly those initiated by the organization, also facilitated development of competencies related to effective performance. In a similar vein, Pless, Maak and Stahl (2011), reported on findings from a study of company-sponsored participation in international service learning programs. They found that after going through the program participants increased in the following domains, all of which are important for global leadership: responsible mindset, ethical literacy, cultural intelligence, global mindset, self-development, and community building. They reported that the processes that facilitated the heightening of these competencies were paradox confrontation and resolution, construction of a "new life-world," and emotional sense making.

A Model for Developing Global Executives

The third model focuses on the interaction and partnership between the individual and the organization. It was developed by McCall and Hollenbeck (2002) on the basis of interviews with global executives (actual global leaders) who worked overseas. International assignments, which are viewed as the most powerful development tool in facilitating global leadership competencies (Gregersen et al. 1998; Hall et al. 2001; Mendenhall et al. 2001), received a great deal of attention in McCall and Hollenbeck's research and model.

Individuals cannot be forced to develop, and they themselves bear the ultimate responsibility for their development. Organizations, however, establish an organizational culture and policies that either enhance or impede development. Due to the experiences organizations provide, they can be the source of both intended and unintended lessons. Therefore, these authors recommend that organizations be both intentional and collaborative about development. Stated simply, this model is based on the idea that the company strategy determines what qualities are required in its leaders, and then talented people are hired and given appropriate experiences and support in order to develop those qualities.

One of their research questions involved testing whether a developmental model based on research on U.S. executives (McCall 1998) would also apply to an internationally diverse group of global executives. They found that the earlier model was relevant for global executives with only one adaptation—the addition of context to the experience component, which you can see in Figure 5.3. Context, in this instance, usually relates to culture. Therefore, they concluded that "this basic process of development is the same for all executives, regardless of the countries they come from or whether the development is for global, expatriate, or local executive work" (McCall and Hollenbeck 2002: 172). Although the basic components of the model are similar for all groups, the specifics of developing global executives do differ significantly—another example of a difference of both degree and kind. "Global executive development is much more complex and unpredictable and requires a greater focus, effort, and resources concentrated over a longer period" (McCall and Hollenbeck 2002: 172). They justify their argument with these observations:

- The global business strategy determines, to an even greater extent, the relevant lessons leaders need to learn.

- A wider range of more difficult developmental experiences has to be available to develop a more talented cadre of executives.

- Development takes place in a more complex, multicultural global environment with more diverse executives.

- The mechanisms for development are more complicated, difficult to administer, and expensive.

The McCall and Hollenbeck model is described below. The starting point chronologically is Business Strategy in the upper right corner.

Business Strategy

An organization's strategy and structure determine the number of international jobs, the types of global executives and their nationalities, and the skills they

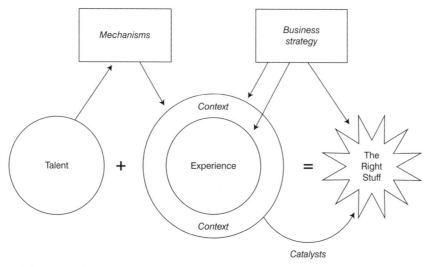

Figure 5.3 A Model for Developing Global Executives

Source: Reprinted with permission. From M. W. McCall, Jr. and G. P. Hollenbeck (2002) *Developing Global Executives: The Lessons of International Experience* (Boston, MA: Harvard Business School Press), p. 173.

will need. If a firm opts to grow via acquisitions and alliances, they need executives with experience working across company borders. If the structure is organized along strict functional lines, it will be difficult to provide executives with the necessary cross-functional experience early in their career. The choice of geographic markets, for example, can determine how many executives of what cultural mix will be needed. The type of work leaders will be expected to do and where they will do it all depends on the business strategy. It informs the Experience and Context as well as The Right Stuff, described next.

The Right Stuff

In this model, "the right stuff" refers to the end-state of development, what leaders have learned. It is determined by the business strategy and therefore varies by company. McCall and Hollenbeck (2002) believe that leaders are "made" (or born, then made) because most of what they need to master can be learned and is learned primarily from global experiences. The usual things that all executives have to know are made more difficult and subtle in a global context. Thus, there is a second category of lessons that relate specifically to the international nature of their jobs and are rooted in cultural differences and the unique demands of expatriation.

Box 5.1 lists the themes and lessons that were reported by McCall and Hollenbeck's sample when they were asked to tell about at least three experiences that had shaped them as international executives and what they had learned from those experiences. The list is not necessarily exhaustive of lessons learned, nor

Box 5.1 The Themes and Lessons of International Experience

Learning to Deal with Cultural Issues and Different Cultures
1. Learning to speak a foreign language
2. Learning about specific foreign cultures and contrasts between specific cultures
3. Learning generic lessons about living and working in foreign cultures

Learning to Run a Business – Strategy, Structure, Processes; Global versus Local; Specialized Knowledge
1. Learning strategies for doing business
2. Learning the specifics of running a business

Learning to Lead and Manage Others – Selection, Development, Motivation, Team Building, Deselection
1. Learning how to establish credibility
2. Learning to select the right people
3. Learning to build and sustain an effective team
4. Learning to make tough calls about people
5. Learning to stay focused – keeping it simple, setting clear goals
6. Learning to keep people motivated and committed, what to delegate and what not to delegate
7. Learning to develop people and the importance of developing people

Learning to Deal with Problematic Relationships – Headquarters, Bosses, Unions, Government, Media, Politics
1. Learning to handle immediate bosses and other superiors
2. Learning to manage the interface with headquarters and the larger organization
3. Learning to handle public appearances and the media
4. Learning to deal with governments and (external) politicians
5. Learning to deal with unions and other types of negotiations
6. Learning about internal politics

Learning about the Personal Qualities Required of a Leader
1. Learning to listen carefully, to ask questions, and to see the world through other people's eyes
2. Learning to be open, genuine, honest, fair; to treat other people with respect; and to trust others
3. Learning to be flexible, to adapt to changing situations, to take changing circumstances into account, to manage multiple priorities and complex relationships, and to think on your feet
4. Learning to assess risks and take them, and to act in the face of uncertainty
5. Learning to persevere, to act with discipline, and to stay calm under tough circumstances
6. Learning to be optimistic, to believe in oneself, to trust one's instincts, to take a stand for what one believes is right, and to accept responsibility for the consequences of one's actions

Learning about Self and Career
1. Learning about likes, dislikes, strengths, weaknesses, and preferences
2. Learning what support you need from family or others, and how to manage the family under the pressure of foreign work
3. Learning to manage your own career and development

are these lessons universal to all global executives. They do indicate the type of lessons learned from global experiences. The authors compared these findings to the lessons learned by a sample of U.S. executives that was carried out in the 1980s. Many of the same lessons emerged from both samples, indicating that, on the surface at least, there is a common skill set shared by global and domestic executives.

The comparison, however, also surfaced significant differences in lessons learned. Cultural lessons composed 15 percent of the lessons learned by global executives; this category never emerged from the domestic executives. Furthermore, global executives reported more "big picture" lessons related to the Strategies for Doing Business category, while the U.S. executives recounted more lessons related to the Learning to Lead and Manage Others category. From this, McCall and Hollenbeck conclude that global executives have a broader perspective on the world, which is why it can be difficult for them to return to a narrower scope in a domestic job once they have worked abroad. Learning to listen carefully and the importance of the family in global work were more significant to global executives than to U.S. executives. McCall and Hollenbeck (2002) argue further that even lessons that seem similar on the surface, such as learning to be flexible, are deeper and broader when learned in the more complex and uncertain global setting. For that reason, there is no substitute for actually working in another country (McCall and Hollenbeck 2002: 180).

Experience

As in the previous two models, experience is found at the center of the model. The significant development experiences identified in McCall and Hollenbeck's work were categorized as foundation assignments (early work experience and first managerial responsibility), major line assignments (business turnarounds, start-ups, joint ventures, alliances, mergers or acquisitions), shorter-term experiences (significant other people, special projects, consulting roles, staff advisory jobs, developmental and educational experiences, negotiations, stint at headquarters), and perspective-changing experiences (culture shock, career shifts, confrontations with reality, changes in scope or scale, mistakes and errors in judgment, family and personal challenges, crises). Exposure to "significant other people" was reported by the largest number of participants (32 percent). These people might have provided either positive or negative lessons. "Especially in global work, opportunities to work in parallel with a predecessor, on-site learning (intentional or not) from a local national, and exposure to others with global careers had important influences and offered important learning opportunities" (McCall and Hollenbeck 2002: 180).

The organization cannot control all of these experiences. Nor do intentionally designed experiences always result in developmental outcomes. However, individually tailoring experiences, thinking ahead about where individuals might need support, and tracking their progress provides a greater possibility that positive lessons will result. An international experience in the early years of one's career was strongly recommended by the participants. The selection of experiences, like "the right stuff," is ultimately determined by the strategy.

Talent

As Figure 5.3 shows, Talent plus Experience equals The Right Stuff. The organization is also responsible for managing talent and ensuring that they provide the right employees with experiences. There are several difficulties in assessing talent in a multicultural global organization: identifying a common standard across cultures, country differences in assessing, promoting and developing managers, wide variability in global executive jobs, and the organization's openness to promoting executives from other nationalities (McCall and Hollenbeck 2002: 185–186). In order to benefit from the diversity, these factors should be considered:

- Career histories have to be interpreted based on their cultural context.

- Preexisting assets should be analyzed to assess where individuals stand now, where they could go, and which experience would contribute the most at this particular point.

- Ability to learn from experience should be evaluated since this relates to taking advantage of the experience.

- Potential for derailment should be analyzed. "Because the traps are more numerous and deadlier in the international context, it is imperative that organizations consider the possibility of derailment when assessing talent" (McCall and Hollenbeck 2002: 187).

Mechanisms

Talent management also requires appropriate Mechanisms, which refer to those policies and practices that aim at "getting the right people into the right experience." McCall and Hollenbeck (2002: 189) believe that organizations have to establish and maintain five parallel processes that serve both short-term business needs and development needs.

1 *Selection* refers to the organization's need to identify people who are ready to assume global positions. There has to be a system to identify and select these people when unexpected staffing needs arise.

2 *Succession* involves replacement plans with lists of potential successors in case an incumbent vacates a job unexpectedly. When this is done in advance, rather than in the midst of an emergency, more thought and care can be taken.

3 *Development* occurs by placing people in jobs that will expand their cultural or business skills, which is often done with people from a culturally diverse background who have a clear interest in international work.

4 *Discovery* mechanisms provide parochial employees with an opportunity early in their careers to ascertain whether they might have a previously unidentified interest in international work.

5 *Recovery* pertains to the organization's efforts to integrate repatriates when they return home from a global assignment.

Catalysts

The last category of organizational supports are developmental catalysts that help executives learn from their experiences. One category of catalysts *improve information*, such as interpreting feedback or providing feedback on development as well as on performance and outcomes. A second category *provides incentives and resources*, like holding people accountable for developmental goals or promoting people who model the desired developmental behaviors. A third category of catalysts *support change* by providing emotional support or viewing change in a systems context. "While perhaps an indirect catalyst, support for the whole family [of an executive on a global assignment] turns out to be important from a learning perspective" (McCall and Hollenbeck 2002: 193).

This model's contribution lies in illustrating the strategic imperatives that drive executive development and the role played by the organization. They "globalized" a domestic model of development, and their international findings provide insight into some of the unique characteristics and challenges of developing global leaders. Given the qualitative nature of their research, future studies could generate hypotheses and test the model with quantitative measures. The work of Furuya and associates (2009) provides some support for the McCall and Hollenbeck model. They found that clarification of the alignment of international assignments with firm strategy and supportive HR management policies was associated with significant global leader competency acquisition and transfer.

Lessons from the Global Leadership Development Models

All three models presume that the demands of global leadership in a complex, ambiguous setting will require flexibility and adaptability. Thus, the ability to learn and learn continuously is critical. The development of this learning capability is best achieved through an experiential approach that emphasizes putting people into work situations that reflect the capabilities they need to develop (McCall 2010). For example, intercultural flexibility is best developed by placing individuals in intercultural settings. In particular, the learning associated with challenging international assignments can result in personal transformation that, in turn, creates a better fit with global work requirements. Because it is "personal" and transformational, the development process for individuals is nonlinear, uncertain, and hard to predict.

We would be remiss not to point out that these models are presumed to be universally applicable, i.e. they describe the developmental process for global leaders regardless of nationality or culture. This is not, however, to suggest that the same experiences, or even the same type of experiences, will be similarly efficacious. Wilson and Yip (2010) find evidence suggesting Indian and Singaporean global leaders may derive very different learning than their U.S. counterparts from identical experiences (Wilson 2008; Yip and Wilson 2008). The key insight, therefore, is that effective use of the model requires an individualized application.

More research is needed on process models of global leadership to determine whether the models presented in this chapter are adequate and borne out by empirical study. A systemic analysis of the factors that promote or impede global leadership development would verify whether the models are comprehensive and avoid a Western bias. There is a strong need for longitudinal research that compares and measures the impact of the transformational experiences at the center of these models. Moreover, organizational aspects of development must be taken into consideration. Firm-specific factors such as the alignment of strategy and HR management processes with the firm's efforts to develop global leadership require particular attention.

The question of what companies have learned from their efforts to develop global leaders is taken up in Chapter 10.

6 Assessing Global Leadership Competencies

ALLAN BIRD AND MICHAEL J. STEVENS

A quick tour of the internet provides some insight regarding the topic of this chapter—the assessment of global leadership competencies. In just 0.27 seconds Google references 503 million websites relating to leadership. Narrow the search to "global leadership" and it takes 0.16 seconds to identify 3.4 million sites. But key in "global leadership assessment," and only 769,000 sites surface. This is a significant change since the publication of the first edition of this book in 2008. At that time, the respective numbers were: 170 million, 983,000, and 64. Some of this change may be attributable to the growth of the internet itself. But it is reasonable to also conclude that there is increasing interest in the subject of global leadership and significant growth in trying to assess global leadership competencies. Nevertheless, as we will discover as we proceed further, when it comes to assessing the competencies associated with effective global leadership, much work remains to be done.

In this chapter we will begin by discussing what "competency" means in the context of global leadership and note significant challenges in identifying and measuring it. We'll then move on to a consideration of a variety of instruments that are currently used by practitioners and scholars.

A comprehensive review of proposed competencies is beyond the scope of this chapter, which has as its central focus a review of assessment instruments. Chapters 1 and 2 both present an overview of the broader research on global leadership, much of which has taken a content view and, hence, has focused on leader characteristics that are, either implicitly or explicitly, put forward as competencies. For a more detailed review of the leadership competency literature, readers should consult Jokinen (2005) and (Osland et al. 2006).

Defining Global Leadership Competency

The pioneering work on competency as a concept in the workplace was carried out by McClelland, who defined it as a set of underlying characteristics that an individual or team possess that have been demonstrated to predict superior or effective performance in a job (1973). McClelland was particularly concerned with identifying behaviors that superior performers possessed and that average or underperformers did not have. Boyatzis (1982) emphasized the causal connection between capabilities a person possessed prior to performance that could be used to predict superior performance in a given situation. Working from this conception of competency, there are three clear standards that must be met to define an individual characteristic or capacity as a competency: 1) it must exist prior to performance; 2) it must be causally linked to performance; and 3) it must be possessed by superior, but not by average or sub-par, performers.

The task domain of global leadership makes it difficult to identify competencies that conform to the three standards presented above. As Osland and associates (2006) note, there is no agreed upon definition for what constitutes global leadership. Even where it is possible to succinctly define a global leader as someone whose job responsibilities include a global scope (Black et al. 1999a), the range of positions to which such a definition applies makes it problematic to circumscribe a narrow range of activities or behaviors. Be that as it may, for our purposes here, it may be useful to adopt Jokinen's (2005: 200) formulation as our definition of global leadership competencies:

> those universal qualities that enable individuals to perform their job outside their own national as well as organizational culture, no matter what their educational or ethnic background is, what functional area their job description represents, or what organization they come from.

As noted in Chapter 1, assessing global leadership competencies presents several distinctive challenges. First, there may be a tendency to over specify the number of competencies required for superior performance in a specific job (Conger and Ready 2004b). For example, Morrison (2000) notes that Chase Manhattan Bank has identified 250 competencies associated with global leadership. Mendenhall and Osland (2002) reviewed the academic scholarship on global leadership and came up with a list of fifty-six competencies. It is reasonable to question whether such lengthy lists are useful or practical.

A second challenge is that both practitioners and academics alike may be inclined to develop competency lists that reflect an idealized performance standard, rather than what is actually possible (Conger and Ready 2004b). This may arise as a consequence of trying to envision what superior performance might look like or what behaviors might lead to it rather than focusing on what has been demonstrated to be superior performance or on what is realistic.

Third, there is a need to distinguish between competency types. In studying expatriate managers—the group single-most associated with global leadership research—Leiba-O'Sullivan (1999) proposes a distinction between stable and dynamic competencies. Stable competencies reflect aspects of personality and are relatively settled and enduring over time. They are difficult, if not impossible, to significantly change. However, they may be broadly applicable, i.e. they may contribute to superior performance across a range of jobs or work situations.

For example, the personality predisposition of optimism is widely accepted as contributing to superior performance across a multitude of managerial positions. By contrast, dynamic competencies are specific skills and abilities that can, to a greater or lesser degree, be taught. They are, however, often more narrowly applicable. For example, typing skills can be taught, though some people will learn how to type more accurately and more quickly than others. Moreover, the ability to type accurately and quickly is less likely to be associated with superior performance across a broad range of managerial positions or situations. The distinction between stable and dynamic competencies is sometimes framed respectively in terms of "soft" versus "hard" competencies or "behavioral" versus "technical."

In the next section we will review several of the more widely used assessment instruments. After presenting the competencies purportedly measured by each, we will attempt to evaluate them in accordance with the three criteria noted above, namely do the competencies exist prior to performance; are they causally linked to performance; and do they distinguish between superior and non-superior performance. We'll do that by looking for empirical evidence that supports their ability to predict performance.

Global Leadership Competency Assessment Instruments

Broadly classified, assessment instruments used in developing global leaders fall into one of three broad categories: cultural difference assessments, intercultural adaptability assessments, and global leadership competency assessments. We consider each type below, and discuss specific assessment instruments.

Cultural Difference Assessments

Although not directly focused on assessing global leader competencies, it is appropriate to recognize that practitioners and scholars have developed a variety of assessments and survey instruments for identifying variations in national cultural values across a range of dimensions. A number of the more widely used instruments (e.g. Maznevski and DiStefano, 1995; Hampden-Turner and Trompenaars 2000; Hofstede 2001), are often construed as a form of indirect competency assessment. In a typical application along these lines, a manager's cultural profile (i.e. score or position on various cultural value dimensions) will be computed and these will be used within the context of a training program to determine developmental needs. In this regard, it is appropriate to view them as competency assessment proxies as they are used to identify areas where the development of hard competencies is presumed to lead to superior performance.

Taras (2006b) has compiled the most comprehensive catalogue of such instruments to date. More than 100 instruments cover the gamut of work- or business-related dimensions on which cultures are likely to vary, including the common—e.g. individualism, power distance, uncertainty avoidance, and universalism—and the not so common—e.g. family integrity, faith in people, and upward influence. Where available, Taras (2006b) also provides the specific items in the instrument as well as Cronbach alpha and test-re-test reliabilities.

It should also be noted in passing that Taras (2006a) has compiled a similarly comprehensive catalogue of surveys and instruments used to assess acculturation. Though less frequently used for global leader competency assessment, acculturation surveys are sometimes used in corporate training and development programs. This catalogue contains information on fifty assessments and also includes Cronbach alpha and test-re-test reliability information where available.

Intercultural Adaptability Assessments

In this section we will consider several instruments that have as their primary focus effective intercultural competence. Instruments that fall into this category are frequently used in conjunction with global manager development programs. Because effective interaction with culturally different others is a critical aspect of effective global leadership in most contexts, the assessment of intercultural competence is highly appropriate. At the same time, it is important to recognize that intercultural competence represents just one aspect of a global leader's competency set.

There are numerous intercultural adaptability assessments that are commercially available, but for which there is scant, if any, research literature. Stuart (2007) provides a practical, though perhaps less-than-critical, review of a range of instruments. A more comprehensive listing of intercultural assessment tools can be obtained from the Intercultural Communication Institute (intercultural.org).

The Cross-cultural Adaptability Inventory

The Cross-cultural Adaptability Inventory (CCAI) was developed by Christine Kelley and Judith Meyers (1995a) as a self-assessment tool for cross-cultural adaptability training and development. Over time it has come to be used for measuring competency acquisition, as in pre- and post-test measures in conjunction with training programs. The CCAI measures four dimensions: flexibility/openness, emotional resilience, perceptual acuity, and personal autonomy. After reviewing the literature and interviewing expert interculturalists, the developers originally settled on five dimensions, but dropped "positive regard" for others when their pilot studies failed to differentiate this dimension from the other four (Kelley and Meyers, 1995b).

Flexibility/Openness. The first of the four dimensions addresses the tendency to be open to others and broad-minded toward people and ideas. It also reflects a willingness to be flexible and nonjudgmental in one's perspective (a = 0.54).

Emotional Resilience. The ability to navigate the unfamiliarity associated with intercultural situations while maintaining positive emotions is the focus of the second dimension. Negative emotional reactions, e.g. culture shocks or bumps, are frequent occurrences when working in intercultural contexts. Emotional resilience reflects an ability to cope, as well as quickly recover from, such situations (a = 0.80).

Perceptual Acuity. Openness to new people and experiences and an ability to cope with stressful situations can be easier when an individual is able to accurately read situations and detect and appropriately respond to verbal and non-verbal signals. The third dimension also refers to an ability to communicate effectively in such situations (a = 0.78).

Personal Autonomy. The final dimension focuses on the possession and maintenance of a strong personal identity in the face of adapting to a new cultural context that involves others whose values may be different than one's own (a = 0.67).

The CCAI includes fifty items and is administered using a paper and pencil format. The survey is self-scored. The average respondent requires about 10 minutes to complete the inventory. There is no mechanism for monitoring social response bias. Results are reported by tallying scores in four columns, with each column representing one of the dimensions. Interpretation of scores requires a facilitator/trainer.

The CCAI has primarily been used in studies attempting to measure the effectiveness of intercultural training programs. For example, Cornett-DeVito and McGlone (2000) used the CCAI to evaluate the effectiveness of intercultural training programs for law enforcement personnel. Similarly, Goldstein and Smith (1999) relied on the CCAI to evaluate the effectiveness of training programs for business professionals. It should be noted, however, that in a recent factor analytic study of the CCAI Davis and Finney (2006) found that inventory items did not support a four factor structure. They conducted further exploratory factor analysis but concluded that no interpretable structure could be identified. There does not appear to be any published research demonstrating the CCAI's ability to predict interculturally effective behavior in managers or in any other group.

Global Competence Aptitude Assessment

The Global Competence Aptitude Assessment (GCAA) grows out of research in conjunction with an article published by Hunter et al. (2006) and from Hunter's dissertation (2004), which used a Delphi technique to identify knowledge, skills, attitudes, and experiences essential to developing global competence. The GCAA identifies eight factors that are divided into two groups associated with competence—Internal Readiness and External Readiness.

The four factors comprising *Internal Readiness* are self-aware, willing to take risks, open-minded, and perceptive and respectful of diversity.

Self-Aware refers to possessing an accurate, i.e. honest and balanced, view of oneself as well as recognizing one's place in society or particular social contexts.

Willing to Take Risks reflects the degree to which one is willing to take unpopular or unconventional positions, willing to risk making mistakes or take on significant challenges, where success may be uncertain.

Open-minded refers to being free from prejudice as well as being receptive to new ideas. Even though one may have opinions or have developed certain attitudes, one should remain open to new ideas and strive not to prejudge others.

Perceptive and Respectful of Diversity reflects an awareness that people differ in many ways and, regardless of difference, are deserving of respect.

The four factors comprising *External Readiness* are globally aware, knowledgeable about world history, interculturally competent, and effective across cultures.

Globally Aware addresses the extent to which one is both knowledgeable about the world and also possesses an awareness of the world as a whole.

Knowledgeable about World History reflects an individual's knowledge and understanding of history about peoples and places throughout the world.

Interculturally Competent is the extent to which one is open to other cultures and flexible in interactions with people from other cultures.

Effective Across Cultures addresses one's ability to function in intercultural contexts, collaborate with people from other cultures and work effectively within and across cultures.

The GCAA includes fifty items and is administered online. The average respondent requires about 15 minutes to complete the inventory. There is no mechanism for monitoring social response bias.

The GCAA has only seen limited use in empirical studies to date, perhaps due to its recent development. In an investigation of geographical knowledge learning, higher GCAA scores were found among thirty-six study abroad students when compared to a sample of forty-six students who did not go on study abroad (Greunke 2010).

Intercultural Effectiveness Scale

The Intercultural Effectiveness Scale (IES) was developed by Allan Bird, Michael Stevens, Mark Mendenhall, Gary Oddou, and Joyce Osland (2008) as an abridged version of the Global Competencies Inventory for general purpose use in assessing intercultural competency. It is primarily used in educational and non-governmental organizational settings, but is also used in corporate contexts, often as an early assessment tool. It has been used for program assessment in university settings as well. The IES measures three dimensions: continuous learning, interpersonal engagement, and hardiness. Each of these factors has two sub-dimensions. The developers sought to develop a more accessible and less costly version of the Global Competencies Inventory; one that would not require special training by administrators or the need for facilitation or coaching.

The first dimension is **Continuous Learning**. This dimension examines how people cognitively approach cultural differences, and the degree to which individuals engage the world by continually seeking to understand themselves and also learn about the activities, behaviors, and events that occur in the cross-cultural environment. Continuous learning has two sub-dimensions. *Exploration* is the extent to which people are open to and pursue an understanding of ideas, values, norms, situations, and behaviors that are different from their own. It reflects a fundamental inquisitiveness, curiosity, and an inner desire to learn new things. *Self-awareness* is the degree to which a person is aware of their personal values, strengths, weaknesses, interpersonal style, and behavioral tendencies, as well as the impact of these things on other people.

Interpersonal Engagement is the second dimension. Developing positive intercultural relationships depends in large part on one's interest in learning about people from other cultures, their customs, values, etc. It is comprised of two sub-dimensions. *Global Mindset* focuses on the extent to which a person is interested in, and seeks to actively learn about, other cultures and people. *Relationship Interest* is the extent to which a person is likely to initiate and maintain positive relationships with people from other cultures.

The final dimension is **Hardiness**. Interacting with people from different cultural backgrounds requires significant effort, which often produces stress, anxiety, and sometimes fear. It has two sub-dimensions. *Positive Regard* measures the degree to which one withholds judgments about situations or people that are new or unfamiliar. *Emotional Resilience* reflects the level of emotional strength and an ability to cope with challenging emotional experiences.

The IES includes sixty items and is administered online or using a paper and pencil format. The average respondent requires about 10 minutes to complete the inventory. There is no mechanism for monitoring social response bias. Results are reported by tallying scores in three columns, with each column representing one of the dimensions. The feedback report provides direction on the interpretation of scores.

The IES has primarily been used in educational settings for both instructional purposes and for program assessment. Its recency—it first appeared in 2009—may explain the lack of published empirical research.

Intercultural Development Inventory

The Intercultural Development Inventory (IDI) was developed by Mitchell Hammer and Milton Bennett based on Bennett's theory (1993), the Development Model of Intercultural Sensitivity (DMIS), which identified six stages of intercultural development and associated competencies that group into two sets— ethnocentric and ethnorelative. The ethnocentric stages, in order of development, are Denial, Defense, and Minimization. The ethnorelative stages are: Acceptance, Adaptation, and Integration. The IDI measures an individual's worldview regarding cultural difference, which may be construed also as a capacity for intercultural competence. The ethnocentric stages can be interpreted as different ways of *avoiding* cultural differences, e.g. denying differences exist, defending one's culture against differences or minimizing the extent or significance of the differences. The ethnorelative stages are ways of *seeking* cultural difference, through first accepting the importance of difference, then adjusting or adapting one's perspective to take difference into account and, finally, by integrating the concept of culture and difference into one's identity. Each of the six stages can also be broken down into sub-stages.

Denial. This stage is characterized by a condition in which one's own culture is taken to be the only culture. Though other cultures may exist, they should be avoided or isolated. People in this stage are disinterested in cultural differences, but when confronted with difference may respond viscerally, seeking to eliminate differences that intrude into their sphere of activity. The two sub-stages of Denial are *Isolation* and *Separation*.

Defense. The second ethnocentric stage reflects a worldview in which one's own culture (or an adopted culture) is experienced as the only good one. Other cultures are seen as being in opposition to one's own culture, i.e. "we" versus "them." Moreover, other cultures are viewed as inferior and one's own as superior. People in this stage may feel threatened by cultural difference. An alternative position in this stage is to view one's own culture as inferior and other cultures as superior, i.e. to experience a reversal of dominant orientation in this stage. The three sub-stages or categories of Defense are *Denigration*, *Superiority*, and *Reversal*.

Minimization. The third stage in the ethnocentric set takes a perspective that one's own culture reflects a deeper element universal to all cultures. Consequently, differences are minimized or suppressed. People in this stage may ignore or mask over important differences. The Minimization sub-stages are *Physical Universalism* ("cultures increasingly share so much in common") and *Transcendent Universalism* ("at heart we are all the same").

Acceptance. The first ethnorelative stage adopts a worldview that sees one's own culture as just one of many complex worldviews. Although one may accept that there are differences and one's own perspective is not superior, this does not mean that a person at the Acceptance stage necessarily agrees with other worldviews. People at this stage are curious about and respectful of differences. The sub-stages for Acceptance are *Acceptance of Behaviors* and *Acceptance of Values*.

Adaptation. In this stage, acceptance of another culture yields both perception and behaviors appropriate for effective functioning in that culture as well as an ability to see the larger world in new ways. Adaptation entails intentional modification of behavior in order to interact with culturally different others. The two sub-stages associated with this stage are *Empathy* and *Pluralism*.

Integration. The ultimate intercultural development stage is Integration, the ability and inclination to move in and out of different cultural worldviews. People who reach Integration may confront issues of cultural marginality as they work to integrate these shifting worldviews into their self-identity. Integration is not the required level of intercultural competence in most situations. It is common, however, among "global nomads" and others with extensive experience working at cultural intersections. The sub-stages of Integration are *Contextual Evaluation* and *Constructive Marginality*.

Based on the DMIS, the IDI was structured with five scales and ten clusters, roughly matching the stages and sub-stages of the DMIS. The IDI scales are comprised of the DD (Denial/Defense) scale, the R (Reversal) scale, the M (Minimization) scale, the AA (Acceptance/Adaptation) scale, and the EM (Encapsulated Marginality) scale (Encapsulated Marginality as Integration).

The IDI includes fifty items, requiring the average person to take 10–15 minutes to complete. The inventory is available in paper and pencil format and, recently, online. There are thirteen language versions—English, Spanish, French, Portuguese, Italian, German, Chinese, Japanese, Korean, Bahasa, Indonesian/Malay, Norwegian, and Russian. Results are reported in terms of level of development for each of the six stages, with developmental level ranging from "unresolved" to "in transition" to "resolved." Ideally, respondents should receive their feedback report as part of a counseling session from an IDI-qualified facilitator.

Research on the validity and reliability of the IDI has found strong support for the internal validity and reliability of the psychometric properties of the instrument (Hammer et al. 2003; Paige et al. 2003). Studies of students (Straffon 2003) and returned Peace Corps volunteers (Kashima 2006) found the IDI predictive of level of intercultural sensitivity. Developers of the IDI also report similar findings for the IDI when used in business settings; however, because these results have not been made public through empirical studies published in peer-reviewed journals it is not possible to confirm their validity.

Multicultural Personality Questionnaire

Developed by Karen van der Zee and Jan-Pieter van Oudenhoven (2000), both at the University of Groningen, the Multicultural Personality Questionnaire (MPQ) measures five dimensions of personality relevant to adjustment and performance of expatriates. Dimensions are drawn from a review of earlier work on expatriate adjustment and from their own research. Moreover, the framing of dimensions is clearly in terms of the effective intercultural adjustment of expatriates.

Cultural Empathy. This dimension relates to one's ability to empathize with people from a culture different from one's own. It also encompasses the ability to empathize with thoughts and behaviors of people from other cultures (a = 0.83).

Open-mindedness. Effective intercultural behavior is also predicated on having an attitude that is open to differing cultural norms and to people from other cultures. Open-mindedness reflects an unprejudiced approach to others (a = 0.84).

Social Initiative. This dimension addresses the way that people approach social situations, recognizing that empirical work has confirmed the importance of taking the initiative and being active in establishing and maintaining relationships with people, both at home and abroad (a = 0.89).

Emotional Stability. The tendency to handle stressful situations calmly rather than with an affective response is important because novel or ambiguous situations can evoke strong emotion (a = 0.84).

Flexibility. The fifth dimension focuses on a person's ability to adjust plans and behaviors easily. Van der Zee and van Oudenhoven (2000) stress the importance of this dimension in a new cultural environment, where one's established ways of doing things are likely to be inappropriate (a = 0.64).

The MPQ contains seventy-eight items and can be administered either online or via paper and pencil format. The average respondent requires 10–15 minutes to complete the instrument. There are English, Dutch, French, German, and Italian versions available. There does not appear to be any monitoring of social desirability response patterns. Results are reported graphically for each dimension using a bar line and a ten-point, scale with ten being highest. One or two sentences of explanation specific to each dimension score is also provided.

The majority of the research on the MPQ has been carried out with students; however, it has been used in conjunction with expatriate assessment as well (Van Oudenhoven and Van der Zee 2003). Two longitudinal studies (Mol et al. 2001; Van Oudenhoven and Van der Zee 2002) conducted with international student samples found that the MPQ was predictive of psychological well-being and social support. A subsequent study of expatriates in Taiwan (Van Oudenhoven et al. 2003) confirmed the MPQ's predictive capability with regard to three facets of personal adjustment (satisfaction with life, physical health, and psychological well-being), job satisfaction, and social support.

Intercultural Readiness Check

The Intercultural Readiness Check (IRC) assessment, developed by Karen Van der Zee and Ursula Brinkmann, is apparently an extension of the Multicultural Personality Questionnaire. The latter instrument was developed with a specific focus on expatriates whereas the IRC seems aimed at application to a broader range of personnel, not just those slated for international assignment.

The original IRC measured six dimensions that the developers argued were relevant to multicultural success (Van der Zee and Brinkmann, 2004): intercultural sensitivity (a = 0.80), intercultural communication (a = 0.84), intercultural relationship building (a = 0.80), conflict management (a = 0.59), leadership (a = 0.70), and tolerance of ambiguity (a = 0.78). Subsequent refinement of the instrument has settled on four dimensions. Reliability alphas on these four dimensions do not appear to have been publicized.

Intercultural Sensitivity. The focus of this dimension is on the awareness and perception of culturally different communication styles, e.g. the ability to notice and accurately read verbal and non-verbal communication. It also measures interest in differing cultural norms and values. This dimension has two facets: *cultural awareness* and *attention to signals*.

Intercultural Communication. This dimension measures one's ability to empathize with people who are culturally different. It is concerned not only with feelings, but also with thoughts and behavior. This dimension has two facets: *active listening* and *adjusting communicative style*.

Building Commitment. Motivating others, nurturing interaction and cooperation, and leading out while maintaining support and commitment from others is the focus of this dimension. The two facets for this dimension are: *building relationships* and *reconciling stakeholder needs*.

Managing Uncertainty. Intercultural situations are characterized by uncertainty around meanings, norms and behaviors. This dimension assesses ability to cope with intercultural situations. The two facets for this dimension are: openness to *cultural complexity* and *exploring new approaches*.

The IRC is a sixty-item instrument and can be administered either online or via paper and pencil format. The average respondent requires 10–15 minutes to complete the instrument. There are English, Dutch, French, German, and Japanese versions. There does not appear to be any monitoring of social desirability response patterns. Results are reported using a graphical presentation and index, with additional commentary provided for each of the four dimensions.

The developers of the IRC provide generalized anecdotal evidence for its predictive capability relative to superior performance in jobs entailing a large intercultural component; however, statistical data supporting these claims has not been made public through empirical studies published in peer-reviewed journals. Nevertheless, the convergent validation of the IRC vis-à-vis the MPQ (Van der Zee and Brinkmann, 2004) suggests a basis for assuming some measure of predictive capability and association with positive outcomes in intercultural situations. Moreover, the authors claim a database of 25,000 respondents drawn from 130 countries and across fourteen industries.

Cultural Intelligence (CQ)

Developed by Christopher Earley and Soon Ang (2003), and predicated on the broader conceptual notion of multiple intelligences, the CQ assessment measures four dimensions relevant to cultural intelligence, which they define as being able to function effectively in cross-cultural situations. Earley and Ang (2003) assert that cultural intelligence constitutes a type of intelligence akin to, but independent from, other previously identified intelligences.

The four dimensions encompass cognitive, metacognitive, motivational, and behavioral elements of effective cross-cultural elements, which is consistent with other conceptualizations of cultural intelligence (Thomas 2006; Livermore 2010).

CQ Drive (Motivational CQ). As the name implies, this dimension relates to one's level of interest or drive in adjusting to cultural differences one encounters. It has three sub-dimensions. *Intrinsic motivation* refers to the degree to which someone derives enjoyment from culturally diverse situations and experiences. *Extrinsic motivation* addresses the degree to which external rewards—e.g. compensation, career advancement—are motivating forces encouraging intercultural action. Finally, *self-efficacy* reflects one's confidence in being able to successfully navigate culturally diverse interactions.

CQ Knowledge (Cognitive CQ). A second element of effective intercultural action is a knowledge of relevant cultural issues, including a general understanding of culture and how it influences perceptions, cognitions, and behaviors as well as specific information regarding the cultures one will be working in. This dimension has two sub-dimensions. *Cultural systems* refers to one's understanding of the ways that societies are arranged, e.g. family structures, social institutions. *Cultural norms and values* addresses one's understanding of cultural norms and underlying values that shape thinking and behavior.

CQ Strategy (Metacognitive CQ). The third dimension of the CQ assessment focuses on how individuals process intercultural situations and select responses. This is labeled the metacognitive dimension because it reflects one's *approach* to navigating situations, rather than to the actual act of navigation. It has three sub-dimensions. *Awareness* refers to the extent to which one is sensitive to the situation. *Planning* measures how one anticipates and prepares for an interaction. Finally, *checking* examines the degree to which one monitors the encounter to determine that behavior aligns with perception and plan.

CQ Action (Behavioral CQ). The final dimension focuses on the adjustment of behavior so that it is appropriately adaptive to the situation. It has three dimensions, which align with the types of behaviors in an encounter: *nonverbal actions*, *verbal actions*, and *speech acts.* The last dimension refers to the specific words and phrases employed.

The CQ consists of twenty items and is administered online. The average respondent requires 10–15 minutes to complete the instrument. A multi-rater version is also available. There are English, Dutch, French, German, and Italian versions available. There is not any monitoring of social desirability response patterns. Results are provided in a twelve-page feedback report that includes comparisons with norms based on worldwide samples. Additionally, the report includes supporting material to aid in further development of CQ dimensions.

The developers (Ang et al. 2004) conducted a variety of statistical analyses to determine the reliability and validity of the CQ. Their reported results are consistent with accepted standards of internal consistency and factor structures. In a study of expatriate adjustment, Templer et al. (2006) found that CQ Drive (Motivational CQ) was predictive of both general and work adjustment in a sample of 157 global professionals working in Singapore. More recently, Ward and associates (Ward et al. 2009) report on a series of empirical studies that raise several questions about the conceptual foundations of the cultural intelligence as measured by the CQ. Though argued to be a distinct intelligence, Ward and associates found that the CQ exhibited a high level of convergence on the EQ, which suggests that CQ may not be a separable construct and, therefore, that construct validity is not tenable. Ward and associates (2009) also reported that CQ, with the exception of Motivational CQ, did not contribute incremental value in explaining social adaptation in a sample of 118 international students in New Zealand. Moreover, CQ added no incremental value in explaining academic adaptation or language acquisition.

Big Five Personality Inventories

In the early 1960s psychologists doing research on personality characteristics carried out a review of a number of empirical studies and found five recurring traits. In the 1980s Costa and McCrae (1985) developed a standardized taxonomy that labeled the five factors as: Extraversion, Agreeableness, Conscientiousness, Neuroticism, and Openness to Experience. There are several terms that apply to this group of personality characteristics such as the Big Five, the Five Factor Model, and Five Factor Theory. It is also important to note that these broad factors—described in greater detail below—encompass a wide range of more discrete personality traits. Consequently, most instruments that measure the five factors also measure a variety of these discrete facets. In the case of the NEO PI-R, for instance, each of the five factors has six facets associated with it.

Whether personality traits are able to predict performance has been an ongoing debate; however, a number of recent meta-analytical studies have found conclusive support for their predictive validity of moderate magnitude. For example, Saulsman and Page (2004) undertook a review of fifteen different studies and found a distinct profile of the five factors for each of ten mental disorders listed in the Diagnostic and Statistical Manual of Mental Disorders (DSM-IV). In the realm of job performance, Barrick and Mount (1991; see also Mount and Barrick 1998) completed a meta-analytic review covering 23,994 subjects from 162 samples in 117 studies and concluded that Conscientiousness consistently predicted performance across all jobs and all occupations. They also found that Extraversion was predictive of superior performance in occupations where social interactions were essential (e.g. sales and management).

Extraversion. This factor refers to a person's orientation toward engagement with the external world. Extraverts are characterized as outgoing, people-oriented, energetic, and action-oriented. They are usually those who talk most in groups and are often assertive in social settings.

Agreeableness. This factor describes the extent to which people value social harmony and cooperation, or are concerned with getting along with others. Optimism and a positive view of human nature and of people as basically trustworthy are also a part of this factor.

Conscientiousness. This factor relates to how a person regulates and controls impulses. The inclination to act spontaneously or to delay gratification is associated with this factor. This factor also encompasses an achievement orientation.

Neuroticism. This factor addresses emotional stability and focuses on whether people experience primarily negative emotions, i.e. anxiety, hostility, anger, or depression. An inclination to respond emotionally to situations is also an aspect of Neuroticism.

Openness to Experience. This factor (which is also sometimes referred to simply as Openness) describes the trait of being creative, having an active imagination, and being open to people and experiences. An appreciation of art, intellectual curiosity, and an interest in complex or sophisticated ideas are also a part of this factor.

There are a variety of instruments that measure the Big Five personality traits, but among the most widely used is the NEO PI-R, developed by Costa and McCrae (De Fruyt et al. 2004). The NEO contains 240 items and measures neuroticism, extraversion, openness, agreeableness, and conscientiousness along with six facets for each of these factors. The assessment takes approximately 45 minutes to complete and is available in a paper and pencil format (with scantron forms for processing). It is also available via software loaded onto a computer, but is not yet online. Though numerous other language versions have been developed for research purposes, it is widely available in English and Spanish for commercial purposes. Distribution and sale of the NEO PI-R is governed by the professional standards of the American Psychological Association, which means users must demonstrate an appropriate level of coursework or advanced training in both the theory and measurement of human personality.

Early studies examining the ability of personality traits to predict expatriate performance were generally negative (Harris 1973; 1975; Brislin 1981). More recently, however, a number of empirical studies have found support for the use of Big Five personality measures in predicting expatriate performance (Ones and Viswesvaran 1999). For example, Caligiuri (1995; 2000) found that emotional stability (Neuroticism) was predictive of expatriate adjustment. Deller (1998) found that ambition (a facet of Conscientiousness) and several facets of Openness were predictive of expatriate job performance. In a similar vein, Sinangil and Ones (1995) also found facets of Conscientiousness and Openness to be predictive of job performance. Dalton and Wilson (2000) studied expatriate managers in the Middle East and found that Agreeableness and Openness were predictive of home-country ratings of performance, but not predictive of host-country ratings.

Global Leadership Competency Assessments

In this section we consider several instruments that have adopted a broader focus and attempt to identify a variety of competencies, not just intercultural competence. As noted for the intercultural adaptability assessments in the preceding section, there are numerous commercial global leadership assessments available, but for which there is scant, if any, research literature. For that reason, they are not considered in this section. In a similar vein, we have not considered the broad range of widely used leadership instruments that were not developed for assessing global leadership competencies, but are nevertheless used in international contexts.

Global Mindset Inventory

The Global Mindset Inventory (GMI) was developed under the direction of Thunderbird School of Global Management's Global Mindset Institute to assess the characteristics needed for global leaders to effectively influence people from cultures different than their own. The conceptual basis for the inventory's dimensions drew upon the collective input of select academicians, as well as responses from hundreds of global executives interviewed for the project. Although the authors of the GMI technical report quite improperly assert that it is "the world's first and only psychometric assessment tool that measures and predicts performance in global leadership positions" (Javidan et al. 2010a: 4), the inventory nonetheless may rightly be recognized for its solid conceptual foundation and rigorous empirical development. A rich and detailed technical report is provided openly at the Institute's website (www.globalmindset.com), and provides exemplary documentation on the process by which the GMI was developed and evaluated for its validity.

According to Javidan et al. (2010b), global mindset is a concept that consists of three broad individual characteristics, having three discrete facets each, arranged as stated below.

Intellectual Capital. This dimension consists of a deep knowledge and understanding of the global business environment, industry and value chain, as well as the capacity to learn and understand the context at a global level (a = 0.94).

Global Business Savvy. This refers to one's grasp of worldwide industry and business operations, the behavior and habits of one's global customers, and the strategic risks associated with operations in different parts of the world (a = 0.94).

Cognitive Complexity. This describes one's capacity for connecting complex scenarios with many elements, along with the capacity to make decisions and act appropriately in the face of many options (a = 0.93).

Cosmopolitan Outlook. This relates to an active interest in the geography, cultures, histories, and socio-economic systems that can be found in many different parts of the world (a = 0.85).

Psychological Capital. This dimension consists of the mental and emotional flexibility, openness to cultural adventure, and self-assurance needed to operate successfully in a new cultural environment (a = 0.89).

Passion for Diversity. This refers to one's proclivity for experiencing new and different parts of the world, unfamiliar cultures, and novel ways of doing things (a = 0.91).

Thirst for Adventure. This describes one's capacity for deriving enjoyment, even pleasure, from multifaceted and unfamiliar environments (a = 0.82).

Self-assurance. This relates to one's level of self-confidence and capacity for taking risks, especially in new situations, as well as the tendency to be energized rather than enervated by a foreign environment or culture (a = 0.78).

Social Capital. This dimension consists of the propensity to develop and maintain authentic relationships with individuals from different cultures or regions of the world, as well as the capacity to build consensus and influence essential stakeholders from cultures and backgrounds that are different from one's own (a = 0.89).

Intercultural Empathy. This refers to one's tendency for understanding and emotionally connecting with people from different cultures of regions of the world (a = 0.89).

Interpersonal Impact. This describes one's capacity to build credibility and maintain social networks when working with people from divergent backgrounds, cultures, and life experiences (a = 0.68).

Diplomacy. This relates to one's facility for conversation, especially through asking and listening (rather than answering), with persons who are different from oneself (a = 0.80).

The current version of the GMI attempts to measure the above dimensions via seventy-six survey questions, fifty of which are referred to by the developers as "global mindset items" and twenty-six as demographic. Once the GMI survey questions have been answered and a profile report is generated, care must be taken not to over-interpret the implications of the profile results. Specifically, while the GMI feedback report uses language that purports to describe a respondent's level of skill or ability on the various GMI dimensions (e.g. knowledge of the global business environment, ability to grasp complex concepts quickly, knowledge of different world cultures, wittiness in tough situations, ability for diplomacy, etc.), the inventory nevertheless simply asks respondents to make self-evaluations (on a five-point scale) of the degree to which they believe they possess these various GMI global leadership competencies. While such self-evaluation surveys often can serve as an appropriate methodology for assessing important individual differences on global leadership competencies, users would be wise to make sure they understand the inherent difference between a respondent's own self-scoring of the possession of GMI knowledge, skills, and abilities, as opposed to the actual possession of those attributes (e.g. self-evaluations of one's diplomacy skills or one's ability to grasp cognitively complex ideas, are not the same as actually possessing those competencies). There is no mechanism for monitoring social response bias in the inventory.

A variety of statistical analyses were conducted to determine that the GMI items indeed have the desired levels of internal consistency and factor structures. The GMI technical report also provides evidence of predictive validity via statistical correlations between GMI scores and performance-related criterion measures at two large companies. The magnitude (or effect size) of the reported correlations appears to be within the ranges consistent with general expectations for such studies (Javidan et al. 2010a); however, it is not clear from the descriptions of these two predictive studies whether the criterion-related performance data were collected from respondent self-reports or from other sources of multi-rater evaluations.

The GMI is internet-based, comes in two formats (a self-assessment and a 360-degree evaluation version), and provides both individual and group reports. Participation in a GMI certification program is necessary to become qualified as an administrator to use the inventory and conduct debrief sessions with respondents. Current information notes that the GMI has been administered to more than 6,000 respondents to date, many of whom are reported to be in a managerial or global executive position. Upon completing the GMI, respondents are encouraged to attend a one-day debriefing workshop to better understand their individual profile, their group's profile, the importance for their organization, and to consider action planning strategies for improving global mindset in targeted areas.

The Global Competencies Inventory

Initially developed in 2000 by Allan Bird, Michael Stevens, Mark Mendenhall and Gary Oddou, the Global Competencies Inventory (GCI) measures seventeen dimensions of personality predispositions associated with effective intercultural behavior and dynamic global managerial skill acquisition. The dimensions are predicated on an elaboration of the expatriate adjustment model developed by Black et al. (1991) and, accordingly, are grouped under three factors—Perception Management, Relationship Management, and Self-management. The three factors and their associated dimensions are presented below. Additionally, the GCI has been mapped on the global management competency model developed by Bird and Osland (2004).

Perception Management. This factor encompasses five dimensions that address how individuals mentally approach cultural differences. How individuals perceive people who are different from them affects how they think about such people and, in turn, how they think about people who are different from themselves influences their opinions, evaluations, and ultimately their behavior toward culturally different others. This factor also assesses how mentally flexible an individual is when confronted with cultural differences that are strange or new, as well as any tendency to make rapid (rather than thoughtful) judgments about those differences. It also evaluates an individual's ability to manage perceptions when faced with situations that are not immediately easy to understand because they differ from expectations. This factor also assesses an individual's natural curiosity toward foreign countries, cultures, and international events, as well as tendencies to draw sharp boundaries between things that are different.

Nonjudgmentalness. This dimension considers an individual's inclination to suspend or withhold judgments about situations or persons that are new or unfamiliar (a = 0.72).

Inquisitiveness. This dimension assesses an individual's pursuit of understanding ideas, values, norms, situations, and behaviors that are different from one's own. It also addresses an individual's capacity to take advantage of learning opportunities (a = 0.84).

Tolerance of ambiguity. This dimension measures the extent to which someone is able to manage ambiguity as it relates to new and complex situations where there are not necessarily clear answers about what is going on or how things should be done. It also evaluates how much someone enjoys surrounding themselves with ideas or things that are new and unfamiliar, rather than feel threatened by them (a = 0.73).

Cosmopolitanism. This dimension measures the level of natural interest in and curiosity about countries and cultures that are different from one's own. It also assesses the degree to which someone is interested in current world and international events and would enjoy traveling abroad (a = 0.85).

Interest Flexibility. This dimension measures flexibility in identifying and adopting new interests, hobbies, and changes in one's daily routine when normal activities and other outlets are not available. The ability to find new interests reflects a willingness and capability to look at things in a different way. An example of interest flexibility would be playing cricket instead of baseball in a country where cricket is more popular (a = 0.83).

Relationship Management. This second factor assesses a person's orientation toward developing and maintaining relationships in general; that is, how aware someone is of others around them, their interaction styles, values, and so on. It also considers one's personal level of self-awareness and awareness of how their behaviors impact others. This factor complements the Perception Management factor because it examines how personal attitudes, values, and beliefs influence the development and management of interpersonal relationships in a cross-cultural environment. Positive relationships in an intercultural environment are essential for effective performance in the global workplace.

Relationship Interest. This dimension measures the extent to which one has a genuine interest in, and awareness of, people who are from other cultures or ethnic groups. It also reflects your desire to get to know them, their values, and why they do what they do (a = 0.76).

Interpersonal Engagement. This dimension considers the extent to which one is likely to initiate and maintain friendships with people from other countries or cultural groups. It also measures how inclined someone is to actively seek out others who are different, as well as have the desire and ability to engage them in interesting conversations (a = 0.80).

Emotional Sensitivity. This dimension measures the capacity to accurately read and comprehend the emotions of others and to understand their feelings from their perspective. It also measures how well one is able to listen genuinely and respond with empathy to the circumstances and challenges they face (a = 0.74).

Self-awareness. This dimension appraises the extent to which one is aware of personal values and interpersonal style, personal strengths and weaknesses, and how one's past experiences have helped shape who one is as a person. It also measures how well someone claims to know himself or herself, how comfortable someone is with themselves, and the extent to which there is an understanding of the impact of personal values and behavior on relationships with others (a = 0.73).

Behavioral Flexibility. This dimension measures your tendency to regulate and adjust your behavior to fit in, and to present yourself to others in ways that create positive impressions and facilitate the building of constructive relationships (a = 0.72).

Self-management. This third factor of the GCI assesses the strength of sense of self-identity and ability to effectively manage thoughts, emotions, and responses to stressful situations. To be effective in cross-cultural situations, one must be capable of understanding, changing, and adapting appropriately to a global work environment and to challenging cultural differences while at the same time having a clear and stable sense of who one is as a person, with an unambiguous understanding of one's most fundamental values. The ability to adapt and change within the context of a stable self-identity is critical to remaining mentally and emotionally healthy in a new culture.

Optimism. This dimension measures the extent to which one maintains a positive outlook toward people, events, and outcomes generally, and views challenges as learning opportunities. New intercultural environments are almost always stressful, so facing such situations with a naturally positive outlook improves one's ability to cope and adjust (a = 0.74).

Self-confidence. The self-confidence dimension assesses the level of personal belief in one's ability to achieve whatever one decides to accomplish, even if it is something that has never been tried before (a = 0.83).

Self-identity. This dimension considers a leader's ability to maintain personal values and beliefs regardless of the situation. A strong self-identity means one has strong personal values and maintains a high sense of personal integrity while at the same time being openly accepting of those who are different, without feeling personally threatened (a = 0.73).

Emotional Resilience. This dimension measures one's level of emotional strength and ability to cope favorably with irritations, setbacks, frustrations, and failures. It also assesses capacity to recover quickly from psychologically and emotionally challenging situations (a = 0.81).

Non-stress Tendency. This dimension measures one's innate capacity to respond with peacefulness and serenity to potentially stressful situations or circumstances, whether they are derived from different sources or from a wide range of stressors (a = 0.81).

Stress Management. Stress Management assesses the degree to which one reports actively utilizing stress reduction strategies and techniques when faced with stressors in daily life, as well as the degree to which one is willing to employ new stress reduction techniques in the future (a = 0.74).

The GCI contains 180 items and is administered online or via paper and pencil format. The average respondent requires 45–60 minutes to complete the instrument. A Social Desirability dimension (a = 0.83) is also measured, though not explicitly reported to respondents. Administrators can use this dimension to determine whether a respondent has answered in a way designed to elicit favorable scores. Results for each of the sixteen dimensions, three factors, and an Overall Competency Score are calculated relative to norms based on the responses of all previous respondents. Prior versions of the instrument reported results using percentile scores. The most recent version (3.0) reports scores by indicating a respondent's position in one of three competency categories (each subdivided into two classes): Low (limited or partial), Moderate (basic or good), and High (high or superior).

Longitudinal research (Furuya, 2006) conducted with samples of Japanese international managers linked Overall Global Competency Scores with higher levels of "hard" global competencies acquisition. Specifically, higher GCI scores were related to higher levels of three types of skill: 1) *global business acumen*, consistent with the formulation put forward by Black et al. (1999a) of savvy use of extensive knowledge about business in a worldwide context; 2) *employee management skills*, which correspond closely to Bird and Osland's (2004) conceptualization of interpersonal skills, i.e. mindful (intercultural) communication, creating and building trust, and teaming; and 3) *global administrative skills*, which corresponds to Bird and Osland's (2004) description of system skills of spanning boundaries, managing change through building community, and leading. Higher scores were also associated with higher levels of skill transfer upon assignment to a new position, increased motivation and work attachment, and to higher levels of general work performance.

The Global Executive Leadership Inventory

Manfred Kets de Vries and his associates developed the Global Executive Leadership Inventory (GELI). The instrument grew out of extensive work with executives involved in training programs at INSEAD (Kets de Vries, Vrignaud and Florent-Treacy 2004). They concluded that most leadership inventories are carried out by means of self-assessment that suffer from an inherent subjectivity bias. They also noted that the gap between a leader's personal assessment of capabilities and the assessments of others was often significant. They settled on a 360-degree feedback approach as a means of identifying levels of competency and also of identifying awareness gaps in those competencies. Drawing on prior leadership research and on interviews with global executives, they identified two broad roles that global leaders carry out, one being primarily charismatic—inspiring, directing, motivating—and one being primarily architectural—designing systems and processes to help make the organization and the people within it effective. These two broad roles were broken down into twelve dimensions, which are presented below.

Visioning. This dimension addresses a leader's ability to develop and articulate a vision and accompanying strategy that encompass the firm's global needs and is accessible and can be embraced by all stakeholders, e.g. shareholders, employees, suppliers, and customers (a = 0.77).

Empowering. Finding ways to empower employees throughout the firm by means of information sharing and delegation of authority comprises the second dimension (a = 0.80).

Energizing. The third leadership dimension involves the ability to energize and motivate employees to bring the firm's mission to reality (a = 0.82).

Designing and Aligning. This dimension focuses on the ability to design organizational structures and control systems appropriate for the effective functioning of the firm at a global level consistent with the firm's mission, vision and strategy. It also encompasses the ability to align employee behavior consistent with organizational culture and values (a = 0.84).

Rewarding and Feedback. Effective global leaders must also be able to establish and implement performance appraisal and reward systems that drive the right employee behaviors on a global level (a = 0.87).

Team Building. This dimension addresses the ability to design, motivate, and focus teams to work effectively across time, space and diversity. It also entails an ability to foster an organizational climate that encourages collaborative effort and the constructive use of conflict (a = 0.85).

Outside Orientation. The seventh dimension emphasizes the ability to direct employee awareness and attention to external constituencies such as customers, suppliers, and other stakeholders, including local communities (a = 0.82).

Global Mindset. Fostering an awareness of and knowledge of the global context in which the firm operates among employees at all levels is yet another capability that global leaders must possess. This dimension also encompasses a sensitivity and ability to work across cultures (a = 0.87).

Tenacity. Effective global leaders must also have courage and persistence in pursuing those ends that serve the firm's purposes and are consistent with firm and personal principles. Leading by example, they should also encourage others to do similarly (a = 0.76).

Emotional Intelligence. The creation and maintenance of trust and the fostering of an emotionally intelligent organization is another capability found in effective global leaders, who know themselves and are able to work with others in a respectful and empathetic manner (a = 0.91).

Life Balance. Global leadership extends beyond the boundaries and mission of the organization and into non-work life. It involves the ability to maintain balance in work and personal life in order to maintain the long-term welfare of the individual. Effective leaders are able to not only model this behavior, but to articulate it in a way that impacts those they work with and are responsible for (a = 0.79).

Resilience to Stress. The final dimension addresses a leader's ability to manage the multiple types of stress—work, life, health, and career—and manage pressures such that balance can be maintained (a = 0.84).

The GELI is designed as a 360-degree feedback assessment. In order to generate effective reports, it is essential that at least two observers—a superior, co-worker, direct report, or acquaintance—complete the observer's version of the instrument. Both the Leader and Observer versions of the GELI contain 100 items and can be administered either online or via paper and pencil format. The average respondent requires 15–20 minutes to complete the instrument. Observers also have the option of providing written comments that elaborate on their survey responses. There are English, Dutch, French, German, and Italian versions available. There does not appear to be any monitoring of social desirability response patterns. The results are presented via a feedback report showing the respondent's scores based on norms drawn from the more than 2,000 executives who initially completed the inventory during its development phase. The respondent's scores are also presented vis-à-vis observers' scores for each of the dimensions. Where sufficient numbers are available, observer scores are presented in aggregate, and by observer group, i.e. superiors, direct reports, colleagues, and others. In this regard, the GELI presents a type of gap analysis similar to that of the GLA.

Research on the internal validity of the GELI found support for the psychometric properties of the instrument (Kets de Vries et al. 2004). Developers of the GELI report that it is highly predictive of executive performance in organizations (Kets de Vries 2005); however, because these results have not been made public through empirical studies published in peer-reviewed journals it is not possible to confirm their validity.

Global Leadership Online

Global Leadership Online (GLO) was developed by Ernest Gundling and associates at Aperian Global based upon the research of he and his colleagues (Gundling et al. 2011). It is used primarily in business settings. GLO measures five dimensions, the initial letters of which form the acronym SCOPE. The dimensions and facets were developed based on the authors' interviews of seventy international assignees. Of the interviewees, fifty-six had been on multiple assignments. The interviewees were drawn from twenty-six countries and had worked in thirty-two different destination countries.

The first dimension is **Seeing Differences**, the ability to notice important cues. This dimension has two facets. *Cultural Self-Awareness* is the extent to which leaders are aware of how their own cultural experiences influence their perceptions. *Inviting the Unexpected,* the second facet, measures a person's openness to new situations, new ideas, and new people and the differences they introduce.

Closing Gaps is the second dimension. Once global leaders identify differences, the next act of leadership involves finding ways to close the gaps between the differences. It is comprised of two facets. *Results through Relationships* focuses on the extent to which a person is able to work through interpersonal relationships and personal networks to achieve results. *Frame Shifting* is the extent to which a person is able to change their cognitive and behavioral styles in order to accommodate different contexts.

The third dimension is **Opening the System**. Leadership across a global organization requires an ability to exercise influence beyond one's personal network; the influence must be extended to the system level and it must bring more people into the process. It has two facets. *Expand Ownership* reflects the extent to which a leader is able to engage others and have them share responsibility for achieving objectives. *Develop Future Leaders* reflects the ability to also foster the development of others who will take on leadership responsibility in the future.

The fourth dimension is **Preserving Balance**, which reflects the requirement of global leaders to address the competing demands of adapting to the context and adding value through what one brings to the context. *Adapt and Add Value* is the extent to which a person can adapt to the demands of the situation *and* also add value by contributing a new perspective or new skills and knowledge. *Core Values* *and Flexibility* reflects an ability to retain one's core values and also understand how to apply those values flexibly to new settings as well as a willingness to incorporate differing facets or nuances of one's core values that may surface through global work.

The final dimension is **Establishing Solutions**. This dimension is focused on the implementation of changes. *Influence Across Boundaries* addresses the ability to work across boundaries, be they business units, functional, or organizational. *Third Way Solutions* is the ability to draw upon all of the other dimensions and facets to craft creative and appropriate solutions.

The GLO includes sixty items, including qualitative responses, and is administered online. The average respondent requires about 15 minutes to complete the inventory. The assessment has two components—a self-assessment and a multi-rater assessment. There is no mechanism for monitoring social response bias. Results are presented in the form of numerical scores that indicate strengths as well as areas for improvements. Qualitative comments from raters are also incorporated into the report.

Information on the reliability and validity of the GLO is not publicly available at this time. The recency of its development also serves as an explanation for the lack of empirical studies published in peer-reviewed journals.

Conclusion

It is important to remember, as was pointed out in Chapter 1, that the field of global leadership is still in its infancy, with no established definition and no accompanying set of clearly defined behaviors. Given the nature of the phenomenon it may be unrealistic to expect that this will be resolved any time soon. Nevertheless, work has already begun on several fronts to identify competencies associated with effective global leadership. With two exceptions—the NEO PI-R and the CCAI— none of the assessments considered in this chapter existed fifteen years ago. Indeed several have appeared in just the past several years. We can anticipate that, as global leadership achieves greater clarity as a concept, more assessments will be developed.

A comparison to the twelve intercultural and global leadership assessments reviewed in this chapter is instructive. Table 6.1 presents basic information about the assessments, their validity, reliability and various aspects of their usage.

For the most part, the assessments considered in this chapter demonstrated sound psychometric properties with regard to internal validity and reliability. Additionally, many also demonstrated convergent and discriminant validity. However, the critical issue is whether or not the characteristics they measure are predictive of superior global leadership performance. On that point, there is a paucity of evidence, though perhaps reason to be optimistic. When not restricted to global leadership,

Table 6.1 Comparison of Intercultural and Global Leadership Assessment Tools

	Cross-Cultural Adaptability Inventory	Global Competencies Aptitude Assessment	Intercultural Effectiveness Scale	Intercultural Development Inventory	Multicultural Personality Questionnaire	Intercultural Readiness Che
Acronym	1. CCAI	2. GCAA	3. IES	4. IDI	5. MPQ	6. IRC
Reliability	Low	Moderate	High	High	High	High
Validity:						
content	Moderate	Moderate	High	High	High	High
predictive	Low	?	Moderate	Not recommended	Moderate	N/A
convergent	?	?	High	High	High	Moderate
face	High	High	High	High	High	Moderate
differential bias	?	?	No	No	?	?
Social Desirability Check	No	No	No	No	No	No
Cost	$6-12	$20	$12	$10	N/A	$200
Usability	Simple	Moderately complex	Simple	Moderately complex	Moderately complex	
Qualification Standards	Required	Not required	Not required	Required	Not required	Not required
Target Audience	Originally for expatriate coaching, and predeparture training, etc.	Education and business settings	Any intercultural setting or cross-cultural encounters	Education, business, government, NGOs and non-profits	Education and business settings	Business settin
Time Requirements	~15 min.	~20 min.	~15 min.	~30 min.	~20 min.	~15 min.
Delivery Method	Online or Paper & Pencil	Online	Online or Paper & Pencil	Online	Online	Online or Pape Pencil
Languages Options	English only	English only	English, Chinese, French, German, Japanese, Spanish	Currently available in 12 languages	English, Dutch, French, German, Italian	English, Dutch French, Germa Japanese
More Information?	Vangent	Global Leadership Excellence, LLC	Kozai Group, Inc.	IDI, LLC	Van der Maesen Personnel Management	IBI (Intercultu Business Improvement)
Dimensions Measured (sub-dimensions are italicized)	Flexibility/ Openness Emotional Resilience Perceptual Acuity Personal Autonomy	Internal Readiness *Self-Aware* *Willing to take risks* *Perceptive and respectful of diversity* *Open minded* External Readiness *Globally Aware* *Knowledgeable about World History* *Interculturally Competent* *Effective Across Cultures*	Continuous Learning *Exploration* *Self-Awareness* Interpersonal Engagement *Global Mindset* *Relationship Interest* Hardiness *Positive Regard* *Resilience*	Denial Defense Minimization Acceptance Adaptation Integration	Cultural Empathy Open-Mindedness Social Initiative Emotional Stability Flexibility	Intercultural Sensitivity *Cultural Awar* *Attention to Si* Intercultural Communica *Active Listenir* *Adjusting Communica* *Style* Building Commitmen *Building Relationship* Reconciling Stakeholder Needs Managing Uncertainty *Openness to Cultural Complexity* *Exploring New Approaches*

Cultural Intelliigence	Big Five Personality Inventories	Global Mindset Inventory	Global Competencies Inventory	Global Executive Leadership Inventory	Global Leaderhsip Online
7. CQ	8. NEO PI-R	9. GMI	10. GCI	11. GELI	12. GLO
Moderate	High	High	High	High	N/A/
High	High	High	High	High	N/A
Moderate	Moderate	Moderate	Moderate	N/A	N/A
High	High	?	High	N/A	N/A
High	Moderate	Moderate	High	High	High
N/A	No	?	No	N/A	N/A
No	No	No	Yes	No	No
Variable cost	$6-10	~$150	$130	$200	N/A
Moderately Complex	Complex	Moderately complex	Moderately complex	Moderately complex	Simple
Required	Required	Required	Required	Not required	Proprietary
General population	General population	Education, business, government, NGOs and non-profits	Intercultural settings or cross-cultural encounters	Global leaders and expatriates	Global leaders and expatriates
~20 min.	~45 min.	~15 min.	~45 min.	~20 min.	~15 min.
Online	Paper & pencil or stand-alone PC software	Online	Online	Online or Paper & Pencil	Online
English	Available in more than 20 languages	English, Mandarin Chinese, Japanese, Russian	English, Chinese, French, German, Japanese, Spanish	English, Dutch, French, German, Italian	English
Cultural Intelligence Center, LLC	PAR, Inc.	Thunderbird School of Global Management	Kozai Group, Inc.	Pfeiffer	Aperian Global
CQ Drive (Motivational CQl) *Intrinsic Motivation* *Extrinsic Motivation* *Self-efficacy* CQ Knowledge (Cognitive) *Cultural Systems* *Cultural Norms & Values* CQ Strategy (Metacognitive CQ) *Awareness* *Planning* *Checking* CQ Action (Behavioral CQ) *Verbal Actions* *Nonverbal Actions* *Speech Acts*	Extraversion Agreeableness Conscientiousness Neuroticism Openness to Experience	Intellectual Capital *Global Business Savvy* *Cognitive Complexity* *Cosmopolitan Outlook* Psychological Capital *Passion for Diversity* *Quest for Adventure* *Self-Assurance* Social Capital *Intercultural Empathy* *Interpersonal Impact Diplomacy*	Perception Management *Nonjudgmentalness* *Inquisitiveness* *Tolerance of Ambiguity* *Cosmopolitanism* *Interest Flexibility* Relationship Management *Relationship Interest* *Interpersonal Engagement* *Emotional Sensitivity* *Self-Awareness* *Behavioral Flexibility* Self Management *Optimism* *Self-Confidence* *Self-Identity* *Emotional Resilience* *Non-Stress Tendency* *Stress Management*	Visioning Empowering Energizing Designing and Controlling Rewarding and Giving Feedback Team Building Outside Orientation Global Mindset Tenacity Emotional Intelligence Life Balance Resilience to Stress	Seeing Differences *Cultural Self-Awareness* *Inviting the Unexpected* Closing Gaps *Results through Relationships* *Frame Shifting* Opening the System *Expand Ownership* *Develop Future Leaders* *Preserving Balance* *Adapt & Add Value* *Core Values & Flexibility* Establishing Solutions *Influence Across Boundaries* *Third Way Solutions*

but considered in the context of performance more broadly defined, there is more evidence to support predictive validity claims. We should anticipate that more empirical research exploring their predictive potential is either currently underway or will be soon undertaken.

Where do we go from here? The chapter began by discussing *competency* as a concept and noted that it involved a link between a pre-existing characteristic or capability and superior performance. The assessments considered here measure a variety of characteristics that could be classified as competencies, but what is sorely missing is a clearly defined set of behaviors that constitute *superior* global leadership. Both the GLA and GELI address this issue by focusing on managerial actions; however, even these two instruments find it difficult to identify the specific set of actions appropriate to a specific position.

Future work might proceed along two lines, both of which involve "flying a little close to the ground." First, it would be useful to learn more about what effective global leaders actually do. As noted in Chapter 2, most empirical research has asked managers what they *think* are the important or critical behaviors. This approach runs into the challenge noted above of developing an *idealized* rather than real or practical understanding of what global leaders do. Research that observes and measures actual performance may be more productive in establishing the behavioral standards necessary to work backward in the causal link to competencies. Second, it might be useful to search for hard competencies, identifiable skills or behaviors that contribute to high performance. Most of the assessments in this chapter focus on soft competencies, i.e. characteristics of personality or worldview or attitude. This may seem appropriate given that global leadership appears to fit into a wide variety of contexts and positions and soft competencies are broadly applicable. For example, do global leaders who engage in more reflexive listening behaviors perform at a higher level than those that do not? Reflexive listening is a hard competency, a skill that can, to varying degrees, be taught. It is also one that we might expect to contribute to more effective intercultural communication, which in turn would contribute to other effective leader behaviors.

7 Leading Global Teams

MARTHA L. MAZNEVSKI AND CELIA CHUI

Most work in organizations today is done by teams. A team is simply a group of people working together to accomplish a task, and there are many variations on this theme. In a new product development team at Boeing or Airbus, team members represent different functions such as basic engineering and production and work together over years in a highly interdependent way to develop and test a new product. In a sales team for Panasonic or Novartis, each salesperson has his or her own territory; team members interact with each other to share ideas and best practices and to work on a limited number of joint accounts. In a global auditing team at Ernst & Young or Deloitte, one auditor from each subsidiary's country develops the accounts for that subsidiary and submits the accounts to a managing partner. The members of this large global audit team interact very little with each other. The managing partner then uses a small and representative "inner team" to bring together all the subsidiary accounts and create a single picture of the global client's operations.

Although teams have always been part of the organizational landscape, they have become increasingly important. Previously, the most important tool for managing people was the hierarchy (Leavitt 2003; Elliot 1989; Weber 1946; 1947): a set of nested levels of authority and responsibility. In a traditional hierarchy, organizations are divided into separate units: each unit has a boss who divides the unit's work into several pieces with a subordinate in charge of each piece; each of those subordinates does the same with his or her part of the organization's work, and so on. The hierarchy is a very simple way of managing people and work. Everyone's task is clearly defined, and everyone knows with whom to communicate about what.

However, hierarchies are notoriously inflexible and in today's era of globalization they fall increasingly short. If the work requirements change—for example, if a supplier changes the specifications on a key component—hierarchies may not clarify who should adapt to the change. If the environment changes—for example, if customer demands shift from one product group to another or a new competitor arrives on the scene—hierarchies may not detect the shift soon enough and resources are unlikely to be allocated appropriately. And if the task requires high levels of interdependence—for example, if basic development of a new drug should take into account how to manufacture the drug—hierarchies fail miserably as they discourage communication across separate business units or functions. The traditional hierarchy, glorified in the first half of the twentieth century, does not manage people to achieve results well in the dynamic and competitive environment of the twenty-first century.

Hierarchies must be supplemented with more informal modes of organization (for further discussions, see also Pfeffer 1995), especially teams. Teams are more dynamic and adaptable to change. They can be temporary, formed quickly to achieve a specific task then disbanded afterwards. Their membership can be fluid, including important skills as they are needed. They can co-exist with other forms of organization; members of teams can and usually do hold other organizational roles simultaneously.

Any leader today must be both a good team member and good at leading teams. Leaders at all levels of the organization are key members of coordination teams, project teams, joint-task teams, and so on. They also find themselves leading such teams at their own level and below. Helping teams perform well, whether as a member or a designated leader, requires a sophisticated understanding of today's teams. And just as leadership itself is more complex in today's global environment than it was previously, teams themselves are also more complex.

In this chapter, we begin by reviewing what we know about team effectiveness: how teams combine the efforts of individual members to create strong results. Then we identify the specific characteristics that differentiate global teams from the more mundane local variety. Next we discuss some specific issues related to global teams in the larger context. Finally, we identify the implications for leaders: what does it take to be a good leader of global teams?

Effective Teams

Although every team is a unique combination of people, tasks, processes, and environment, there are some characteristics that effective teams share no matter what their configuration. Earlier team research, mostly using laboratory studies, identified what we call here the basic conditions of team performance. More recent research, which has incorporated extensive field studies of real teams, has added insights about high performing teams in more complex environments. Although global teams are highly complex, they are teams first. To take advantage of the opportunities offered by their global configuration, global teams must first get the basics right. To optimize performance, they can develop further characteristics and processes that manage complexity (e.g. Maznevski and Jonsen 2006). The relationship between Basic Conditions and High Performance Characteristics is shown in Figure 7.1.

Basic Conditions of Team Performance

For teams to meet their basic objectives, certain conditions must be met (e.g. Govindarajan and Gupta 2001; Canney Davison 1994; Bettenhausen 1991): the task must be well-defined, the team members must have the right combination of skills; members must develop appropriate roles; and, they must engage in effective processes. Often these processes are referred to by the handy rhyme: "forming,

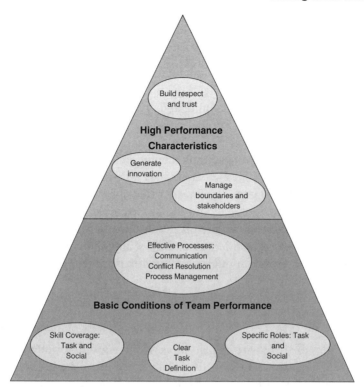

Figure 7.1 Team Performance

storming, norming, performing" (Tuckman 1965); however, not all effective teams experience the so-called stages the same way and it is more important to understand the underlying processes.[1]

Defined Task and Objectives

It goes *almost* without saying that team members must know clearly what their task and objectives are, in order to achieve them. Unfortunately, though, many teams do not understand their objectives well or do not agree on them. Sometimes this is due to lack of clear communication from leaders. The leader presents a briefing or mandate that is clear to him- or herself, but is difficult or ambiguous to interpret from the point of view of the team. Often, team members have different interpretations of the task and objectives. For example, a marketing professional may think that a successful product launch is defined by high market share, while a finance professional may think it is defined by profitability; these two objectives are potentially conflicting, but many teams neglect to clarify common goals and definitions before working together.

---

1   The "forming" stage encompasses task definition and team composition; the most intense "storming" usually occurs during role assignment; "norming" is when team processes are running smoothly; and when "performing" a team puts together roles and processes to achieve performance.

Team Composition

It should also be obvious that teams need the right combination of skills among members and this includes the right technical skills, as well as functional and geographical knowledge. It is equally important to have a mix of skills related to managing tasks, such as planning and driving towards milestones, and social skills, such as facilitating participation and resolving conflicts. Team composition is related to some aspects of team effectiveness, such as influencing the level of team creativity and innovation implementation (Somech and Drach-Zahavy 2011) and team performance (Woolley et al. 2007). But teams frequently have significant skill overlaps and skill gaps. Teams are often composed based on convenience rather than careful assignment, and sometimes the necessary skill combination is simply not available. Team members must assess the adequacy of their capabilities, and gaps should be closed by adding members or developing the skills or knowledge necessary through training or experience.

Roles

Roles are sets of specific responsibilities within a group for interacting with others to complete the task. To be effective, teams need members to take responsibility and be accountable for different aspects of achieving results. Some roles help guide the team's processes, such as discussion facilitator, workplace organizer (e.g. for shared workspace on the network) or meeting chairperson. Others are related directly to the task itself, such as idea generator, subject expert, and decision maker. There are several classifications of roles, but research suggests that the most important thing for teams to remember is to have and reinforce both task-related roles *and* process-related or social roles (the latter are more often neglected than the former). There is also debate as to whether roles should be explicit and formally assigned, or implicit and informally emergent. In fact, teams can perform well in either case. In a team whose members are experienced in working on teams, who communicate effectively and easily with each other, and whose skill balance is appropriate for the team, roles often emerge and team members flow easily into an effective dynamic. In this case, assigning roles formally is not necessary (although members may prefer it anyway). In a less experienced team, or one in which communication is more difficult and/or agreement on the team objectives is not clear, it is usually better to assign roles explicitly and respect their boundaries.

Processes

A team moves from initial objectives to achievement of results by discussing, gathering information, deciding, and implementing. The three most important processes in a team to facilitate achieving results are communication, conflict management, and managing progress. All three have been studied extensively in laboratory and field settings.

Effective communication is the transmission of meaning as it was intended (Maznevski 1994). Team performance is higher to the extent that each member understands the others' perspectives and the information brought to the team, and to the extent that all members are kept informed of progress in the team in a continuous way. Team members can only act in a cooperative way if they know what they are cooperating *about* and what they are contributing *to*. To accomplish this, communication must be an active process, with extensive questioning, checking, and paraphrasing from all parties involved. Many teams find that having a member responsible for facilitating communication is extremely helpful in ensuring effective communication.

Conflict is the expression of differences in opinion or priority due to opposing needs or demands (Tjosvold 1986). The effect of conflict on a team is complex (e.g. De Dreu and Weingart 2003; Jehn 1994; 1995). Other things being equal, task-related conflict—disagreement and discussion about facts and priorities directly related to the task—tends to enhance team performance (e.g. Kostopoulos and Bozionelos 2011; De Dreu 2006; Jehn and Mannix 2001; cf. De Dreu and Weingart 2003). Social or person-related conflict—disagreement and discussion about people in the team—tends to decrease team performance (e.g. Hulsheger et al. 2009; Jehn 1995). It seems that teams need "the right amount" of conflict. Not enough conflict decreases performance because perspectives are not questioned or improved upon. Many teams assign a formal role of "devil's advocate" to prevent such groupthink. Too much conflict decreases performance because it prevents convergence on a decision and implementation, and teams that experience too much conflict can enhance their performance by assigning someone to facilitate and even mediate such conflict. However, no research has been able to determine exactly how much is "the right amount" of conflict.

Research on managing progress has been conducted both by team researchers as "task strategy" or "task management," and within the field of operations as "project management." Teams are more likely to achieve results if they plan a clear process with activities, milestones, and deliverables, and if they track progress according to this plan, adapting it when necessary. There are many guides, software programs, and formal processes available for helping teams manage progress, depending on the task and team setting.

These four conditions—task definition, composition, roles, and processes—are necessary for performance in any team, whether it is in Brazil or in China, an assembly-line team or a top management team, a short-term response team or a multi-year development team. Whenever a team is underperforming, it is useful to check these basic conditions first: they are too often taken for granted. For teams with simple, routine, or stable tasks, these four conditions are usually sufficient to predict performance. However, teams that face more challenging tasks or environments must address a further set of issues.

Beyond the Basics: Achieving High Performance

To perform well in more complex situations, teams must develop three characteristics in addition to the basic conditions. They must build respect and trust among members, engage in innovative and creative processes, and manage outside the team boundaries well. These aspects of team performance have been less researched than the basic conditions, partly because they are much more difficult to study. Their implementation depends on the team, and they can look quite different from one team to the next. However, when we look across quantitative, qualitative, and anecdotal studies, some important patterns emerge.

Building Respect and Trust

In a team, respecting someone is appreciating his or her contribution to the team. Such respect can come from recognizing a high level of skill or knowledge in an area one is already familiar with; for example, one engineer may recognize strong engineering expertise in another, and therefore appreciate the second engineer's contributions. Less commonly, respect can derive from acknowledging a high level of skill or knowledge in an area one is *not* familiar with. For example, a marketing professional with extensive expertise about reading the market but no engineering expertise may respect a product development engineer with such knowledge. It is more difficult for people to respect those whose expertise is different because it is harder to understand the contribution of such expertise and to evaluate its level. Good communication and conflict resolution usually lead to the development of such respect (and vice versa) (e.g. Keller 2001).

Trust is a positive attitude about other team members, specifically a belief that a team member would make decisions, even in the absence of other team members, that optimize the team's interests. When team members trust each other, they allow themselves to be vulnerable; that is, they put themselves at risk of being hurt by the team because of their belief that team members would always try to act to help the team and its members (Mayer et al.1995). Respect is a prerequisite for building trust, but trust goes further. Trust is developed through a series of positive experiences, building from predictability and reliability (I respect your knowledge, and I can rely on you to do your part and to do what you committed to do) to deep-level personal trust (I can rely on you to make big decisions on my behalf). Sharing similar work values can also enhance trustworthiness among team members (Chou et al. 2008). It is important to remember that trust cannot be built without taking risks; team members can only demonstrate to each other that they will act in the team's interests if other team members let them take unsupervised actions.

Respect and trust facilitate team effectiveness in many ways (Chou et al. 2008). They can enhance efficiency in a team (e.g. Govindarajan and Gupta 2001), increase commitment to the team and its decisions, and set the foundation for innovative processes that allow the team to build synergy beyond the individual contributions. When team members respect and trust each other, they do not second-guess each others' contributions, and they have a more positive perception of team performance (Costa et al. 2001). They are able to act independently of each other to fulfill task requirements, including implementation. Respect and trust are particularly important when the task is impossible for team members to achieve individually, even given enough time. For example, in some manufacturing teams, each person can feasibly do every part of the task, but labor is divided for the sake of efficiency. In such a team, respect and trust are less important than in a team doing a multifunctional strategy-development task, in which each member must contribute something completely different, must lobby on behalf of the team with different parts of the organization, and must implement effectively in different parts of the organization. Even in teams whose tasks can be done by all members, respect and trust are important to the extent that team performance is more important than the sum of individual performances. For example, with the manufacturing team, if the team can perform much more efficiently with joint efforts and if team performance is rewarded or valued more than individual performance, then respect and trust are important for performance in this team too.

Generating Innovation

High performing teams must go beyond communication of ideas and resolution of conflicts to generate new approaches. Innovation is developing novel solutions that create value. Although some innovations are truly big ideas and revolutionary to their field, most are the application of ideas from one situation to another that is quite different, or the novel combination of ideas to address a specific challenge. Innovation requires a combination of creativity and deep understanding of the challenge the innovation is trying to address (e.g. O'Reilly et al. 1998). Creativity is the consideration of a wide variety of alternatives and criteria for evaluating alternatives, as well as the building of novel and useful ideas that were not originally part of the consideration set.

Many group techniques combine creativity with structured problem solving to achieve high quality innovation. All involve using ideas brought to the group only as a starting point, explicitly trying to build on each others' ideas, and developing alternatives no one in the group had thought of previously. For example, Ideo, the world's most award-winning design firm, uses a process called the "Deep Dive" to create innovative solutions to design challenges: anything from developing a new toothbrush to revising the way insurance claims are processed (Kelley et al. 2001). The first step is a deep and careful examination of the challenge from all points of view, paying particular attention to features the end-users need. The second step is a structured brainstorming exercise to generate as many ideas as possible. Third, the team creates prototype solutions to the challenge and tests them in a variety of contexts. From the results of the prototype, a final solution is created and implemented.

Innovative teams get the basic conditions of team performance right, and move beyond. Because innovation requires taking risks in generating new ideas and trying them out, innovative teams must have high levels of respect and trust. They also tend to use roles more fluidly than teams who are less innovative, experimenting in a trusting way with different responsibilities in the team in addition to different types of expertise. Innovative teams manage their task processes in a way that combines fluidity with discipline: they are disciplined in their understanding of the task objectives and the importance of final timelines, and they are fluid and flexible in their information gathering and task management during the project itself. Finally, teams that innovate well—generate novel approaches that create good value—also manage their boundaries well, as we will examine next.

Managing Boundaries and Stakeholders

For a simple, routine, and stable task, a team can sometimes take the task mandate and fulfill it without looking outside the team. However, most team tasks require extensive interaction between members and various parties outside the team. Effective teams must manage these boundaries well (Ancona and Caldwell 1992). The three most important aspects of boundary management are resourcing the team, gathering information, and implementing solutions. Often these activities are characterized by a high need for knowledge management and transfer (Hajro and Pudelko 2010). Teams need many different types of resources, including members with particular skill sets, access to information, technology for conducting research or meetings, administrative support, travel, and so on. Usually, a large part of these resources must originate from outside the team. Furthermore, because most organizational teams' task mandates are to achieve something for the organization, the team inevitably requires information from different parts of the organization. Teams also gather information from outside the organization itself, for example by benchmarking best practices from other companies or by conducting market research. Finally, teams must hand off their output to someone outside the team, whether it is simply by creating a report for a more senior manager or actually implementing the solution.

Boundaries and stakeholders must be managed carefully (e.g. O'Sullivan and O'Sullivan 2008; Freeman 2004; Driskat and Wheeler 2003; Ancona and Caldwell 1992). Effective teams map out the external relationships they need, and strategically assign members to be responsible for different relationships on behalf of the team. Teams generally face two types of challenges in working with stakeholders across boundaries. First, because teams often operate outside the hierarchy, they may lack direct authority to obtain resources and information and to implement solutions. To achieve the team mandate, therefore, teams must make benefits clear from the perspective of the source: "If you provide us with this information, we will be better able to build a solution that meets your needs"; or must provide reciprocal benefit: "If you provide these resources for us, one of our team members will help you out on your next project." Because different team members typically interact with different external stakeholders at different times and places, this aspect of boundary and stakeholder management requires high levels of respect and trust among team members.

The second challenge teams typically face is interpreting and incorporating external perspectives into the team (Maznevski and Athanassiou 2006). Such perspectives rarely come in a form that is ready-made for the team's task and operations. For example, a team may have a mandate to assess the potential in a new market segment. However, because the segment is new, it is unlikely that data already exists about this segment. The team will have to derive an analysis of the potential by integrating information and opinion from many different sources. Bringing information and resources into the team from external sources shares many requirements with innovation. Team members must trust and respect each other so they can build on each others' expertise and take risks in interpreting ambiguous information in various ways. Furthermore, team members must be open-minded enough to accept different stakeholders' perspectives. Cross-cultural awareness and multilingual skills are thus key underlying competences for effectively working across boundaries in global teams (Hajro and Pudelko 2010).

Although there is no easy formula for team performance, teams who fulfill the four basic conditions are well on their way to at least mediocre performance. Teams with more complex tasks must also pay attention to going beyond the basics with respect and trust, to create value by interacting outside the team and innovating.

Global Teams: More Barriers, More Opportunities

Global teams represent a subset of "teams" in general. While teams are groups of people working together to accomplish tasks, global teams are groups whose members represent different countries and/or whose tasks are multinational in nature. Everything described above with respect to teams applies to global teams, but global teams are more extreme. Global teams face higher barriers to effective performance, and it is much more difficult for global teams to achieve both the basic conditions and the characteristics of high performing teams. On the other hand, the characteristics and contexts of global teams provide more potential for high performance and for creating an important impact within organizations. Global teams that perform well make a big difference to their companies. Two characteristics of global teams particularly differentiate them from teams in general: their composition and their distribution. Below, each of these characteristics will be described and their implications for performance discussed. The discussions are summarized in Table 7.1.

Table 7.1 Diversity and Dispersion: Overcome Barriers to Take Advantage of Opportunities

	Barriers	*Opportunities*
Diversity	Tendency towards: • Less effective communication • Increased conflict • Lower alignment on task	Potential for: • Increased creativity and innovation • More complete and comprehensive perspectives, stakeholder coverage
Dispersion	Difficult to achieve and maintain basic team conditions, due to: • Limited communication • Invisible relationships • Logistical challenges	Potential for: • More complete and comprehensive perspectives, stakeholder coverage • Focused, objective, balanced communication

Diverse Composition

Global teams, on average, have much more diverse composition than teams in general do (Schneider and Barsoux 2003). This diverse composition has enormous implications: it provides great potential for higher performance by promoting creativity and innovation (Albrecht and Hall 1991; Payne 1990) and by bringing in new perspectives and connection to external stakeholders; at the same time, it makes smooth team interactions much more difficult. Empirical research has shown that while work team diversity influences communication behaviors that can have negative effects on internal team dynamics, it is also beneficial to team performance (see Jackson and Joshi (2011) for a review). Diverse teams therefore tend to perform either better or worse than homogeneous teams, depending on how they are managed (Staples and Zhao 2006; DiStefano and Maznevski 2000; Earley and Mosakowski 2000; Thomas 1999; Thomas et al. 1996). Interestingly, the most common reaction to diversity is to suppress it (e.g. Richard and Johnson 2001; Tsui and O'Reilly 1989), that is, to focus only on similarities. This moves a team from low performing or value destroying, to the medium performance of homogeneous teams—an improvement, but still misses the potential offered from diversity.

Global teams are diverse in terms of nationality, but also because they are generally created to address strategic tasks that are usually diverse in terms of function, and their members often represent business units with different priorities and needs. This triple-dose of diversity means that global teams cannot suppress their differences, the way more local teams often can and do. It also means that the potential for high performance is even greater than for teams with less diversity. Functional and business unit differences are evident; although they are difficult for teams to manage, they are generally clear and their effects quite rational. These differences can be dealt with using careful application of the normal group processes described above. Cultural differences, however, usually affect dynamics deep below the surface (Harrison et al. 1998) and must be dealt with differently.

Impact of Cultural Diversity

People from different cultures bring different expectations to the team. We learn these expectations through years of experiences in families, schools, communities, and other cultural institutions and, like other aspects of culture, people tend not even to be aware that they hold these expectations. Comparative research shows us that although all cultures use teams, cultures differ from each other quite widely in terms of how they tend to work in teams (see Zhou and Shi (2011) for a review). Different cultures even use different metaphors to describe teams; for example, some cultures think of teams as families, while other cultures compare business teams to sports teams.

One of the most important differences among cultures is related to how roles are defined and managed. For instance, in more hierarchical cultures, such as Japan and Brazil, it is generally assumed that a team must have a single leader and that the leader must have hierarchical decision-making authority within the team. If the team is not managed this way, it is believed that the team will devolve into chaos and inefficiency. In other cultures, such as Scandinavian cultures, it is assumed that team leadership should be more emergent, fluid, and shared, with different people taking the lead at different points in the team's task. More individualistic cultures, such as America and France, tend to define specific task-related roles clearly so as to identify individual areas of accountability. In these cultures, team members are comfortable differentiating individual performance within the team, rewarding some more than others. More collective cultures, such as Singapore, Malaysia, and Thailand, tend to define roles more fluidly with people contributing to the team as they can and with higher accountability for the group than for individuals. In these cultures, teams prefer to reward everyone on the team the same. These differences, of course, affect the ease with which team members from different cultures agree on roles within the team, one of the basic conditions for team performance.

Another set of important differences among cultures is related to acceptable norms for communication and conflict resolution. In some cultures, such as many Latin cultures, it is acceptable to express one's ideas at any time, even speaking at the same time as others and with openly expressed emotion; in other cultures, such as many East Asian cultures, it is only acceptable to speak when asked a question, and it is never acceptable to speak at the same time as others— silence is preferable. In many cultures, showing excessive emotion is considered inappropriate. For example, members of collective cultures tend to be more sensitive towards the affective influence of their team members than those in individualistic cultures (Ilies et al. 2007). The different perception of power across cultures can influence the type of conflict resolution strategies used (Kaushal and Kwantes 2006). Some cultures, such as many Nordic cultures, show respect for each other by expressing conflict only indirectly (it is important not to hurt each others' face or feelings); while others, such as the neighboring Dutch, show respect by expressing disagreement openly (it is important not to waste each others' time on trivial agreement). With such widely varying norms for communication, it is difficult for culturally diverse teams to communicate effectively, to send and receive meaning as it was intended. And with such widely varying norms for showing respect in conflict resolution, it is difficult to resolve conflicts constructively.

These differences can be exacerbated by what is called faultlines (Lau and Murnighan 1998): rifts in teams that are created by alignment of different types of differences. For example, a global team may consist of two production engineers, two marketers, and two R&D scientists, from the U.S., Japan, and Germany. If the engineers are from the U.S., the marketers from Japan, and the scientists from Germany, then the functional and cultural divisions are aligned and there are likely to be three sub-groups within the team who find it very difficult to collaborate. On the other hand, if each of the functions is represented by people from different countries, the sub-groups will be less evident and differences will be easier to bridge.

Given these challenges, it is even more important for global teams to build respect and trust than it is for other teams to do so. Research shows that multicultural teams who develop a collaborative and cohesive climate do perform well, outperforming homogeneous teams (e.g. Mullen and Copper 1994; Mudrack 1989). Such respect and trust help team members appreciate that their differences are related to different ways of expressing and working together, not different objectives. But as noted above, it is more difficult to build respect and trust among people who are different from each other than among people who are similar to each other!

Managing Cultural Diversity in Teams Effectively

Research in this area suggests that global teams must explicitly address and manage *both* their similarities *and* their differences; they must *both* create social cohesion *and* acknowledge and respect individual differences. Diverse teams that focus only on their differences create great rifts within the team and find it difficult to converge or align. Teams that focus only on their similarities, though, in an effort to maximize social cohesion, also underperform—they do not take advantage of their differences. Moreover, their suppressed differences eventually arise in the context of deep and personal conflicts, hurting the team and its performance.

The starting point is for team members to map out their similarities and differences, especially with respect to culture, function or expertise, and business unit perspective. Mapping is creating a picture of the team's diversity, using charts and, where possible, data from personality or cultural dimension assessments. If done with an open mindset and motivation, this mapping process itself helps to create respect and trust as team members explore their different perspectives. The team can then identify in which areas it is easily aligned, and areas where different members will contribute differently. Recent research suggests that teams should develop tight alignment around task-related issues, such as the definition of the task and objectives, while encouraging and respecting diverse perspectives around contributions to the task and ways of getting it done and social needs within the group.

Once the differences are mapped, then team members must *bridge* these differences using effective communication techniques. Especially important is decentering, or speaking and listening from the others' point of view. For example, an American, through mapping, may understand that her teammates from East Asia prefer to express conflict indirectly. However, she may not be able to bridge that difference by decentering: she may say "I know you find it difficult to be direct in conflict, but it's okay to do it with me, I won't be offended." If the American were truly decentering, she would find ways to ask questions and check for agreement that allow the East Asians to express conflict indirectly. Referring to a decision about direction, for example, she might ask a teammate "How do you think people in your office would react to this decision?" This question would allow a teammate to express his own disagreement indirectly as a hypothetical third person's opinion and not his own. Equally important in bridging is refraining from blame. Problems and miscommunication in diverse teams are inevitable, and it is a natural reaction to blame others for the problem, or to attribute low motivation or other negative characteristics to them. In effective multicultural teams, team members do not blame each other when such problems arise, but engage in creative dialogue to try and understand which types of differences contributed to the misunderstanding. In this way, effective teams turn problems into opportunities for learning about each other.

It is particularly important for diverse teams to experience pieces of the task quickly, to develop respect and reliability and create a foundation for trust. For example, the more quickly team members are assigned different aspects of information-gathering then come together to share initial results, the more "data" team members have about each other to build roles, processes, and eventually trust.

Diverse global teams experience great challenges overcoming the barriers raised by diversity. But remember that team members are often motivated by the differences—there is no doubt that being a member of a global, diverse team is interesting and an excellent learning experience (e.g. Tjosvold and Yu 2007; McLeod et al. 1996). Effective leaders of global teams can leverage this motivation and, addressing the principles outlined here, can help such teams achieve their potential.

Dispersed Distribution

In addition to diverse composition, global teams are typically characterized by dispersed distribution: their members are usually based in different locations, often spanning many time zones and climates, and many members travel frequently.

Communication and coordination, therefore, present major challenges for global teams. On the other hand, due to their dispersion and travel, members have access to a wide variety of resources and networks, and therefore can provide a broader variety of inputs to the team and links with its stakeholders.

Dispersed teams, who rely on information and communications technology to conduct much of their work together, are often referred to as "virtual teams." Although research in this field is relatively new it has been extensive, and we can provide relatively clear advice on how to manage the virtual aspect of global teams. Early research compared virtual teams with face-to-face teams and, in laboratory situations, generally found that face-to-face teams outperform virtual ones (e.g. Warkentin et al. 1997). This research identified barriers raised by communications technology and how to overcome them. Later research has accepted that virtual teams are inevitable—because companies create virtual teams whenever there is a need to bring together people who are geographically distributed, the tasks are often different from those assigned to face-to-face teams and comparing their performance is neither possible nor relevant. This latter stream of research has examined the dynamics of such virtual teams and identified the key factors contributing to their performance (e.g. Carte and Chidambaram 2004; for further discussions and references, see also Jonsen, Maznevski and Canney Davison 2012).

Impact of Virtual Communication

Communication over technology is much less rich than face-to-face communication, even if visual technology such as video conferencing or webcams are used. Subtle nonverbal communication, such as body language and tone of voice, is greatly constrained by technology. Virtual teams therefore find it more difficult to communicate effectively, especially complex and context-sensitive information regarding the task itself, and emotional information regarding team processes (e.g. Kezsbom 2000). And even though most managers conduct a high proportion of their teamwork virtually, most report that they do not like or prefer this mode of communication. It is a "necessary evil."

Even though most managers are uncomfortable with virtual communication, research has shown there are only two aspects of team performance that are so difficult to achieve virtually that they should be done face to face if at all possible: building relationships of trust and commitment (e.g. Johnson et al. 2009), and sharing deep-level tacit knowledge. Everyone has heard stories of relationships, including marriages, being built over the internet; however, this kind of relationship building is still the exception, not the norm. Reliability and predictability can be developed virtually through the kind of task experiences identified earlier, and in fact it is even more important for virtual teams to develop this quickly than for diverse teams to do so. But the deep trust that allows a team member to be vulnerable to others is extremely difficult to build without personal contact. Therefore, if a global team's task requires members to have this level of trust and commitment to each other—and most do—then the team must meet face to face.

Second, tacit knowledge is extremely difficult to share over technology. Tacit knowledge is the type of knowledge that is contextually embedded and cannot be articulated explicitly. Explicit knowledge can be written down in manuals, spreadsheets, patent applications, and so on, and can be transferred relatively easily from one person to another in such forms. Explicit knowledge is copyable and inexpensive; in fact, it can be found free of charge all through the internet. Tacit knowledge takes explicit knowledge and puts it in context, in use. Tacit knowledge comes from experience, and incorporates wisdom and judgment. It is not copyable, and it tends to be expensive. For example, a chemical engineer just graduated from university has high levels of explicit knowledge: he knows all the latest techniques and applications for combining elements; but he has less knowledge of the complex contexts of different applications. A chemical engineer who has been working on field applications for fifteen years may have less explicit knowledge than the young graduate (that is, she may not know all the latest techniques), but she has more tacit knowledge about how different compounds react to the multitude of variables in different manufacturing contexts. Tacit knowledge is best transferred during face-to-face interactions, which allow for questions, dialogue, and the richness of nonverbal communication. Therefore, if a global team's task requires high levels of tacit knowledge transfer and development—and most do—then the team must meet face to face.

Create a Heartbeat

The question is not, then, "should we meet face to face?", but "when should we meet face to face, and what should we do with that time?" Most teams believe they should get together at the team's launch, then whenever there is a crisis, conflict, or a major decision point: "This team is important, and so whenever we really need to see each other, when things aren't going well, we make the effort to jump on a plane and see each other." In fact, high performing teams do something quite different. They schedule regular meetings and stick to the schedule, for example meeting once every three to four months for two days each time. They create a team heartbeat with a regular rhythm (e.g. Malhotra et al. 2007). During their face-to-face meetings they do *not* present sales reports or simple updates; instead, they engage in discussions and actions to build shared tacit knowledge and strong relationships. They might visit customers or suppliers together, work on an innovation process, or share cases about best practices or reviews of failures. These activities pump the equivalent of oxygen through the team. Research has shown that teams who have a strong heartbeat can manage all other tasks virtually in between their face-to-face meetings, and that this is both less expensive and more effective than getting together "whenever we need to" (Maznevski and Chudoba 2000).

Discipline and Focus

When working over technology, the most important message is to maintain discipline and focus. Face-to-face teams can use the immediacy of personal contact to create a sense of urgency and momentum; virtual teams must create it deliberately themselves. Identifying roles, developing a project plan, monitoring progress—all the processes discussed earlier in this chapter—must be accomplished with great deliberation in virtual teams. Interestingly, teams who develop good discipline and focus find that working over technology can actually facilitate team performance, rather than hinder it. When meeting times are limited, people tend to prepare more effectively and stay focused throughout the meeting. When nonverbal cues are limited, people focus on the spoken or written word and remain much more task focused. Because of this, virtual teams often have lower levels of personal conflict than face-to-face teams. The use of structured communication tools such as conference calls, emails, and web meetings tends to decrease the dominance of extraverts and native language speakers, giving each member more of a chance to participate in a way he or she feels comfortable. This "performance bonus" can only be achieved, though, when the team has built relationships, shared tacit knowledge, and developed discipline and focus.

Which Technology?

Virtual teams often search for the "one best technology" that will solve all the members' challenges. So far, though, that technology has not yet emerged. Some recent advances such as voice and video over broadband internet hold promise, as they add richness to normally sparse electronic communication. However, global teams usually face different infrastructures in different countries, company firewalls, people traveling, and other complications which make it difficult for them to rely on these advances. Effective virtual teams use a range of technology, matching different technologies to different aspects of the team's task. They might use email for asynchronous communication, phone for one-to-one discussions, web meetings for joint discussions (some members using the phone and others using the internet for the voice aspect), and a shared workspace for keeping documents. They might also combine or sequence technologies in specific ways; for example, a good technique for communicating effectively across cultures is to first exchange email background about a topic, then to discuss it on the phone to develop a dialogue with questions and answers in real time, then to follow up on email to ensure that the main points were shared. In addition, high performance teams also take team members' personality characteristics into account and match technology with personal preferences well (Jonsen et al. 2011). Recent research has shown a relationship between technological communication, personality characteristics, and performance (Turel and Zhang 2010; Jacques et al. 2009). When choosing technologies, teams should select ones (and provide training if necessary) that all team members can use and that will be supported as needed.

Like diverse composition, distributed configuration raises enormous barriers and opportunities for global teams. But also in parallel with diversity, team members are often motivated by this extra challenge, especially at the beginning of a team's life. Working with people in different locations adds variety and new perspectives, and many people find it inspiring to connect with people in other places. Effective global team leaders can take advantage of this momentum to get the team working well together and, using the findings discovered by research about dispersed teams, can turn the challenges into opportunities for high performance.

Global Teams and Organizational Performance

So far we have considered the effectiveness of global teams themselves; but it is also important to examine their impact on the overall performance of organizations. To this end, we will discuss two specific topics here: top management teams, and connected teams.

Top Management Teams—Are They Really Teams?

The top manager and his or her direct reports are usually referred to as the Top Management Team (TMT). The overall corporation has a global TMT, and each business unit also has a TMT which may be global or local, depending on the company's structure. The TMT's mandate is to decide on the overall direction and strategy of the company (or business unit, within the company strategy), and to take responsibility for implementing it. Team members usually act independently from each other in terms of implementation—if the TMT members are heads of geographic units then they implement within their regions; if they are heads of product group units then they implement for their own product areas; and so on. In fact, if the company's reward structure focuses mainly on business unit performance then the TMT members may actually compete with each other for resources needed to implement the strategy in their own units. For this reason, there is often debate as to whether the TMT is *really* a team (e.g. Katzenbach 1997).

A lot of research on TMTs has focused on the relationship between team composition and company performance (e.g. Carpenter et al. 2004; Elron 1997), using publicly available data. This research has shown that functional diversity is usually associated with slightly higher performance, but that other sources of diversity do not affect company performance (see Cannella et al. 2008). However, this research stream cannot sort out whether the source of diversity is suppressed or used as an opportunity within the team. A few studies have indicated that effective communication and conflict resolution are associated with high performing TMTs (i.e. those whose organizations perform well), but the impact is hard to determine.

Anecdotal evidence, experience, and some more in-depth research studies suggest that a company or business unit whose TMT behaves like an effective team tends to perform better in the long term than one whose TMT behaves like a group of independent (or even competing) individuals. When TMT members follow the basic conditions and adhere to the high performance characteristics described above, and when they use diversity and dispersion as opportunities, they are more likely to develop strategies that take into account the organization as a whole and that are more adapted to the current environment. In such TMTs, team members are better at helping each other to implement, for example by sharing ideas, people, and other resources. For example, one study found that when those who have the most influence in the TMT also have the most international expertise, a global TMT's company is more likely to perform well. In the short term, a company can perform well when its TMT members act independently or compete; however, when the environment changes and the company must drive changes or react, then the company is better off with a "real" team as its TMT.

Connected Teams Create Global Organizations

Today's multinational organizations typically share some negative characteristics, including impersonality and heavy complexity. Multinationals are large and distributed, and it is often difficult for their members—especially those outside of headquarters—to relate to other parts of the company. Moreover, the use of virtual workers is becoming much more common, such as salespeople with independent territories who only see another member of their own company a couple of times a month or even less. The complexity also makes these organizations heavy and unwieldy, and managers have difficulty getting information where it is needed, when it is needed. Many senior managers today are trying to learn how to motivate people and share information in this difficult situation, to maintain commitment and collaboration so that the opportunities of globalization will not be lost under the burdens. Effective global teams have some important "side effects" related to creating global organizations. "Connected teams" refers to global teams who pay attention to, and nurture these higher-order benefits.

First, members of effective global teams tend to feel more committed to the organization as a whole than do people who are not members of such teams. When people have personal *and* performance-related connections with others in different parts of the organization, those other parts of the organization seem less distant and more real. Team members make the organization more tangible for each other. This may seem trivial, but for a leader trying to enhance and coordinate performance in a multinational organization, this commitment to the company and the individuals within it goes a very long way.

Second, most managers today are members of two or more global teams. As we discussed at the beginning of this chapter, global teams often cross the hierarchy and join people from different parts of the organization. Because of this, the multiple global teams that each manager is part of tend to cross *different* parts of the company. Each manager (team member), therefore, is a potential conveyor of knowledge across boundaries, and global teams can be conduits for knowledge sharing and organizational learning. This perspective is summarized in Box 7.1. As for all other potential benefits of global teams, this knowledge sharing does not happen automatically. In fact, members of global teams tend to focus on the task at hand—which is difficult enough—and not pay attention to passing on knowledge about other aspects of company performance. But as global teams start to master their own task their conversations often turn to "what else is happening at your end?" Effective global leaders and teams encourage this learning, and in fact, sophisticated multinational companies see its advantages and facilitate it deliberately.

It is easy to argue that team performance is key to organizational performance: work is done by teams—teams make decisions and implement them—and if teams perform well then so will the organization. In this section we have illustrated two ways that effective global teams contribute to the performance of the organization beyond their own task mandates: the special case of TMTs, and connected teams.

Leading Global Teams

We began this chapter by arguing that effective global leaders must be good both at being global team members and at leading global teams. Throughout this chapter we have identified the characteristics of effective global teams, and global leaders can use the ideas in the chapter as somewhat of a checklist:

- Have the basic conditions been met?

- Does the team have high performance characteristics?

- Is the team capturing the opportunities inherent in its diversity and distribution?

- If the team is a TMT, is it acting like a high performing team to ensure the whole organization benefits?

- Are the members leveraging the team as a connected team?

But every global team is different, and therein lies the importance of leadership. Beyond the basic conditions, there are no hard and fast rules about global teams. All global teams should develop trust and respect, the path for doing that in each team is different. All global teams should be innovative, but the focus of their innovation, the end-user, is different. All global teams must manage external stakeholder relationships, but all have different sets of stakeholders. And so on.

Box 7.1 Connected Teams

Most managers are on two or more distributed teams, but tend to see these as separate teams or matrixed teams. This is typically how connected teams are shown, emphasizing the distinct nature of the different teams:

	USA and Canada	Latin America	Europe	Asia	Middle East and Africa
Marketing	A	F			S
Production	B		J	N	
Logistics	C	G	K		T
R&D	D		L	P	
Finance	E	H	M	Q	U
Call Centers				R	V

For example, person A is on the "USA and Canada" team, and also on the "Marketing" team.

Here are the same teams shown as a network. Shapes the same shade of gray are in the same geographical team, and the same shape are in the same functional team. This network emphasizes the interconnections between team members and highlights the opportunities for learning and distribution of knowledge.

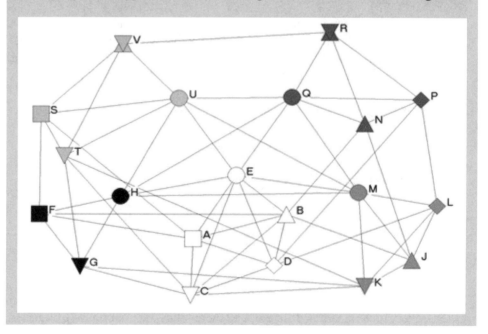

In literature, global and multinational leaders are generally seen to be responsible for defining the goals and direction of the team, organizing and supporting the team in accomplishing their goals, and guiding the implementation of their goals (Fink et al. 2004; Zaccaro et al. 2001). Team leaders with good communication styles can even mitigate the negative effects of geographical differences, and research suggests that team leaders should communicate more regularly with their globally dispersed teams as well as create team norms that encourage communication amongst team members (Cummings 2007). Recent research (e.g. Maznevski et al. 2006) has even begun to suggest that, in global teams, the traditional leadership role tends to be distributed across more people than in traditional teams. In traditional teams, the "leader" tends to be the hierarchical head of the team, the meeting chairperson, the discussion facilitator, the decision maker, the discipline enforcer, the direction setter, and often other roles as well. It seems that global teams may be too complex and dynamic for one person to take on all of these roles.

Experienced leaders of global teams find themselves either assigning some of these roles to others, or facilitating the emergence of multiple leadership roles within the team. Although this research is still not conclusive, it resonates well with experienced leaders and probably represents an emerging trend. This would be yet another complexity for leaders of global teams, but, as with diversity and distribution, could create an opportunity for higher performance if well managed.

This infinite variety of teams and the ambiguity of leadership roles prevent the checklist from being applied like a recipe. It is more like a field guide of which characteristics to pay attention to, and which leadership tools might be most effective in different situations. The application is up to the leader, who must match the tools with the situation, including the combination of members, task, and external stakeholders. This implies that leaders of global teams must constantly observe and check the condition of the team, monitoring also its context (which includes cultural contextual awareness), and situation.

As emphasized elsewhere in this book, cultural competency is important to global team leadership. Studies have shown a positive relationship between multinational team performance and the degree of cross-cultural competency of their leader (Matveev and Nelson 2004). One way of increasing cultural awareness is international experience: team leaders who have had international experience are likely to possess a higher level of cultural competence and empathy (Schwer 2004). A team leader's cultural intelligence has been shown to influence team members' perceptions of leader performance and team performance (Groves and Feyerherm 2011). Naturally, leaders who can communicate better with their global followers will be better able to influence the motivation of their team members to exploit, explore, and transfer knowledge within the team.

Global teams are inherently unstable, and monitoring can help the astute leader benefit from the instabilities (they are chances to take advantage of flexibility!)

rather than be limited by them. The leader must provide some consistency of direction, but guide the team dynamically according to its needs and opportunities.

Like global leadership in general, leading global teams is a craft that combines the science of conditions and opportunities in teams—the checklist—with the art of applying the right processes at the right time. Leaders who are open to and careful about learning will develop the skills needed for this craft.

8 Global Leadership Knowledge Creation and Transfer

ALLAN BIRD AND GARY R. ODDOU

After five years performing at a high level, an expatriate manager was transferred back from his assignment in Bonn, Germany to his firm's New York headquarters. He had grown significantly and had acquired an extraordinary amount of knowledge. He had developed an extensive understanding of German banking regulations and practices. He had developed a far-flung network of contacts—people who could open doors, provide counsel, or solve problems. Moreover, as a result of this assignment he had a deeper understanding of what the company was trying to accomplish with its global strategy, and he saw ways to more effectively and efficiently implement this strategy in Europe. He was poised to take more of a leadership role by both using what he knew and sharing it with others.

To his surprise, upon his return to New York he was put on a six-month temporary assignment assisting in the training of new employees in the U.S. His superiors appeared to have little idea of how to capitalize on his German experiences within the context of existing training programs, nor could he identify ways to apply his hard-won insights within his new assignment. By the time he received a longer-term assignment working with African subsidiaries, a large portion of the learning acquired on his prior assignment had eroded. For instance, his German network of friends, so critical to the firm knowledge base there, had already begun to dissipate. Key contacts had moved or were no longer in position to help him or the company. As a result of the poor management of his transition, he developed negative feelings toward his company and his motivation to help and apply his learning also dissipated.

The purpose of this chapter is to acquaint you with the role of knowledge creation and transfer in global leadership. Many models of global leadership competency (cf. Bird and Osland 2004; Black et al. 1999a; Brake 1997; Kets de Vries and Florent-Treacy 1999) emphasize the important role that knowledge plays in effective leadership. Surprisingly, this aspect of global leadership has not been well researched. This chapter addresses the issue of knowledge creation and development and also explores the transfer of knowledge. The transfer of knowledge is considered both in terms of the individual—the application of previously acquired knowledge to new situations—and the organization—the interest and receptivity of the organization to the capture and use of knowledge the repatriate might have acquired.

Careers, Development, and Knowledge Creation

In this section we explore the relationship between knowledge creation and the development of a knowledge capability necessary for effective global leadership. We begin by reviewing Nonaka's theory of knowledge creation and then link it to global leadership development.

In 1994, Bird proposed that a knowledge perspective be used to better capture the significance of career experience and development in career research. He argued that the traditional definition of career as "the evolving sequence of a person's work experiences over time" (Arthur et al. 1989: 8) ignored the essential substance of a career. He reasoned that type, duration, length, and sequence of work experiences were but outward markers of a career, and that a more meaningful understanding of careers could be constructed by focusing on the knowledge that was accumulated or discarded over time. The arc of a career could be understood in terms of the inflows, outflows, and transformations of individual and organizational knowledge that derive from sequences of work experiences.

Subsequently, Bird (2001) applied the "careers as repositories of knowledge" perspective to international assignments as a way of understanding the role they might play in developing global leaders. Adopting this perspective, international work experiences constitute the primary mechanism by which knowledge creation relevant to global leadership took place (Bird 2001).

It is impossible to conceptualize careers as repositories of knowledge apart from a view of organizations as knowledge creators (Argote and Ingram 2000; Inkpen and Dinur 1998). The experience of individuals forms the substance from which knowledge is created (Nonaka 1991a). When a firm competes on the basis of cost, quality, or product differentiation it is competing on the ability to distinguish its products or services from that of its competitors. The ability to differentiate is embedded in an invisible asset: its knowledge base (Prahalad and Hamel 1994). That knowledge base is derived, in turn, from the experience of the individuals affiliated with that firm (Nurasimha 2000). Ultimately, all advantages are informational in nature. Maintaining competitiveness and sustaining an ongoing ability to differentiate requires firms to develop their human resources in ways that enhance the supply of information and knowledge available to the firm. Firms that revitalize themselves through knowledge creation and transfer set themselves apart from competitors (Argote and Ingram 2000).

Perhaps the most important way that organizations create knowledge is by shaping employee work experiences and then eliciting experience-based learning in ways that allow it to be shared throughout the organization and lead to the accomplishment of organizational objectives. Framed in this way, a key activity of line managers and human resource development policies that support them is to give direction to the knowledge-generating activities of employees by creating meaning, i.e. by making sense of experiential data (Louis 1980b; Weick 1996).

Explicit Knowledge and Tacit Knowledge

There are two ways that organizations and individuals transmit knowledge. When knowledge is transmitted to others through formal, systematic language—when it is articulable—it can be called "explicit" (Polanyi, 1966). Explicit knowledge is impersonal and independent of context. For example, a mathematical equation conveys knowledge by means of an impersonal (it is not rooted in any person or situation), formal (there are rules governing the structure of equations), systematic language (mathematical symbols).

Tacit knowledge describes information that is embedded in people's experiences and which is difficult to communicate to others. By definition, tacit knowledge is personal—it is gained only through first-hand experiences and also is rooted in action and commitment (Nonaka 1991a). It is accessible to its possessor primarily in the form of intuition, speculation, and feeling. When Polanyi (1966: 4) states, "We know more than we can tell," he is describing the sum of an individual's understanding that cannot be articulated to others.

Tacit knowledge has two variants that are relevant to acquiring knowledge critical for global leadership. First, one type of tacit knowledge is reflected in deeply held beliefs, paradigms, schemata, or mental models (Nonaka 1990). This knowledge helps us make sense of the world and influences our perceptions of what are appropriate values, attitudes, and behaviors. A second type is technical, and consists of skills, techniques, and know-how that are context-specific. Both types are important to global leadership and to the development of global leaders. It is also important to note that a large share of the tacit knowledge that individuals possess remains beyond one's ability to make explicit (Winograd and Flores 1986).

Types of Knowledge Creation

Various types of interaction between these two basic knowledge types—tacit and explicit—gives rise to four types of knowledge creation (Nonaka 1991a), as shown in Figure 8.1. Sequenced together, the four create a cycle of knowledge creation.

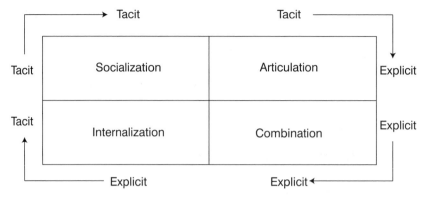

Figure 8.1 Typology of the Knowledge Creation Process

Source: A. Bird (1994) "Careers as repositories of knowledge: A new perspective on boundaryless careers." *Journal of Organizational Behavior*, 15(4): 329. John Wiley & Sons Limited. Reproduced with permission.

Tacit-to-Tacit

Knowledge creation involving the transmittal of tacit knowledge between individuals represents the first type. Studying under a master craftsman, apprentices may learn not only through spoken words or instructions, but through observation and imitation as well. These processes of socialization lead to knowledge creation through the expansion of the apprentice's knowledge, i.e. newcomers imbue or modify what is learned via socialization by filtering it through their own understanding. Notwithstanding this process, however, little new knowledge is created through socialization. Moreover, the socialization form of knowledge creation is time-consuming and difficult to manage, more so when large numbers of people are involved.

Explicit-to-Explicit

Knowledge that is explicit can be easily transmitted. The explicitness often makes *combination* of different knowledge transparent and easy. For example, collecting information about the financial performance of various overseas business units (explicit knowledge) brings about the creation of new knowledge: how the firm as a whole is performing in overseas markets (explicit knowledge). Combination of explicit knowledge creates new knowledge through synthesis. Unlike socialization, the new knowledge created often tends to be less significant in its scope.

The two most profound knowledge creation types involve the transition from tacit to explicit or explicit to tacit. This is also the locus where individuals' work experiences hold the potential to make their largest contribution to the organization.

Tacit-to-Explicit

Articulation is the conversion of tacit knowledge to explicit knowledge. It is significant for organizations because when knowledge that was previously inaccessible is made explicit it can be shared. In a furniture company, for example, when a master cabinetmaker is able to articulate the thinking and techniques behind his particular style of woodworking, that information can be widely disseminated within the organization. Designers can incorporate the new knowledge into future products. Additionally, the information might even be shared with other cabinetmakers thereby enabling them to make pieces of comparable workmanship. It may even be possible to incorporate this knowledge into the design of equipment and processes such that workmanship that could only be achieved by individual craftsmen can now be produced through machine-driven manufacturing.

Explicit-to-Tacit

The acquisition and subsequent application of explicit knowledge to an individual's own unique situation results in an expansion of the tacit knowledge base. In addition to *internalization* of explicit knowledge, this knowledge creation may lead to a reframing of what is known that constitutes knowledge creation as well. It is also important to note that transference of knowledge from explicit to tacit can lead to self-renewal of the employee and a deepening commitment.

There are similarities between tacit-to-tacit and explicit-to-tacit knowledge creation types. The primary difference between "socialization" and "internalization" lies in the informational source. In the socialization (tacit-to-tacit), a master or role model is the primary information source contributing to new knowledge creation. New knowledge is initially being created through replication, with the receiver's knowledge base contributing little to the newly created knowledge. In the case of explicit-to-tacit knowledge creation, the receiver's knowledge base contributes most of the information. By helping the receiver to see things in a different light or think in a different way (both being forms of new knowledge), explicit knowledge stimulates learning.

International Assignments as Spirals of Knowledge Creation

Through iteratively cycling through the four knowledge creation modes it is possible to trace the knowledge arc of a career path. Different experiences spark shifts from one mode to another. Nonaka (1991b) provides an example of how this sequencing of knowledge creation modes plays out. In doing so, he outlines the nature of experience in each mode as well as the modal shifts in describing the experience of one team member on a product development team at Matsushita Electric Company charged with improving the design and performance of a home bread-making machine. Though a prototype had been developed, it produced unacceptable bread. The crust was hard and the inside was doughy. One team member, Ikuko Tanaka, suggested they study the technique of Osaka International Hotel's baker, who had a reputation for making the best bread in Osaka. She arranged to work as an apprentice with the baker. One day she noticed that the baker had a distinctive technique of stretching the dough when kneading it. She returned to the product development team and shared her insights. Acting on this new understanding, they made several modifications in the bread-maker's design. Matsushita engineered the "twist dough" method into its design and came out with a new machine that set a sales record for kitchen appliances.

Nonaka (1991b: 99) continues:

1   First, (Ikuko Tanaka) learns the tacit secrets of the Osaka International Hotel baker (socialization).

2   Next, she translates these secrets into explicit knowledge that she can communicate to her team members and others at Matsushita (articulation).

3   The team then standardizes this knowledge, putting it together into a manual or workbook and embodying it in a product (combination).

4   Finally, through the experience of creating a new product, Tanaka and her team members enrich their own tacit knowledge base (internalization). In particular, one of the things they come to understand in an extremely intuitive way is that products like home bread-making machines can provide genuine quality. That is, the machine must make bread that is as good as that of a professional baker.

It is interesting that Nonaka uses a project team experience to illustrate the sequence of knowledge creation modes (Nonaka, 1994). This has implications for understanding knowledge creation as part of a global leadership development process, particularly as enacted through international assignments. When individuals join a project or work team they may experience a form of *socialization*. Dialogue within the team, in turn, leads to *articulation*. As ideas and concepts generated by the team are incorporated into existing knowledge bases or joined with existing data there is a modal shift to *combination*. Experimentation with various new combinations of knowledge may lead to "learning by doing" that becomes *internalization*. In a similar vein, leaders who venture out into the global context often undergo a profound socialization as they work to adjust to their new surroundings and the requirements of their new work. As they acquire some facility or proficiency, they will likely share their experiences and observations with others, leading to *articulation* of their newly acquired tacit knowledge. Combining this knowledge with explicit knowledge about their work context, organization, competitive environment, and so forth involves a process of *combination.* As they fully incorporate all of this learning, they will have internalized this understanding, resulting in more knowledge creation.

As individuals repeat this sequence of work experiences their store of knowledge grows. Development, then, can be understood as the path of an individual's work experiences through the various knowledge creation modes. The sequences of modes can be visualized as an outwardly expanding spiral.

Four Types of Knowing

Though the knowledge creation cycle provides a description of the developmental trajectory work experiences may take, it does not delineate the content of that development. Knowing that work experiences involve moving through a sequence of knowledge creation modes does not tell us anything about the types of knowledge embedded in that development. A way of categorizing types of knowledge that is particularly useful for understanding knowledge acquisition and transfer related to developing global leaders can be found in Kidd and Teramoto's (1995) four-class taxonomy of "knowings." Each of the four is discussed below.

Know Who

This refers to a person's social capital. It is the actual and potential resources embedded within, available through, and derived from the network of relationships an individual is able to access. Examples of *know who* would include such knowledge as having a contact in the Chinese government willing to make introductions on one's behalf to local, state-owned enterprises or being acquainted with key individuals in the Ireland Development Agency. Knowing who involves a relationship with others *and also* the ability to tap into resources through those relationships.

Know How

Know how covers knowledge related to a person's set of skills and understanding about how to accomplish tasks or how to do work. For example, methods for structuring payment protocols to take into account the effects of hyperinflation in Argentina represent one type of know how. Another would be methods for giving or saving *face* in Chinese business relationships.

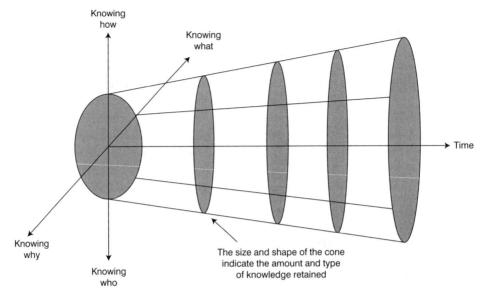

Figure 8.2 Four Types of Knowing Over Time

Source: G. K. Stephens, A. Bird, and M. E. Mendenhall (2002) "International careers as repositories of knowledge: A new look at expatriation." In D.C. Feldman (ed.) *Work Careers: A Developmental Perspective* (San Francisco, CA: Jossey-Bass), p. 303. Reprinted with permission by John Wiley & Sons, Limited.

Know What

This addresses the nature and extent of a person's understanding about specific projects, products, services, or organizational arrangements. Knowledge of the firm's supply chain management procedures and the various suppliers and transportation services in Malaysia or an understanding of the structure of the South African subsidiary's information system constitute types of *know what.*

Know Why

This relates to the nature and extent of a person's identification with the firm's culture, intention, and strategy. For instance, knowing why the firm chose to set up a manufacturing operation in Honduras rather than Kenya. Knowing why gives meaning and purpose to organizational and individual action.

Through time, the volume and value of each type of knowing may increase or decrease. Additionally, specific types of knowledge may be acquired, lost, and recovered. Figure 8.2 presents a graphic depiction of an idealized career developing over time.

Types of Knowing in International Assignment and Global Leader Development

The "careers as repositories of knowledge" perspective offers significant value for the study of global leader careers, particularly from a developmental standpoint. Two recurring themes in research on global leadership development have been the use of international assignments—with their extensive range of new experiences as a mechanism for growth—and the role of knowledge acquisition.

Personal experience is the essential element in knowledge creation and the basis for all tacit knowledge. Each phase of knowledge creation draws on the current or past experience of individuals. Nevertheless, the value of experiences is variable. Frequently, experiences such as driving to and from work, for example, provide little that is useful for new knowledge creation. The experiences most likely to lead to significant knowledge creation possess three characteristics—variety, quality, and affective intensity (Nonaka 1994). All three are present in the experiences associated with international assignments and leading in a global context.

Variety refers to the range of experiences acquired over a given period of time. International assignments, unlike most other work experiences, provide extraordinary opportunities for variety. Living and working in another country present a wide range of new experiences. Often managers encounter a mixture of customs, norms, beliefs, and attitudes across a wide range of situations and circumstances. The physical environment itself is likely to be quite different, with differing climate, terrain, and weather. Additionally, there will be new foods and beverages to sample and adjust to. Possibly there will be a new language to learn. More importantly, there will be a new position with new colleagues, new reporting relationships, and new responsibilities and demands, and, perhaps most importantly, there will be a new organizational culture with new rules and processes about how things are done, who the key people are, and the determinants of credibility. Typically, the more important things to learn and the most difficult to ascertain are the tacit acquisitions.

As a result of these new encounters, the quality of experiences is likely to be richer and deeper than in previous, non-international assignments. Moreover, managers are likely to pay greater attention to and reflect longer on these experiences because their expectations about anticipated outcomes are more likely to be under-met or over-met in overseas assignments (Black et al. 1991). Additionally, mistakes and failures are likely to be more frequent (Mendenhall 2001b), leading managers to re-evaluate core assumptions about themselves, others, and about their work context. Managers may also find they experience unexpected successes (Mendenhall 2001b).

The heightened quality of experience, with its attendant amplified attention and deeper reflection, in turn, increases the probability that individuals will experience greater knowledge creation. In other words, international assignments spur knowledge creation, particularly around self-knowledge because they evoke stronger affective reactions than other types of assignments (Mendenhall 2001b). The knowledge creation may be further enhanced because of the heightened emotional impact that international assignment experiences often carry.

International assignments can be characterized as infrequent events that provide managers with significant opportunities and material for tacit knowledge creation. No doubt, this explains why Osland (1995) characterizes international assignments as transformative experiences for many managers. For these managers, the experiences of an international assignment have no comparable counterpart in prior work they have done. It is this poignancy of experience—the extent of variety, the depth of quality, and the intense emotionality—that may also help explain why research on global leadership development has emphasized the importance of international assignments, but has had difficulty in understanding how best to study the knowledge acquired through those experiences.

Application to Global Leadership Development

International assignments associated with global leadership development possess unique properties when viewed through the lens of knowledge creation. This section considers those distinctive properties and explores their implications.

Syntactic and Semantic Issues

Work experiences have both a syntactic and semantic aspect, to borrow two terms from linguistics. Syntax refers to the structure of a sentence; semantics to its meaning. Human resource managers must consider both the structure of work experiences and their meaning, if international assignments are to lead to significant knowledge creation beneficial to global leadership development and the overall competitiveness of the firm. Syntactic dimensions of work experience include such things as the duration of the assignment, the sequencing of assignments, and the structure of assignments. There are several important issues to consider here.

The duration of international assignments may often be arbitrarily established. Short-term assignments of nine months or less are usually based on the completion of a particular task or project, while long-term assignments often follow a standard length of two to three years. In setting the length of the assignment there is frequently little regard for the impact on knowledge acquisition or dissemination (Black et al. 1999b). Clearly not all international assignments are alike in terms of the variety, quality, and intensity of experience they provide, which means that the knowledge creation process may vary in length as well. For example, similar cultures, legal regulations, and a common language may make it possible for a

U.S. manager to quickly learn how to get a new subsidiary fully operational in New Zealand. That same manager may take considerably longer to accomplish the same feat in China. The difference is not solely one of culture, language, and/or legal regulations, but also involves the acquisition of the right sorts of experiences that will allow useful new knowledge to be created. In a related vein, whether a particular culture is characterized by high- or low-context communication preferences may influence, in turn, whether the most effective knowledge creation methods will be tacit or explicit (Dulek and Fielden 1991). Chinese culture is characterized by a communication style in which much of the message is embedded in the situation rather than in explicit written documents or verbal exchanges (Hall 1966). U.S. managers in China may need to acquire a substantial range of local experiences before they are able to accurately make sense of what is going on around them. In China, the most effective knowledge creation type early in the assignment may be the tacit-to-tacit exchange—socialization— whereby a newly arriving manager works closely with a local Chinese manager or experienced expatriate. That same manager, when assigned to Australia, may be able to create knowledge through combination (explicit-to-explicit), as the U.S. manager and local counterparts share their understanding of plant set-up and management.

Sequence is another issue that human resource managers should consider when using international assignments in developing global business leaders. Gunz (1989) suggests that, though many large organizations carry out career planning to identify logical sequencing of positions and promotions for managerial personnel, the knowledge creation process does not factor into that planning. An international assignment may be appropriate as the next step on a career path headed to the top of the organization, but inappropriate for moving a manager through the next phase of the knowledge creation cycle or providing a manager with the right type of experiences. For example, after eighteen months in a domestic department where he focused on mortgaged-based securities, one manager at a U.S. investment bank was transferred to Tokyo where his new position was to oversee a Japanese securities trading operation. There was little, if any, room within the new assignment for internalization of knowledge acquired in the previous position.

Disruption in the knowledge creation process may also occur upon repatriation (Black et al. 1999b; Gupta and Govindarajan 1991; Stroh 1995), particularly if personnel in the receiving unit are not open to the experiences of the repatriate. Adler (2002) calls this the "xenophobic response," wherein colleagues' and supervisors' fear and rejection of the new knowledge repatriates contribute subsequently constrains the transfer of knowledge. Many firms find it difficult to access with any depth of understanding what a manager has learned or to position the manager so that international experiences can be effectively used in broader knowledge creation activities. The case of the American manager returning from Germany that opened this chapter provides an obvious instance of disruption of the knowledge creation process and also of a firm's inability to tap into or transfer knowledge.

It is ironic that, though firms send managers on international assignment to get experience that will lead to knowledge acquisition in a wide variety of ways, many firms seem incapable of appreciating how successful they have been, often underestimating the growth in knowledge that managers have experienced. Repatriates report that work takes on broader significance. Moreover, they have a changed perspective of their role within the firm and within the world as well as a changed understanding of where the firm fits in the world. Both of these transformations—awareness of a broader significance and reinterpretation of their role within the firm and the firm's place in the world—point to the development and growth of a global mindset (Levy et al. 2007), which has been identified as an essential characteristic of global leadership (Osland et al. 2006).

Employee Transformation

There are three aspects of international assignment experiences that help to explain the significant transformations managers may undergo (see Table 8.1). The commingling of work and non-work experiences, common to both short- and long-term assignments, often lead to learning and insight about oneself, one's family, about global business operations and the world in general. In turn, these insights inevitably extend to a changed view of the work setting, an understanding of cross-cultural differences, the development of a more extensive and global network, the meaning of work, and the nature of foreign organizations. Short-term assignments that don't include the relocation of the family, but which include extended absences or the development of local social support systems may also lead to a new perspective on work, the company, and larger "purpose of life" issues. Oddou (2002) gives a fairly comprehensive list of the transformations expatriates usually experience.

A second aspect of international assignments that influences transformation is the compression into a short span of time of myriad novel, intense, significantly different experiences. Compression of so many powerful experiences may lead to a proliferation of new mental maps, an explosive increase in the repertoire of schema and scripts for dealing with a multitude of commonplace and not-so-commonplace events. Typical of this phenomenon in a more superficial way is the matter of the proper way to greet people in a business setting. Prior to an international assignment in Japan, a typical U.S. manager would probably employ a handshake as the most common form of greeting and introduction. After working in Japan for several months or years, that same manager would return home with an expanded set of greetings and introductions that would now include bows of various depths and rigidity as well as handshakes of varying strength and duration.

Other transformations can relate to very deep-seated values or attitudes. For example, an expatriate in Vietnam was having a conversation with a Vietnamese colleague one day. The Vietnamese colleague asked him how he could support the U.S. president with respect to the war in Iraq. When asked to clarify, the

Table 8.1 Repatriate Resource Capabilities and Application Potential

Resource Type	New Resource Capabilities	Application Value
Cognitive	• New global knowledge (of foreign operations, interdependencies, etc.) • New broader and different perspectives or worldview • Increased ability to conceptualize diverse information • Increased cognitive complexity	• Understanding of the foreign culture • Understanding of the foreign operation • Clearer and more accurate worldview • Personal understanding of the interdependencies of global business operations
Relational	• New sources of information (e.g. people contacts) • New quality or depth of relationships	• Names of individuals in the foreign operation (internal to the firm and those external—politicians, community leaders, other firms' personnel) that can be sources for gathering information more efficiently and accurately • Favor-granting relationships with individuals in the foreign operation (internal to the firm and those external—politicians, community leaders, other firms' personnel) that can be helpful in exploiting opportunities and defending against threats
Attitudinal	• Increased self-efficacy	• More initiating behavior • Greater self-reliance when necessary • Increased sense of "can-do-it"
Behavioral	Managerial skills: • More effective communication skills • More effective motivation skills • More effective planning skills • More effective organizing skills	• Greater ability to consider diversity in planning tasks • Greater understanding of different communication styles • Better understanding of and ability to manage or work with people with different motivations

Vietnamese colleague said that the expatriate's president was responsible for killing civilians just like Saddam Hussein. Neither one was better than the other, the Vietnamese colleague stated. This perspective was a completely new one for the expatriate. He had always defined whether something was good or bad based on the results or the intent. The Vietnamese colleague, however, represented a cultural viewpoint that intent counted for nothing if the results were not also good. Although this example was not readily applicable to the expatriate's job in a tangible way, the ability to understand a very different perspective enabled him to better accept that there are other views to events that he had never questioned. Such increased mental flexibility is a valuable characteristic to acquire for any businessperson, but is particularly important for global leaders (Black et al. 1999a).

Because many, if not most, firms do not view repatriate knowledge as a valuable resource or competitive advantage, such gains can be of little consequence to the firm. Kang et al. (2010) found that in domestic contexts with monocultural project teams, the more difficult, tacit, and important knowledge was perceived, the more effort an organization made to obtain it. However, significant differences exist between this kind of context and that of an employee returning from an international assignment. Most of the differences have to do with the transition process, coming from the outside to the inside. Organizations appear to be challenged to recognize the value of knowledge created outside the context in which it could be applied. In fact, repatriates report that firms seldom take a strategic perspective when positioning them upon return (Downes and Thomas 1999; Forster 1999; Harzing 2001), reducing the likelihood that their hard-earned knowledge will be applicable to their new situation. A case study of a Spanish bank revealed that the bank showed little interest in what repatriates learned abroad; repatriates felt their knowledge was "undervalued or not wanted at all" (Bonache and Brewster 2001:159). Upon re-entry, repatriates typically do not get to use much of the knowledge acquired in foreign assignments (Harvey 1989; Osland 1995; Stroh and Caligiuri 1997). However, a recent study of Japanese repatriates found that those who were able to transfer the global competencies they learned abroad reported higher levels of commitment (Furuya, Stevens, Oddou, and Bird 2009). Repatriates are often dissatisfied with their re-entry, and their turnover rate is much higher than that of their domestic counterparts (Black and Gregersen 1999; Price Waterhouse 1997; Stroh et al. 1998). If they resign, firms lose repatriate knowledge assets, most likely to a competitor.

These losses are of the types discussed earlier. *Knowing who* losses may occur as some friendships, acquaintances, and relationship networks wane. *Knowing what* losses may take place as a manager's knowledge of some products and services or specific aspects of some organizational arrangements are forgotten, become outdated, or are no longer relevant. As a manager's identification with the firm shifts or changes, understanding of what is relevant or strategic may be lost. Finally, the move to a new position and new responsibility may result in less practice and application of well-developed skills so that knowledge of certain techniques or the ability to use some skills may wither. In short, international assignments are a time of both knowledge growth and development and also loss and decay.

The failure on the part of firms to value and actively draw out repatriate knowledge greatly limits its successful transfer. Repatriates in Berthoin Antal's (2001) study identified three major barriers. First, a lack of interest and the absence of processes or structures to communicate knowledge hindered the dissemination of repatriate knowledge. Second, the lack of a global mindset in the parent firm, coupled with a lack of real dedication to being multinational constituted another set of barriers. However, failure to assign repatriates to jobs that utilized their international expertise was perhaps the most significant obstacle. Thus, she recommends adding another stage to the expatriation-repatriation process—knowledge sharing—that would occur after re-entry and involve an active knowledge management process (Berthoin Antal 2001).

It is important to note here that much of the work on knowledge creation and transfer has been framed in terms of international assignees—primarily expatriates; however, recent research on another type of international assignee—inpatriates—is opening up new lines of inquiry. Reiche and associates (Reiche et al. 2009b) have identified the role of inpatriates in the mediation of knowledge flows within global organizations. They also identify the ways in which inpatriates access their personal social capital (which we refer to as *knowing who*) to enhance the inter-unit intellectual capital of the organization associates (Reiche et al. 2009a).

In the following section, we will explore those variables that are important to address in order to facilitate the transfer of repatriate knowledge. Although researchers have suggested HR tools that could facilitate repatriate knowledge transfer (Lazarova and Tarique 2005; Tsang 1999), we actually know very little about the conditions under which repatriate knowledge might be captured by the firm.

Scholars have complained that our knowledge of how organizations manage their personnel lacks good conceptual underpinning (Kochan et al. 1992; Welch 1994), which is certainly true for repatriate knowledge transfer.

A Communication Perspective on the Repatriate Knowledge Transfer Process

Transferring information is a type of communication process—whether explicit or tacit. In the explicit communication of knowledge, the repatriate can write the information down and pass it along to others, for example. With tacit knowledge, although the repatriate might not write information down, he/she acts in such a way that the information can be observed, and, therefore, communicated and captured. It is useful, then, to use as a basic framework, the early work that Shannon and Weaver (1949) did on the components of a basic communication model. This approach has precedence in light of researchers who have used a communication model to study knowledge or information flows in other contexts (Bryant and Nguyen 2002; Gupta and Govindarajan 2000). Further, Minbaeva's (2005) literature review noted that the knowledge transfer process in MNCs is affected by the characteristics of the knowledge (the message), the knowledge sources and transferors (the sender), the recipients (the receiver), and their relationship (the context). The nature of the knowledge (explicit or tacit) to be transferred is, of course, an important part of the transfer process. This has previously been addressed in earlier sections of this chapter. The following discussion will focus on the rest of the communication model. The research work by Oddou et al. (2009) provides the principal basis for this discussion.

The essence of the Oddou et al. (2009) model can be found in Figures 8.3 and 8.4.

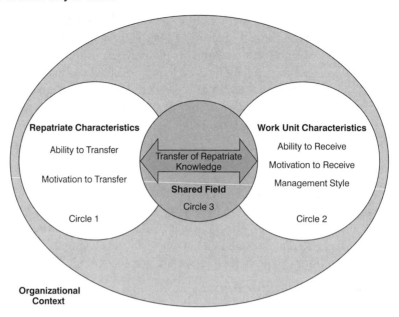

Figure 8.3 The Repatriate Knowledge Transfer Model

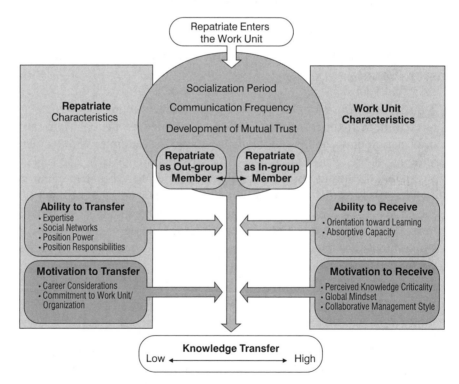

Figure 8.4 The Repatriate Knowledge Transfer Process

Figure 8.3 shows the roles of the repatriate and the organization and reflects the importance of the shared context that allows the transfer to take place. In Figure 8.4, essentially, the model suggests that to the degree that the repatriate has certain ability and motivation characteristics, becomes an in-group member and is part of an organization that has the ability and motivation to acquire knowledge, there will be successful knowledge transfer within the field of the shared context. A summary of some of the literature supporting each of these three major parts will follow.

Repatriate Characteristics

First, the model suggests the repatriate has the ability and motivation to transfer the learning acquired from the international experience.

Motivation to Transfer Knowledge

The repatriate's motivation has been found to relate to personal career interests, i.e. self-centeredness (Lazarova and Tarique 2005). For example, a repatriate who is focusing on a promotion or other organizational reward is more likely to want to look for opportunities to improve the organization. Another important motivation where similar behaviors are manifested is personal commitment to the firm: being other-centered (Meyer and Allen 1997), demonstrating organizational citizenship and commitment, including altruism and other intrinsic factors (Liu 2010; Mogotsi et al. 2011; Wang and Yang 2007). Self-esteem, absorptive ability, and tendency to trust have also been found to relate to knowledge sharing characteristics (Shu and Chuang 2011). However, what makes acquiring trust more challenging in a repatriate context is that the new repatriate has little basis for trusting or being trusted if s/he is returning to a new context. Furthermore, given the typical treatment repatriates often receive upon re-entry by the firm, there is a question about how much commitment they will have to their new environment.

Ability to Transfer Knowledge

The other major repatriate "characteristic" is the repatriate's *ability* to transfer knowledge. Variables that have traditionally been viewed as relating to the ability to influence include one's perceived competence or expertise (Cross and Prusak 2003; French and Raven 1959). The greater the perceived expertise of the individual, the more potential influence he or she can have. The social networks of which one is a member (Boisot 1998) and the depth of the relationship (Hu 2009) is also a factor. Au and Fukuda (2002) found that individuals who held boundary spanning roles (i.e. were members of social networks) had more organizational power than those who didn't. Certainly, the repatriate who is in a project management position and interacting regularly with six or seven people from different areas has the potential to influence more than a repatriate who returns as an outside salesperson working primarily with external clients. In addition, the actual position one has and how it might be related to the acquired knowledge the repatriate has obtained is important. For example, Berthoin Antal (2001) found that when re-entry jobs have international dimensions and are similar to the foreign assignment, the repatriates' knowledge is more relevant to their work and to their co-workers.

Firm Characteristics

Motivation

Firms are composed of people and systems. Therefore, it is important to address both aspects when considering knowledge transfer. The people who are most in contact with the repatriate are those who are more likely to allow or encourage or otherwise accept and apply the knowledge of the repatriate. Some of the more important aspects about these individuals that relate to knowledge transfer include: 1) the relevance of the repatriate's knowledge that the repatriate's colleagues perceive for their work milieus (Zander and Kogut 1995); 2) colleagues' openness to learning new information in general (Berthoin Antal 2001); and 3) how collaborative the work culture is and the nature of the leadership style of the repatriate's manager (Politis 2001).

Ability

Organizations have systems that include policies and procedures, as well as informal routines created by their organizational culture. These "routines" affect the organization's ability to absorb information (Zahra and George 2002). More than likely, such routines are a reflection of the attitudes of the members of the organization. Gold et al. (2001) found that organizations that reflected the importance of continuous improvement, experimentation, and openness to new ideas were related to learning organizations. Organizational routines need to be created around these activities.

Shared Context

When the repatriate returns to the company and is given a particular work setting, the repatriate and colleagues in that work setting share a context. How the individual and the organization share that context is meaningful for the transfer of knowledge (Wood 1997). Kodama (2005a) refers to this as shared space and argues that it is necessary in order to create a context for knowledge creation. In an effort to determine why some firms were able to capitalize on personnel mobility to enhance knowledge transfer and others not, they found that a shared context was the differentiating factor (Pan and Wang 2010).

Although shared context is not necessarily a physical space, it is a space in which ideas can be exchanged, discussed, and possibly applied. Such a space is created from trust. Trust between two parties is critical in knowledge transfer (Andrews and Delahaye 2000; Argote et al. 2003) and one that creates a consistent atmosphere of openness in a knowledge market (Cross and Prusak 2003)

Implications for Knowledge Transfer

Based on our understanding of what variables affect knowledge transfer, a number of things can be done to enhance this process; these recommendations include:

1   Firms can attempt to create more strategic planning around the careers of their international assignees. The position upon repatriation should be related in responsibility to the acquired knowledge and skills gained in the foreign assignment. In fact, this process might start in the selection of the assignee, ensuring that the knowledge to be gained in the foreign assignment is strategic to the employee's growth and the firm's needs. This will create continuity in the knowledge creation process. It will also likely hasten the process of engendering trust among employees within the work unit and increase the repatriate's commitment to the organization.

2   Firms can institute, as a few do, debriefing sessions where the repatriate gives a debriefing to the firm upon return, explaining what was learned and experienced, what networks were developed that might be of use, etc. This can also be achieved by the repatriate's manager using a very collaborative management style to create a spirit of openness and cooperation.

3   Firms can also create routines such as knowledge-sharing sessions around themes. Such sessions can be carried out during lunch hours and be company sponsored. Themes can be country-focused or issue-focused. Doing these kinds of things creates routines in the organization that facilitate knowledge transfer and absorption.

4   Firms can train the managers of repatriates about the issues surrounding reacculturation and culture shock so as to facilitate the repatriate's return and resocialization process into a new work culture. Doing so will likely increase the repatriate's personal commitment to the firm and also allow opportunities to discuss experiences and learning.

5   Firms could incorporate the inclusion of a "back-home project" in which the expatriate, as a transition back to the home country and organization, is given a relevant project to work on before actually returning from the foreign

assignment. This might allow more opportunities to transfer learning as well as better prepare the expatriate for network development and socialization.

Conclusion

In conclusion, today's world of global business requires that companies must "innovate by learning from the world" (Doz, Santos and Williamson 2001: 1). Today's economy is often referred to as a knowledge economy, knowledge that firms must recognize, capture, and manage in order to create a sustainable competitive advantage (Inkpen and Dinur 1998). Exposure to new ideas and business practices as well as foreign cultures and markets via international assignments contributes to the creation of knowledge that can be used to build and sustain competitive advantage (Tallman and Fladmoe-Lindquist 2002) and transform individuals that make them more valuable employees of the organization (Oddou and Mendenhall 1991; Osland 1995).

The motivation and ability of the repatriate to transfer the knowledge acquired in the international assignment combined with the ability and interest of the firm to learn and apply new information are keys to the transfer process. Without such transfer, the ability to build and sustain a competitive advantage is less realizable. Firms can do a number of things to increase the likelihood of knowledge transfer, including selecting the appropriate person to take the foreign work experience, training their managers to understand the personal challenges these individuals experience upon return, and creating organizational routines that will create a knowledge-sharing environment.

9 Leading Global Change

JOYCE S. OSLAND

There is no more delicate matter to take in hand, nor more dangerous to conduct, nor more doubtful in its success, than to be a leader in the introduction of changes. For he who innovates will have for enemies all those who are well off under the old order of things, and only lukewarm supporters in those who might be better off under the new.

(Machiavelli 1515)

We have to be willing to cannibalize what we're doing today in order to ensure our leadership in the future. It's counter to human nature, but you have to kill your business while it is still working.

(Lew Platt, former CEO of HP)

Leadership professor Jim Clawson believes that being a leader boils down to one's point of view, rather than one's title or status (2006: 4). In his opinion, the leadership point of view has three elements: "1) seeing what needs to be done; 2) understanding all the underlying forces at play in a situation; and 3) having the courage to initiate action to make things better" (Clawson 2006: 6). This chapter is all about making organizations better and making a difference, which fits with our definition of global leaders as change agents. One can readily argue that it is more difficult to see what needs to be done on a global level and understand all the underlying forces in a more complex setting. It's undoubtedly more problematic to successfully change the mindset and behavior of followers and partners who come from diverse cultural and organizational backgrounds. Global leaders face the arduous task of catalyzing and steering change efforts and aligning extremely large and far-flung multinational corporations. While leading and managing change is always challenging, no matter where it takes place, we make the assumption that it is more difficult in a global setting. That said, global leaders are in a position to have a broad impact with their ideas and to foster the agility, innovation, and rapid learning capacity crucial to business survival and success.

In this chapter, we'll talk about the universal aspects of managing change as well as the factors that seem particularly important in global change efforts. Since innovation and change go hand in hand, we will describe how global leaders can promote and lead innovation. To understand the context in which global change occurs, we'll begin by summarizing the cultural differences that influence change and innovation.

The Role of Culture in Change

Change interventions that work in one country do not always succeed elsewhere (Faucheux et al. 1982; Weick and Quinn 1999). To avoid failure, several cultural factors should be taken into consideration in global change efforts. Culture affects not only the predisposition to change but how change itself is viewed and implemented.

Cultures vary in their beliefs about how change occurs (Bartlett and Ghoshal 2000). When most European and Japanese companies want to make a change, they follow this process: 1) focus on changing the attitudes and mentalities of their key people; 2) modify the flow of communication and decision-making processes; and 3) consolidate the changes by realigning the structure to mirror the changes that have already occurred. U.S. companies, however, take a different approach based on different assumptions about change. They begin by modifying the organizational structures with the hope that a new structure will cause changes in interpersonal relationships and processes, leading eventually to changes in individual attitudes and mentalities. Bartlett and Ghoshal (2000) note, however, that these different national biases seem to be disappearing as global companies learn different approaches from one another.

There is limited research on cultural differences and global change. We can, however, infer from the research on culture the likely impact of certain cultural beliefs and values. Table 9.1 summarizes the cultural value dimensions that seem to influence predisposition to change.

Cultures vary in their level of comfort with change and whether they see change as basically positive or negative. Cultures who have a preference for order and who are high in uncertainty avoidance should be more likely to avoid change and the risks that it entails. High uncertainty avoidance cultures are less comfortable with ambiguity and risk (Hofstede 1980b). For this reason, it is helpful to clearly delineate the change process for them so they know what to expect at each stage. Members of cultures characterized by flexibility and low uncertainty avoidance, should be more open to change. Due to their history, some countries are more likely to develop these values and be more comfortable with change. For example, the historical origins of the U.S. made change an important cultural value. "In the Old World [Europe] respect came from a valuable heritage, and any change from that norm had to be justified. In America, however, the *status quo* was no more than the temporary product of past changes, and it was the resistance to change that demanded an explanation. A failure to change with the times was more than just a private misfortune; it was a socially and organizationally subversive condition. This attitude still persists in America, 'particularly in the corporate world'" (Bridges 1995: 20). This is not an unmixed blessing; it might explain, in part, why some U.S. firms go on to launch repeated change projects without first ensuring that previous projects are completely implemented. Countries are not prisoners of history or culture, and

Table 9.1 Cultural Dimensions Related to Change

More Disposed to Change	Less Disposed to Change
• Low uncertainty avoidance	• High uncertainty avoidance
• Flexibility	• Order
• Mastery	• Harmony
• Future-oriented	• Past-oriented
• Internal locus of control	• External locus of control
• Human nature as mutable	• Human nature as immutable

Factors that Influence Implementation

1 Human nature as trustworthy vs. untrustworthy
2 Low or high power distance
3 Importance of hierarchy
4 Communication styles
5 National history

attitudes toward change can evolve or radically transform, as seen in the rapid transformations occurring in Asia.

Kluckhohn and Strodtbeck (1961) categorized cultures according to their perspective on time as either past-, present-, or future-oriented. Future-oriented cultures are seen as being more open to both change and innovation because their focus lies on the need to adapt to what is coming next. We usually expect more resistance to change in cultures that value the past and tradition. Historical precedent receives more attention than innovations. In past-oriented cultures, managers are expected to be less proactive about making changes, and change processes may take more time (Osland 2004).

The same is true of cultures that believe people are at the mercy of uncontrollable forces rather than masters of their own destiny. Cultures whose members are characterized by external focus of control (also called outer-oriented) believe that other forces, such as fate or luck, control one's destiny (Rotter 1966; Hampden-Turner and Trompenaars 2000). Accordingly, we would expect them to be less likely to initiate change or be highly proactive in their strategy and planning efforts. Employees may not be held as personally accountable for accomplishing changes since this is not viewed as completely within their own control. In contrast, cultures whose members believe that people control their own destiny, internal locus of control (also called inner-oriented), tend to take matters into their own hands and are more likely to see themselves as change agents.

A culture's relationship with its environment can impact the target of change. Do they believe in mastering the environment or living in harmony with it (Kluckhohn and Strodtbeck 1961)? Cultures with a preference toward mastery are generally more dynamic, competitive, and likely to use technology to change the environment and accomplish their goals. They are more likely to dam rivers to obtain hydroelectric power than to refrain out of concerns about upsetting the delicate balance of nature by altering the river. The latter is more characteristic of cultures that value harmony with nature. Rather than changing the environment, they believe in understanding and working with it.

A culture's beliefs about human nature also impact the target of change efforts. Cultures see humans as either mutable (capable of change) or immutable (incapable of change) (Kluckhohn and Strodtbeck 1961). In cultures where human nature is viewed as immutable or unchanging, there may be less confidence that change projects involving new behaviors and mindsets are feasible. They are more likely to subscribe to the belief that "You can't teach an old (or even young) dog new tricks." By contrast, members of cultures who believe that human nature is mutable will likely put more faith in training and behavioral change.

A related view of human nature can affect the change implementation process. Kluckhohn and Strodtbeck (1961) differentiated between cultures that saw humans as basically good, mixed, or evil. We believe it is more helpful to characterize this dimension as trustworthy versus untrustworthy and associate it with the length of time needed to build trust in different cultures. In cultures where human nature is viewed as basically good, or trustworthy, trust in general comes more quickly. In cultures that believe human nature is basically evil, or untrustworthy, it takes longer to build trust. Since trust in leaders and change agents is essential in change projects, it seems logical that trusting cultures may be quicker to go along with change projects and assume the leader has the best interests of the organization in mind. In cultures that see humans as untrustworthy, we hypothesize that it will take longer to build trust and commitment to the change, unless the leader already enjoys the followers' trust.

Power distance is another cultural factor that can influence the change process. High power distance cultures accept that power is distributed unequally, whereas low power distance cultures believe in equality and a more even distribution of power (Hofstede 1980b). Power distance values can determine who is invited to the table to provide input and plan the change and who will lead the change. Will egalitarian values hold sway or will only those at the very top of the organization be involved in planning and leading change? Schwartz (1994) noted that in hierarchical cultures, the social fabric is maintained by a hierarchical structure of ascribed roles. Any change with the potential to disturb this hierarchy by changing the roles or the distribution of power could be viewed as threatening, provoking more resistance to change. Although resistance to change varies in terms of degree and cause, it is a natural reaction to change and part of the adaptation process.

Participation and equality and power sharing are among the core values of organization development (OD) consulting, which leads organizations through planned change. These values are congruent with low power distance, but not high power distance. In low power distance cultures, participation is generally the best way to allow employees to feel some sense of ownership of the change process and thereby reduce resistance to change. They can then see themselves as architects of the change rather than a victim. Employees from cultures characterized by high power distance, however, are more likely to expect leaders to make decisions without their input and are less satisfied when empowerment programs are put in place. Research found less satisfaction resulting from empowerment in high power distance Asian cultures than in low power distance Canada (Eylon and Au 1999) and again in high power distance India compared with the U.S., Poland, and Mexico (Robert et al. 2000).

Communication differences should also be considered in change projects. Style differences can prevent people from accurately perceiving, analyzing, and decoding intercultural communication. People in collectivist cultures are more likely to encounter situations in which there is a preference for high context, indirect, and self-effacing (modest) communication and silence (Ting-Toomey 1999). They show greater concern for saving face and not standing out from the group (e.g. the Japanese saying, "The nail that sticks up is hammered down"). In contrast, people in individualistic cultures are more likely to encounter situations characterized by a preference for low context, direct, and self-enhancing communication and talkativeness (Ting-Toomey 1999). These communication styles are defined in Table 9.2. One can readily imagine change-related situations in which global leaders would want to communicate their vision and receive

Table 9.2 Communication Style Differences

Low versus high context	Pertains to the extent to which language is used to communicate the message. **Low context:** relies on explicit verbal messages to convey intention or meaning. The onus lies on the speaker to send a clear, easily decoded message. (Examples: Germany, Switzerland, U.S.) **High context:** relies mostly on information contained in the physical context or internalized in the person. The onus lies on the listener to "read" meaning into the message. (Examples: Asia, Latin America.)
Direct versus indirect	Pertains to the extent to which language and tone of voice reveal or hide the speaker's intent. **Direct:** speakers specify their intentions in forthright statements. (Examples: Western cultures.) **Indirect:** speakers hide their meaning in nuances in their verbal statements. (Examples: Eastern and Middle Eastern cultures, most of Latin America.)
Self-effacing versus self-enhancing	Pertains to how one refers to one's effort or performance. **Self-effacing:** emphasizes the importance of humbling oneself via verbal restraints, hesitations, modest talk, and the use of self-deprecation. (Examples: Asian cultures.) **Self-enhancing:** emphasizes the importance of boasting about or drawing attention to one's accomplishments and abilities. (Examples: Arab, African-American.)
Silence	Pertains to the meaning of silence. **Silence conveys a message.** It can mean respect for someone of a higher status, careful consideration of the speaker's words, displeasure with a child's behavior, harmony, etc. (Examples: China, Japan, Korea.) **Silence has no meaning.** Therefore, it is usually filled with words. (Examples: Latin America, U.S.)

Source: Based on research by S. Ting-Toomey (1999) *Communicating across Cultures* (New York: Guilford).

input and feedback without running the risk of misunderstandings due to cultural communication problems.

Global leaders should also consider national history in change efforts. Countries that have sovereignty issues, for instance, can be particularly sensitive to changes imposed by a foreign headquarters. Hungary's political structure and state-owned companies exert a strong influence on views of change and its implementation, and one can expect special considerations in managing change in transition economies (Fehér and Szigeti 2001).

We have a few caveats about culture. There are still other cultural values, unique to a specific culture, that could influence change efforts. The value dimensions in Table 9.1 can provide us with the "first best guess" (Adler and Gunderson 2008) about the preferences and behavioral predispositions of another culture with regard to change; however, they will not allow you to predict behavior with total accuracy. These cultural values describe modal preferences, but there are many individual differences within cultures. Secondly, cultures are much more complex than these value dimensions convey; other factors can trump these values in specific contexts (Osland and Bird 2000). Thus, global change agents need to consider other factors and seek more information to have a full understanding. These cultural value dimensions should, however, be on a global leader's radar screen whenever organizational change is under discussion.

Is culture an insurmountable obstacle to change? No. It is possible to work around and leverage cultural beliefs and values. For example, you can empower employees to implement change in a high power distance culture when the change is tied to other values in the culture. Total Quality Management (TQM) was successfully implemented in Morocco because authority figures were used as role models and TQM was linked to Islamic values and norms (Gelfand et al. 2007). Without a deep knowledge of the culture, it would not have been possible to leverage them. In a Central American TQM project, the general manager absented himself from key problem-solving meetings so that senior managers would more openly share their opinions. Had he been present, they would have deferred to him unquestioningly. He was wise enough to realize that this modification was necessary in a high power distance culture (Osland 1996). While expert leaders understand and respect cultural constraints, they also know when and how to get around them. Percy Barnevik, former CEO of ABB, described this expertise in an interview:

> Global managers have exceptionally open minds. They respect how different countries do things, and they have the imagination to appreciate why they do them that way. But they are also incisive, they push the limits of the culture. Global managers don't passively accept it when someone says, "You can't do that in Italy or Spain because of the unions," or "You can't do that in Japan because of the Ministry of Finance." They sort through the debris of cultural excuses and find opportunities to innovate.
>
> (Champy and Nohria 1996: 67)

To do so, global leaders may have to adapt their own change-related behavior to match the cultural scripts used in different locations, find ways to leverage cultural differences, and contextualize the change in ways that are appropriate for different cultures. We will discuss contextualization later in the chapter.

Change Management

Change management, which is based on behavior science knowledge, is a concerted, planned effort to increase organizational effectiveness and health. It involves an intentional and structured transition to a desired end-state. Organizational change is usually categorized in terms of magnitude as either incremental or transformative. Incremental change (also known as first-order change) is linear, continuous, and targeted at fixing or modifying problems or procedures. Transformative change (also called second-order change or gamma change) modifies the fundamental structure, systems, orientation, and strategies of the organization (Burke and Litwin 1992). Transformative change is radical, generally multidimensional and multilevel, and involves discontinuous shifts in mental or organizational frameworks. To borrow Wilbur's (1983) analogy, whereas incremental change is analogous to rearranging the furniture in a room to make it more comfortable or functional, transformative change questions whether this is even the room or floor where we should be. Given the complexities of global organizations, Champy and Nohria (1996) contend that incrementalism is a luxury businesses can no longer afford; to avoid falling behind, they recommend radical change and moving ahead quickly.

Change Process Models

The process of change is often viewed in terms of unfreezing, moving, and refreezing (Lewin 1947). *Unfreezing* entails overcoming inertia and developing a new mindset. This stage is accompanied by stress, tension, and, once people's defense mechanisms have been breached, a strong felt need for change. In the *moving* stage, the change begins, which involves relinquishing old ways of behavior and testing out new behaviors, values, and attitudes that have usually been proposed by a respected source. As one would expect, this stage is characterized by confusion. *Refreezing* occurs when the new behavior is reinforced, internalized, and institutionalized or, to the contrary, rejected and abandoned. Whatever the outcome, this stage represents a sense of returned equilibrium.

In a study of multinational organizations, the framework was modified as follows: *incubation* (questioning the status quo), *variety generation* (middle-up experimentation) leading to *power shifts* (change in the leadership structure), and then the process of *refocusing* (Doz and Prahalad 1987). Ghoshal and Bartlett (1996) observed the following sequential and overlapping process—

simplification, integration, and regeneration—in successful large-scale strategic transformations at GE, ABB, Lufthansa, Motorola, and AT&T. Simplification involves a more laser-like change focus that clarified the strategy, such as GE's "being number one or two in the industry." In the integration phase, shared values and realigned cross-unit relationships bring people together. Jack Welch's focus on inter-unit collaboration and the sharing of best practices in GE is a good example of integration. In regeneration, the last phase, efforts are made to build an organization that is capable of renewing itself. This was the purpose of Welch's "boundarylessness" push at GE (Ghoshal and Bartlett 1996).

Kotter and Cohen (2002) provide a more detailed breakdown of the sequential stages in the change process used in successful change efforts:

1   Increase urgency—unfreezing occurs by demonstrating the need for change with undeniable evidence, something they can see, touch, and feel that touches their emotions.

2   Build the guiding team—a group powerful enough to guide the change is created and teambuilding is used to build a trusting, effective team.

3   Get the vision right—the guiding team creates a succinct, inspiring, moving, and appropriate vision for the future.

4   Communicate for buy-in—the change is communicated in ways that are simple and heartfelt and that take into consideration the feelings of those who will be affected.

5   Empower action—obstacles are removed from their path so that more people feel able to contribute their efforts to the change and are rewarded for doing so.

6   Create short-term wins—easy, visible, and early successes build momentum, lessening the likelihood of resistance and increasing the support of powerful players.

7   Don't let up—people make wave after wave of change, tackling ever more difficult challenges until the vision is realized.

8   Make change stick—change is institutionalized by the organizational culture, storytelling, promoting change heroes, socializing new recruits, and ensuring continuity.

One of the most important contributions of this model is Kotter and Cohen's (2002) finding that leaders have to include the emotional aspects of change to be successful. For example, building a rational business case for change is not enough. The feelings that block change require incontrovertible evidence that touches people's emotions and helps them feel the need for urgency.

Not everyone views change as an orderly progression, in part because they view the reality of change as more haphazard and dependent on luck and circumstance. Some describe change as a "strategic layering" process, in which firms continuously build capabilities in response to environmental demands (Evans and Doz 1989). Another school of thought views change as a spiral process. Management teams focus on a change initiative until it looks as if they might be going too far in that direction. Then, to avoid the pathologies that could result from the initial change effort, they switch their focus to something else (Evans et al. 2002). The top management team of a firm in the midst of decentralizing, for example, may switch its attention to integration mechanisms when decentralization begins causing too many coordination problems. When the integration mechanisms begin to look too cumbersome, they will spiral on to another focus.

Unlike change in a single location or operations in a single country, global change involves a broader range of action. This means that global leaders have to anticipate changes to a greater degree. The process of looking ahead to predict future needs and adjustments is called anticipatory sequencing (Evans and Doz 1989). The challenge of building the future into the present is daunting, as noted in the epitaph for a change agent, "How are you supposed to change the tires on a car when it's going 60 miles per hour?"

Another approach to global corporate change is contingent in nature (Pettigrew 2000), and acknowledges both local differences and the difficulty of balancing global/local tensions. Global firms need global standards and centralization around core aspects, but they also need local innovation and modifications and decentralization (Ghoshal and Bartlett 1999). Pettigrew (2000) contended that too many change efforts ignore local contextual issues and take a universalistic approach to change. Higgs and Rowland (2005) found limitations with the linear approach and support for the contingent approach. Based on a subsequent case study, they recommend that leaders build capability for the change in teams and individuals and establish networks that facilitate opportunities for learning and dialogue. In terms of leader behavior, it is more effective to "frame changes and articulate clearly the core principles and values underpinning the changes and to distinguish these 'hard rules' from areas in which local input and differentiation is feasible within the process of implementing strategy" (Higgs and Rowland 2009: 55).

Box 9.1 summarizes basic lessons about successful domestic and international organizational change.

Successful Global Change

Research conducted by Prosci with more than 1000 organizations from fifty-nine countries shows that people must achieve five building blocks in order for change to be realized successfully. These building blocks, known as the ADKAR Model, consist of these factors (Hiatt 2006):

Box 9.1 Common Lessons about Change

Leadership

- There has to be a vision for the change so that people have a purpose to believe in.
- Top management support for planned change, or at least benign neglect, is crucial.
- In addition to top management support, there needs to be a "critical mass"—the smallest number of people or groups who must be committed to a change for it to occur.
- Thoughtful management of resistance to change is the responsibility of change leaders.
- The more discretion managers have, the more changes they will make.
- Leaders have to be self-aware.
- Leaders have to be role models for the change.

Communication

- The end result of the change must be clearly communicated so people are willing to leave behind what they know for something new.
- It is almost impossible to "over-communicate" a change—people need to hear about it several times in a variety of mediums before the message is accurately received.

Trust

- Lasting change won't happen unless there is a sufficient level of trust within the organization.

Context

- Change almost always requires reexamining and rethinking the assumptions people hold about the environment, the way the organization functions, and their working relationships with other people. There is often a mourning period before people can let go of the way things used to be.
- Change requires new assumptions, attitudes, behaviors, and skills, which must eventually be institutionalized so the change can endure.
- Constant change is a source of stress for employees, so organizations have to balance both change and continuity.

Tactics

- Since tactics that work in one part of the organization cannot always be transferred successfully to another area, standardized change efforts may not be possible.

- Multiple interventions are necessary—one is seldom sufficient.
- People have to possess the skills required by the change, which may necessitate training.
- Evaluation and incentive systems have to support the change and reward the desired behaviors.
- Changing one element in a system will not work unless we bring all the other elements into alignment to support the change.

Implementation process

- Change is a process rather than an event or a managerial edict.
- A good idea is not enough—the change process has to be skillfully managed for implementation to be effective.
- The change process occurs in multiple steps that cannot be bypassed.
- While there are linear steps in planned change, implementation is seldom linear.
- Changes require a fertile context—an organizational culture with values and norms that complement the change and a climate of renewal and growth.
- Changes need time to take root.
- Change is hard to sustain; some innovations succeed initially but conditions eventually revert to their previous state.
- Change requires perseverance.
- There are costs associated with any change, and we can expect a predictable slump in performance before a successful change starts to show results.

Resistance

- Resistance is a natural response to change.
- Three common types of resistance are: blind, ideological, or political.
- Changes often upset the political system in organizations and come into conflict with the vested interests of people who prefer the status quo.
- Allowing people to participate in some aspect of the change process and educating them about the change are positive ways to reduce resistance.

Sources: A. Armenakis and A. G. Bedeian (1999) "Organizational change: A review of theory and research in the 1990s." *Journal of Management*, 25(3): 293–315; W.W. Burke (2002) "The organizational change leader." In M. Goldsmith, V. Govindarajan, B. Kaye, and A. Vicere (eds) *The Many Facets of Leadership* (Upper Saddle Creek, NJ: Financial Times Prentice Hall), pp. 83–97; T. C. Cummings and C. G. Worley (2004) *Organization Development and Change* (Cincinnati, OH: South-Western); T. Jick and M. Peiperl (2003) *Managing Change: Cases and Concepts* (Boston, MA: Irwin); and E. Lawson and C. Price (2003) "The psychology of change management." *The McKinsey Quarterly*, June Issue: 31–41.

1 Awareness—of why the change is needed.

2 Desire—to support and participate in the change.

3 Knowledge—of how to change.

4 Ability—to implement new skills and behaviors.

5 Reinforcement—to sustain the change.

There is very little empirical research on global change efforts. Therefore, the research findings in this chapter are supplemented with information from interviews and case studies of global leaders who are successful change agents. These sources indicate that the factors shown in Box 9.2 play an especially important role in global change or have special meaning in a global context (Osland 2004). Many of these are universal change lessons that are equally important in domestic settings.

Some of these factors are present in the following story of change efforts by Paolo Scaroni. Scaroni successfully turned around two firms, Pilkington (UK glassmaker) and Enel (Italian electric utility) before taking the CEO position at ENI, an Italian oil and gas company (Ghislanzoni 2006). When asked for his advice on leading change, his answer was to keep things simple and avoid complexity. At Pilkington, he built a community and integrated and centralized finance and purchasing. Scaroni dubbed this "Building One Pilkington" and repeated this message over and over. In another turnaround at Enel, he refocused around core competencies to avoid distraction and decrease the problems to a manageable number.

ENI was in good shape when Scaroni took over, but he believes that organizations can always be improved. His challenge was to foster growth and make changes in an organization that did not need to be turned around. The specific change he wanted to make was completing the integration process that would definitively signal ENI's transformation from a holding company.

Scaroni created a sense of urgency by setting stretch goals that were reinforced by mechanisms like bonuses and the compensation system. When the business environment is intensely competitive, this creates an inherent sense of urgency. In less competitive environments,

> the only thing you can do to create the appropriate sense of urgency is to benchmark yourself against others so you can see what others have been doing and where you should be doing better. Stretch targets are always a good way to get people to improve quickly.
>
> (Ghislanzoni 2006: 61–62)

Box 9.2 Key Factors in Global Change

- Leaders as catalysts
- Vision that is clear, motivating and linked to performance goals
- Change message that is easily grasped and repeated
- Building a community and generating trust
- Clear expectations and operationalization of the vision at all organizational levels
- Alignment of organizational design components to complement changes
- Use of teams to drive the change
- Accountability for results at all levels and for units and individuals
- Measurement and evaluation during the process
- High standards of performance
- Results-driven approach
- Reinforcement systems
- Persistence
- Creating a context for change by modifying the organizational culture and establishing vehicles for learning and participation
- Cultural contextualization of the change

Scaroni was asked whether he had employed a different leadership style at ENI than he had at Pilkington or Enel.

> Not really. I normally try to find three or four strategic concepts that sum up the direction in which the company should be moving, build up an organization that believes in these concepts and repeat, repeat, repeat them throughout the organization. I am convinced that communication is a very powerful tool for running very large organizations such as this one. It works fine if people know exactly where they are going, but in order to know this, they need to be able to grasp some easy concepts. If it takes more than one minute to explain a strategy, something is wrong. In my view, it has to be that simple. Successful things are simple; I have never seen successful things that are very complicated. You provide simple guidelines and then repeat them throughout the organization.
>
> (Ghislanzoni 2006: 59)

Scaroni's strategic goals involve changing both the mindset and behavior of thousands of employees. While this is the essence of global change, it is never an easy task. The next section describes in greater depth the factors that play a critical role in global change.

Leaders as Catalysts

Kotter (1990c) once stated that leadership, unlike management, is about coping with change. Leaders are catalysts, as we see in former BP CEO John Browne's description of how leaders can institutionalize breakthrough thinking:

> The top management team must stimulate the organization, not control it. Its role is to provide strategic directives, to encourage learning, and to make sure there are mechanisms for transferring the lessons. The role of leaders at all levels is to demonstrate to people that they are capable of achieving more than they think they can achieve and that they should never be satisfied with where they are now. To change behavior and unleash new ways of thinking, a leader sometimes has to say, "Stop, you're not allowed to do it the old way," and issue a challenge.
>
> (Prokesch 2000: 302–303)

Champy and Nohria (1996) claim that a leader must possess these personal traits to manage change:

- driven by a higher ambition

- able to maintain a deep sense of humility

- committed to a constant search for the truth

- able to tolerate ambiguity, uncertainty, and paradox

- personally responsible for the consequences of their actions

- highly disciplined in their everyday lives

- always authentic.

Most of these characteristics, such as humility, authenticity, inquisitiveness, and cognitive complexity, were identified in Chapter 3's global leadership competency lists. Global leaders have to live with ambiguity and paradox when making changes because the need to take quick action may preclude the luxury of extensive diagnoses. The results of major changes are seldom completely predictable. Discontinuous thinking and a global mindset help leaders come up with the right change goals and tactics at the right time. Good change agents know that they must first understand and then change peoples' mental maps in order to implement a change. This involves mindful communication and the ability to engender trust, which rest on authenticity. Finally, the articulation of a vision and the ability to communicate this vision are key competencies for global leaders, as seen in the following sections.

Creating the Right Vision

The capability that was most valued in a large study of global managers from eight countries was *the ability to articulate a tangible vision, values, and strategy* (Yeung and Ready 1995*)*. The other five capabilities they identified all contribute to successfully managing global change: *being a catalyst for strategic change, being results-oriented, empowering others to do their best, being a catalyst for cultural change,* and *exhibiting a strong customer orientation*. Closeness to the customer helps identify the right vision and promote a culture that is open to change. Larry Bossidy, former CEO of Honeywell and Allied Signal, said,

> I think that the closer you come to the customers, the more you appreciate the need to change. And the more inwardly focused you are, the less you understand that need. As we get more and more customer focused, we don't have to preach about the need to change. People know it.
>
> (Tichy and Charan 1995: 247–248)

Without a clear vision for global change, employees will not leave "the known for the unknown" and change their behavior. Stories from successful global CEOs reveal: 1) a clear vision for change that made sense to followers, 2) that they communicated over and over again, 3) accompanied by a blueprint for achieving the vision.

Selecting the right change target depends on the environmental scanning and creative abilities of the global leader and others in the organization. In some firms, the top management team or employee groups help with this function, even though leaders are ultimately responsible for ensuring that it takes place and is accurate. Senior management at Nokia assigns 5–15 themes of critical interest to the firm to cross-functional strategic planning teams, involving as many as 400 employees every six months (Gratton and Ghoshal 2005). The teams interview experts inside and outside Nokia and summarize their findings in reports called Strategy Road Maps. As with strategic planning, consensus is building that determining the vision for change should be a participative effort rather than the sole responsibility of one leader.

> Conditions associated with the global economy's new competitive landscape— shorter product life cycles, ever-accelerating rates and type of change, the explosion of data and the need to convert it to useable information—prevent single individuals from having all the insight necessary to chart a firm's direction… Insightful top managers recognize that it is impossible for them to have all of the answers, are willing to learn along with others, and understand that the uncertainty created by the global economy affects people at the top as well as those lower down in the organization.
>
> (Ireland and Hitt 2005: 65)

Change targets should be results driven (e.g. increase market share) rather than activity based (e.g. train 1000 employees in emotional intelligence). The change should be closely linked to business issues and performance so employees can readily see its relevance. Changes are more likely to succeed if they are in line with the organization's history and core values (except when those values are part of the problem and modifying the organizational culture is the change goal). Understanding the organization's culture also clarifies what should *not* be changed because it serves as the organizational glue or strongly relates to key success factors. Alan Lafley, former P&G CEO, stated that the company's purpose and values were not going to change, but strategy and execution would be improved—*"So I was very clear about what was safe and what wasn't"*(Gupta and Wendler 2005: 4).

One of the ways a single person can begin to influence a large organization is to envision a feasible and powerful future and paint a picture of that vision for others. Larry Bossidy is a proponent of the "burning platform" theory of change in which the leader is the catalyst. When an oil rig catches fire and the foreman orders the workers to jump into the ocean, they don't automatically obey. Fear of the ocean or sharks and so forth will hold them back until they see the flames actually burning the platform.

> The leader's job is to help everyone see that the platform is burning, whether the flames are apparent or not. The process of change begins when people decide to take the flames seriously and manage by fact, and that means a brutal understanding of reality. You need to find out what the reality is so that you know what needs changing. I traveled all over the company with the same message and the same charts, over and over. Here's what I think is good about us. Here's what I'm worried about. Here's what we have to do about it. And if we don't fix the cash problem, none of us is going to be around. You can keep it simple: we're spending more than we're taking in. If you do that at home, there will be a day of reckoning.
>
> (Tichy and Charan 1995: 247–248)

Bossidy increased the perceived need for change by highlighting the "creative tension" (Senge 1990) that results from perceiving the gap between the ideal situation (the organization's vision) and an honest appraisal of its current reality. By focusing attention on problems or opportunities and taking their change story to many groups of employees at all levels in the organization, global leaders can "turn up the heat" and create a sense of urgency.

As OD consultant Richard Beckhard stated:

> For change to be possible and for commitment to occur, there has to be enough dissatisfaction with the current state of affairs to mobilize energy toward change. There also has to be some fairly clear conception of what the state of affairs would be if and when the change was successful. Of course, a desired state needs to be consistent with the values and priorities of the client system. There also needs to be some client awareness of practical first steps or starting points toward the desired state.
>
> (Beckhard 1991: 664)

Communicating the Vision

Bossidy's earlier statement, "I traveled all over the company with the same message and the same charts, over and over" (Tichy and Charan 1995: 248) is typical of global leaders. To personally convince employees about the need to embrace the change, the message has to be consistent and repeated. Without consistency, the message is distorted as it is passed up and down hierarchies and across cultural borders, much like the children's game of "Telephone." Without repetition and the commitment demonstrated by leaders, employees "sit out" change efforts, assuming that this is just another in a long line of management fads that will pass when a new CEO is named or when the current top management team's attention is drawn to a more pressing issue. Sharing evidence and making a case for change that touches people's emotions to increase the level of dissatisfaction with the status quo, reiterating the perceived need for change, and painting a vivid picture of the desired end-state are essential parts of the unfreezing process.

The change message is communicated more effectively when it contains a simple metaphor or slogan that travels well across cultures. Even though P&G hires the smartest students from the best schools, Lafley says the need to communicate at a "Sesame Street level of simplicity" was one of his most significant lessons after becoming CEO (Gupta and Wendler 2005).

> So if I'd stopped at, "We're going to refocus on the company's core businesses," that wouldn't have been good enough. The core businesses are one, two, three, four. Fabric care, baby care, feminine care, and hair care. And then you get questions: "Well, I'm in home care. Is that a core business?" No. "What does it have to do to become a core business?" [industry global leader, best structural economics in industry, consistent growth rate, and cash flow return on investment] So then business leaders understand what it takes to become a core business.
>
> (Gupta and Wendler 2005: 3)

The simplicity and repetition is needed in part due to P&G's diversity and size— 100,000 people from over 100 cultures. But Lafley was also trying to "unclutter employee thinking" so they can stop, think, and internalize the strategy and go on to make their own decisions (Gupta and Wendler 2005: 3).

The following example of a bank transformation includes lessons about communicating the vision. Hired to improve a large European retail bank with 30,000 employees, the new CEO began by setting performance targets (Lawson and Price 2003). This was not sufficient for the change he had in mind. Unless the employees changed both the way they worked and their mindset, they would not be able to offer better customer service at a lower cost. The bank's culture had to be transformed from a bureaucracy to a "federation of entrepreneurs" who quickly solved customer problems.

The first step was to develop a convincing story to provide employees with a purpose to believe in. The CEO drafted his story and improved it with feedback from his executive directors. In turn, each of them created a version of the story for their area and delegated the responsibility for one aspect of the story to a team member, who developed a performance scorecard for each deliverable.

The story was then retold by the employees' immediate boss all the way down the hierarchy, giving emphasis to the relevant points for each different audience. In other words, how could each unit and employee provide better service with fewer costs? This process, called dialogue-based planning, was a series of sense-making efforts that involved several iterations, feedback on the stories, and both upward and downward communication flows. For example, employees reported that out-of-order document imagers frequently prevented them from making customer copies efficiently. These were replaced in each branch and that information was added to the story as an example of a change that helped both employees and customers. For the CEO, the secret to having employees believe and accept the story was to have it describe "how life could be better for all of the bank's stakeholders, not just investors and analysts" (Lawson and Price 2003: 37).

The tactics that come to mind for communicating a change may be limited to persuasive speeches, newsletters, and memos. However, change agents also influence and communicate change by (Armenakis, Feild and Harris 1999):

- encouraging the participation of those who will be impacted by the change in the process;

- supporting human resource management practices (hiring criteria, performance appraisal systems, compensation, employee development programs);

- giving importance to symbolic activities (rites and ceremonies, celebrations);

- instituting diffusion practices (best practice programs and transition teams);

- managing internal and external information; and

- instituting formal activities that demonstrate support for change initiatives (modified organizational structures and new job descriptions).

Corrado Passera, former CEO of Banca Intesa recommends using the press to communicate change successes in turnarounds of large organizations:

> Change will only be effective if people are really convinced that they are working for a successful business. Internal results undoubtedly matter, but even they won't count for much if everyone keeps reading in the newspapers

that the business is still a poor performer… People will not believe you unless you can change the organization's image in the media.

(Ghislanzoni and Shearn 2005: 77)

Building a Community

Charles Handy, noted British management thinker, predicts that companies in the future will not be property owned by shareholders but communities to which people belong. Rather than workers, employees will be citizens with rights and a share of the profits that they create (Handy 2001). While they may not go as far as Handy predicts, successful global leaders do indeed create communities. This theme is heard repeatedly in global leader interviews, witness Scaroni's slogan "Building One Pilkington" (Ghislanzoni 2006). Here's a similar mention of community building from a global leader, "I had to create one culture and one integrated organization…nearly every day I was meeting with parts of the organization, explaining what we wanted to achieve, giving feedback, listening to their concerns and doubts" (Higgs and Rowland 2009: 51). The leaders of large, multicultural, and geographically distant organizations have to bring the members of their heterogeneous groups together before they can act in concert. "A sense of community may be the 'glue' in global organizations that builds enough consistency to risk major changes and survive the unanticipated consequences inherent in change efforts" (Osland 2004: 134). Wellsfry (1993) found that building work communities in organizations led to innovation, action, and change in a dissertation on global leaders.

Community is borne out of shared values, shared language, trust, and a sense of belonging and identification. The trust that accompanies community building lays the groundwork for successful change. Employees seldom exert themselves for leaders they do not trust, which underscores the need for integrity and credibility. Trust is also an issue for the teams charged with carrying out change projects. One of the authors did a series of organizational change seminars in various countries that were attended by change teams from different firms. As facilitators, we readily observed that some teams were highly competitive and dysfunctional, while others operated like effective teams with a high level of trust. When we checked back informally on the teams' progress, we were not surprised to find that the changes directed by the dysfunctional teams were less successful. Their preoccupation with personal agendas and feuds translated into less energy to devote to their change project and less attention to the external forces that threatened their projects. Transformational change can be a difficult, even treacherous journey and is best undertaken with trustworthy companions in community.

The vision itself can contribute to building a community. When former CEO Sir Colin Marshall announced his vision that British Airways (BA) would be "the world's favorite airline," BA was actually ranked close to the bottom of the barrel.

Instead of laughing at this goal, his employees were motivated by it. Many people prefer working for successful rather than poorly performing organizations for the sake of their self-esteem and the opportunity to make positive contributions. Therefore, change targets, even bodacious ones like this, unleash employee motivation and can bring them together if the blueprint for change is clear and the process is carefully managed. Marshall wanted to signal a change in BA's culture from a sole focus on technology and airline safety to a customer focus. One of the interventions that helped them successfully make this transition was a two-day "Managing People First" session that focused on relationship building. About 150 people from various departments and locations were invited, which built community. Marshall demonstrated his commitment and perseverance by attending every one of these sessions.

> I spent two to three hours with each group. I talked with people about our goals, our thoughts for the future. I got people's input about what we needed to do to improve our services and operations. The whole thing proved to be a very useful and productive dialogue. We found it so valuable, in fact, that in cases when I was away, we offered people the opportunity to come back and have a follow-up session with me. So I really did talk to all 110 groups in that five-year period.
>
> (Burke 2002: 93)

When a sense of community is lacking in an organization, employees are less likely to make the effort or the necessary sacrifices to realize a vision. Even when people recognize the need for change, self-interest or inertia can prevail if there is no perception that this harms the community. Therefore, many successful changes incorporate community building, as shown in the following example of a "grassroots" change in which a global leader tried to bypass the bureaucracy and change the mindset and behavior of the frontline employees and work directly with them (Pascale 1999).

Steve Miller, group managing director of Royal Dutch/Shell Group of Companies, set up a "retailing boot camp" for 6–8 person teams at a time from six different operating companies throughout the world. After receiving training to identify and take advantage of market opportunities, the teams went home to apply their new skills. Sixty days later they returned to present their analyses and plans to the other teams and provide feedback to one another. They had another sixty days to perfect their business plans, which they then presented in a fishbowl session with Miller and his direct reports; the other teams observed so they could learn vicariously from each team's interchanges with senior management. In exchange for promised results, Miller and his staff approved their plans and made financial commitments to support them. The teams returned to the field to implement their plans and returned in two months for a follow-up session in which they analyzed and learned from what succeeded or failed. Thus, this was a plan to empower, challenge, provide resources, and hold frontline people accountable (Pascale 1998).

One result was US$300 million worth of audited results to Shell's bottom line. Another outcome was that the corporate culture became more participative and innovative. The third consequence was community building for the grassroots teams, senior management, and, by extension, their individual networks. Shell had never before taken mid-level employees and exposed them to employees from different countries or to senior management. As Miller stated:

> The whole process creates complete transparency between the people at the coal face [Shell's term for its frontline activities in the worldwide oil products business] and me and my top management team. At the end, these folks go back home and say, "I just cut a deal with the managing director and his team to do these things." It creates a personal connection, and it changes how we talk with each other and how we work with each other. After that, I can call up those folks anywhere in the world and talk in a very direct way because of this personal connectedness. It has completely changed the dynamics of our operations.
>
> (Pascale 1998: 110)

Operationalizing the Change

Percy Barnevik, former ABB CEO, and his team spent 200 days a year communicating their vision and message and helping units figure out what the vision meant in terms of their own work (Ghoshal and Bartlett 1996). This is called operationalizing the vision. Not only does it set clear expectations for each employee and unit, it also helps align the organization and symbolizes the leader's commitment to change. A vision without a blueprint for change simply frustrates employees.

Organizational Alignment

Sometimes the change goal or target is to better align the organization. Much of Scaroni's integration efforts at ENI were directed at internal alignment. Even when the change target has an external focus (e.g. market share, new strategic direction), however, organization design components have to be aligned. For example, a new strategy usually requires concurrent, complementary changes in policies, employee skills, staffing, systems, cultural norms, and structure (Pascale and Athos 1981). Organizations are interdependent systems; changing only one component can result in the systemic resistance that occurs when other components of the organization block the change. For instance, if employees do not possess the skills to use a new IT tool and these skills are not evaluated in the performance management system, implementation will fail. The compensation mechanisms that reinforce new ways of thinking and behaving demanded by a change should simultaneously reward personal results, group results, short-term results, and long-term results (Ghislanzoni and Shearn 2005). Ensuring the "fit" among components is a key aspect of institutionalizing change. In a study of 500 of the largest

European firms, there were significant performance benefits only in the firms that changed structures, processes, and boundaries simultaneously (Whittington et al. 1998). The firms that changed only structures and boundaries but failed to make their processes complementary not only failed to improve their performance—they were worse off *after* the change!

Given the rapidly changing environment, global leaders have to expect to carry out ongoing alignment. Organizational evolution usually consists of periods of incremental change punctuated by discontinuous or revolutionary change. Thus, global leaders and managers face the paradoxical demands of "increasing the alignment or fit among strategy, structure, culture, and processes, while simultaneously preparing for the inevitable revolutions required by discontinuous environmental change" (Tushman and O'Reilly 1996: 11). In addition to paying attention to the future, this entails a willingness to tear apart what has just been painstakingly cobbled together. As we saw in Lew Platt's quotation in the beginning of the chapter: "We have to be willing to cannibalize what we're doing today in order to ensure our leadership in the future" (Evans et al. 2002: 423). While alignment is a necessity for institutionalizing change, it can also be a barrier to future change if leaders are not willing to cannibalize it. In this sense, alignment can be viewed as a double-edged sword.

Measurement

Following the truism that "people do only what is measured," successful global change projects have a clear, understandable focus that can be measured. Changes should be monitored with a reasonable number (three to five) of carefully thought out metrics. The use of metrics like the Balanced Scorecard allows Multinational Corporations (MNCs) to target critical success factors and hold employees accountable for achieving them. Recommended general metrics measure the most important performance and health indicators, such as:

- financial performance

- operations (quality and consistency of key value-creation processes)

- organizational issues (depth of talent, ability to motivate and retain employees)

- state of product market and position (quality of customer relationships)

- the nature or relationships with external parties, such as suppliers, regulators, and non-governmental organizations (Dobbs et al. 2005: 67).

Leaders should remember to include several types of measures: performance measures, evaluation of the change itself, and systemic measures of the long-term health of the organization. The concern for organizational health implies a longer time horizon that lays the groundwork for the future (Dobbs et al. 2005). Review processes that are carefully monitored also allow global leaders to keep tabs on the progress of change in far-flung MNCs.

Taking a long-term view of change is important since some changes that are successful in the short run may eventually revert back to the status quo; other changes look like failures in the short term only to prove successful years later. Thus, "when" a change is measured makes a notable difference.

Change Tactics and Contextualization

Accounts of global change produce seven general guidelines:

1 Begin with the basics of planned change.

2 Know your company well enough to understand which interventions and tactics will be most effective.

3 Understand when solutions and interventions have to be universal (global or corporate-wide) or particularistic (local).

4 Contextualize training and tactics when made necessary by cultural differences.

5 Modify mindsets and abilities via training that is culturally appropriate.

6 Establish specific, measurable goals.

7 Provide rewards and incentives for change.

Goss, Pascale and Athos (1996), consultants who specialize in helping firms make the changes they will need for the future, have this specific advice for staying out ahead:

1 *Assemble a critical mass of key stakeholders.*

2 *Conduct an organizational audit* to identify assumptions, influential functional units, key systems that drive the business, core competencies or skills, shared values, and idiosyncrasies.

3 *Create urgency and discuss the undiscussable* so employees are motivated to question basic assumptions.

4 *Harness contention* to jumpstart the creative process.

5   *Engineer organizational breakdowns*, like setting impossible deadlines, so organizational problems become visible.

Such general tactics are very constructive, but they have to be adapted to fit the conditions and history of the specific organization. ABB's philosophy on global change, shown below, represents the lessons learned from their own experience with cross-border mergers. Other companies have learned different lessons or operate in different conditions.

1   Immediately reorganize operations into profit centers with well-defined budgets, strict performance targets, and clear lines of authority and accountability.

2   Identify a core group of change agents from local management, give small teams responsibility for championing high-priority programs, and closely monitor results.

3   Transfer ABB expertise from around the world to support the change process without interfering with it or running it directly.

4   Keep standards high and demand quick results (Barnevik in Champy and Nohria 1996: 81).

One of the challenges of global change is that not all solutions and interventions are effective throughout a firm's global operations. The vision cannot be operationalized the same way given local differences that are influenced by culture, history, and local business practices. No matter how well-designed corporate-wide solutions and interventions are, they may require some type of contextualization—modification to fit the local context. This is one of the major lessons about global change. Those who know the local people and culture best need the autonomy and discretion to tailor the change effort so it is appropriate. In the European bank transformation example, each boss developed his or her own story to communicate and operationalize the vision.

Training is a common change tactic because changes require a different mindset, new skills, or new ways of working. Broad-scale training programs signal a deep commitment to the change by the company and send a strong symbolic message to employees.

> However, training programs in global firms have to be contextualized to ensure their relevance and acceptability to different cultures. For this reason, training designs should include room for learning to go in more than one direction. Global change and training are more than the transmission of knowledge from an expert source to a non-expert receiver. Instead, global change is a matter of knowledge creation among different communities; it involves mutual learning.
> (Tenkasi and Mohrman 1999)

Global firms benefit most when training sessions produce general lessons, recommendations for the rest of the company, and shared knowledge about necessary local adaptations.

Creating a Context for Change

Organizational scholars have long accepted Ashby's (1956) concept of requisite variety, which states that organizations have to be as complex as their environments. This is one of the arguments for the development of a global mindset in the workforce. The complexity of employee views in a global firm should equal the complexity of the global environment. Heterogeneous, complex perspectives help firms to perceive opportunities, problems, and solutions that a homogeneous mindset cannot see. In addition, the innovation and creativity so central to many successful change efforts is stifled when employees cannot contribute their diverse views.

The social architecture aspect of a global leader's role involves building an organizational culture with these characteristics that set the stage for change (Osland 2004):

- entrepreneurship—to foster initiatives and a concern for performance;

- diversity—to attract and retain employees of all types so different views can be heard;

- learning and innovation—to promote renewal and growth and ward off stagnation and obsolescence;

- participation—so diverse views can be heard and employees can express their ideas and feel a sense of ownership;

- trust—so employees believe in the wisdom and fairness of their leaders and colleagues;

- collaboration—so that employees are willing to contribute their efforts to the change effort.

Honda is an example of a firm that successfully created a context for change through its organizational culture and *waigaya* sessions.

> Contrary to what many Westerners might think about the importance of consensus in Japanese culture, institutionalized conflict is an integral part of Japanese management. At Honda, any employee, however junior, can call for a waigaya session. The rules are that people lay their cards on the table and speak directly about problems. Nothing is out of bounds, from supervisory

deficiencies on the factory floor to perceived lack of support of a design team. Waigaya legitimizes tension so that learning can take place.

(Goss et al. 1996: 107–108)

Organizational cultures that value learning are more open to change and innovation. If companies are actively learning, the need for change becomes obvious. As BP CEO John Browne stated,

Learning is at the heart of a company's ability to adapt to a rapidly changing environment. It is the key to being able both to identify opportunities that others might not see and to exploit those opportunities rapidly and fully.

(Dess and Picken 2000: 31)

Taking the time to learn what will be successful before leaping to a global implementation plan is another way to benefit from a learning orientation. Action learning, which brings together diverse global teams to study specific issues and make recommendations, is a practice of learning organizations (Dotlich and Noel 1998), as well as a component of global leadership training programs. The Nokia teams that produce Strategy Road Maps are a good example of action learning.

Innovation

Global change and learning organizations are closely tied to innovation. We have mentioned previously the challenge global leaders face in building organizations that simultaneously manage the present and create the future. In large part, innovation is the solution. Innovation, which is defined as the implementation of new ideas at the individual, group, or organizational level, is closely linked to organizational survival in the global economy. At a 2006 leadership forum, then IBM CEO Samuel Palmisano commented: "The way you will thrive in this environment is by innovating—innovating in technologies, innovating in strategies, innovating in business models." In IBM's survey of CEOs and government leaders, innovation, particularly with respect to new business models, was a major topic of interest and an area that requires personal leadership.

With product innovation, if you stand up on your soapbox and you cheer a little bit, that will certainly help. But the reason I think that the CEOs have to lead this is because, fundamentally, the biggest breakthroughs are a result of changing the business model and the processes and the culture.… Go back even 10 years ago. Was it natural for IBM to go collaborate around the future of innovation or the future of our technologies? … Was it natural for IBM to join into the open-source community to talk about standards around lots of technologies? These weren't natural things to occur. …If the CEO doesn't give people permission to go change behavior and to collaborate, then it's not going to happen. Everybody is looking for the signal. They want to know whether things are really changing fundamentally.

(Palmisano in Hamm 2006)

In addition to signaling that innovations have to be taken seriously, leaders create the architecture needed to foster innovation, follow up on innovations, and repeatedly communicate their importance and publicize successes and failures (Loewe and Dominquini 2006). While leaders play a crucial role in innovation, they are never the sole reason why some companies are more innovative than others.

Boston Consulting, at the behest of *BusinessWeek*, surveyed 1070 executives and asked them to name the most innovative companies in the world outside their own industry (*Businessweek Online* 2006). Five common themes emerged as lessons from the nominated firms: 1) opening the doors of R&D labs to work with customers, suppliers, and expert networks, 2) leadership from the top to drive and protect innovation, 3) using a variety of innovation metrics, 4) redesigning the organization to foster coordination and collaboration, and 5) customer insight, based on a close connection with customers and techniques that get at how customers think.

Innovation paid off financially for the Thompson Reuters 2011 Top 100 Global Innovator companies (PRNewswire 2011). They added 400,000 new jobs in 2010 and their average revenue outperformed the S&P 500 by 5.7 percent. Forty percent are U.S. firms, 31 percent are Asian, and 29 percent are European.

Despite the proven worth of innovation, research shows that, according to employee evaluation, most companies are not good at innovation (Loewe and Dominiquini 2006). Only 85 percent of new ideas ever get to market, and 50–70 percent of those that do are failures (Booz Allen and Hamilton 1982; Cooper 2001; Tucker 2002). "While operating around the world may help companies generate ideas for innovations, the complexity of the global network is likely to render the evaluation and optimal exploitation of innovation ever more difficult" (Koudal and Coleman 2005: 22). To increase global markets and reduce costs, organization functions, including R&D, are geographically dispersed to an unprecedented degree. Thus, it's no wonder that the ability to coordinate innovation across complex global operations was identified as the key success factor in a study of 650 firms (Koudal and Coleman 2005). Additionally, those firms that invested heavily in innovation infrastructure showed profits up to 70 percent higher than those who did not. They put their money into 1) product development capabilities; 2) supply chain process infrastructure like flexible manufacturing, design quality, and the use of common platforms; 3) sophisticated information systems used to synchronize and support innovations across the value chain; and 4) into closer collaboration with customers and suppliers (Koudal and Coleman 2005). Mondi, a European paper and packaging firm, is an example of investing in technology to support innovation. The firm has a web-based "Innovation Zone" where employees contribute ideas that others build upon and improve (Koudal and Coleman 2005).

Best Buy took an innovative approach to learning about customer insight. Innovation teams generated hundreds of new ideas by observing the behavior of consumers in their normal habitat. Instead of focusing solely on their typical customer—young male "techies"—employees went to observe the American Girl Store in Chicago to understand what draws girls and their mothers to this destination retail store. They also went to Amish country and to poor barrios in Mexico City to comprehend the frustrations of less technologically proficient people (Loewe and Dominiquini 2006: 26).

Innovation cannot be limited to employees who work in R&D or product development. It's an expectation of all employees, as shown in Whirlpool's logo: "Innovation from everyone everywhere." Truly innovative firms make a concerted effort to hire creative personalities. Lotus Development was an extremely successful start-up founded in 1982 to market Lotus 1-2-3. When the firm hit 1000 employees, they started hiring primarily outside MBAs from *Fortune 500* companies who transplanted the management techniques appropriate for routine work in big firms. Subsequently, Lotus had difficulty developing and marketing new products. Mitchell Kapor, chairman of the board and former CEO, and Freada Klein, head of organizational development and training, put to the test one of their own hypotheses for the diminished creativity. They tested it by carrying out an experiment. They took the résumés of the first forty people hired at Lotus, changed the names on the résumés and put them into the current applicant pool. None of these "applicants" even made it to the interview stage because their backgrounds had too many "wacko and risky things." Instead of linear business careers, they had eclectic experiences like community organization, transcendental meditation teaching, and clinical psychology. To Kapor and Klein, this was evidence that Lotus was systematically weeding out applicants like the creative people who were responsible for the firm's only hit product (Sutton 2001: 8).

Getting creative people through the door and hiring them is only the first step. Research has identified a long list of organizational conditions, shown in Table 9.3, that either enhance or repress individual creativity in organizations. They can be categorized as designing complex jobs, rewarding creativity, adopting a managerial style that fosters creativity, creating an organizational culture, and developing a structure that promotes collaboration, interaction, trust, and unleashes creativity. It has to be easy for employees to present their ideas and get a hearing for them without fighting bureaucratic requirements. John Chambers, Cisco CEO, has birthday breakfasts with employees that give him an opportunity to get feedback and hear ideas (Shalley and Gilson 2004). The organizational culture has to reward risk and refrain from punishing people for errors. Associated Enterprises celebrated mistakes by bestowing an award, the "screw-up of the week," accompanied by an ugly statue that traveled around the office. Thomas Edison once said, "I make more mistakes than anyone else I know, and sooner or later, I patent most of them." Google, definitely an example of a culture that rewards creativity, allows employees to spend 20 percent of their work week developing their own ideas.

Table 9.3 Contextual Effects on Creativity

Creativity Enhancers	*Creativity Killers*
Focus on intrinsic motivation	Excessive focus on extrinsic motivation
Creativity goals	Limits set by superiors
Developmental feedback	Critical evaluation
Supportive supervision	Close, controlling supervision
Healthy competition	Competition in a win-lose situation
Participative decision making	Control of decision making
Hire creative individuals	Control of information
Enriched, complex jobs	Time pressure
Provision of necessary resources, particularly time	Political problems
Clear organizational goals	Emphasis on the status quo
Instructions to employees to be creative	
Recognition and rewards for creativity	
Encourage risk taking	
No punishment for failure	
Autonomy	
Productivity	
Workforce diversity	
Opportunities for internal and external interaction	
Diverse teams skilled at working together	
Supportive climate	
Organizational culture that promotes innovation	
Flexible, flat structures	
Close interaction and relationships with customers	

Source: J. S. Osland, D. Kolb, I. Rubin, and M. Turner (2006) *Organizational Behavior: An Experiential Approach,* p. 325. (©2006. Printed and electronically reproduced by permission of Pearson Education, Inc., Upper Saddle River, NJ.)

The SAS Institute in North Carolina, the world's largest privately held software company, is a good example of a company that manages creativity and innovation well (Florida and Goodnight 2005). SAS has 10,000 employees and 40,000 customer sites worldwide. The company sells its services in an innovative fashion via subscriptions. Since 98 percent of the subscriptions are renewed, their income is steadier and more predictable. So is their workforce. Their turnover rate is only 3–5 percent in an industry that averages 20 percent; they figure this saves them US$85 million annually in recruitment and replacement costs. Their revenues grow annually. CEO Jim Goodnight credits SAS's success and creativity to three guiding principles (Florida and Goodnight 2005).

1. Help employees do their best work by keeping them intellectually engaged and by removing distractions.

According to an *Information Week* survey, IT workers are motivated more by challenging jobs than by salary and financial incentives. SAS keeps its employees stimulated via training, employee white papers on new technologies, a constant stream of new products, and internal R&D expos where technical staff educate nontechnical staff about new products.

SAS asks workers each year what non-work tasks distract them from their work. Their answers guided the establishment of in-house medical facilities for workers and their families, a day care center and a cafeteria where kids can eat lunch with their parents, workout facilities, and a Work-Life Department that helps workers' children make the right college choice and finds home health care for workers' elderly parents. Dry cleaning, massage, haircut, and auto-detailing services are also available on site at a discount. SAS believes these programs, plus flexible work hours that allow employees to meet their family needs, pay off in higher employee retention and productivity.

The company keeps bureaucratic requirements to a minimum and understands that creativity requires downtime. An SAS proverb is: "After eight hours, you're probably just adding bugs (errors)." SAS believes that creative capital is built by long-term relationships among developers, support staff, salespeople, and customers. Therefore, they focus on careful selection and retention. Their hiring decisions, which can take months to make, are designed to ensure that prospective employees fit the culture. All employees receive the same benefits package, and no jobs are outsourced. "SAS recognizes that 95 percent of its assets drive out the front gate every evening. Leaders consider it their job to bring them back the next morning" (Florida and Goodnight 2005: 127). Goodnight claims that they "hire hard, manage open, and fire hard." Employees are not terminated when they make errors but for failing to meet performance standards after receiving a second chance with a corrective action plan.

2. Make managers responsible for sparking creativity and eliminate arbitrary distinctions between "suits" (managers) and "creatives" (employees doing creative work).

All SAS managers do hands-on work in addition to managerial responsibilities. Even the CEO still writes code to send a symbolic message that everyone in the firm is a creative, despite their job assignment, on the same team working toward the same goal. The manager's role is to stimulate creativity by asking good questions, convening groups to exchange ideas, removing obstacles, and getting employees what they need to accomplish their work.

3. Engage customers as creative partners to enable the company to deliver superior products.

Because SAS is privately held, they track customer satisfaction and opinions, rather than stock prices, which then guide the 26 percent of their budget devoted to R&D. SAS surveys customers annually on desired new features and stores customer complaints and suggestions in a database. This information is fed into product design and updates. At user conferences, SAS aims for creative interchanges.

> SAS may be the only company that prints the names of its software developers in product manuals. Customers can—and do—call them up. And because employee loyalty is so high, the developers actually answer the phone: they haven't moved down the road to start-up number seven.
>
> (Florida and Goodnight 2005: 131)

SAS aims to build mutual loyalty in customers by releasing products only when they are bug-free.

SAS takes an integrative approach by aligning all the puzzle pieces that culminate in innovation—hiring and retaining creative employees, creating a culture designed especially for creatives, fostering a managerial style that catalyzes and enables creativity, partnering with customers, building long-term relationships, and investing heavily and consistently in innovation infrastructure.

Conclusion

The research on global change leadership is more anecdotal than empirical and therefore warrants further study. The role of global leaders in innovation has received less attention than domestic leaders, although much more is known about innovation from a strategic and product development point of view. Our message in this chapter is that global leaders are especially skilled at catalyzing and managing global change and designing innovative organizations. They practice many of the universal lessons about change management, while placing more emphasis on the following areas. Although we have not repeated the lessons of Chapter 7, "Leading Global Teams," global leaders rely heavily on teams to carry out their vision. From accounts of successful global change agents, they also rely on inspiring visions that have to be carefully crafted to cross cultural and organizational boundaries without losing their meaning. Perhaps the most surprising finding is how much time and travel global leaders devote to communicating the vision and working with employees at various levels to operationalize the vision and clarify what that means for themselves and their work unit. This signifies a great deal of persistence and commitment. Furthermore, their efforts in this regard also generate trust and build the community that lays the groundwork for change.

The organizational architecture identified as a competency of global leaders in Chapter 3 is very evident in both global change and innovation. Global leaders align the various organizational components to support changes and then take the puzzle apart and realign them yet again to anticipate future needs. They build organizational cultures that support change and innovation and create a context for change so that it is not an uphill battle and so that the need for change becomes self-evident to many employees. The size and complexity of global organizations makes architectural design and modification a challenging task. Thorough alignment also requires persistence.

Global leaders take cultural differences and local history and conditions into consideration when planning and implementing change. Rather than allow cultural difference to be an obstacle, they leverage cultural values that support the desired change. Implementation plans, and training in particular, are contextualized so they are appropriate for the local context.

To be effective change agents, global leaders require knowledge related to future trends and knowledge about change management and innovation, the impact of culture, and a deep understanding of the organization. Change agents and leaders also need self-knowledge in the form of self-awareness. A leader's vision comes from reflection on the tasks they find most engaging and what they see as their purpose in life. There is a truism that it is impossible to change an organization without changing oneself in the process. This is captured best by an African proverb:

> When I was a young man, I thought I would change the world.
> When I was middle-aged, I thought I would change my village.
> Now that I am an old man, I think I will change myself.

10 Global Leadership Development

GARY R. ODDOU AND MARK E. MENDENHALL

The nature of competition and the forces of innovation shift the frontiers of science, business and technology at a rate we've never seen before, which is why expertise is not static. To be competitive, any individual—like any company, community or country—has to adapt continuously, learning new fields and new skills …We need a workforce model that recognizes this shift. As always, the really hard part is culture and mindset.

(Sam Palmisano, IBM chairman, president and chief executive officer, 2007)

In 2008 IBM launched a company-wide initiative to completely change its cultural DNA. The goal? To become a truly "globally integrated enterprise." White and Rosamilia (2010) noted that IBM had "seen massive shifts in where revenue is generated, spurring the need to grow leaders with global mindsets wherever they are located" (p. 2). This realization led to a new cultural initiative where all IBMers had to play a part, and thus all needed to develop "a global mindset with common corporate values as the glue" (p. 2).

As a result, an essential component of IBM's change strategy involves the mission critical element of developing global leaders and increasing intercultural competence in all IBM employees (White and Rosamilia 2010).

We will return to IBM's strategy for accomplishing this lofty goal later in this chapter. IBM is not the first company to recognize that in order to compete in the age of globalization it needs executives, managers, and employees who possess global skills commensurate to the demands of their job descriptions. This need became clear to some firms as early as the 1990s.

Almost two decades ago, Alcatel, a French telecommunications giant and competitor of IBM's, went on a merger and buying spree probably never before seen. In a very short time, not only did it have its 200 operations in France but it had acquired over 700 subsidiaries in the rest of the world in well over thirty different countries. These mergers with, and acquisitions of, foreign operations created significant management challenges for Alcatel. The telecommunications giant was struggling with the immediate issues of standardization versus localization. It needed to build a common corporate culture yet allow decentralization as appropriate. It needed to understand how to manage foreign units that wanted greater independence yet also encourage cross-unit collaboration in order to leverage experience economies among its vast domestic and foreign operations. To manage such an operation, Alcatel needed a new management mentality, one that would reflect a keener understanding of countries—their cultures, politics, economics; of the individual operations they acquired— their history, their organizational cultures, their distinctive competencies; of management and organizational principles—balancing the needs of local independence with system interdependence.

The biggest, single, long-term challenge Alcatel had to deal with over that next decade—and the one many more firms are struggling with today—was how to identify, select, and develop its managers to make sure they had the right mentality to manage this complex organization in an ever-increasing dynamic and competitive world. In Alcatel's case, the need to identify and develop a new breed of leaders was motivated as a result of its acquisitions, but it was also reacting to movements of deregulation, greater global competition, privatization of industries in France, and pan-European markets. Many firms today face the same issues, not because their current leadership has implemented a strategic plan but simply as a result of the environmental changes that are in constant flux, making the world, as IBM's Palmisano stated in the opening quote, an almost impossible place to predict. New markets, changing governments, fluctuating economies, growing regulations, new competitors, more complex capital sourcing, changing population patterns, disrupted cargo routes, and many other things have created a landscape that is ever changing and increasingly complex to understand. No one person can manage it. No single country mindset can understand it.

Alcatel realized it needed to develop global leaders in the early 1990s. IBM realized it needed to develop global leaders in 2007. Should not all large firms with worldwide operations have realized this with the onset of globalization years ago? What seems to occur is that top management teams come upon the realization for the need for global leadership development (GLD) at different times, and perhaps for different reasons; what is clear, though, is that since the later 1980s, the trend toward trying to meet the challenges of globalization has been unchanging.

In 1997 Black et al. studied Fortune 500 companies and concluded that 85 percent said they did not have adequate numbers of capable global leaders. Further, of those few "global leaders" they *did* have, only about 30 percent of them were rated as having the necessary competencies to really be effective. Very significantly, the human resource directors of these firms in the survey rated "having effective global leaders" as the number one priority of their firms. Mendenhall et al. (2003) found similar conditions extant in large global firms across industries. In a more recent study by Development Dimensions International (2008) that encompassed thirty-five industry sectors, with HR professionals and leaders from seventy-six countries, they found that although 75 percent of executives surveyed identified improving or leveraging global talent as a top business priority, only 50 percent of the organizations had a process to identify high-potential leaders and only 39 percent had a program to accelerate their development.

Unlike IBM and others, most organizations clearly are lagging in the implementation of programs and policies to identify and develop their future global leaders. However, it is not just medium and large organizations with foreign markets that need global leaders at the helm. Even the smallest of businesses need to be aware of the global business arena. A restaurant that gets it shrimp from South America needs to understand the issues related to sourcing from foreign countries and have alternate plans in case tariffs close off its sources of shrimp or changing global climate patterns alter the sea temperature in that part of the world and lessen the availability of shrimp, thereby increasing the cost or requiring searching for another source. In the surfboard industry, Clark Foam, a very small firm, was the clear majority supplier of surfboard blanks to surfboard manufacturers worldwide. In 2006, it closed its doors almost overnight. Other users of surfboard blanks were caught totally unprepared. At the retail level surfboard prices almost doubled overnight (and have never come down with the increase in supply). Had they understood the dynamics of today's volatile marketplace, surfboard manufacturers, from one-person operations to larger-scale manufacturers, would have already been sourcing from foreign suppliers as well. Indeed, almost all of the new suppliers came from foreign countries. Without an understanding of global sourcing, even small firms or seemingly insignificant industries will not be able to operate most efficiently or profitably.

In this chapter we will, however, focus on the development of global leaders in larger firms, including general leadership methods that apply to GLD and conceptual issues that underlie effective GLD, and provide two examples of very different GLD practices and how they each can positively affect GLD.

GLD Methods

Firms' general approaches to developing global leaders has usually involved altering existing traditional leadership development approaches to try to incorporate a global perspective in their managerial cadres. From a review of the literature and of current company *traditional* leadership development programs benchmarked against best practices, the following appear to be the most common components (Day and Halpin 2001):

- 360 degree feedback

- executive coaching

- job assignments

- mentoring

- networking

- reflection

- action learning

- outdoor experiences.

For many firms, all of these are still part of their approach to developing leaders who operate in multiple markets and/or simply across country boundaries in one capacity or another. If modified appropriately, such methods can become an important part of GLD. Adapting what used to be general leadership methods requires a change of mindset, though. For example, mentoring is more effective if a less experienced manager is being guided by someone with significant learning accrued from global business experience rather than by someone who has risen through the organization when global markets were not really necessary for adequate profit.

Executive coaching will be more effective if the coach has had international work experience as well and can relate the issues the manager might be struggling with to the context of global business and the competencies needed to be effective. Action learning projects need to involve members of the firm from different countries, such as with global teams tasked to analyze global operations of the firm or some other relevant issue. Reflection needs, in part, to be based on survey instruments that are specifically designed to indicate one's intercultural competencies as well as one's cultural profile as it compares and contrasts to other cultures with which one works. Job assignments need to include international ones, where the manager is exposed to cultural and business differences and also has the opportunity to develop global networks of people. Outdoor, experiential exercises are best done with international team members.

One of the primary challenges will be whether firms can appropriately modify their general leadership development programs to address the peculiar requirements of GLD.

In addition to understanding the complexity inherent in global leadership situations and how that can affect leadership development, it's also important to see the commonalities, across the different global leadership models that have been proposed. Most or all of the models extol the importance of the individual's personal competencies (e.g. tolerance of ambiguity, integrity, maturity, etc.), with particular emphasis on their desire to continually learn, and all of them emphasize the importance of being able to effectively develop and manage relationships. Additionally, the importance of business experience and acumen is underscored by each of them, representing a tripartite dimensionality that the global leadership program design must address.

The previous discussion has primarily addressed common practices to develop leaders and the competencies needed by global leaders. Relative to the *process* of

GLD and how those competencies are acquired, we will examine the following aspects of GLD in the sections that follow: 1) the basic types of learning contexts and approaches, 2) the conceptual process and outcomes of effective training that leads to transformation, and 3) the different strategies that firms can use to "globalize" their managers.

Learning Context of GLD Methods

Learning the kind of competencies needed for global leaders can be had through multiple forums, each with its advantages and disadvantages. Although classroom type training can efficiently disseminate information, research shows that only approximately 20 percent of our education comes through formal classroom training, 30 percent through information exchanges with others, and 50 percent from personal work experience (Dodge 1993). Classrooms can gather in-company personnel from all around the world and help company managers forge networks efficiently as well, which can then contribute to that 30 percent of information exchange. Further, current issues affecting the firm can be delivered by leading-edge experts. However, few of us recall much of what we hear or see in a classroom. Efficient delivery does not mean effectively learned. Experiential education, conversely, activates both the intellectual and emotional memories. Experiential education involves giving managers exposure to actual business operations in geographically dispersed, functionally different operations of the firm. They confront cultural differences that actually impact their real performance—it's a case study in "living color." The lessons learned, though requiring much more time, are learned for a lifetime.

Through such experiences, a network can be developed that is much deeper, though perhaps not as inclusive as the network available in company seminars, for example. Such experiences also test the mettle and capabilities of the manager in real-life business experiences. Because experiential education involves intellectual and emotional memory, the lessons learned are not easily forgotten. In summary, both classroom (e.g. seminars) and experiential education are important and complementary and have a part in the development of global leaders.

Conceptual Process and Outcome of Effective GLD Programs

As has been discussed, most firms have a fairly common set of learning approaches they use to train their personnel. The underlying process that creates the learning, however, is rarely made explicit. Nonetheless, there is a process at the conceptual level that is critical to training and learning. For GLD programs to be effective, they must address this process and recognize the value it brings. Black and Gregersen's proposed model for GLD (2000) embodies the essential elements of this learning process: *contrast, confrontation, and replacement* (Black and Gregersen use the term *remapping* instead of "replacement"). Mezirow first identified this process of transformation in the late 1970s (Mezirow 1978): exposure to a disorienting dilemma (contrast), self-examination and exploration of options (confrontation), and provisional trying of new roles and building competence and self-competence in those roles in order to arrive at a stage of reintegration based on one's new perspective (replacement or remapping). Taylor (1994) cited Mezirow (1978) on this topic of transformation:

> The process of becoming critically aware of how and why our assumptions have come to constrain the way we perceive, understand, and feel about our world; changing these structures of habitual expectation to make possible a more inclusive, discriminating, and integrative perspective; and, finally, making choices or otherwise acting upon these new understandings.
>
> (p. 167)

For us to learn, we must acquire new information and become able to see the same thing from a different perspective. As individuals with certain cultural maps about how the world works and how business operates, we need to experience contrasts to those views and confront our beliefs and assumptions. Without such contrasts that lead to confronting our traditional way of seeing or doing, there can be no change. Joyce Osland (1995; 2000) described this process as "Letting go" and "Taking On" in Chapter 2 (see Table 2.2). Although her focus is on the experience that international assignees go through as they confront differences and have to deal with them, it is the same process for anyone undergoing change. Consider the following example of a German purchasing agent.

Case Scenario: Contrast, Confrontation, and Replacement

A purchasing agent in Germany who now has to deal with the *contrasting* inconsistencies in communication with a supplier in Malaysia because of local power outages and differences in notions of urgency is forced to *confront* his mental map of how business is done in other parts of the world. To be effective in dealing with the agent's Malaysian counterpart, the agent must *replace* his previous notion (i.e. mental map) that business can be conducted with the same methods and communications, resulting in the same efficiency everywhere in the world. However, a changed mental map can occur at different levels—at a superficial level or a deep level. A superficial level change might be something along the lines of the agent's realization that Malaysia has a poor electricity infrastructure, negatively affecting the timeliness of communications, and secondly that the Malaysian vendor is not very motivated. Such a remapping is superficial because it localizes the difference in operating methods to a particular person and to a physical infrastructure issue rather than a deeper underlying cultural issue that often is the more important variable affecting the efficiency of operations.

A deeper-level replacement of the purchasing agent's mental map would relate to an improved understanding of not only the physical infrastructure but of the cultural "infrastructure" as well. Managers in developed countries place great value on urgency because of the value on customer service in the highly competitive world they operate in. This value puts pressure on the manager to get the rest of the world to conform to that assumption about competition—that the customer is king. This is a belief that fits well with the concept that planning is critical and the ability to satisfy the customer is a competitive edge. For a deeper-level understanding to occur, the purchasing agent might have to ask others about the interaction or do some research (be learning oriented), or be observant over time to see patterns that develop across individuals and contexts in dealing with Malaysia (demonstrating a tolerance of ambiguity and nonjudgmental attitudes). Understanding that Malaysia is a high context culture, where relationships are critical and in-groups and out-groups differentiate the level of responsiveness between two people would represent a much deeper level of remapping.

One of the author's brother-in-law and sister came to stay with him and his wife in France recently. The author and his wife had developed good friendships with many of the neighbors in the village and so invited them to dinner sometimes. Because the French don't usually invite others for dinner until 7pm, and it's often not until 7:30 that the meal actually starts, dinner often goes until 11pm or later. Meals in France are a time to socialize and renew friendships. Eating can be secondary, although the food is always a topic of conversation. This meant that the author's relatives and accompanying teenagers did not get to bed until much later than usual. So the teenagers got up late as well—to the consternation of the brother-in-law. Why did we have to start so late? Why does it have to go so late? He would try to move things along faster and get us to start the dinner earlier. Despite the author's explanations for why the French eat later than Americans and why they eat this way, he could not internally accept it and it became a source of frustration for him the entire time. He was, in essence, unwilling to confront his assumptions that eating was essentially to replenish one's energy supply rather than develop deeper relationships and that eating dinner should occur earlier in the evening to allow an earlier bedtime. Without confronting his cultural assumptions about these things, there was no possibility of changing his perspective.

Whether the context is a social situation or a business operation, a deeper level of remapping represents a fundamental level of learning that can then be applied to multiple contexts. For example, the author's brother-in-law could expect sales calls in a French business environment to last much longer than he was used to in the U.S. because they often are done over a meal. The purchasing agent doing business in Malaysia can expect a similar lengthy process to ensue in other high context cultures that emphasize the hierarchy of relationships and the need to ensure good relationships before making final decisions. In both these instances, more fundamental lessons at this level of learning include the consideration of a culture's values. In the purchasing agent's situation, for example, it is important when planning an operation, when there is a critical interdependency that involves foreign operations and great distances, to allow for more time and for greater possibilities for things to go wrong (the "remapping"), and it is critical to develop a good relationship with the agent's counterpart in the foreign country (in this case, Malaysia) in order to be better informed and have better access to information that might be helpful.

It is important to help managers understand that a superficial addition to their existing mental maps (e.g. Malaysia requires more time) is not as efficient or effective as actually replacing the mental map with a more sophisticated one. Kurt Lewin (1947) referred to this process of confronting our mental maps and replacing them with new ones as "unfreezing," "changing" and "refreezing" within a context of dynamic stability. That dynamic stability applied to GLD and the change process to become a global leader is at the heart of the "contrast, confrontation, and replacement" process.

The German purchasing agent experienced a contrast to his usual way of doing business and had to confront the situation (unfreezing). In this case, he could either try to force the Malaysian salesman to change the situation in Malaysia (unlikely) or change his own perspective on how to work with the Malaysian company more effectively ("changing" in Lewin's terminology and "replacement" or "remapping" in our previous discussion). When we experience a contrast in customs, beliefs, etc. that doesn't allow us to conduct business the way we are used to, we have forces that continue to push toward doing business the old way and we have forces that are pushing us to do business in a new way (i.e. resulting in a dynamic stability). The German continues to feel pressure from his own company to obtain the necessary supplies in a timely manner. That pressure doesn't disappear and motivates the German to continue to act in his normal way. However, there are also pressures that are pushing the German to realize that he cannot always expect to realize the same time economies in Malaysia as he normally could in his own country. Those pressures, by contrast, motivate the German to act in a way different from his customary behavior.

These competing pressures force a reconstruction of the previous "map." The conclusion or learning arises from creating a better understanding of all the variables at play and an effective way to work within that new context (changing). Finally, as our new way or new "map of the world" is reinforced through additional similar experiences across individuals, countries, and business operations, it becomes a new, usable "legend" that helps us more effectively manage our businesses and relationships (refreezing). And the process must continue so that our "legend" becomes increasingly refined and accurate because, as noted in Chapter 1, the global context will continually change over time.

In terms of GLD it may be useful to merge concepts from both content and process theories reviewed earlier in the book (Chapter 3) in designing GLD curricula. The process theories focus on global leadership as a transformational process—of letting go and taking on new mental constructs and models.

Enablers of Transformation

To accomplish the kind of transformations we're speaking of does not occur automatically just because one experiences a contrasting experience that creates a confrontation. In other words, the German purchasing agent does not automatically move from one type of approach to time and relationships (the German's) to another (the Malaysian's). In fact, it's possible—or even likely—that the German will simply make a quick judgment about the Malaysian culture being inefficient. Such stereotypes are common and certainly do not allow for the development of a new understanding. In Lewin's terms, there is no "unfreezing" and therefore no "changing" that occurs.

In order for there to be a transformation, the individual needs to have certain competencies that enable this process. For example, if the German purchasing agent is able to *tolerate ambiguity*, the agent is less likely to draw quick, and most likely inappropriate, conclusions about the Malaysian vendor. This allows the agent time to inquire about the challenges the vendor might be facing or the specific cultural context in which the vendor lives. Such an inquiry demonstrates another enabling competency: *curiosity or openness*. To actually discover the relevant information to better understand the Malaysian's culture, the German might have to initiate conversations with the vendor, himself, or with people familiar with Malaysian culture. This, in turn, demonstrates another enabling competency: *interpersonal initiation*. If the agent takes a strong interest in the vendor, himself, rather than in the issue as a general cultural concept, the German further demonstrates another competency that can lead to an effective transformation: *relationship development*. Wanting to develop and effectively manage their vendor–purchasing agent relationship is more likely to lead to a cooperative, long-term collaboration.

Thus, having these and other enabling competencies are absolutely necessary for appropriate transformations to occur in managers seeking to become effective global leaders (for a more in-depth discussion of the transformation process associated with GLD, please see Chapter 5). The enabling competencies help ensure appropriate transformations, and transformations lead to better global managers and leaders. A complete GLD program needs to include a diagnosis of the leader's enabling competencies as well as experiences that can more easily lead to meaningful transformations. (For an in depth discussion of the various enabling competencies, see Chapter 4).

Kozai Learning and Transformation Model

The Kozai Group (2008) developed a useful model that indicates the process most individuals tend to follow through the learning process to develop greater global leadership competencies; it is illustrated in Figure 10.1.

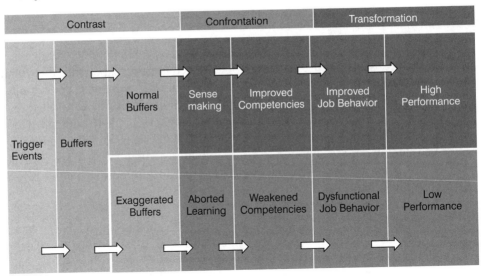

Figure 10.1 The Kozai Learning and Transformation Model

The first step in the transformation process is to experience events that act as trigger events, that is, ones that can cause us to step back, reflect, react to situations foreign to us or otherwise trigger a process that leads to sense making and a greater understanding of the context and players that triggered the sense-making process. This is the same as Mezirow (1978) described as "a disorienting dilemma." As the model indicates, after a given trigger, individuals typically do one of two things: they react defensively or dismissively (Exaggerated Buffers) and essentially abort the sense-making process. This might involve judging, stereotyping, or otherwise evaluating in a way that negates any value to the experience. In those circumstances, nothing is learned and behavior is unchanged. (Hence, being *nonjudgmental* is another enabler of transformation.) Other individuals think about the situation and become interested in understanding it better (Normal Buffers); they analyze the variables at play, try to characterize the players involved in an objective fashion, and so on, and learn something at both the surface and deeper level that they can carry with them into their next experiences. This learning in turns builds new knowledge, increases their competencies, and also their performance levels.

Strategies for Globalizing Personnel

Regardless of the enabling competencies an individual might have, for this change or developmental process to occur, firms need to strategize to put their personnel into situations where this transformation process of contrast—confrontation—replacement can happen. In the latter part of the 90s, Oddou et al. (1998) queried multinational Japanese, U.S., and European firms about their methods for developing their personnel to become more globally qualified. Their research showed that there were five main training elements that were part of the process of globalizing personnel:

- international business travel

- international business seminars with in-company personnel

- international business seminars with non-company personnel

- international project teams/task forces

- international assignments (both expatriation and inpatriation).

These methods appear to continue to be the primary ones firms initiate to develop a global mindset in their employees or that are part of chance experiences employees have that can result in the same. An additional method, however, that has gotten increased attention and application is sending individual high potentials to developing countries on "hardship" type assignments where their global competencies are tested and further developed—or they fail and fall out of the system.

In the following sections two of the aforementioned methods of globalizing personnel will be discussed. The purpose of this is to show how these two methods enable the process of transformation even though they are in many ways on opposite ends of the spectrum: international business travel and international assignments. International business travel tends to be very short term (a few days to a couple of weeks) and can be very superficial in a cross-cultural learning sense, because there is far less need to learn the local language, learn the local customs, and understand more than superficially the foreign counterparts and their organizational culture. The employee is often personally taken care of from arrival to departure without having to venture into the foreign culture and problem solve on her/his own. Rarely does the international business traveler need to learn the transportation system or where to shop for this or that. Quite often, the international business traveler is little more than a tourist in a business context.

Many firms and many businesspersons, themselves, create these kinds of cultural bubbles and isolate themselves from having to come in contact with the local culture. They are picked up at the airport by a chauffeur who waits for them at the exit with their name on a white piece of paper. They follow the chauffeur in and out of buildings and parking spaces to the car that awaits them. The chauffeur takes care of the luggage, opens the door to the car for the businessperson to step in and speeds away, negotiating the signs and distances on the way to the hotel or the company she/he is visiting. If it's to a hotel, the hotel employees usher the business traveler to the reception desk and from there to the room itself, without possibly ever having to figure out anything on her/his own. A similar process occurs at the company site when the traveler arrives there. And so it goes for many business travelers. There is no need to use their analytical abilities to figure things out, no need to ask or try to ask in the foreign language about directions or transportation, no need to translate signs directing them to certain places, no need to navigate traffic into the city, and so on. In other words, the traveler may not be confronted with and therefore have to deal with any direct contrasts between his/her own culture and that of the foreign land. As such, without confrontation there is no real meaningful contrast, no unfreezing or change and certainly no replacing of one's mental maps of how things are done, what is right and wrong, what works and what doesn't work.

Leveraging Travel for GLD

For traveling to be part of GLD, it has to be designed strategically to do so. The company or traveler has to build in time to the travel for mistakes and discoveries to be made. The businessperson has to be willing to take risks and able to manage negative emotions or tensions that are created in trying to find his or her own way. The businessperson has to observe carefully the actions and words of others and the effects they have. He or she has to figure out ways to try to build trust quickly by being open, accepting and appropriately appreciative. Damiran (1993) speaks of this kind of traveler as a contrast to the tourist as follows:

> A traveler and a tourist can visit the same city, but experience it very differently. A tourist's goals are typically to see all the sights, learn their names, make and collect stunning pictures, eat the foods, and observe the rituals of the city. A traveler, on the other hand, seeks to understand the city, to know and live briefly among the people, to understand the languages, both verbal and nonverbal, and to participate in the rituals of the city. At the end of equally long visits, the tourist is likely to have seen more monuments, but the traveler is more likely to know how to use the public transportation.

J. Bonner Ritchie (Oddou, Mendenhall, and Ritchie 2000) recounted an experience he had as a traveler that broadened his global mindset. While walking through the Muslim Quarter in the Old City of Jerusalem, he stopped to look at a brass vase. He asked the shopkeeper the price. Upon hearing the price, even though he wasn't seriously in the mood for buying, Bonner said "too much." The shopkeeper asked how much he would offer. He said he wasn't sure as he began walking down the street. The shopkeeper followed and threw out a lower figure: "60 shekels." Bonner, willing to play the game, responded "25 shekels." The merchant in turn said "40 shekels." They went through another round and settled at 35 shekels.

The important part of his experience was not the transaction, though without the transaction, no development would have occurred. After settling on a price, because the shopkeeper had noticed that Bonner seemed uncomfortable with the bidding negotiation, he asked Bonner why that was so. The merchant reminded Bonner that in the U.S. Americans do not buy homes or cars based on a fixed price, so why would negotiation be omitted from other transactions. He suggested it was not only more enjoyable to prolong the interaction but it was fairer to do so. Surprised, Bonner asked him why it is fairer. The merchant responded that this way, the seller and buyer can arrive at a price that is mutually acceptable and that such a price is going to reflect the buyer's ability to buy and need to buy—it will likely be a higher price for someone who has more money and a greater need and a lower price for someone who is poorer or with less of a need. And so, the merchant reasoned, a lower price was not a better deal but a fairer deal.

Bonner had entered the negotiation with a sense of discomfort because doing business this way for this type of product was not his normal way. Though not a lot was at risk in this situation, Bonner had to confront the effectiveness of his usual way of buying such products with the local way of doing so and figure out what was equitable. Bonner's assumption that a fixed price meant a fair price is a cultural belief he had been accustomed to in the U.S. The fairness was in a reasonable profit margin the merchant determined and the clarity of the price so the buyer can make an "informed" decision. It gives all the responsibility to the buyer, in a sense, to determine fairness. Bonner didn't want to be taken advantage of by paying a higher price than he should, particularly because he was a foreigner and suspected the merchant might try to gouge him in order to gain a higher profit margin than should be expected. Bonner was assuming this way of doing business gave the merchant all the responsibility and power to determine what was fair. From this traveler transaction, Bonner learned that "fairness" was a clear factor embedded in negotiations in such contexts, that equity or fairness was best reached in a more flexible, fluid context where the needs and motivation of the two parties could be understood in a conversation. This cultural *contrast* resulted in Bonner's *confronting* his understanding of "fairness" and "responsibility" in reaching equitable transactions. He gained a better appreciation for cultures that are more flexible and allow individual circumstances to influence transactions to reach a greater sense of equity.

This change in Bonner's mental map (*replacement* or *remapping*) would never have occurred had Bonner not ventured beyond his hotel room and hotel restaurant or if he had allowed himself to always be "protected" by a host employee who could have intervened. Bonner never would have had to learn another perspective.

International Assignments

On the other side of the spectrum from international travel is an international assignment (IA). It is commonly agreed upon that IAs are the best experience and the greatest proving ground to develop global management competencies (McCall and Hollenbeck 2002). International assignments are the longest type of exposure to foreign business and culture (1–3 years usually) and require a tremendous amount of interaction and integration into all aspects of the culture. The international assignee lives the culture every single day.

Still, as will be discussed in the following section, an international business traveler who is curious and motivated to learn can have an adventure that goes well beyond the experience of a tourist. Such assignments require the greatest degree of integration with the culture. It is the necessity of integration that causes the greatest degree of culture shock. By definition, culture shock is the absence of familiar "markers," which causes a disorientation and inability to perform according to habitual expectations. In the *general* culture, an expatriate must normally deal with differences in language, rules of the road, shopping, on down to such mundane but essential things as differences in car insurance and the payment of utility bills and more. Within the *work environment*, the assignee might also deal with language differences but he or she more certainly deals with work culture differences, performance appraisal systems, meeting behavior, and so forth. The assignee might or might not have family members with him or her. Family members each are dealing with another subset of the culture and will bring additional and supplementary contrasts to the cultural experience.

When one of the authors of this chapter was in France with his family, they moved into the home they were to be in for six months while on an assignment there. The washing machine had just broken down. They were given a number of the repairman to call by the previous family. He called and the repairman said he would be out within a couple of days. The repairman never came. He called again after a few more days and the repairman said he'd be out right away, but that it was taking longer because the washing machine was German and he had to order the part from Germany (he had never even come out to the house to see what was wrong to even know what part might have to be ordered!). Either way, he never came. The author's wife began to complain and was getting upset with him from having to do so much wash by hand (because they didn't know where to go to wash them—if there were any public washing machines even available). He called the repairman again and told him (in good French) that the repairman was unprofessional. With that, the repairman got upset and both of them hung up their phones, mutually dissatisfied.

One day, about two weeks later, while eating at the parents' home of the people whose house they lived in, the mother asked how everything was and he told her except for the problem with the washing machine, things were great. She asked what was wrong and they explained what had transpired. She immediately said not to worry, that the repairman had been a previous employee of theirs for many years in their import–export firm, and that she would call him. He came out the next day with a replacement washer.

There was a lesson to be learned there. But the lesson wouldn't have been learned had the author not had to personally *confront* the *contrast* in the "repair process" in France and the U.S. In the U.S., he was used to a repair person making an appointment and usually coming approximately when the appointment was made. When that didn't happen in France, he had to confront the difference but without any explanation for why the repairman behaved this way. When he saw how quickly his previous employer got him to come, he began to realize that this is a country where relationships could mean everything. The author had no relationship with the repairman and so there was apparently no obligation—he could take as long as he wanted and it was acceptable. The mother of the people whose house they lived in had a long relationship with him. That previous relationship apparently was enough to motivate the repairman to do something even though he was no longer in their employ.

The author now had to modify his understanding of how things can get done (*replacement*). In the U.S., the relationship between repairman and the customer is a neutral one. However, because customer service is a competitive advantage for business survival in the U.S., a deep relationship is not needed. The required relationship is established simply by being a customer—business is business. This notion was in stark contrast to his experience in France where the relationship is established over years of familiarity, and not by virtue of being classified as a customer over a phone conversation. And so to get things done in a country like France, the author realized he had to establish and maintain relationships. He had to replace his mental model of supplier–customer relationships to fit a broader definition. As an expatriate, this was just one of the many "maps" that was altered during his time in France.

Strategies for Globalizing Personnel and GLD

You might recall the common elements of GLD programs cited earlier: 360 degree feedback, executive coaching, job assignments, mentoring, networking, reflection, action learning, and outdoor experiences. How do these elements support or enable the potentially strategic globalizing training methods? First, you might recall that all of the strategies firms were using in Oddou et al.'s (1998) research among Japanese, European, and US MNCs are job assignments of one type or another. Job assignments provide the experiential context that generates the cultural contrasts that lead to one's confronting the "normal" way with a "different" way (unfreezing).

The more *experiential* (or action/"outdoor" learning), or more holistic (emotional, behavioral, and intellectual) the experience or contrast that characterizes the experience, the greater the impact. In addition, the greater the number of *sources* of feedback that tells the manager his or her behavior or decision was or was not appropriate (360 degree feedback), the more impact the contrast will also be. These contrasts cause us to reflect and possibly seek out perspectives from mentors or coaches to help us understand the contrast and how to manage it. All this can more easily lead to the unfreezing and changing of our mental maps. Of course, in the process of working with foreign counterparts in these job assignments, the manager is also building global networks, another important common component of general leadership models. Figure 10.2 illustrates these relationships.

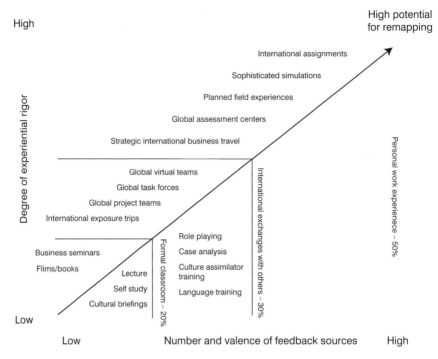

Figure 10.2 Relationship of Experiential Rigor and Number of Feedback Sources on Mental Remapping Potential in Global Leadership Development Programs

It has been said that "the primary objective of global leadership training is stretching someone's mind past narrow domestic borders and creating a mental map of the entire world" (Black and Gregersen 2000). To accomplish this, most GLD programs take an eclectic approach to the challenge of developing global leaders, with an emphasis on classroom and information exchange types of approaches. As was discussed earlier, Dodge (1993) found that 20 percent of managerial learning is best suited for classroom type scenarios, and 30 percent involves exchanging information with others, and learning from them. More in-depth learning occurs from actual, personal work experience—if it is facilitated in a productive way.

Recent research on global leaders bears out the notion that developmental activities at the higher end of the continuum in Figure 10.2 facilitate global competency development. Caligiuri and Tarique (2011) studied 420 global leaders and, among other findings, reported that "high contact" experiences that were initiated by the organization such as lengthy expatriate assignments, working as global team members, and mentoring by people from another culture, etc., helped managers develop critical global leadership competencies. Thus, the careful structuring of developmental experiences that have embedded within them the key learning triggering mechanisms that have been previously discussed are critical to GLD.

Let's now look at two multinationals' GLD programs (PricewaterhouseCoopers and IBM) as best practice cases where more in-depth GLD occurs. It should be noted that space limits reviews of other programs that could be categorized as best practices as well; for example, Pfizer's Global Health Fellows Program, Cisco's Leadership Fellows Program, and Accenture's Development Partnerships Program are all examples of firms who have designed GLD programs taking the principles discussed in this chapter into consideration (Dowling and Breitfelder 2010).

PricewaterhouseCoopers

PricewaterhouseCoopers (PwC) is a global firm, made up of legally independent firms in over 100 countries. Co-owners of each firm are designated as partners, and they constitute 5 percent of the more than 160,000 people PwC employs worldwide. From 2001 to the present over a hundred partners have gone through PwC's GLD program, Ulysses (Pless et al. 2011). PwC runs a variety of global leadership competency development training programs, but for the purposes of this chapter, we will focus only on the Ulysses Program, which is designed to enhance the global leadership competencies of their partner-level executives. Pless et al. (2011) state that

> The overarching goal of the Ulysses program is to promote responsible leadership within PwC's global network of firms and to develop partners of the firm into well-rounded leaders who are aware of their responsibilities in society and capable of interacting effectively and ethically with various stakeholders in the global marketplace.
>
> (pp. 240–241)

The core concept of the Ulysses Program is simple and straightforward: form partners into teams of three or four and send them to developing countries for two months to work on challenging assignments with local and international organizations. For example, in Africa, partner teams have worked in Cameroon, Eritrea, Ghana, Kenya, Madagascar, Namibia, South Africa, Uganda, and Zambia on projects that involve combating HIV/AIDS, enhancing agriculture production, growing rural electricity, facilitating landmine removal, mental health development, providing ongoing clean drinking water, institutionalizing women and children protection services, eye care, rural development, and more. Partner teams have carried out similar types of projects in Cambodia, China, East Timor, India, Belize, Ecuador, Paraguay, Peru, and Moldova (Pless et al. 2011). After partners are nominated and selected to participate in this program there are five phases or stages to the Ulysses Program; they are summarized in Figure 10.3.

Each phase is designed to prepare participants for challenges faced in later phases of the developmental process. For example, in the induction phase, yoga training is given to prepare the participants to relieve the intense stress that they will face working 24/7 in their service-learning environment. Also, they receive

Phase	Focus	Length
Preparation	360 Feedback, team formation, team project assigned, team coaching	8 weeks
Induction	Project briefing, yoga training, personal coaching, personal development plan, team building, project planning	7 days
Field Assignment	Teams implement plan in field, coaches visit in field	8 weeks
Debriefing	Celebrate and report results to other teams, learning through debriefing with coaches, record team-learning narratives, develop individual vision statements, engage in yoga and meditation	8 days
Alumni Networking	Regional alumni meetings, global alumni meetings bi-yearly, alumni special interest groups, follow-up visits, surveys, and events	Ongoing

Figure 10.3 Conceptual Design of PwC's Ulysses Program

Source: Adapted from N. M. Pless, T. Maak, and G. K. Stahl (2011) "Developing responsible global leaders through International Service Learning Programs: The Ulysses experience." *Academy of Management Learning and Education*, 10(2): 242.

individualized coaching to help them strategize how they will approach, cope, deploy their expertise, and learn global leadership skills during their time overseas. After their assignment ends, during the debriefing stage the focus is on learning activities that help the participants in individual and collective sense making of their experience in order to "lock in" their learning and to be cognitively, affectively, and behaviorally aware of the degree to which they have developed and expanded their global leadership competencies (Pless et al. 2011).

Pless and her colleagues were able to study the impact of the Ulysses Program on its participants. Their findings indicate that, indeed, the program produced heightened levels of global leadership skills. As the Mezirow (1978) and Kozai Learning and Transformation models show, they found that global leadership skills occurred because of the operation of "triggering mechanisms," and that these mechanisms were threefold in nature; namely, 1) being forced to resolve tensions and paradoxes in the new, unfamiliar environment; 2) having to construct a new "life-world" in order to make sense of the new environment in order to successfully achieve their project task; and 3) being forced to cope with adversity and the attendant strong emotions that were triggered by that adversity (Pless et al. 2011). Their findings support the notion that crucible experiences are powerful vehicles for the development of global leadership competencies (for a more in-depth discussion of the role of crucible experiences in GLD, see Chapter 5).

More specifically, Pless and her colleagues found that: 1) significant learning took place in the areas of cultural intelligence and intercultural competence development; 2) participants had heightened levels of tolerance, openness to different cultural norms and perspectives, and nonjudgmentalness; 3) significant increases occurred in the areas of cosmopolitan thinking and the ability to grasp and manage complexity; and 4) participants showed heightened abilities to reconcile global and local imperatives, as well as evidencing significant learning gains in moral reflection, self-awareness, and the role of leaders as global citizens (Pless et al. 2011: 249). From their study, they concluded the following:

> … international service-learning programs that involve cultural immersion at a relatively deep level through daily interaction and collaboration with local stakeholders can help managers … Experiencing the heightened ambiguity, challenging ethical dilemmas, and cultural paradoxes associated with working in a developing country can trigger a transformational experience and produce new mental models in managers—new world-views, mind-sets, and perspectives … A substantial portion of Ulysses participants reported that the program helped them to broaden their horizons, learn more about themselves, adapt to a new culture, learn how to perceive the world through the eyes of people who are different, and work effectively with a diverse range of stakeholders—qualities which are essential for leading responsibly in a global and interconnected world.
>
> (Pless et al. 2011: 252)

IBM's Globally Integrated Enterprise Leadership Development Program

In 2008, IBM embarked on a huge change initiative to become a truly globally integrated enterprise (GIE). IBM realized that to be competitive in the twenty-first century their "work must be far more collaborative, far more attuned to a multiplicity of cultural differences, far more fluid and less hierarchical" (White and Rosamilia 2010: 3). As part of this quest, one of the major elements in their plan is to provide more of their employees with opportunities to enhance their global leadership skills, and offer more varied global experiences earlier in careers.

To figure out how to accomplish this task, IBM consulted with numerous constituencies to create a model of what skills different employees need to have to be GIE-type leaders. They spoke with and listened to hundreds of IBM employees in more than thirty countries, their clients and business partners, academic scholars, university students who were potential future hires at IBM, and government leaders. The GLD model that was created from this approach focuses on two primary factors: 1) providing more employees with enhanced global skills; and 2) offering more varied global experiences earlier in careers.

Providing More Employees with Enhanced Global Skills

The desire is to "embed cultural intelligence and adaptability throughout IBM" (White and Rosamilia 2010: 6) according to the job roles that employees hold. Their model for accomplishing this is shown in Figure 10.4. IBM employees

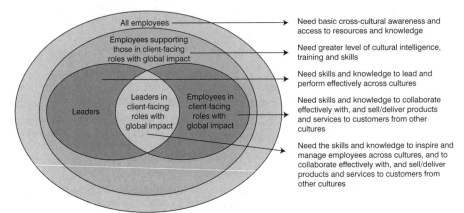

Figure 10.4 IBM's Global Leadership Skills Development Model

Source: White and Rosamilia (2010).

are expected to identify their own global skill gaps and to develop them with assistance from IBM support personnel. Tracking measures have been implemented for accountability purposes; for example, IBM is trying to track global skill development by 1) measuring improvements in global competencies over time; 2) assessing employee satisfaction based on employee feedback; and 3) assessing increases in availability in their workforce of global skills to meet business needs (White and Rosamilia 2010: 7).

Offering More Varied Global Experiences Earlier in Careers

A comprehensive delineation of all aspects of IBM's global leadership competency development program is not feasible in this chapter; however, we will focus on IBM's development of their Corporate Services Corps (CSC) Program, which focuses on developing senior and high potential executives' global leadership skills, as a "best practice" example. White and Rosamilia (2010: 9) note that:

> In 2009, nearly 10,000 IBM employees from 63 countries applied for 500 spots in the CSC. Forty-one teams of IBM employees worked in 13 countries with non-profits, small businesses and non-governmental organizations. Dozens of participants have since posted audio, video and photos of their volunteer experiences on company Web pages to demonstrate how the CSC experience changed how they think about their company, work and their own place in the world. The company intends to expand the program to include 20 percent more participants in 2010.

CSC is viewed within IBM as being its version of the Peace Corps; however, IBM differentiates activities of the CSC from other companies' service-learning programs. While other firms focus on pro bono work, the CSC is "community service with a business bent: rather than delivering basic goods like food or housing, IBM is donating expertise and focusing on results" (IBM 2008: 1). IBM has sent teams to Romania, Ghana, Vietnam, the Philippines, and Tanzania to work on projects such as helping the Africa Wildlife Foundation develop strategy and providing the business expertise of IBM team members to local small and micro-business operations to assist them in supply chain operations, financial management processes, and in exporting. The focus is on helping local businesses and organizations become more productive and developing global competencies in IBMers as they engage with local cultural, social, business, and governmental environments (IBM 2008).

The original 2008 plan involved a six-month total program span: Phase 1 involved three months of self and team preparation; Phase 2 involved one month working in the country; and Phase 3 involved two months of post-country work. Assessments of the first CSC Program launched in 2008 found that participants showed strong increases in the following competencies: appreciation of differences in the world, value of working cross-culturally, enhanced leadership skills, and emotional resilience (Marquis and Kanter, 2008). Also, IBM reported in 2010 the following general results of the overall GIE initiative (White and Rosamilia 2010: 12):

1 an increase of global leaders have emerged throughout IBM

2 an increase of collaboration at the country level between senior leaders and local leaders in effective execution of corporate strategy

3 an expansion and deepening of global client relationships

4 an increase in the creativity of client solutions around the world

5 an increase in understanding in employees of IBM's global strategy, their role as global citizens, and how they fit into IBM's global strategy

6 an increase in the degree to which employees collaborate with peers.

The capstones of the broader GLD programs of PwC and IBM seem to meet the development criteria espoused in this chapter; each forces participants to engage in the contrast, confrontation, and replacement process in a deep and meaningful way, which over time seems to produce beneficial GLD outcomes in the participants. But, unlike PwC and IBM, what if a company is not able to spend the resources and time and intensity on their GLD efforts?

Union Bank of Switzerland

Contrast these comprehensive programs to the Seitenwechsel ("perspective change") program that was run by the Union Bank of Switzerland (UBS) in the late 1990s (Mendenhall and Stahl 2000: 258). Part of the ongoing management development efforts of this firm was to broaden and expand the perspectives of their managers so as to better understand people who were different from them. UBS managers were assigned to work for one week, full-time, with not-for-profit agencies that dealt with various social problems; for example, some managers were assigned to work with terminally ill HIV patients while others were required to care for the homeless at government-sponsored shelters. In other cases, managers were assigned to work with juvenile delinquents or with immigrants from war-ravaged countries who were seeking asylum.

Though often painful and challenging, this experience provided powerful contrasts to the managers, and challenged them to expand their perspectives and worldviews. The results indicated that this intensive simulation experience helped the UBS managers to significantly "reduce subjective barriers and prejudices, learn more about themselves, broaden their horizons, and increase their interpersonal skills—all of which are competencies associated with global leadership" (Mendenhall and Stahl 2000: 258). Interestingly, 60 percent of the managers who participated in the Seitenwechsel program continued to support the institution that they served in after the program finished (Mendenhall and Stahl 2000).

The Seitenwechsel program is an excellent example of a GLD technique that can be classified in the "personal work experience" dimension of managerial learning. Managers were placed in situations where they had to extend the reach of their existing competencies to handle, cope, and be productive in milieus that were alien to them. Thus, it is possible to develop global leadership competencies without sending people overseas per se. Also such in-depth simulations can be used to increase the number of managers who are trained to develop global competencies, as this type of global leadership competency training does not require managers to be sent overseas on either long- or short-term assignments, which can be quite expensive and budget-prohibitive.

Can Global Leaders be Developed?

The answer to the above question would seem to be a straightforward "Yes!" based on the descriptions and findings of the three case studies reviewed above. As Caligiuri and Di Santo (2001) note, the undergirding assumption or raison d'être of GLD programs is that global leadership competencies can be developed through experiential development processes. However, Debrah and Rees (2011) observed that: "Perhaps the most contentious aspect of the literature on the development of global leaders/managers is the issue of whether all managers can be trained and developed to acquire global perspectives" (pp. 389–390).

This debate stems from the same disagreement that exists among some scholars and practitioners in the general field of leadership, that is, the notion that some people simply will never be able to become leaders no matter how devoted an organization is to try and develop them into leaders. We report below the following arguments from Debrah and Rees' 2011 summary of this issue.

Caligiuri (2006) has contended that it is likely that individuals' abilities to develop global leadership competencies are dependent upon their aptitude, knowledge, skills, abilities, and personality traits. Personality traits that may influence competency development are viewed by most scholars as being immutable, and do not change much over time (Caligiuri 2006; Furuya et al. 2009). If this is so, then the implications for firms is to carefully select employees to enter GLD programs based on their "developmental readiness factors," and to exclude employees from working globally who are less suited to do so (Caligiuri 2006; Debrah and Rees 2011; Gregersen et al. 1998; Ng et al. 2009). Earlier we reported that Caligiuri and Tarique (2011) found that "high contact" programs produced global leadership competencies in the global leaders in their sample; however, there is a caveat to that general finding—"certain experiences are better than others (i.e. those that are high contact) and that certain people benefit more from those experiences (i.e. those with extraversion, emotional stability, and openness)" (Caligiuri and Tarique 2011: 1). They found that there is a "dynamic interplay" between personality traits and activities that are high contact in nature, and that this interplay allows for global competencies to be developed and for global leadership outcomes. They argue that:

> Global leadership development programs should identify those individuals with the requisite individual characteristics (e.g. personality) and then offer high-contact cross-cultural experiences to those identified. Multinational organizations (MNCs) are encouraged to 1) assess their potential global leaders for personality characteristics and, having selected carefully, 2) promote high-contact culturally oriented experiences.

So, were the employees of PwC, IBM, and UBS simply those who were more predisposed to develop global competencies than their counterparts due to personality make-up? Do these types of people tend to be nominated by their superiors to be admitted into GLD programs more often than those who are not predisposed for global competency development? Is that why the best practices are best practices—because inadvertently these companies tended to select participants who were predisposed to be more likely to succeed?

Or, did the design of these programs elicit deeper level competency triggering processes within people *despite* their developmental predispositions? A moderation of this stance would be that well-designed programs have the capability to facilitate improvement in any or most individuals—but at varying levels; that is, predisposed individuals would reach higher global competency levels, but less predisposed people would nevertheless improve their global competency levels as well, just not to the same heights as those who were highly predisposed.

In the end, this is an empirical question, and a gap in the literature exists on this issue that needs filling by future research studies. To date, studies have not tended to measure predisposition levels for global competency development in participants and then tracked their *pre-*, *during-*, and *post-*global leadership competency development outcomes.

Exploratory research also indicates the possibility that developing leadership and global leadership competencies may also be influenced by the degree of fit between "national culture" and "leadership competency development method" (Wilson and Yip 2010; Yip and Wilson 2008; 2010). Their findings suggest that though some leadership development processes are universal across cultures (e.g. challenging assignments, developmental relationships, hardships, coursework and training, and personal experience), other variables come into play differentially across cultures in leadership development processes. For example:

> Hardships include crisis, work-related mistakes, career setbacks, and ethical dilemmas. The types of experiences categorized as "hardships" are cited less frequently in India and Singapore than in the United States. Do managers genuinely experience fewer hardships in some countries? Does that mean that leaders from those countries are less likely to learn the unique lessons produced by hardships?
>
> (Wilson and Yip 2010: 53)

Thus, depending on the culture in question, some of the five processes above move from figure to ground, and vice versa, in their preference and importance to participants in terms of leadership development. Also, leadership development processes beyond the universal five mentioned above exist in some cultures and not in others; thus, the manner in which an individual would most likely go about trying to develop global competencies may differ significantly across national culture; for example, in the case of Indian executives they found that "familial relationships — such as with parents, uncles, and cousins—are cited more frequently as sources of leadership learning than is the case with executives from other countries" (Wilson and Yip 2010: 53).

For most global organizations, GLD programs tend to take on a "one-size-fits-all" paradigm—even in the case of the best practices firms we highlighted in this chapter. And this may be efficacious for employees who have internalized the global work culture and values of the organization in which they work. However, the work of Wilson and Yip suggests that employees may also have deeper, emotionally preferred ways of developing leadership competencies that may or may not be congruent with the organization's GLD program. Paying close attention to these cultural preferences may be important—even critical—to developing global competencies across a global workforce. Wilson and Yip (2010: 53) observed that

> Our current models of leader development draw primarily on the experiences of senior executives from United States and Western European corporations. Does the use of individualism as a tacit frame of reference for current research truncate a more complete understanding of leader development?

Conclusion

As the world becomes increasingly interdependent, complex, uncertain, and dynamic, the challenge to understand and operate within that world will become ever more difficult. Firms typically have responded to this environment by creating strategic allies in foreign countries in order to operate more easily in global markets. However, creating strategic foreign allies also increases the need to interact effectively on an operational basis with foreign counterparts in the strategic alliance. This requires managers who can understand and work with people who are different from them and who must work in a cultural milieu that is also different. Simultaneously, forging alliances with foreign firms can decrease the need to develop a keen understanding of that foreign culture, itself, because the strategic ally is better positioned to do so. This might only postpone or inhibit the probable necessity of mutual understanding.

Another response to the kind of environment reflected in our current global marketplace is organizational redesign. Alcatel, for example, was struggling with some design issues to try and address a very complex global operation: overall centralization versus decentralization of authority and communications within the corporation; common culture versus decentralized work cultures in a context of allowing some foreign operations more autonomy given their cultural needs and the business they were in. Some of these challenges can in part be taken care of by redesigning reporting relationships, creating new organizational structures for problem solving across cultures, and so on.

In both these common ways to respond to an ever challenging global marketplace, the more the managers (and all employees, for that matter) have a global mindset, the more effective the strategies will be, as well as the operations and the specific working relationships of employees representing a diverse set of values and mindsets. Global leadership training is essential. As both former (Black et al. 1999a) and more recent research (Development Dimensions International 2008) has clearly pointed out, the recognition of the need to train more global leaders far exceeds firms' current ability to identify and develop them.

As more entrants come into the marketplace, we will need increasing numbers of these individuals. The more the training creates contrasts by confronting managers with different ways of being and doing, the more the manager will likely change and evolve to have a greater mental map of the world to achieve greater effectiveness and efficiency. This is consistent with the more recent trend highlighted by the examples in PwC and IBM to send global leader potentials on short-term hardship assignments and McCall and Hollenbeck's (2002) finding that international assignments are the best ways to develop global leaders. This is a tough world in which only well developed, tough global leaders will survive.

11 Responsible Global Leadership

GÜNTER K. STAHL, NICOLA M. PLESS, AND THOMAS MAAK

As the world works to recover from the effects of the recent economic crisis and, according to some, the parallel crisis of management ethics (e.g. Fry and Slocum 2008; Waldman and Galvin 2008), business leaders have come under more scrutiny than ever before. This situation is partly due to the highly publicized corporate scandals and instances of management misconduct that eroded public faith and fuelled legislative reactions, including the Sarbanes–Oxley Act. Scandals have brought to the forefront the recognition that leaders of organizations may be acting irresponsibly more often than previously thought (Bansal and Candola 2003; Brown and Treviño 2006; Schwartz and Carroll 2003). There is also a growing awareness that the costs of managerial misconduct are enormous, whether in terms of the loss of business, damaged corporate reputations, alienated customers, litigation costs, or damages paid (Arnott 2004; Ebersole 2007; Leatherwood and Spector 1991; Zolkos 2002).

In extreme cases, such as the Enron stock crash, the collapse of the entire company and the ensuing loss of jobs, pensions, and value of annuities and retirement funds resulted from irresponsible behavior by corporate leaders. Managerial misconduct also may have less direct and visible consequences, such as negative work climates, demoralized employees, or difficulties attracting, recruiting, and retaining talent (Stahl et al. 2008). For society, the indirect costs may take the form of loss of confidence in the marketplace, loss of government revenue in the case of bailouts, and a tarnished image of corporate leadership (Waldman and Galvin 2008). Irresponsible behavior by business leaders thus affects a range of stakeholders, including investors, employees, customers, and larger society.

The quest for responsible leadership is not only a response to recent business scandals and calls for more ethical managerial conduct but also a result of changes and new demands in the global marketplace (Pless et al. 2011; Puffer and McCarthy 2008; Waldman and Galvin 2008). One demand is the expectation of stakeholders that corporations and their leaders will take a more active role as citizens in society and contribute to the "triple bottom line" (Elkington 1997) by creating environmental, social, and economic value (Bansal 2002; Hart and Milstein 2003). In essence, these calls acknowledge that leadership exerts its influence in a global stakeholder environment and therefore demand that leaders "contribute to the creation of economic and societal progress in a globally responsible and sustainable way" (EFMD 2005: 3). As the growing number of public–private partnerships, social innovations, and leadership initiatives (e.g. "Tomorrow's Leaders Group of the World Business Council for Sustainable Development"; "The Global Business Coalition on HIV/AIDS") indicates, more and more business leaders accept their responsibility to help find solutions to pressing global problems, such as poverty, environmental degradation, pandemic diseases, and human rights protections. Surveys of senior executives conducted by the strategy consultancy McKinsey and Co. (McKinsey 2006; 2010) reveal, however, that a knowing–doing gap persists with regard to responsible leadership: executives recognize their broader responsibilities as global citizens, but they also struggle to cope effectively with the wider social, political, and environmental issues facing today's business leaders.

The trend by which more and more managers operate in a global environment further compounds this challenge. As various authors have pointed out (e.g. Beechler and Javidan 2007; Bird and Osland 2004; Lane et al. 2009; Levy et al. 2007; McCall and Hollenbeck 2002; Mendenhall 2008), the challenges facing managers in the global arena are considerably more demanding than those encountered in a domestic environment, because the global context increases the valence, intensity, and complexity of several dimensions for leaders, namely,

- A setting characterized by wider-ranging diversity.

- Greater need for broad knowledge that spans functions and nations.

- More stakeholders to understand and consider when making decisions.

- Wider and more frequent boundary spanning, both within and across organizational and national boundaries.

- A more challenging and expanded list of competing tensions both on and off the job.

- Heightened ambiguity surrounding decisions and related outcomes/effects.

- More challenging ethical dilemmas related to globalization.

Extending this complexity even further, executives of global corporations must balance various needs, such as global integration and local responsiveness, to ensure global consistency in corporate social responsibility (CSR) approaches and initiatives while also being sensitive to local cultural norms and expectations (Donaldson and Dunfee 1999; Husted and Allen 2006; Pless et al. 2011). In addition to the competencies identified in global leadership literature (see Chapter 3), dealing effectively with these challenges requires moral judgment (Brown and Treviño 2006), an ability to balance contradictions (Marquardt and Berger, 2000), and decision making rules to determine when different is simply wrong (Donaldson 1996).

These two major trends in international business—globalization and the quest for responsible leadership—in turn raise two fundamental questions: What are the qualities that predispose business leaders to act responsibly in an increasingly complex, global, and interconnected world? And how can organizations develop these qualities in their current and future leaders? In this chapter, we provide tentative answers to both the "what" and the "how" questions for developing responsible global leaders. To date, global leadership research has not adequately addressed these questions, and the ethical dimensions and social responsibility aspects of global leadership remain underexplored. Various authors stress the importance of qualities such as honesty and integrity and highlight that both personal and company standards are far more prone to being compromised in a global context (e.g. Black et al. 1999a; McCall and Hollenbeck 2002). However, for the most part, research has failed to address the complex ethical dilemmas that face global leaders, their choices for resolving those dilemmas, or ways to develop responsible global leadership in organizations.

We begin by exploring what it means to be a "responsible" leader, specifically by considering the challenges and dilemmas facing executives in four key CSR domains: diversity, ethics, sustainability, and citizenship. We describe three prototypical approaches to CSR—global, local, and transnational—and discuss their implications for global executives, with a particular focus on the tensions and possible trade-offs between globally integrated and locally adapted CSR strategies, the constraints they impose on managerial behavior, and the competencies they require in global leaders. We conclude by discussing approaches for promoting responsible global leadership in organizations and offering recommendations for how organizations can effectively prevent, manage, and control the risks of irresponsible leader behavior.

What Is Responsible Global Leadership?

Despite a large, rapidly growing body of research on behavioral decision making and managerial ethics (for reviews, see Kish-Gephart et al. 2010; Maak and Pless 2006; O'Fallon and Butterfield 2005; Stahl 2011; Tenbrunsel and Smith-Crowe 2008), no generally accepted definition of "responsible leadership" exists. While some authors adopt an ethics lens, focusing on the morality of managers' actions (e.g. Jones 1991; Treviño et al. 2003), others take a broader citizenship perspective and consider managers' propensity to engage in actions that enhance societal well-being (e.g. Crilly et al. 2008; Maak and Pless 2006). Brown and Treviño (2006: 595), in their review of extant literature on ethical leadership, conclude that research remains "underdeveloped and fragmented, leaving scholars and practitioners with few answers to even the most fundamental questions, such as 'what is ethical leadership?'"

Most definitions of social responsibility represent one of two schools of thought: proponents of a shareholder primacy model (e.g. Friedman 1970; McCloskey

1998; Sundaram and Inkpen 2004) argue that maximizing stockholder value is the only, or most important, goal that executives should consider when making decisions. Critics of this position (e.g. Donaldson and Preston 1995; Freeman and McVea 2001; Grant 1991) insist that a single-minded focus on shareholder value maximization imposes costs on various other constituencies, such as employee layoffs, barely acceptable wages and working conditions, environmental pollution, and so on. Therefore, according to this second school of thought, business leaders should make decisions that consider the needs and demands of broader sets of stakeholders. To bridge the gap between the shareholder primacy model and stakeholder theory, Schwartz and Carroll (2003) have proposed a multi-domain approach to CSR, in which the three core domains of economic, legal, and ethical responsibilities exhibit some degree of overlap (see Figure 11.1). Thus, executives may engage in multiple domains and address the needs of multiple stakeholders simultaneously.

In this chapter, we focus mainly on the ethical responsibility domain but also consider the economic and legal dimensions of CSR when necessary. The latter are by no means less important for defining the obligations of businesses in society, but there is less disagreement about the economic and legal responsibilities of business leaders. The notion of an economic responsibility, in terms of delivering an appropriate level of financial returns to shareholders, is accepted by both stakeholder theory and traditional economic views, and both views accept the need to adhere to laws and regulations in society (Freeman and McVea 2001; Waldman and Siegel 2008). From a leadership point of view, the more interesting and controversial aspects of CSR pertain to the nature and extent of those obligations

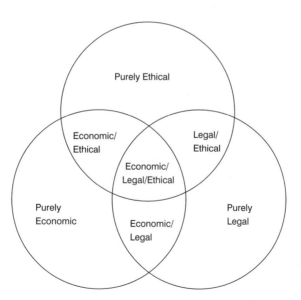

Figure 11.1 Three-Domain Model of Corporate Social Responsibility

Source: M. S. Schwartz and A. B. Carroll (2003). "Corporate social responsibility: A three-domain approach." *Business Ethics Quarterly*, 13, 503–530

that extend beyond economic and legal responsibilities. These responsibilities reflect the expectations placed on business leaders by corporate stakeholders and society as a whole. Vogel (2005) thus speaks of a market for virtue, in which businesses and their leaders compete for values and ethical standards. Such ethical responsibilities are ill-defined and vary across institutional and cultural contexts. As Vickers (2005: 30) noted, "global corporations operate in nations where bribery, sexual harassment, racial discrimination, and a variety of other issues are not uniformly viewed as illegal or even unethical."

CSR Domains and Associated Leadership Challenges

The demand for global executives to act in accordance with the needs and expectations of a multitude of stakeholders, both locally and globally, creates significant leadership challenges that constitute four major areas: diversity, ethics, sustainability, and citizenship.

The Diversity Challenge

The need to interact with and manage a multitude of stakeholders, spread across the globe, means that managers of global organizations confront a diversity of values, perspectives, and expectations. Responding effectively to this diversity requires broad knowledge about constituencies, a willingness to include different voices into the corporate dialogue and decision-making process, and the capacity to balance multiple and often competing stakeholder interests. It also requires a simultaneous consideration of the ethical, economic, and legal dimensions of doing business in different countries and regions (Schwartz and Carroll 2003). Multiple stakeholders with multiple agendas exist at multiple levels (Aguilera et al. 2007; Devinney 2009), so global managers often find themselves torn in trying to address the expectations of different constituencies. Badaracco (1992) shows that myriad stakeholder demands confronting executives of global corporations often include conflicts of right versus right (i.e. various legitimate demands compete), not right versus wrong.

The case of a senior executive of a large German bank illustrates some of the challenges involved in leading responsibly in an environment characterized by multiple, and partially conflicting, stakeholder expectations:

> Robert Heinen, the general manager of the Japanese branch of the German DCN Bank (names have been changed), faced a decision about whether to work to increase the proportion of women in higher management levels in this branch. On the one hand, the bank's core values and corporate credo emphasized diversity and equal opportunity. During his four-year tenure as general manager, the branch had recruited many women, and he generally found them to be competent and hard working. The annual performance

and potential evaluations that the bank had recently introduced to review its global talent pool showed that the young Japanese women working in this branch on average scored higher in terms of both performance and leadership potential than did men in similar positions. These results had prompted an intense debate among the bank's senior managers. Previously, only one woman had been promoted to senior management, and women made up less than 10 percent of the high-potential pool. Shouldn't this number be much higher, in light of the results of the talent review? However, a previous effort to enhance the career advancement of women in the branch had encountered strong opposition, not only from the bank's predominantly Japanese clients but also from high-ranking government officials with whom the bank's senior executives had to interact. Many male employees resented reporting to a female manager, and some had openly voiced their displeasure with Heinen's decision to promote women to management positions, declaring they would rather quit than work for a female boss. After long and controversial discussions, in which the German expatriates strongly advocated the need to promote gender equality and their Japanese counterparts equally forcefully argued against any "radical" and "culturally inappropriate" management actions, Heinen decided that the time was not yet right to promote a significant number of female employees to management positions.

(Stahl 1998)

How should the general manager have balanced his obligations to the various parties affected by his decision: young Japanese women, whose career prospects were at stake; the bank's corporate customers and male Japanese government officials, who were unaccustomed to dealing with female executives; the expatriate managers who comprised his management team and insisted on fair and equitable treatment of all employees; and the predominantly male employees, who resisted any attempts to promote gender equality and increase the proportion of female managers in this branch? These stakeholders all had different expectations and vested interests; it was clear that in meeting some obligations, the executives of this bank would inevitably fail to meet others. Thus,

> After carefully weighing the pros and cons of the various options, Robert Heinen decided that a long-term approach was needed to tackle the problem. He and his management team launched a three-year program aimed at improving career opportunities for women in this branch. The program, "Making DCN Bank Japan a Great Place to Work for Women," included training and career coaching for women, changes in career development systems and promotion criteria, and efforts to build awareness about gender issues and create acceptance among male employees. Heinen and his team went to great lengths to demonstrate that gender equality was a top management priority, and he made it a point to personally introduce recently hired or newly promoted female managers to key customers and important government officials. Through this program, DCN Bank Japan significantly increased its proportion of female managers and reduced turnover rates among

women. In addition, internal surveys showed that team productivity, job satisfaction, and personal motivation among women improved.

(Stahl 1998)

This case illustrates that effectively responding to the needs of a diverse set of stakeholders requires an ability to balance different, and often conflicting, stakeholder demands and expectations. It also highlights the virtue of patience and cultural sensitivity as necessary factors in implementing global CSR initiatives and overcoming resistance at the local level.

The Ethics Challenge

Executives operating in a global, multicultural environment face complex ethical issues and moral dilemmas, often stemming from questions such as (DeGeorge 1993; Donaldson 1989):

- Shall we apply the same technological, environmental, and safety standards in developing countries?

- How should we deal with gifts from business partners, in particular in cultures where such giving is highly regarded?

- How should we react to bribery attempts by government officials?

- Is there a way to adhere to fundamental moral principles, such as human rights, while also being sensitive to cultural differences?

The scenario facing an operations manager for Levi-Strauss in Bangladesh illustrates the challenges when trying to make ethical decisions across geographic, cultural, and legal boundaries:

> After running an ethical audit, the operations manager discovered that two of his contractors employed children under 14 years of age. This practice was allowed under local law, but it violated International Labor Organization standards and company values and guidelines, which required such employment practices to be terminated. Inquiring further into the causes of child labor, he discovered that termination of their employment would likely drive the children to look for other jobs, most likely worse ones (perhaps even prostitution) and thus create further physical, psychological, and emotional hardships. He also realized that most of the children were the main providers of food and resources for their families, and sometimes the only breadwinners. Terminating their jobs would jeopardize the well-being of the whole family. In light of this challenge, he proposed that the factories should continue to pay the children's salaries while Levi-Strauss covered the costs for their education, until they reached legal working age.
>
> (Sources: Buller et al. 2000; Pless and Maak 2012; Schoenenberger 2000)

This case exemplifies a classic dilemma that cannot easily be reconciled. Simply enforcing compliance with existing global rules and regulations would lead to terrible hardship for the children and their families. But adhering to local standards and continuing to employ children was not an option. Ethical decision making requires managers to balance global and local perspectives and come up with morally imaginative solutions that align the interests of diverse stakeholders and reconcile moral differences on a higher level (Johnson 1993; Werhane 1999).

The Sustainability Challenge

Sustainability or sustainable development has emerged from the discussion on environmental management, closely related to the discourse on global warming and climate change (Gore 2007; Stern 2007). It is defined as "development that meets the needs of the present without compromising the ability of future generations to meet their needs" (Brundtland 1987). This definition contains a temporal dimension that stresses environmental stewardship, in terms of the long-term orientation required to ensure that future generations can thrive and flourish, even though this stakeholder group lacks a voice. It also raises the question of the extent to which leaders and corporations are responsible to not-yet-born members of society (Pruzan and Miller 2006). This long-term perspective stands in sharp contrast with pressures from financial markets to maximize short-term gains, as was aptly illustrated by the recent global economic crisis.

Despite such pressures, the number of companies that have implemented sustainable business practices is growing rapidly. Consider the environmental turnaround at Interface Inc., the world's largest manufacturer of commercial floor coverings:

> In the early 1990s Ray Anderson, then the CEO and now the chair of Interface, was asked to give a presentation on sustainable development at Interface. He was caught off guard and later openly admitted that he did not have much to say on the topic. By sheer coincidence, a book by Paul Hawken landed on his desk around the same time, entitled *The Ecology of Commerce*. As he began to read it, a thought dawned on him: He was a plunderer of the Earth. "Some day," he now likes to say in his frequent speaking appointments, "they will put people like me in jail." Anderson realized that he was exploiting the Earth's natural resources without thinking about the ecological footprint his company would leave for coming generations. For him, reading Hawken's book was an epiphany. In the years since, he set forth to lead one of the biggest and most fundamental transformations in modern business, inspiring innovations that have affected many other organizations and industries, to create the biggest, cleanest, most innovative, and most profitable industrial carpet manufacturer in the world. It is by no means a small achievement. The business of producing commercial carpet and floor tiles is a toxic one; it uses nylon and adhesives that are primarily created from oil and chemicals. In 1994, Interface was

using more than 500 million pounds of raw material each year, producing more than 900 million tons of emissions and 2 billion liters of wastewater (Rothman and Scott 2003). The challenge thus has been to identify ways to save resources, overcome technology barriers, get suppliers on board to deliver environmentally friendly raw materials, keep employees motivated and engaged, realize quick wins, and convince shareholders that the process would be profitable. The successful change initiative under Anderson's leadership has been guided by a mission of becoming a zero-emission business by 2020. In the process, Anderson also realized that "the sustainability initiative has been amazingly good for business." Thus what began as a "mid-course correction" (Anderson 1998) is now spearheading the company's "new industrial revolution" to create the ultimate sustainable enterprise that not only reconciles economic, environmental, and social bottom lines but enhances all of them at the same time.

(Maak and Pless 2008)

A dramatic overhaul of a company's business model in response to stakeholder concerns was an exception in the 1990s but, today, we find heightened awareness of the consequences of global warming and other environmental threats, as well as significant pressure to protect and preserve the natural environment. The increasing activism of powerful stakeholders, including international environmental NGOs, requires that global corporations and their leaders engage in dialogue with various stakeholders and eventually react to societal demands (Spar and La Mure 2003; Zadek 2004). Interface has illustrated that firms can benefit when they actively contribute to the triple bottom line (Elkington 1997) by creating environmental, social, and economic value.

The Citizenship Challenge

Many corporations work hard to be seen as good corporate citizens, engaging in community work, investing in infrastructure, and providing volunteer opportunities for their employees in their local communities. However, in a global environment, the citizenship responsibilities of corporations go beyond giving back to local society. In particular, considering the influence of large MNCs—some of which have more power than most nation-states (a widely cited data indicates that five of the ten largest economies in the world are corporations, not countries; World Trade Organization 2011)—these firms and their leaders are expected to recognize and assume political co-responsibility (Maak 2009; Scherer et al. 2006). This responsibility is not limited to the countries in which they operate but also applies to socio-political issues in the global arena, especially with respect to human rights, social justice, and environmental protections.

The following case provides an example of the citizenship challenge that leaders of MNCs operating in countries characterized by weak institutions, underdeveloped legal systems, and corrupt governments can face:

In 1995 Shell and its local subsidiary SPDC (Shell Petroleum Development Company of Nigeria Limited), which was co-owned by the military dictatorship that ran the Nigerian government, were accused of shirking their responsibilities to the indigenous Ogoni people, who had been living for centuries as farmers and fishers in the Niger Delta, on land where Shell and its partners exploited oil resources. Instead of giving back to the Ogoni and providing them with jobs and infrastructure, oil exploitation and gas flaring resulted in the destruction of their ecological habitat, causing severe health problems among locals. Furthermore, the company came under pressure because it did not try to stop the military government, the operation's co-owner, from executing the writer and civil rights activist Ken Saro-Wiwa, who had founded and led the Movement for the Survival of Ogoni People (MOSOP), an NGO representing the rights and interests of the Ogoni people. In a show trial, Saro-Wiwa had been falsely accused by the dictatorship of responsibility for the death of other activists. Shell's approach to dealing with accusations from local stakeholders such as MOSOP was to hide behind a pure economic-technical business orientation, stressing its position as a nonpolitical, private actor and asserting that its actions were consistent with Shell's global code of conduct. The way Shell handled the situation created the impression that it was collaborating with a corrupt government, which provoked a global outcry and seriously damaged Shell's reputation.

(Pless and Maak 2005)

In May 2009, fourteen years after the execution of Saro-Wiwa and eight fellow Ogoni activists, a court case opened in New York City accusing Shell of condoning human rights violations committed by the former military government and collaborating with the authorities who arranged the executions (Green and Peel 2009). The trial raised again the question of Shell's political co-responsibility for the murder of the Ogoni activists and, more generally, the political role that companies play when they do business in rogue states. In essence, the Shell Nigeria case exemplifies the need to be aware of the political role that comes with economic power, especially in less developed political contexts, and be prepared to take on political co-responsibility.

The above described leadership challenges in the areas of diversity, ethics, sustainability, and citizenship highlight that global executives must act in accordance with the expectations and legitimate demands of a diverse set of stakeholders. These challenges are more complex in a global context, because pressures to adapt or fit in often combine with incomplete and inaccurate understanding of the local operating contexts.

When global executives engage in unethical or illegal activities, it often reflects a naive form of cultural or political relativism. For example, managers may accept bribery or unlawful conduct because they think it is acceptable in the host country or will not be discovered by the inadequate control systems and lax enforcement setting (Donaldson 1996; Puffer and McCarthy 2008). Other managers make the opposite mistake and uncritically apply global standards, rules, or policies to situations that require culturally sensitive handling. When Shell engaged in a business partnership with the Nigerian government, it should have realized that, by doing so, it was entering the political arena, creating some political responsibility and accountability for itself. In contrast, when the Levi-Strauss manager in Bangladesh attempted to address the problem of child labor, he could not simply apply global standards but needed a sustainable solution that could eliminate the problem while also demonstrating cultural sensitivity. In the global arena, both cultural relativism and ethical imperialism are likely to lead instead to inappropriate, irresponsible leadership behavior.

In the next section, we elaborate on these ideas and present three approaches to responsible global leadership.

The Challenge of Responsible Global Leadership: Balancing Global and Local Requirements

Recently, several scholars (e.g. Arthaud-Day 2005; Husted and Allen 2006; Stahl et al. 2009) have proposed that MNCs must respond to pressures for global integration and local responsiveness with respect to CSR, just as their business strategies respond to the pressures for integration and responsiveness in product markets (Bartlett and Ghoshal 1989; Prahalad and Doz 1987). Companies competing in the global marketplace thus face a fundamental dilemma, namely, how to balance the need for global consistency in CSR approaches with the need to be sensitive to local conditions. Building on the framework of transnational CSR proposed by Arthaud-Day (2005), we look at three prototypical approaches to CSR and discuss their implications for the challenges facing executives in the global arena. Figure 11.2 illustrates the three approaches and highlights the tensions and possible trade-offs between globally integrated and locally adapted CSR strategies.

The Global CSR Approach

If headquarters' perspective and demands for global consistency and integration prevail over local concerns, a global CSR approach is implied. The perceived advantages derived from the global integration of CSR activities must clearly outweigh the perceived benefits of meeting the needs of salient stakeholders in countries where the firm operates. The MNCs that follow the global approach to CSR tend to establish universal guidelines or codes of conduct and apply them to every cultural context in which they do business (Arthaud-Day 2005). The viability of this approach rests on the assumption of a universal standard of responsible behavior that transcends the norms and values of particular societies (Donaldson and Dunfee 1999; Frederick 1991). Examples of such universal norms and values are those that appear in the UN Global Compact (e.g. support

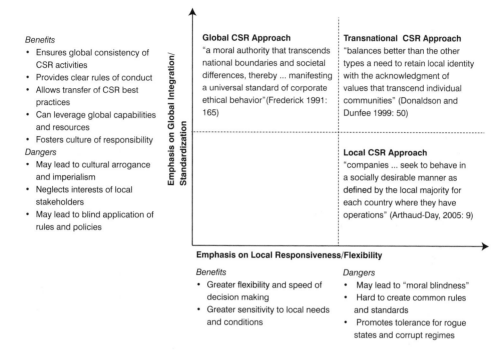

Figure 11.2 Approaches to CSR in Global Organizations

and respect the protection of international human rights) or the UN Millennium development goals (e.g. ensure environmental sustainability), but they are also implicit in corporate policies, mission statements, and ethics codes (e.g. "We act with the highest standards of integrity at all times and do not enter into any form of fraudulent activity wherever we do business"). Donaldson and Dunfee (1999: 52) call these universal principles "hypernorms," asserting that they are based on values "acceptable to all cultures and all organizations."

The potential benefits of a global approach to CSR are evident. It establishes clear rules of behavior, raises awareness of the importance of responsible conduct among employees worldwide, increases trust in the firm's leadership and control mechanisms, helps the company prevent and manage risk, fosters a culture of responsibility within the global organization, and ensures global consistency in managerial decision making and behavior. However, such global consistency comes at a price. A global CSR approach can lead to cultural arrogance and ethical imperialism, which directs executives to act everywhere in the same way that "things are done at headquarters." As Donaldson (1996: 52) has noted, "when cultures have different standards of ethical behavior—and different ways of handling unethical behavior—a company that takes an absolutist approach may find itself making a disastrous mistake." A global CSR approach also makes it more likely that managers use their companies' global policies to legitimize actions that are detrimental to the interests of local stakeholders or turn a blind eye to human rights abuses in the countries where they operate. The case of Shell

Nigeria is instructive in this regard. Shell's management decided not to interfere with local government, insisting on its nonpolitical role and hiding behind its global code of conduct. Ignoring its political co-responsibility and allowing the execution of Ken Saro-Wiwa resulted, thirteen years later, in a lawsuit in New York, "hailed as a milestone moment in the movement towards corporate accountability and human rights" (Center for Constitutional Rights 2011) and settled by a payment of US$15.5 million. The Shell case illustrates that a global CSR approach does not absolve companies of responsibility for the impact of their operations on human rights or the welfare of the local communities in the countries where they operate.

The Local CSR Approach

The locally oriented approach to CSR is in some ways the mirror opposite of the global approach. It emphasizes the need for sensitivity and responsiveness to local conditions when conducting business in different contexts (Arthaud-Day 2005; Solomon 1996). Executives of companies that have implemented a local CSR approach thus seek to behave in a socially desirable manner, as defined by the local majority for each country where they conduct operations (Naor 1982), and attempt to work as cooperatively as possible with the government and other stakeholders of the host country.

The main benefits of this approach compared with the global CSR approach are its greater responsiveness to the interests and concerns of stakeholders in the host country. The greater flexibility and responsiveness with respect to CSR derived from a local approach is not without issues though. In practical terms, this approach makes it very difficult to create or apply any universally accepted code of conduct (Manakkalathil and Rudolf 1995), or even to determine what is ethically right or acceptable. As Donaldson (1996: 49) acknowledges, "[c]ultural relativism is morally blind." If there is no right or wrong per se and everything is relative, there is no common standard by which to judge the morality of an action and guide managerial decision making. Moreover, in combination with weak institutions, inadequate regulations, and ineffective law enforcement in the countries where MNCs operate, a local CSR approach may lead to disastrous decisions at the local level.

The Chinese baby milk scandal provides a case in point. The New Zealand dairy cooperative Fonterra, which owns a 43 percent stake in a Chinese company that had sold contaminated milk powder, was accused of failing to go public quickly enough when it learned of the scandal—waiting until after the 2008 Olympic Games were nearly finished before formally notifying New Zealand authorities. When Fonterra executives received the information, they held three meetings to try to persuade Shijiazhuang health officials in China to raise the alarm, all without success. The central government had issued directives to suppress "bad news" during the Beijing Olympics. The whistle was finally blown by the New Zealand government on

September 9, 2008, six weeks after Fonterra discovered the contamination, and a recall was issued. Paul French, director of Access Asia, a Shanghai-based consumer consultancy, blamed "the worst failure to whistleblow ... ever" on Western executives who believed that they had to avoid making their local partners in China "lose face" at all costs (Spencer and Foster 2008).

The Fonterra case illustrates, somewhat paradoxically, that global executives' attempts to work within a system and act in a locally sensitive manner can lead to decisions that put both the company and its stakeholders in harm's way. This danger is particularly acute in cases in which executives interpret their responsibilities to local stakeholders narrowly, forging strong, cooperative relationships with local government but ignoring the legitimate concerns of other, less powerful stakeholders in the host country.

The Transnational CSR Approach

A transnational approach adopts a hybrid strategy, resting on the assumption that global and local approaches to CSR are not mutually exclusive (Arthaud-Day 2005). In many cases, economic needs, political pressures, and stakeholder expectations demand that companies respond to both global issues and local concerns simultaneously, thereby acknowledging that diverse stakeholders and conflicting value systems require complex CSR responses (Husted and Allen 2006; Logsdon and Wood 2005). In essence, a transnational CSR approach demands that companies develop a global template for their CSR activities to ensure consistency across the organization but allow executives of local subsidiaries to adapt that template according to their specific needs and circumstances. Global policies and codes of conduct may be enacted in different ways, depending on the local conditions and cultural norms. IBM, for example, despite its strong emphasis on diversity, does not have gay and lesbian policies in some Asian countries (Stahl et al. 2008). According to IBM executives, issues related to sexual orientation are not well accepted or openly discussed in many Asian countries, which makes it difficult to implement such policies in an Asian context. However, other policies and programs related to diversity are considered "non-negotiable" and implemented worldwide with few, if any, local adaptations. Such transnational flexibility in diversity practices enables IBM to build and leverage local talent in a way that remains consistent with local norms but still sufficiently globally standardized to ensure that all parts of the organization attract, develop, and retain diverse talent.

Thus, agreement on the fundamentals (e.g. for IBM, a consensus about the importance of fair treatment of all employees and the need to capitalize on the talents of diverse workforces) does not preclude sensitivity to local norms and customs. Although the transnational approach is not without problems—in particular, it is often difficult to strike an appropriate balance between global consistency and local adaptation—this approach appears best able to guide managerial decision making and behavior, as well as to help executives address their responsible leadership challenges in the global arena.

To conclude, a local approach to CSR may promote a naive form of relativism (e.g. "when in Rome, do as the Romans do") with disastrous consequences, as illustrated by the case of the Fonterra baby milk scandal. The global CSR approach may lead to ethical imperialism and a neglect of local stakeholder interests. The transnational approach instead seems to balance the need for global consistency and local responsiveness with respect to CSR principles, standards, and practices.

Competencies Required for Responsible Global Leadership

Table 11.1 summarizes the key competencies required for responsible global leadership. It clearly is not exhaustive in terms of listing all personal characteristics (e.g. personality traits, abilities, motives) that might support a firm's CSR strategy or promote responsible leadership within a global organization (for a detailed overview of individual-level influences, see Stahl 2011). Rather, we attempt to include characteristics that differentiate best among the three approaches and thereby to illustrate that different CSR strategies require different types of managers, with different competencies, perspectives, and experiences. A transnational approach to CSR is most demanding in terms of required managerial and leadership skills, in that it requires managers to reconcile the different, and often conflicting, expectations of their global and local stakeholders.

As indicated by Table 11.1, executives implementing a transnational CSR strategy must possess all the competencies needed to achieve success at global and local levels. For example, managers should approach local stakeholders in open and nonjudgmental ways, understanding their needs and perspectives, and respond effectively to legitimate demands and expectations (i.e. local approach to CSR). These capabilities require, among other things, some culture-specific knowledge, intercultural sensitivity, and perspective-taking skills—qualities sorely missing in Shell's handling of the Saro-Wiwa case. Yet global executives also must keep a big picture in mind, consider the needs of global stakeholders, and be able to

Table 11.1 Competencies Required to Support Different CSR Approaches

Global CSR Approach	Local CSR Approach	Transnational CSR Approach
• Strong commitment to head office • Understanding of global stakeholders' needs • Big picture thinking • "Helicopter" view • Understanding of universal ethical standards • Integrity and behavioral consistency	• Strong commitment to local stakeholders • Nonjudgmental and open to different views • Local knowledge and experience • Intercultural sensitivity and perspective-taking skills • Adaptability and behavioral flexibility	Global + Local Approaches, plus... • Dual citizenship • Global mindset • Ability to balance paradoxes and contradictions • Tolerance of uncertainty • Multicultural identity • Long-term orientation • Moral imagination

adopt a "helicopter" view to avoid being trapped into narrow, local thinking (i.e. global approach to CSR), as occurred when Fonterra's executives responded to the baby milk scandal. When it comes to making critical decisions that affect the overall organization and the firm's global stakeholders, executives must appreciate universal ethical standards, which can serve as the moral compass to guide decision making and behavior.

However, as we saw in the Levi-Strauss child labor case, a transnational CSR orientation requires more from managers than just an understanding of universal ethical standards and local norms and customs. To reconcile the tensions between centralization and decentralization, global integration and local flexibility, commitment to the firm's global stakeholders and commitment to the needs of local stakeholders, managers need to be able to develop what Black and Gregersen (1992) have called "dual citizenship": an ability to identify with and understand both local and global realities, viewpoints, and requirements. This form of citizenship should go hand in hand with the ability to tolerate uncertainty and cope with cultural paradoxes and ethical dilemmas (Donaldson 1996; Pless et al. 2011; Stahl et al. 2009). It requires a global mindset and thus cosmopolitan thinking, as well as the capacity to understand, mediate, and integrate multiple cultural and strategic realities (Levy et al. 2007). Finally, this approach requires moral imagination by the manager (Werhane 2008), a quality that can help a manager resolve ethical dilemmas and align the conflicting interests of diverse stakeholders by developing novel and synergistic solutions that transcend established global policies or local practices.

Approaches to Promoting Responsible Leadership in Global Organizations

Companies can take several steps to promote responsible global leadership in their organizations, as well as to effectively prevent, manage, and control the risks of irresponsible managerial behavior.

Assessment and Selection

When recruiting, selecting, and promoting managers, organizations must recognize the individual-level variables, such as personality traits, motives, and values, that best predict managers' propensity to engage in responsible or irresponsible behavior. For example, firms might use personality tests and integrity tests (Munchus 1989), along with situational interviews, to help determine which employees are more likely to act responsibly or irresponsibly in a global environment. In situational interviews, the interviewer describes a situation (e.g. an ethical dilemma facing an expatriate manager) and asks applicants how they would handle it. Stahl (2001) has developed the Intercultural Assessment Center (IAC) survey, which assesses candidates on a range of competencies that are critical for responsible global leadership, including nonjudgmental attitudes, behavioral flexibility, and tolerance of ambiguity, through individual and group exercises (e.g. negotiation simulations, role plays, situational questions).

Training and Development

An area of particular importance for promoting responsible managerial behavior is leadership development and training. Recently, management scholars and educators (Ghoshal 2005; Giacalone and Thompson 2006; Mintzberg 2004; Mintzberg and Gosling 2002; Pfeffer 2005) have begun to question the assumptions underlying traditional management education, which seemingly contributed to a moral vacuum while also failing to prepare managers and students for the leadership challenges that they would face in modern corporations. Although many personality traits, attitudes, and values associated with responsible global leadership (e.g. integrity, nonjudgmental attitudes) are relatively fixed and hard to change, training and development activities can help ensure that managers of all types act more responsibly. After an employee has joined an organization, induction programs, individual coaching by superiors, and other socialization practices can ensure that the newcomer learns the values, expected behaviors, and social knowledge needed to become an effective, responsible member of the organization (Cohen 2010). For example, training programs might focus on awareness of various facets of sexual harassment, to increase understanding of the risks of sexual harassment for both the employee and the organization (Pierce et al. 2004).

A promising new trend in management education is the use of service learning programs and consciousness-raising experiences to prepare managers for the social, ecological, and ethical issues they are likely to encounter (Mirvis 2008; Pless and Maak 2009). For example, PricewaterhouseCoopers' Ulysses Program aims to develop leaders who are capable of assuming senior leadership roles in the global arena and who

> understand the changing role of business in influencing the economic, political, social and environmental well-being of communities and markets across the world, and our responsibility to work in collaboration with a broader group of stake-holders to achieve sustainable success through responsible world-wide business practices.
>
> (PwC 2008)

The program sends senior executives and partners on assignments in developing countries to work with a host organization (usually a nonprofit organization) on predefined service projects in areas such as health, poverty alleviation, sustainability, and rural development. To ensure learning from these experiences, the program uses an integrated service learning approach. Thus the field assignments are integrated into a learning design, with a one-week preparation phase prior to the assignment and a one-week debriefing phase after the trip. Furthermore, the program uses a variety of learning methods and assessment tools, including 360-degree feedback, coaching, team building, project-based learning, yoga and meditation, storytelling sessions, and reflective exercises to achieve learning at the cognitive, affective, and behavioral levels.

The findings of an evaluation study (Pless et al. 2011) support the effectiveness of the Ulysses Program in developing competencies that are critical for responsible global leadership, including intercultural sensitivity and a global mindset, self-awareness and self-management skills, and "ethical literacy" that encompasses moral imagination, ethical decision making, and service orientation. As we illustrate in Figure 11.3, learning through this program occurred at the cognitive, affective, and behavioral levels. Furthermore, PwC identified several learning mechanisms that seemed particularly significant in the context of international service learning programs, such as the experience of dealing with cultural paradoxes and ethical dilemmas. Collectively, these findings suggest that international service learning programs that involve cultural immersion at a relatively deep level, through daily interaction and collaboration with local stakeholders, can help managers develop responsible global leadership capabilities and be effective means of developing a transnational orientation. A growing number of companies, including IBM, Novo Nordisk, and Unilever, have implemented similar programs to support their global CSR and sustainability strategies and promote responsible leadership in their organizations (Colvin 2009; Googins et al. 2007).

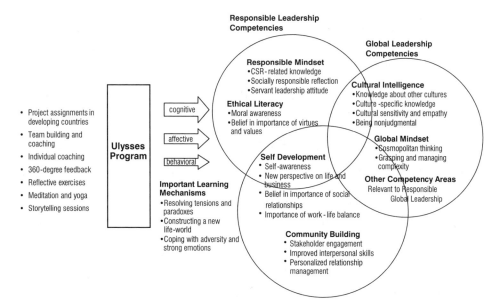

Figure 11.3 Developing Responsible Global Leaders: PwC's Project Ulysses

Source: N. M. Pless, T. Maak, and G. K. Stahl (2011) "Developing responsible global leaders through International Service Learning Programs: The Ulysses experience." *Academy of Management Learning and Education*, 10(2): 242.

Performance Management and Control Systems

In terms of control systems, top management teams can actively promote responsible behavior and discourage irresponsible behavior by communicating integrity as a core value, creating and enforcing company policies and codes of conduct, and implementing performance management and reward systems that hold managers accountable for their irresponsible behavior (Cohen 2010; Crane and Matten 2007).

An interesting trend in performance management is that companies increasingly recognize that new business models and changes in the marketplace necessitate the incorporation of softer, nontangible, behavioral-based performance measures, within an objective setting and performance appraisal process. Companies as diverse as Oracle, Shell, KPMG, and GlaxoSmithKline actively promote cultures that value not only short-term financial performance but also the intangible aspects of long-term value creation, with an emphasis on both key performance targets and how to achieve those targets (Stahl et al. 2008). Desired competencies include, for example, the ability to see things that others don't, inspiring trust and loyalty in the team, leading by example, and acting in socially responsible ways.

Consistent with this trend, some companies have introduced a "values-based" performance management system, which assesses and compensates employees according to not only how well they perform but also their shared values. For example, the pharmaceutical firm Novartis's performance management system combines the extent of achievement of individual performance objectives (the what) and the values and behaviors required to deliver those results (the how). Thus, Novartis managers are assessed on and rewarded for their shared values, such as candor, trust, and integrity (Chua et al. 2005). Many other excellent companies similarly have come to realize that they must balance priorities—the financial success of the company with principles of fair play, sustainability, or social responsibility—and thus have adopted similar systems.

Conclusion

Executives of global organizations are often ill prepared for the wider social, political, ecological, and ethical issues they face. In this chapter, we have discussed what it means to be a "responsible" global leader by considering the challenges facing executives in the global arena and the choices they have about how to meet those challenges. We have evaluated existing approaches to promoting responsible leadership in global organizations, looked at the competencies critical for responsible global leadership, and offered recommendations for how organizations can prevent, manage, and control the risks of irresponsible leader behavior. If responsibility is "at the heart of what effective leadership is all about" (Waldman and Galvin 2008: 327), then companies would be well advised to take advantage of these tools and approaches, as well as to better prepare their current and future leaders for the leadership challenges arising in an increasingly complex, global, and interconnected world.

12 Looking to the Future

B. SEBASTIAN REICHE AND MARK E. MENDENHALL

A variety of scholars have delineated gaps that exist in the field of global leadership (Beechler and Javidan 2007; Khilji et al. 2010; Morrison 2000; Osland et al. 2006), which usually fall into one of the following categories:

1 *Characteristics of global leadership*: distinguishing between the roles and behaviors of global managers and global leaders, definitively answering the question of whether and how global leaders differ from domestic leaders, developing models that integrate the constructs of global mindset and global leadership, identifying the cognitive processes related to global leadership.

2 *Global leadership competences*: refining the identification of global leadership behaviors, identifying global leadership capabilities in both teams and organizations, developing more rigorous global leadership assessment instruments, investigating the relationship between global strategy and specific types of global leadership skills.

3 *Effectiveness of global leadership*: delineating situational contingencies' effects on global leadership effectiveness and global leadership styles, delineating antecedents of global leadership effectiveness, constructing decision models that aid in the determination of the number of global leaders that firms need, investigating the learning processes of global leaders and how they share their learning within their organizations, and clarifying how global leadership explicitly influences competitive advantages for organizations.

We do not disagree with the recommendations offered above—all of these research streams would be of great benefit to the field; however, many—if not all—of these proposed research foci would be aided significantly if the construct of global leadership itself could be clarified. The issue of defining global leadership has already been addressed in Chapter 1; however, addressing it again in this chapter is necessary because this issue is perhaps the most critical research gap in the field.

Learning from Past Mistakes

Many scholars operating in the field of global leadership began their careers studying expatriate performance. For decades they and other scholars have been studying expatriate adjustment, performance, and commitment, yet they did not actively attempt to define the independent variable of their study—*expatriates*. If described at all in their research studies, expatriates were defined by their demographic characteristics (e.g. citizenship, age, gender, previous overseas work experience, etc.). Over time, as the field evolved, scholars began to realize they might be studying different types of expatriates, and the realization slowly emerged that, "Wait a minute, what do we mean when we say, *expatriate*? Self-initiated expatriates? Short-term expatriates? Long-term expatriates? Flexpatriates? Inpatriates? Or academic versus diplomatic versus missionary versus business versus study abroad versus military expatriates?" It turned out that the conceptual ways in which the construct *expatriate* could be sliced were many and varied, and it logically followed that general models of expatriation may not address all the nuances of expatriate adjustment, identity, and embeddedness associated with the varying species of expatriates (Kraimer et al. 2012; Reiche et al. 2011; Tharenou and Caulfield 2010). The field is growing in terms of the concepts related to expatriation that are studied—a state that has in many ways breathed fresh new life into the domain—but the concepts may not all apply (or apply in different ways) to the different forms of assignees/global employees.

All of this could have been mostly avoided if scholars had focused initially on carefully trying to delineate the core construct of their field instead of assuming that everyone in the field implicitly understood the construct. Now, scholars are having to double back after years of studying expatriates to work out exactly how to best define their construct (Konopaske, Mendenhall and Thomason 2010).

It is important to learn from the field of expatriation and not repeat the same mistake in the field of global leadership. To date there has not been a lively debate in the field regarding what *global* leadership means. We offer ourselves and our colleagues as an "Exhibit 1" case example of this state of affairs. Sometimes, when we are discussing a businessperson we are studying, one of us will say something like, "This person is very impressive, but she is not a global leader—she is really an expatriate." Then, one of us will respond with a statement something like, "Wait a minute, this person is really exhibiting high-level, nuanced global leadership competencies—I think that makes her a global leader." A good-natured debate then ensues that leaves the matter of definition unresolved. While these debates are intellectually stimulating, they reflect an unfortunate reality—right now scholars in the field tend to work based on their idiosyncratic, implicit definitions of global leadership. The dimensions of these implicit definitions often collectively overlap, but there are almost always important divergences as well. Implicit assumptions regarding what is *global* and what is *leadership*, and what is *global leadership* currently do not harmonize sufficiently within the scholarly community and are not explicit enough to act as a heuristic catalyst for the field's profitable evolution.

A sampling of attempts to date to define *global leadership* and/or *global leaders* is given in Table 12.1. For illustration purposes, we have included the definition of the construct proposed in Chapter 1 in this book along with other samples of

Table 12.1 Representative Definitions of Global Leadership from the Literature

Author	Definition
Adler 1997	Global leadership involves the ability to inspire and influence the thinking, attitudes, and behavior of people from around the world … [it] can be described as "a process by which members of the world community are empowered to work together synergistically toward a common vision and common goals resulting in an improvement in the quality of life on and for the planet." Global leaders are those people who most strongly influence the process of global leadership.
Beechler and Javidan 2007: 140	Global leadership is the process of influencing individuals, groups, and organizations (inside and outside the boundaries of the global organization) representing diverse cultural/political/institutional systems to contribute towards the achievement of the global organization's goals.
Brake 1997: 38	Global leaders—at whatever level or location—1) will embrace the challenges of global competition, 2) generate personal and organizational energies to confront those challenges, and 3) transform the organizational energy into world-class performance.
Caligiuri 2006: 219	Global leaders, defined as executives who are in jobs with some international scope, must effectively manage through the complex, changing, and often ambiguous global environment.
Caligiuri and Tarique 2009: 336	Global leaders [are] high level professionals such as executives, vice presidents, directors, and managers who are in jobs with some global leadership activities such as global integration responsibilities. Global leaders play an important role in developing and sustaining a competitive advantage.
Gregersen et al. 1998	Leaders who can guide organizations that span diverse countries, cultures, and customers.
McCall and Hollenbeck 2002: 32	Simply put, global executives are those who do global work. With so many kinds of global work, again depending on the mix of business and cultural crossings involved, there is clearly no one type of global executive. Executives, as well as positions, are more or less global depending upon the roles they play, their responsibilities, what they must get done, and the extent to which they cross borders.
Mendenhall, Osland, Bird, Oddou, Maznevski, Stevens and Stahl (see Chapter 1 in this volume)	Global leaders are individuals who effect significant positive change in organizations by building communities through the development of trust and the arrangement of organizational structures and processes in a context involving multiple cross-boundary stakeholders, multiple sources of external cross-boundary authority, and multiple cultures under conditions of temporal, geographical, and cultural complexity.
Spreitzer et al. 1997: 7	An executive who is in a job with some international scope, whether in an expatriate assignment or in a job dealing with international issues more generally.

In some cases these definitions have been edited, for purposes of readability and clarity, and thus have left out citations within the actual definitions where the authors credit the ideas of others for parts of their definitions. Please see the definitions in the published articles for these citations.

definitions from well-known contributions to the literature, though this is by no means a complete review of all published definitions of the construct.

The field faces an additional obstacle to that of its parent field of leadership: the need for clarity regarding an additional element of its construct—the term, "global" (Jokinen 2005). By attaching the concept of *global* to the construct of *leadership*, scholars choosing to work in this field have doubled their theoretical burden—now they must not only attempt to deal with what *leadership* is, but also to delineate what *global* means!

The construct of leadership is fuzzy enough; attaching a sub-construct to it that matches its obtuseness is not in the best interests of the field. Others have even added further constructs, as in the case of responsible global leadership (Pless et al. 2011). Given the unsuccessful logjam of efforts to uncover an elegant and comprehensive definition of the construct of leadership, it is our contention that spending effort on operationalizing the construct of *global* may be in the best interest of the field. If the concept of *global* is not adequately defined, and scholars go forward assuming that everyone else perceives *global* to mean the same thing as their personal, implicit definition of it, the field may wind up in the same quandary as their sister field of *expatriation*.

The Dimensions of "Global"

In general, the definitions in Table 12.1 lack conceptual elegance. Though there are overlapping assumptions about the meaning of *global*, the attempt to define this element of the definition is usually quite cumbersome. There has been a kind of "kitchen-sink" approach to defining the term that involves listing what the authors consider to be its dimensions. Some authors emphasize that global leaders must deal with *more of* the same type of issues that domestic leaders deal with, such as cross-boundary stakeholders, sources of external cross-boundary authority, and cultures. The implied primary difference between domestic leaders and global leaders is that the international scope of their job demands enhances the multiplicity and type of boundaries that must be continually crossed by the leader. This "multiplicity of boundary spanning" is a common feature of many constructs of *global* in definitions of *global leadership*.

In addition to the above approach, definitions of global leadership also commonly include the notion of *global* as being the context in which leaders must lead. Adler (1997) prefers the traditional dictionary definition of the term *global*, that is, "being of the planet," and her definition emphasizes the notion of leadership in the "world community." Most other scholars are less sanguine in their constructions; they choose to equate *global* with the concept of *globalization* and instead focus on the nature of this phenomenon in their definitions. For them, *global(ization)* tends to be seen as a context that is nonlinear, constantly changing, complex, and ambiguous by nature. However, the authors of these studies do not carefully delineate the dimensions of the *global(ization)* context. Similar to the past tendency in the field of expatriation, scholars tend to implicitly assume that everyone else understands what they mean by the term, *global*. For example, it is likely that the "multiplicity of boundary spanning" factor is the primary dimension of *global(ization)* in the view of some scholars; other scholars, however, may view this as a separate factor that interacts with other, more fundamental conditions inherent in *global(ization)*. Similarly, scholars may work off different conceptualizations of the type of boundaries that global leaders span, including organizational, cultural, linguistic, institutional or even religious boundaries. In summary, scholars have not generally been inclined to carefully delineate what they mean when they use the term *global* with the terms *leaders* or *leadership*. This is, of course, not an unusual state of affairs in a nascent field. We will not propose a comprehensive solution to the problem of the construct definition of *global* in this chapter, but rather will offer an intermediate recommendation for consideration.

Towards a Construct Definition of Global

While we like Adler's 1997 definition of global leadership and its focus on process, its planetary scope may limit its applicability to organizational studies research as her definition requires scholars to be able to isolate primary global leaders that exist within the process of global leadership. From a nonlinear dynamics perspective, anyone and everyone on the planet is an active element of the global leadership process, and isolating those who in actuality influence the process most significantly may prove to be a difficult task. For example, those who may *seem* to influence the global leadership process (e.g. Bill Gates, the Dalai Lama) may in reality not do so as much as we may assume, but rather are icons that reflect media bias regarding who the media choose to programmatically feature in their stories and programs. Delineating global leaders in terms of the actual outcomes of their influence on the overall global leadership process will be a difficult task for scholars to accomplish.

Our inclination is to seek after an integrating approach to the construct that merges portions of the conditions of "multiplicity of boundary spanning" and "global(ization)" that were heretofore discussed as being major elements of most current definitions of *global*. To do this, we propose that the construct of complexity proposed by Lane et al. (2004) may prove beneficial for this purpose. As noted earlier in Chapter 1, they argued that globalization is a term that has been used to attempt to describe what is in reality "increased complexity," and they hold that there are four dimensions of complexity that together in a systemic, ongoing "combining" cause a plethora of business challenges that often are unforeseen and inherently unpredictable to executives; these dimensions are multiplicity, interdependence, ambiguity, and flux. For a more in depth discussion of these dimensions that combine to form complexity, please see Chapter 1.

Thus, we propose that complexity is a defining dimension of the term *global* in the construct of *global leadership*. In other words, simply holding a title or positional authority within an organization does not automatically qualify someone as being a global leader—even if within that job there is responsibility with an international scope. Rather, it is the degree of complexity associated with the nature of one's international responsibilities that is one of the key dimensions of the sub-construct of *global*.

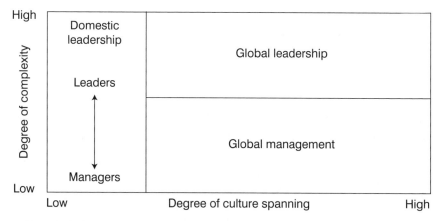

Figure 12.1 Defining Dimensions of the Term "Global"

We also propose that another defining dimension in the sub-construct of *global* is the degree of the "culture spanning" required of the individual in their role. By *culture spanning* we refer to the degree to which individuals must spend significant time and effort, both physically and virtually, in countries, cultures, and sub-cultures that differ from that of the culture they would define as their primary home culture in order to achieve the goals associated with their job description. For a conceptualization of these two dimensions of the sub-construct of *global*, please see Figure 12.1.

As illustrated in Figure 12.1, where degree of culture boundary spanning is low, individuals working in such contexts, despite the level of complexity in their roles, would be regarded as domestic leaders. Thus, though they may have high levels of ambiguity, interdependence, flux, and multiplicity in their work, this is complexity that operates mostly within domestic bounds, or at least with less international flavor than other contexts. Degree of complexity can also be hypothesized as being a condition that separates leaders from managers, thus acting as a differentiating variable between these two domains of administration. If so, complexity may act as one of the variables that theoretically, conceptually, and practically distinguish leadership from management, a long, ongoing debate in the general field of leadership.

In Figure 12.1, degree of complexity also differentiates between global management activities and global leadership activities. One of the challenges in the field is how global leaders should be distinguished from global managers or other global workers. In the proposed rubric, the degree to which an individual must engage in culture spanning and at that same time must handle high levels of complexity in the workplace is the primary factor of differentiation. Thus, we hold that scholars must first assess the level of complexity, using the four dimensions of complexity proposed earlier, and also assess the degree of culture spanning the individual must engage in to successfully perform before labeling a person a global leader for research purposes.

This framework, though basic in nature (and to some overly simplistic), nevertheless provides scholars with a template to follow when selecting global leaders for their research samples. Presently, no such qualification seems to exist in the field; if a scholar thinks someone is a global leader then they are assumed to be a global leader. The framework illustrated in Figure 12.1 places an assessment criterion on researchers to argue the case for inclusion into their sample based on complexity and culture spanning. If all scholars would do this in their research studies, this in and of itself would be a major step forward in the field.

In the Eye of the Beholder

A case one of the authors commonly uses in his classes depicts the situation of Michelle Goffin, a 23-year-old recent college graduate, who applies for and accepts a position as Director of the Children's Convalescent Home (CCH) in Georgetown, Guyana (Dietz et al. 2007). She arrives and finds herself in the middle of a political tug-of-war between the past manager of the CCH who will not step down and the Board of the Guyana Red Cross Society (GRCS). Four months after her arrival, Goffin is able to finally step into the role for which she was hired, and finds an organizational mess. She immediately throws herself in to putting things in order, and to do so she must maintain positive political relations with the GRCS, develop relationships of trust with the staff and the children, assess and work with dysfunctional parents, negotiate with local contractors for renovations to be made to the buildings of the CCH, reorganize the organizational structure of CCH, and overcome a massive mutiny on the part of the staff after her organizational change initiatives undergo a serious setback. All the while she finds herself in this context with no mentors, little expertise regarding Guyanese culture, and no meaningful financial resources to bring to bear on the challenges she faces.

Some scholars in the field would likely contend that she is not a global leader because she is in one country, dealing primarily with one culture, and that her job does not have international scope—it is essentially a domestic job, but a domestic job in a developing country. In other words, she is an expatriate—not a global leader. Other scholars would contend that she is a global leader because the kinds of skills she needs to be successful in her role are the exact same skills necessary for a global leader to be successful, ergo she is a global leader. Some would agree with the latter evaluation, but buffer it with the idea that she is more of a global leader "in training," while others would fall widely across the spectrum in between these two poles. Using the framework illustrated in Figure 12.1, however, would require scholars to assess this scenario somewhat differently.

First, they would need to ask the following question: "To what degree is Goffin dealing with complexity?" That is, to what degree is her work life rife with interdependence, multiplicity, flux, and ambiguity? From an external, objective perspective we know that her competitors are in many cases those for whom she works—people in power who she must keep appeased yet whom she must rely on for support; also, she must manage relationships with the hospital, suppliers, parents of the children in the home, her staff, government officials who oversee children's services, and other volunteers. She also has to reorganize the CCH, and there is no ideal organizational framework to draw from—she has almost an infinite variety of organizational design options from which to select. This multiplicity of stakeholders also creates a system of interdependencies in which she must exist as a manager—these are not separate working parts of but rather the dynamic reality in which she finds herself. Ambiguity for her is a daily reality— lack of information clarity, unclear cause and effect relationships, multiple ways of interpreting the same data, and major differences in cultural and sub-cultural norms compared to those of Canada all adds up to challenging levels of ambiguity. Additionally, she was tasked with assessing whether children should be taken into the CCH, when children should be returned to their parents, etc., none of which she had received formal training for prior to her arrival in Guyana. Add to this the fourth dimension of flux—a constantly changing, unpredictable environment—and most reasonable people would argue that Goffin was living and working in a state of medium to high level of complexity.

Then, the second question must be asked: "To what degree is her work requiring her to span cultures?" While she did not have to work in multiple countries, she was living and working outside of her home country in a developing nation whose social and work norms (not only on the national level, but also at the sub-culture level—familial, socioeconomic, bureaucratic, educational, etc.) were new to her. Given this analysis, our guess would be that most scholars would rank culture spanning as being in the semi-moderate range for Goffin.

Probably, most external analyses of Goffin's overall situation would place her somewhere in the realm illustrated by the lighter oval in Figure 12.2.

However, what if Goffin was queried during her work assignment about these two dimensions? How would she characterize the degree of complexity and culture spanning required of her to be successful? Of this we can never know for certain, but given the intensity of the challenges she faced, with no prior training to prepare her for the nature and variety of the daily problems she was confronted with in her role, it is likely that she would have characterized her context as being high in complexity and fairly high on culture spanning. Our estimation of the realm of her likely self-analysis range is illustrated in Figure 12.2 by the darker oval.

This brings up an intriguing issue in the field: Whose analysis should we pay most attention to as scholars? Self-analyses of complexity and culture spanning likely are important for those scholars and practitioners interested in developing global leadership competencies in managers. The global leadership development process models discussed in Chapter 5 indicate that "crucible experience-like" processes tend to trigger the potential for global competency acquisition. If so, it may not be as important what the objective assessment is of managers' context to determine

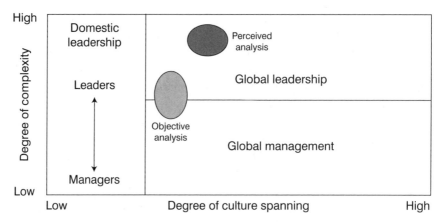

Figure 12.2 Perceived versus Objective Analysis of "Global"

whether it is a "global leadership situation," but rather how managers themselves perceive the nature of their contexts. For global leadership development at any rate, the eye of the beholder may be the most significant assessment; thus, before including a manager into a "global leader" versus "non-global leader" sampling process, scholars may need to refine the populating of their samples using "perceived" and/or "objective" assessments of the construct of global leadership.

In this final chapter, we have revisited what we believe is one, if not *the* most important issue that is currently limiting the field of global leadership from further advancing: the lack of a rigorous and widely accepted definition and operationalization of the construct of global leadership itself. To that end, we have offered two dimensions along which global leaders can be characterized and differentiated from domestic leaders and managers, and we have raised the question of locus of assessment of these dimensions. Explicitly addressing these elements may help scholars to more convincingly argue the case for their main unit of analysis under study, while also contributing to the development of a common body of research. We believe that it is not only the transition from purely domestic to global leadership that is characterized by a "quantum leap" (Bird and Osland 2004: 61), but that we should equally aim for no less in our research efforts to better understand the phenomenon of global leadership. This book provides a modest starting point towards this direction.

Bibliography

Adler, N.J. (1994) "Competitive frontiers: Women managing across borders." In N.J. Adler and D.N. Izreali (eds) *Competitive Frontiers: Women Managers in a Global Economy.* Cambridge, MA: Blackwell: 22–40.

Adler, N.J. (1997) "Global leadership: Women leaders." *Management International Review,* 37(1): 171–196.

Adler, N.J. (1998) "Did you hear? Global leadership in charity's world." *Journal of Management Inquiry*, 7(2): 135–143.

Adler, N.J. (2001) "Global leadership: Women leaders." In M. Mendenhall, T. Kuhlmann, and G. Stahl (eds) *Developing Global Business Leaders: Policies, Processes and Innovations.* Westport, CT: Quorum Books: 73–97.

Adler, N.J. (2002) *International Dimensions of Organizational Behavior*, 4th Edition. Cincinnati, OH: South-Western/Thomson Learning.

Adler, N. and Bartholomew, S. (1992) "Managing globally competent people." *Academy of Management Executive*, 6(23): 52–64.

Adler, N.J. and Gundersen, A. (2008) *International Dimensions of Organizational Behavior.* Cincinnati, OH: South-Western College.

Adler, P. (1975) "The transitional experience: An alternative view of culture shock." *Journal of Humanistic Psychology*, 15: 13–23.

Adsit, D.J., London, M., Crom, S., and Jones, D. (1997) "Cross-cultural differences in upward ratings in a multinational company." *The International Journal of Human Resource Management,* 8(4): 385–401.

Aguilera, R., Rupp, D.E., Williams, C.A., and Ganapathi, J. (2007) "Putting the 'S' back in corporate social responsibility: A multilevel theory of social change in organizations." *Academy of Management Review*, 3: 836–863.

Albrecht, T.L. and Hall, B.J. (1991) "Facilitating talk about new ideas: The role of personal relationships in organizational innovation." *Communication Monographs*, 58: 272–288.

Alldredge, M. and Nilan, K. (2000) "3M's Leadership competency model: An internally developed solution." *Human Resource Management*, 39(2/3): 133–146.

Ancona, D.G. and Caldwell, D.F. (1992) "Bridging the boundary: External activity and performance in organizational teams." *Administrative Science Quarterly*, 37: 634–661.

Anderson, B.A. (2005) "Expatriate selection: Good management or good luck?" *International Journal of Human Resource Management,* 16(4): 567–583.

Anderson, R.C. (1998) *Mid-course Correction, Towards a Sustainable Enterprise: The Interface Model.* Atlanta, GA: Peregrinzilla Press.

Andrews, K.M. and Delahaye, B.I. (2000) "Influences on knowledge processes in organizational learning: The psychosocial filter." *Journal of Management Studies*, 37(7): 797–810.

Ang, S., Van Dyne, L., Koh, C., and Ng, K.Y. (2004) "The measurement of cultural intelligence." Paper presented at the Academy of Management Meeting. New Orleans, LA.

Argote, L. and Ingram, P. (2000) "Knowledge transfer: A basis for competitive advantage in firms." *Organizational Behavior and Human Decision Processes*, 82: 150–169.

Argote, L., McEvily, B., and Reagans, R. (2003) "Managing knowledge in organizations. An integrative framework and review of emerging themes." *Management Science*, 49: 571–582.

Argyris, C. (1979) "How normal science methodology makes leadership research less additive and less applicable." In J.G. Hunt and L.L. Larson, (eds) *Crosscurrents in Leadership*. Carbondale, IL: Southern Illinois University Press: 47–63.

Armenakis A. and Bedeian A.G. (1999) "Organizational change: A review of theory and research in the 1990s." *Journal of Management*, 25(3): 293–315.

Armenakis A.A., Harris S., and Feild H. (1999) "Paradigms in organizational change: Change agent and change target perspectives." In R. Golembiewski (ed.) *Handbook of Organizational Behavior*. New York: Marcel Dekker.

Arnott, R.D. (2004) "Ethics and unintended consequences." *Financial Analysts Journal*, 60(3): 6–8.

Arthaud-Day, M.L. (2005) "Transnational corporate social responsibility: A tri–dimensional approach to international CSR research." *Business Ethics Quarterly*, 15(1): 1–22.

Arthur, M.B., Hall, D.T., and Lawrence, B.S. (1989) *Handbook of Career Theory*. New York: Cambridge University Press.

Arthur, W. Jr., and Bennett, W. Jr. (1997) "A comparative test of alternative models of international assignee job performance." In Z. Aycan (ed.) *New Approaches to Employee Management. Expatriate Management: Theory and Research Vol. 4.* Greenwich, CT: JAI Press: 141–172.

Ashby, W.R. (1956) *An Introduction to Cybernetics*. New York: Wiley.

Au, K.Y. and Fukuda, J. (2002) "Boundary spanning behaviors of expatriates." *Journal of World Business*, 37(4): 285–296.

Aycan, A. (2008) "Cross-cultural approaches to leadership." In P.B. Smith, M.F. Peterson, and D.C. Thomas (eds) *The Handbook of Cross-Cultural Management Research*. Los Angeles, CA: Sage, 219–238.

Aycan, Z. and Kanungo, R.N. (1997) "Current issues and future challenges in expatriation research." In Z. Aycan (ed.) *New Approaches to Employee Management—Theory and Research, 4th Edition*. Greenwich, CT: JAI Press: 245–260.

Badaracco, J.L. (1992) "Business ethics: Four spheres of executive responsibility." *California Management Review*, 34: 64–79.

Bansal, P. (2002) "The corporate challenges of sustainable development." *Academy of Management Executive*, 16(2): 122–131.

Bansal, P. and Candola, S. (2003) "Corporate social responsibility: Why good people behave badly in organizations." *Ivey Business Journal*, March/April: 1–5.

Barrick, M.R. and Mount M.K. (1991) "The Big Five personality dimensions and job performance: A meta-analysis." *Personnel Psychology*, 44: 1–26.

Bartlett, C.A. and Ghoshal, S. (1989) *Managing Across Borders: The Transnational Solution*. Boston, MA: Harvard Business School Press.

Bartlett, C.A. and Ghoshal, S. (1994) "What is a global manager?" In *Global Strategies: Insights From the World's Leading Thinkers*. Boston, MA: Harvard Business School Press: 77–91.

Bartlett, C.A. and Ghoshal, S. (2000) *Transnational Management*. Boston, MA: Irwin McGraw-Hill.

Bartlett, C.A., Doz, Y., and Hedlund, G. (1990) *Managing the Global Firm*. New York: Routledge.

Bartunek, J.M., Gordon, J.R., and Weathersby, R.P. (1983) "Developing 'complicated' understanding in administrators." *Academy of Management Review*, 8(2): 273–84.

Bass, B. M. (1985) *Leadership and performance beyond expectation*. New York: Free Press.

Bass, B.M. (1990) Bass and Stogdill's Handbook of Leadership: Theory, Research and Managerial Applications, 3rd Edition. New York: Free Press.

Bass, B.M. (1997) "Does the transactional–transformational leadership paradigm transcend organizational and national boundaries?" *American Psychologist*, 52(2): 130–139.

Bateson, M.C. (1994) *Peripheral Visions: Learning along the Way*. New York: HarperCollins Publishers.

Beckhard, R. (1991) "Strategies for large system change." In D.A. Kolb, I.M. Rubin, and J.S. Osland (eds) *The Organizational Behavior Reader*. Upper Saddle River, NJ: Prentice–Hall: 662–674.

Beechler, S. and Javidan, M. (2007) "Leading with a global mindset." In M. Javidan, R. Steers and M. Hitt (eds) *Advances in International Management: Special Issue on Global Mindset,* 19: 131–169.

Behrens, A. (2009) *Culture and Management in the Americas*. Stanford, CA: Stanford University Press.

Bennett, J. and Salonen, B. (2007) "Intercultural communication and the new American campus." *Change,* 39(2): 46–50.

Bennett, J.M. (2009) "Cultivating intercultural competence: A process perspective." In D. Deardorff (ed.) *The SAGE Handbook of Intercultural Competence*. Thousand Oaks, CA: Sage: 121–140.

Bennett, M.J. (1993) "Towards ethnorelativism: A developmental model of Intercultural sensitivity." In R.M. Paige (ed.) *Education for the Intercultural Experience*, 2nd ed. Yarmouth, ME: Intercultural Press: 21–71.

Bennis, W. (1989) *On Becoming a Leader*. Reading, MA: Addison-Wesley.

Bennis, W. (1997) "Cultivating creative genius." *Industry Week*, 246(15): 84–89.

Bennis, W. and Thomas, R.J. (2002) *Geeks and Geezers: How Era, Values and Defining Moments Shape Leaders*. Cambridge, MA: Harvard Business School Press.

Bennis, W.G. (1959) "Leadership theory and administrative behavior: The problem of authority." *Administrative Science Quarterly*, 4: 259–260.

Berry, J.W. (1983) "Acculturation: A comparative analysis of alternative forms." In R.J. Samuda and S.L. Woods (eds) *Perspectives in Immigrant and Minority Education*. New York: University Press of America: 65–78.

Berthoin Antal, A. (2001) "Expatriates' contributions to organizational learning." *Journal of General Management*, 26(4): 62–84.

Bettenhausen, K.L. (1991) "Five years of groups research: What we have learned and what needs to be addressed." *Journal of Management*, 17: 345–381.

Bikson,T.K., Treverton, G.F., Moini, J., and Lindstrom, G. (2003) *New Challenges for International Leadership: Lessons from Organizations with Global Missions*. Santa Monica, CA: RAND.

Bingham, C.B., Felin, T., and Black, J.S. (2000) "An interview with John Pepper: What it takes to be a global leader." *Human Resource Management*, 36(2/3): 173–292.

Bird, A. (1994) "Careers as repositories of knowledge: A new perspective on boundaryless careers." *Journal of Organizational Behavior*, 15(4): 325–344.

Bird, A. (2001) "International assignments and careers as repositories of knowledge." In M. Mendenhall, T. Kühlmann, and G.K. Stahl (eds) *Developing Global Business Leaders: Policies, Processes and Innovations*. Westport, CT: Quorum.

Bird, A. and Osland, J. S. (2004) "Global competencies: An introduction." In H. Lane, M. Maznevski, M. Mendenhall, and J. McNett (eds) *Handbook of Global Management*. Oxford: Blackwell: 57–80.

Bird, A., Stevens, M.J., Mendenhall, M.E., and Oddou, G. (2002) *The Global Competencies Inventory*. St. Louis, MO: The Kozai Group, Inc.

Bird, A., Stevens, M., Mendenhall, M., Oddou, G., and Osland, J. S. (2008) *The Intercultural Effectiveness Scale*. St. Louis, MO: The Kozai Group, Inc.

Bird, A., Mendenhall, M., Stevens, M., and Oddou, G. (2010) "Defining the content domain of intercultural competence for global leaders." *Journal of Managerial Psychology*, 25(8): 810–828.

Black, J.S. (1988) "Work-role transition: A study of American expatriate managers in Japan." *Journal of International Business Studies*, 19(2): 274–291.

Black, J.S. (2006) "The mindset of global leaders: Inquisitiveness and duality." In W.H. Mobley and E. Weldon (eds) *Advances in Global Leadership*, vol. 4: 181–200.

Black J.S. and Gregersen, H.B. (1990) "Expectations, satisfaction and intention to leave of American expatriate managers in Japan." *International Journal of Intercultural Relations*, 14: 485–506.

Black, J.S. and Gregersen, H.B. (1992) "Serving two masters: Managing the dual allegiance of expatriate employees." *Sloan Management Review*, 34: 61–71.

Black, J.S. and Gregersen, H.B. (1999) "The right way to manage expatriates." *Harvard Business Review*, 77(2): 52–54, 56, 58, 60–62.

Black, J.S. and Gregersen, H. (2000) "High impact training: Forging leaders for the global frontier." *Human Resource Management*, 39(2/3): 173–184.

Black, J.S., Mendenhall, M., and Oddou, G. (1991) "Toward a comprehensive model of international adjustment: An integration of multiple theoretical perspectives." *Academy of Management Review*, 16(2): 291–317.

Black, J.S., Morrison, A., and Gregersen, H. (1999a) *Global Explorers: The Next Generation of Leaders*. New York: Routledge.

Black, J.S., Gregersen, H., Mendenhall, M., and Stroh, L. (1999b) *Globalizing People through International Assignments*. New York: Addison-Wesley Longman.

Blakeney, R., Oddou, G., and Osland, J. S. (2006a) "The effects of repatriate characteristics on knowledge transfer." Paper presented at the Academy of Management meetings, Atlanta, GA.

Blakeney, R., Oddou, G., and Osland, J.S. (2006b) "Repatriate assets: Factors impacting knowledge transfer." In M. Morley, N. Heraty, and D. Collings (eds) *International HRM and International Assignments*. New York: Palgrave Macmillan: 181–199.

Boisot, M.H. (1998) *Knowledge Assets: Securing Competitive Advantage in the Information Economy*. Oxford: Oxford University Press.

Bonache, J. and Brewster, C. (2001) "Knowledge transfer and the management of expatriation." *Thunderbird International Business Review*, 43(1): 145–168.

Booz Allen and Hamilton (1982) *New Products Management for the 1980s*. New York: Booz Allen and Hamilton.

Bossidy, L.A. (1996) "The CEO as coach: An interview with AlliedSignal's Lawrence A. Bossidy." In J. Champy and N. Nohria (eds) *Fast Forward: The Best Ideas on Managing Business Change*. Cambridge, MA: Harvard Business School Press: 247–248.

Boyacigiller, N.A. and Adler, N.J. (1997) "Insiders and outsiders: Bridging the worlds of organizational behavior and international management." In B. Toyne and D. Nigh (eds) *International Business: An Emerging Vision*. Columbia, SC: University of South Carolina Press: 396–416.

Boyatzis, R.E. (1982) *The Competent Manager: A Model for Effective Performance.* New York: John Wiley and Sons.

Brake, T. (1997) *The Global Leader: Critical Factors for Creating the World Class Organization.* Chicago, IL: Irwin Professional Publishing.

Bridges, W. (1995) "Managing organizational change." In W.W. Burke (ed.) *Managing Organizational Change.* New York: American Management Association.

Brislin, R.W. (1981) *Cross-cultural Encounters: Face-to-face Interaction.* New York: Pergamon.

Brown, J. F. (2007) *The Global Business Leader.* New York: Palgrave Macmillan.

Brown, M. and Treviño, L.K. (2006) "Ethical leadership: A review and future directions." *The Leadership Quarterly*, 17: 595–616.

Brownell, J. (2006) "Meeting the competency needs of global leaders: A partnership approach." *Human Resource Management*, 45(3): 309–336.

Brundtland, G.H. (1987) *Our Common Future: The World Commission on Environment and Development.* Oxford: Oxford University Press.

Bryant, S. and Nguyen, T. (2002) "Knowledge acquisition and sharing in international strategic alliances: The role of trust." Paper presented at the annual meeting the Academy of Management, Washington, DC.

Buller, P.F., Kohls, J.J., and Anderson, K.S. (2000) "When ethics collide: Managing conflicts across cultures." *Organizational Dynamics*, 28(4): 52–65.

Burke, W.W. (2002) "The organizational change leader." In M. Goldsmith, V. Govindarajan, B. Kaye, and A. Vicere (eds) *The Many Facets of Leadership*, Upper Saddle Creek, NJ: Financial Times Prentice Hall: 83–97.

Burke, W.W. and Litwin, G.H. (1992) "A causal model of organizational performance and change." *Journal of Management*, 18: 523–545.

Burns, J.M. (1978) *Leadership.* New York: Harper & Row.

Busco, C., Frigo, M.L., Giovannoni, E., Riccaboni, A., and Scapens, R.W. (2006) "Integrating global organizations through performance measurement systems." *Strategic Finance*, 87(7): 30–35.

BusinessWeek Online. (2006) "The world's most innovative companies." http://www.businessweek.com/magazine/content/06_17/b3981401.htm (accessed January 1, 2006).

Buss, A.H. (1989) "Personality as traits." *American Psychologist*, 44(11): 1378–1388.

Caligiuri, P. (2000) "The Big Five personality characteristics as predictors of expatriate's desire to terminate the assignment and supervisor-rated performance." *Personnel Psychology*, 53: 67–89.

Caligiuri, P. (2004) "Global leadership development through expatriate assignments and other international experiences." Paper presented at the Academy of Management, New Orleans, LA, August.

Caligiuri, P.M. (1995) *Individual Characteristics Related to Effective Performance in Cross-Cultural Work Settings (Expatriate).* Unpublished doctoral dissertation, Pennsylvania State University, PA, University Park.

Caligiuri, P.M. (2006) "Developing global leaders." *Human Resource Management Review*, 16, 219–228.

Caligiuri, P. and Di Santo, V. (2001) "Global competence: What is it and can it be developed through global assignments?" *Human Resource Planning*, 24(3): 37–35.

Caligiuri, P. and Tarique, I. (2009) "Predicting effectiveness in global leadership activities." *Journal of World Business*, 44: 336–346.

Caligiuri, P. and Tarique, I. (2011) "Dynamic competencies and performance in global leaders: Role of personality and developmental experiences." SHRM Foundation Research Grant. http://www.shrm.org/about/foundation/research/Pages/SHRMFoundationResearchCaligiuri.aspx (accessed August 5, 2011).

Cannella, A. A. Jr., Park, J.H., and Lee, H.U. (2008) "Top management team functional background diversity and firm performance: examining the roles of team member colocation and environmental uncertainty." *Academy of Management Journal,* 51: 768–784.

Canney Davison, S. (1994) "Creating a high performance international team." *Journal of Management Development*, 13: 81–90.

Cappellen, T. and Janssens, M. (2005) "Career paths of global managers: Towards future research." *Journal of World Business*, 40: 328–360.

Cappellen, T. and Janssens, M. (2008) "Global managers' career competencies." *Career Development International*, 13(6): 514–537.

Cappellen, T. and Janssens, M. (2010) "Characteristics of international work: Narratives of the global manager." *Thunderbird International Business Review*, 52(4): 337–348.

Carey, C.E., Newman, P., and McDonough, L. (2004) "Global leadership capability: An Asia-Pacific perspective." *Performance Improvement*, 43(8): 13–18.

Carpenter, M. A., Geletkanycz, M. A., and Sanders, W. G. (2004) "Upper echelons research revisted: antecedents, elements, and consequences of top management team composition." *Journal of Management,* 30: 749–778.

Carte, T. and Chidambaram, L. (2004) "A capabilities-based theory of technology deployment in diverse teams: Leapfrogging the pitfalls of diversity and leveraging its potential with collaborative technology." *Journal of the Association for Information Systems*, 5: 448–471.

Catalyst. (2011) http://www.catalyst.org/publication/433/women-on-boards (accessed February 5, 2012).

Catalyst. (2012) http://www.catalyst.org/publication/271/women-ceos-of-the-fortune-1000 (accessed February 5, 2012).

Center for Constitutional Rights. (2011) http://ccrjustice.org/files/6.16.09%20Final%20 factsheet%20case%20against%20shell.pdf (accessed September 1, 2011).

Champy, J. and Nohria, N. (1996) *Fast Forward: The Best Ideas on Managing Business Change.* Cambridge, MA: Harvard Business School Press.

Charan, R., Drotter, S., and Noel, J. (2001) *The Leadership Pipeline.* San Francisco, CA: Jossey-Bass.

Chen, G.M. and Starosta, W.J. (1999) "A review of the concept of intercultural awareness." *Human Communication*, 2: 27–54.

Cheung, C. and Chan, A.C. (2005) "Philosophical foundations of eminent Hong Kong Chinese CEOs' leadership." *Journal of Business Ethics*, 60: 47–62.

Chou, L.F., Wang, A.C., Wang, T.Y., Huang, M.P. and Cheng, B.S. (2008) "Shared work values and team member effectiveness: The mediation of trustfulness and trustworthiness." *Human Relations,* 61(12): 1714–1742.

Chua, C.H., Engeli, H.-P., and Stahl, G.K. (2005) "Creating a new identity and high-performance culture at Novartis: The role of leadership and human resource management." *Mergers and Acquisitions: Managing Culture and Human Resources*. Stanford, CA: Stanford Business Books, Stanford University Press: 379–398. Retrieved from http://search.ebscohost.com/login.aspx?direct=trueanddb=ecnandAN=0827873andsite=ehost–live

Clawson, J.G. (2006) *Level Three Leadership: Getting Below the surface.* Upper Saddle River, NJ: Prentice-Hall.

Clawson, J.G. (2009) *Level Three Leadership: Getting Below the Surface, 6th edition.* Upper Saddle River, NJ: Prentice Hall.

Cohen, E. (2007) *Leadership without Borders.* Singapore: Wiley.

Cohen, E. (2010) *A Necessary Partnership for Advancing Responsible Business Practices: CSR for HR.* Sheffield: Greenleaf Publishing Limited.

Coleman, J.S. (1988) "Social capital in the creation of human capital." *American Journal of Sociology*, 94: S95–S120.

Collings, D.G., Scullion, H., and Morley, M.J. (2007) "Changing patterns of global staffing in the multinational enterprise: Challenges to the conventional expatriate assignment and emerging alternatives." *Journal of World Business*, 42(2): 198–213.

Colvin, G. (2009) "How to build great leaders." *Fortune,* November 19.

Conger, J.A. and Ready, D.A. (2004a) "Rethinking leadership competencies." *Executive Forum*, Spring Issue: 41–47.

Conger, J. and Ready, D. (2004b) "Rethinking leadership competencies." *Leader to Leader*, 32: 41–48.

Cooper, R.G. (2001) *Winning at New Products: Accelerating the Process from Idea to Launch*. Cambridge, MA: Basic Books.

Cornett-DeVito, M. and McGlone, E. (2000) "Multicultural communication training for law enforcement officers: A case study." *Criminal Justice Policy Review*, 11: 234–253.

Corporate Leadership Council. (2000) "The new global assignment: Developing and retaining future leaders." *Executive Inquiry.* Washington, DC: Corporate Leadership Council.

Costa, A.C., Roe, R.A., and Taillieu, T. (2001) "Trust within teams: The relations with performance effectiveness." *European Journal of Work and Organizational Psychology*, 10(3): 225–244.

Costa, P. and McCrae, R. (1985) *The NEO Personality Inventory: Manual, Form S and Form R*. Lutz, FL: Psychological Assessment Resources.

Costa, P.T. and McCrae, R.R. (1992) "Four ways five factors are basic." *Personality and Individual Differences*, 13: 653–665.

Coutu, D.L. (2004) "Putting leaders on the couch: A conversation with Manfred F.R. Kets de Vries." *Harvard Business Review*, 82(1): 65–71.

Crandall, B., Klein, G., and Hoffman, R.R. (2006) *Working Minds: A Practitioner's Guide to Cognitive Task Analysis*. Boston: MIT Press.

Crane, A. and Matten, D. (2007) *Business Ethics: Managing Corporate Citizenship and Sustainability in the Age of Globalization*. Oxford: Oxford University Press.

Crowley-Henry, M. (2007) "The Protean career." *International Studies of Management and Organization*, 37(3): 44–64.

Crilly, D., Schneider, S.C., and Zollo, M. (2008) "Psychological antecedents to socially responsible behavior." *European Management Review*, 5: 175–190.

Cross, R. and Prusak, L. (2003) "The political economy of knowledge markets in organizations." In M. Easterby-Smith and M. Lyles (eds) *The Blackwell Handbook of Organizational Learning and Knowledge Management*. Malden, MA: Blackwell: 454–472.

Cummings, J.N. (2007) "Leading group from a distance: how to mitigate consequences of geographic dispersion." In S. Weisband and L. Atwater (eds) *Leadership at a Distance: Research in Technologically Supported Work*. Mahwah, NJ: Lawrence Erlbaum Associates: 33–50.

Cummings, T.C. and Worley, C.G. (2004) *Organization Development and Change*. Cincinnati, OH: South-Western.

CWDI. (2011) "2011 Report Women." http://www.globewomen.org/cwdi/cwdi_2011_ Fortune%20Global%20200%20Press%20Release.html (accessed February 5, 2012).

Dalton, M. and Wilson, M. (2000) "The relationship of the five-factor model of personality to job performance for a group of middle eastern expatriate managers." *Journal of Cross-Cultural Psychology*, 31(2): 250–258.

Dalton, M., Ernst, C., Deal, J., and Leslie, J. (2002) *Success for the New Global Manager: What You Need to Know to Work Across Distances, Countries and Cultures*. San Francisco, CA: Jossey-Bass and the Center for Creative Leadership.

Dalton, M.A. (1998) "Developing leaders for global roles." In C.D. McCauley, R.S. Moxley, and E. Van Velsor (eds) *The Center for Creative Leadership Handbook of Leadership Development.* San Francisco, CA: Jossey-Bass: 379–402.

Damiran, S.K. (1993) "School and situated knowledge: Travel or tourism?" *Educational Technology*, 33 (3): 27–32.

Dansereau, F., Graen, G.B., and Haga, W. (1975) "A vertical dyad linkage approach to leadership in formal organizations." *Organizational Behavior and Human Performance*, 13, 46–78.

Davis, S. and Finney, S. (2006) "A factor analytic study of the Cross-Cultural Adaptability Inventory." *Educational and Psychological Measurement*, 66 (2): 318–330.

Day, D.V. and Antonakis, J. (2011) "Leadership: Past, present, and future." In D.V. Day and J. Antonakis (eds) *The Nature of Leadership.* Thousand Oaks, CA: Sage Publishing: 3–25.

Day, D. and S. Halpin (2001) "Leadership development: A review of industry best practices." *Technical report 1111. U.S. Army Research Institute for the Behavioral and Social Sciences.* Army Project # 622785A950.

Deardorff, D.K. (2006) "Identification and assessment of intercultural competence as a student outcome of internationalization." *Journal of Studies in International Education*, 10(3): 241–266.

Debrah, Y.A. and Rees, C.J. (2011) "The development of global leaders and expatriates." In A.W.K. Harzing and A. Pinnington (eds) *International Human Resource Management, 3rd edition.* London: Sage Publications: 377–408.

De Dreu, C.K.W. (2006) "When too little or too much hurts: evidence for a curvilinear relationship between task conflict and innovation in teams." *Journal of Management,* (32): 83–107.

De Dreu, C.K.W. and Weingart, L.R. (2003) "Task versus relationship conflict, team performance and team member satisfaction: A meta-analysis." *Journal of Applied Psychology*, 88: 741–749.

De Fruyt, F., McCrae, R.R., Szirmák, Z., and Nagy, J. (2004) "The Five-Factor personality inventory as a measure of the Five-Factor Model: Belgian, American and Hungarian comparisons with the NEO-PI-R." *Assessment*, 11: 207–215.

DeGeorge, R.T. (1993) *Competing with Integrity in International Business.* Oxford: Oxford University Press.

Deller, J. (1998) "Personality scales can make a difference in expatriate selection: The case of Germans working in Korea." Paper presented at the International Congress of Applied Psychology, San Francisco, August.

Deller, J. (2006) "International human resource management and the formation of cross-cultural competence." *International Management Review*, 2(3): 20–28.

Den Hartog, D.N., House, R.J., Hanges, P.J., Ruiz-Quintanilla, S.A., Dorfman, P.W., and Associates (1999) "Culture specific and cross-culturally generalizable implicit leadership theories: Are the attributes of charismatic/transformational leadership universally endorsed?" *Leadership Quarterly*, 10(2): 219–256.

Den Hartog, D.N. and Dickson, M.W. (2004) "Leadership and culture." In J. Antonakis, A.T. Cianciolo, and R.J. Sternberg (eds) *The Nature of Leadership.* Thousand Oaks, CA: Sage: 249–278.

Denison, D., Hoojiberg, R., and Quinn, R. (1995) "Paradox and performance: Toward a theory of behavioral complexity in managerial leadership." *Organization Science*, 6: 76–92.

Dess G.G. and Picken J.C. (2000) "Changing roles: Leadership in the 21st century." *Organizational Dynamics,* 28(3): 31.

Development Dimensions International, Inc. (2009) "Global leadership forecast 2008/2009: Overcoming the shortfalls in developing leaders." http://www.ddiworld.com (accessed September 22, 2010).

Devinney, T.M. (2009) "Is the socially responsible corporation a myth? The good, the bad, and the ugly of corporate social responsibility." *Academy of Management Perspectives*, 23(2): 44–56.

Dickson, M.W., Den Hartog, D.N., and Castaño, N. (2009) "Understanding leadership across cultures." In R. Bhagat and R. Steers (eds) *Handbook of Culture, Organization, and Work.* New York: Cambridge University Press: 219–244.

Dietz, J., Goffin, M., and Marr, A. (2007) "Red Cross Children's Home: Building capabilities in Guyana (A)." Case No. 9B02C042. Richard Ivey School of Business: University of Western Ontario.

Dinges, N.G. and Baldwin, K.D. (1996) "Intercultural competence: A research perspective." In D. Landis and R.S. Bhagat, (eds) *Handbook of Intercultural Training, 2nd edition.* Thousand Oaks, CA: Sage: 106–123.

DiStefano, J.J. and Maznevski, M.L. (2000) "Creating value with diverse teams in global management." *Organizational Dynamics*, 29: 45–63.

Dobbs, R., Leslie, K., and Mendonca, L.T. (2005) "Building the healthy corporation." *McKinsey Quarterly*, 3: 62–71.

Dodge, B. (1993) "Empowerment and the evolution of learning." *Education and Training*, 35 (5): 3–10.

Donaldson, T. (1989) *The Ethics of International Business*. New York: Oxford University Press.

Donaldson, T. (1996) "Values in tension: Ethics away from home." *Harvard Business Review*, 74: 48–62.

Donaldson, T. and Dunfee, R. (1999) "When ethics travel: The promise and peril of global business ethics." *California Management Review*, 41(4): 45–63.

Donaldson, T. and Preston, L. (1995) "The stakeholder theory of the corporation: Concepts, evidence, and implications." *Academy of Management Review*, 20: 65–91.

Dotlich, D.L. and Noel, J.L. (1998) *Action Learning: How the World's Top Companies are Re-Creating Their Leaders and Themselves.* San Francisco, CA: Jossey-Bass.

Dowling, D.W. and Breitfelder, M. (2010) "From corporate university to corporate peace corps." *Harvard Business Review Blog Network*, June 4, 2010. http://blogs.hbr.org/imagining-the-future-of-leadership/2010/06/from-corporate-university-to-c-1.html. (accessed September 7, 2011).

Dowling, P. and Welch, D. (2004) *International Human Resource Management: Managing People in a Global Context 4th ed.* London: Thomson Learning.

Downes, M. and Thomas, A.S. (2000) "Knowledge transfer through expatriates: the U-curve approach to overseas staffing." *Journal of Managerial Issues,* 12(2): 131–150.

Doz, Y. and Prahalad C.K. (1987) "A process model of strategic redirection in large complex firms: The case of multinational corporations." In A.M. Pettigrew (ed.) *The Management of Strategic Change.* Oxford: Basil Blackwell: 63–83.

Doz, Y., Santos, J. and Williamson, P. (2001) *From Global to Metanational: How Companies Win in the Knowledge Economy.* Cambridge, MA: Harvard Business Press.

Drath, W.H. (1998) "Approaching the future of leadership development." In C.D. McCauley, R.S. Moxley, and E. Van Velsor (eds) *Handbook of Leadership Development,* San Francisco, CA/Greensboro, NC: Jossey-Bass/Center for Creative Leadership: 403–432.

Dreyfus, H.L. and Dreyfus, S.E. (1986) *Mind over Machine: The Power of Human Intuitive Expertise in the Era of the Computer.* New York: Free Press.

Driskat, V.U. and Wheeler, J.V. (2003) "Managing from the boundary: The effective leadership of self-managing work teams." *Academy of Management Journal*, 46: 435–457.

Dulek, R.E. and Fielden, J.S. (1991) "International communication: An executive primer." *Business Horizons*, 34(1): 20–29.

Earley, P.C. (1980) "Social loafing and collectivism: A comparison of the United States and the People's Republic of China." *Administrative Science Quarterly*, 34(4): 565–581.

Earley, P.C. and Ang, S. (2003) *Cultural Intelligence: Individual Interactions across Cultures*. Stanford, CA: Stanford University Press.

Earley, P.C. and Gibson, C.B. (1998) "Taking stock in our progress on individualism-collectivism: 100 years of solidarity and community." *Journal of Management*, 24 (3): 265–304.

Earley, P.C. and Mosakowski, E.A. (2000) "Creating hybrid team cultures: An empirical test of transnational team functioning." *Academy of Management Journal*, 43: 26–49.

Ebersole, G. (2007) "Ten most significant risks and costs of unethical behavior in business." http://ezinearticles.com/?Ten-Most-Significant-Risks-and--Costs-of-Unethical-Behavior-in-Businessandid=427722 (accessed March 31, 2010).

EFMD. (2005) "Globally responsible leadership: A call for engagement." http://www.efmd.org/html/Responsibility/cont_detail.asp?id=041207trlvandaid=051012qnisandtid=1andref=ind (accessed October 18, 2005).

Elbow, P. (1973) *Writing Without Teachers*. New York: Oxford Press.

Elkington, J. (1997) *Cannibals with Forks: The Triple Bottom Line of 21st Century Business*. Oxford: Capstone.

Elliot, J. (1989) *Requisite Organization. The CEO's Guide to Creative Structure and Leadership*. Arlington, VA: Cason Hall.

Elron, E. (1997) "Top management teams within multinational corporations: Effects of cultural heterogeneity." *Leadership Quarterly*, 8: 393–412.

Emerson, V. (2001) "An interview with Carlos Ghosn, President of Nissan Motors, Ltd. and Industry Leader of the Year." *Journal of World Business*, 36: 3–10.

Endicott, L., Bock, T., and Narvaez, D. (2003) "Moral reasoning, intercultural development, and multicultural experiences: Relations and cognitive underpinnings." *International Journal of Intercultural Relations*, 27: 403–419.

Evans, P. and Doz, Y. (1989) "The dualistic organization." In P. Evans, Y. Doz, and A. Laurent (eds) *Human Resource Management in International Firms: Change, Globalization, Innovation*. London: Macmillan: 219–242.

Evans, P., Pucik, V., and Barsoux, J.-L. (2002) *The Global Challenge: Frameworks for International Human Resource Management*. Boston: McGraw-Hill.

Eylon, D. and Au, K.Y. (1999) "Exploring empowerment cross-cultural differences among the power distance dimension." *International Journal of Intercultural Relations*, 23: 373–385.

Fantini, A.E. (2000) "A central concern: Developing intercultural competence." http://www.sit.edu/publications/docs/competence.pdf (accessed January 3, 2003).

Faucheux, C., Amado, G., and Laurent, A. (1982) "Organizational development and change." *Annual Reviews of Psychology*, 33: 343–370.

Fehér, J. and Szigeti, M. (2001) "The application of change management methods at business organizations operating in Hungary: Challenges in the business and cultural environment and first practical experience." In D. Denison (ed.) *Managing Organizational Change in Transition Economies*. London: Lawrence Erlbaum Associates: 344–361.

Fennes, H. and Hapgood, K. (1997) *Intercultural Learning in the Classroom*. London and Washington: Cassell.

Fink, G., Neyer, A.K., Kölling, M., and Meierewert, S. (2004) *An Integrative Model of Multinational Team Performance.* EI Working Papers/ Europainstitut, 60. Vienna: Europainstitut, WU Vienna University of Economics and Business.

Fiske, A.P. (1992) "The four elementary forms of sociality: Framework for a unified theory of social relations." *Psychological Review*, 99(4): 689–723.

Florida, R. and Goodnight, J. (2005) "Managing for creativity." *Harvard Business Review*, 83: 124–131.

Fondas, N. (1997) "Feminization unveiled: Management qualities in contemporary writings." *Academy of Management Review*, 22(1): 257–282.

Forster, N. (1999) "Another 'glass ceiling'? The experiences of women professionals and managers on international assignments." *Gender, Work and Organization*, 6(2): 79–90.

Frederick, W.C. (1991) "The moral authority of transnational corporate codes." *Journal of Business Ethics*, 10: 165–177.

Freeman, R.E. (2004) "The stakeholder approach revisited." *Zeitschrift für wirtschafts- und unternehmensethik*, 5:228–241.

Freeman, R.E. and McVea, J. (2001) A stakeholder approach to strategic management." In M. Hit, R.E. Freeman, and J.S. Harrison (eds) *The Blackwell Handbook of Strategic Management*, Oxford: Wiley-Blackwell: 189–207.

French, J.R.P. and Raven, B. (1959) "The bases of social power." In D. Cartwright (ed.) *Studies in Social Power*, Ann Arbor, MI: University of Michigan Press: 150–167.

Friedman, M. (1970) "The social responsibility of business is to increase its profits." *New York Times Magazine*, September 13, 126.

Friedman, R.A. and Polodny, J. (1992) "Differences in boundary spanning roles: Labor negotiations and implications for role conflict." *Administrative Science Quarterly*, 37(1): 28–47.

Fry, L.W. and Slocum, J.W. (2008) "Maximizing the triple bottom line through spiritual leadership." *Organizational Dynamics*, 37(1): 86–96.

Furnham, A. and Ribchester, T. (1995) "Tolerance of ambiguity: A review of the concept, its measurement and applications." *Current Psychology*, 14(3): 179–199.

Furuya, N. (2006) *Repatriation Management Effectiveness: A Mechanism for Developing Global Competencies through a Comprehensive Process of Repatriation.* Unpublished dissertation. University of Tsukuba, Japan.

Furuya, N., Stevens, M. J., Oddou, G., and Bird, A. (2005) "The effects of HR policies and repatriate self-adjustment on global competency transfer." Paper presented at the Annual Meetings of the Academy of International Business, Quebec City, Canada.

Furuya, N., Stevens, M., Oddou, G., Bird, A., and Mendenhall, M. (2006) "Predictors and outcomes of Japanese repatriation effectiveness: Managing the learning and transfer of global competencies." *2006 Best Papers Proceedings of the Association of Japanese Business Studies*, Beijing, China.

Furuya, N., Stevens, M., Oddou, G., Bird, A., and Mendenhall, M. (2007) "The effects of HR policies and repatriate adjustment on global competency transfer." *Asia-Pacific Journal of Human Resources*, 45: 6–23.

Furuya, N., Stevens, M., Bird, A., Oddou, G., and Mendenhall, M. (2009) "Managing the learning and transfer of global management competence: Antecedents and outcomes of Japanese repatriation effectiveness." *Journal of International Business Studies*, 40: 200–215.

Gardner, H. (2006) *Changing minds: The Art and Science of Changing Our Own and Other People's Minds (Leadership for the Common Good).* Boston, MA: Harvard Business Press.

Gardner, W.L., Lowe, K.B., Moss, T.W., Mahoney, K.T., and Coglisser, C.C. (2010) "Scholarly leadership of the study of leadership: A review of the *Leadership Quarterly's* second decade, 2000–2009." *The Leadership Quarterly*, 21: 922–958.

Gelfand, M., Erez, M., and Aycan, Z. (2007) "Cross-cultural organizational behavior." *Annual Review of Psychology*, 58: 479–514.

Ghislanzoni, G. (2006) "Leading change: an interview with the CEO of Eni." *McKinsey Quarterly*, 3: 54–63.

Ghislanzoni, G. and Shearn, J. (2005) "Leading change: An interview with the CEO of Banca Intesa." *The McKinsey Quarterly*, 3: 73–81.

Ghoshal, S. (2005) "Bad management theories are destroying good management practices." *Academy of Management Learning and Education*, 4: 75–91.

Ghoshal, S. and Bartlett, C.A. (1996) "Rebuilding behavioral context: A blueprint for corporate renewal." *Sloan Management Review*, 37(2): 23–37.

Ghoshal, S. and Bartlett. C. (1999) *The Individual Corporation. A Fundamentally New Approach to Management.* London: HarperCollins.

Giacalone, R.A. and Thompson, K.R. (2006) "Business ethics and social responsibility education: Shifting the worldview." *Academy of Management Learning and Education*, 5: 266–277.

Gill, A. and Booth, S. (2003) "Identifying future global leaders," *Strategic HR Review*, 2(6): 20–25.

Gill, S. (2012) *Global Crises and the Crisis of Global Leadership.* Oxford: Cambridge University Press.

Gitsham, M. (2008) "Developing the global leader of tomorrow." Conference presentation at the 1st Global Forum for Responsible Management Education, United Nations, New York, December 4–5, 2008.

Gitsham, M. (2009) "Report of 1st Global Forum for Responsible Management Education," United Nations, New York, December 4–5, 2008. Ashridge Business School and the European Academcy of Business in Society: Ashridge Faculty Publications.

Gold, A.H., Malhotra, A., and Segars, A.H. (2001) "Knowledge management: An organizational capabilities perspective." *Journal of Management Information Systems*, 18(1): 185–214.

Goldsmith, M., Greenberg, C., Robertson, A., and Hu-Chan, M. (2003) *Global Leadership: The Next Generation.* Upper Saddle River, NJ: Prentice-Hall.

Goldstein, D. and Smith, D. (1999) "The analysis of the effects of experiential training on sojourners' cross-cultural adaptability." *International Journal of Intercultural Relations*, 23: 157–173.

Googins, B.K., Mirvis, P.H., and Rochlin, S.A. (2007) *Beyond Good Company.* New York: Palgrave Macmillan.

Gore, A. (2007) *An Inconvenient Truth: The Planetary Emergency of Global Warming and What We Can Do About It.* New York: Rodale Books.

Goss, T., Pascale, R.T., and Athos, A. (1996) "The reinvention roller coaster: Risking the present for a powerful future." In J. Champy and N. Nohria (eds) *Fast Forward: The Best Ideas on Managing Business Change.* Cambridge: Harvard Business School Press: 124–139.

Govindarajan, V. and Gupta, A.K. (2001) "Building an effective global business team." *Sloan Management Review*, Summer Issue: 63–71.

Graen, G.B. and Hui, C. (1999) "Transcultural global leadership in the twenty-first century: Challenges and implications for development." In W.H. Mobley, M.J. Gessner, and V. Arnold (eds) *Advances in Global Leadership, 1.* Greenwich, CT: JAI Press.

Graen, G.B. and Uhl-Bien, M. (1995) "Relationship-based approach to leadership: development of leader-member exchange (LMX) theory of leadership over 25 years: Applying a multilevel multi-domain perspective." *Leadership Quarterly*, 6(2), 219–247.

Graf, A. (2004) "Screening and training inter-cultural competencies: Evaluating the impact of national culture on inter-cultural competencies." *The International Journal of Human Resource Management*, 15(6): 1124–1148.

Grant, C. (1991) "Friedman fallacies." *Journal of Business Ethics*, 10: 907–914.

Gratton, L. and Ghoshal, S. (2005) "Beyond best practice." *MIT Sloan Management Review*, 46(3): 49–57.

Green, M. and Peel, M. (2009) "Shell faces Saro-Wiwa death claim." *Financial Times*, April 3.

Green, S., Hassan, F., Immelt, J., Marks, M., and Meiland, D. (2003) "In search of global leaders." *Harvard Business Review*, 81(8): 38–45.

Gregersen, H., Black, J.S. and Morrison, A.J. (1997) "Developing global leaders for competitive advantage." *Strategic Human Resource Development Review*, 1: 77–102.

Gregersen, H.B., Morrison, A.J., and Black, J.S. (1998) "Developing leaders for the global frontier." *Sloan Management Review*, 40: 21–32.

Greunke, E.J. (2010) *The Global Project: Observing Geographic Literacy Obtained by Study Abroad Learning.* Masters thesis. Western Kentucky University.

Groves, K.S. and Feyerherm, A.E. (2011) "Leader cultural intelligence in context: testing the moderating effects of team cultural diversity on leader and team performance." *Group & Organization Management*, 36(5): 535–566.

Gudykunst, W.B. (1994) *Bridging Differences: Effective Intergroup Communication 2nd edition.* London: Sage.

Gundling, E., Hogan, T., and Cvitkovich, K. (2011) *What is Global Leadership: 10 Key Behaviors that Define Great Global Leaders.* Boston, MA: Nicholas Brealey Publishing.

Gunz, H. (1989) "The dual meaning of managerial careers." *Journal of Management Studies*, 26: 225–250.

Gupta, A. and Govindarajan, V. (1991) "Knowledge flows and the structure of control within multinational corporations." *Academy of Management Review*, 16: 768–792.

Gupta, A.K. and Govindarajan, V. (2000) "Knowledge flows within multinational corporations." *Strategic Management Journal*, 21: 473–496.

Gupta, R. and Wendler, J. (2005) "Leading change: An interview with the CEO of P&G." *McKinsey Quarterly*, July: 1–6.

Hajro, A. and Pudelko, M. (2010) "An analysis of core-competences of successful multinational team leaders." *International Journal of Cross Cultural Management*, 10(2): 175–194.

Hall, D.T., Zhu, G., and Yan, A. (2001) "Developing global leaders: To hold on to them, let them go!" In W. Mobley and M.W. McCall, Jr (eds) *Advances in Global Leadership*, vol. 2. Stamford, CT: JAI Press.

Hall, E.T. (1966) *The Hidden Dimension.* New York: Doubleday.

Hall, E.T. and Hall, M.R. (1990) Understanding Cultural Differences. Yarmouth, ME: Intercultural Press.

Hames, R.D. (2007) *The Five Literacies of Global Leadership.* West Sussex, England: Wiley.

Hamm, S. (2006) "Innovation: The view from the top." *BusinesWeek Online.* http://www.businessweek.com/magazine/content/06_14/b3978073.htm (accessed January 2, 2006).

Hammer, M.R. (2005) "The intercultural conflict style inventory: A conceptual framework and measure of intercultural conflict resolution approaches." *International Journal of Intercultural Relations*, 29(6): 675–695.

Hammer, M. (2007) "Intercultural sensitivity and development." Presentation at Army Research Institute Culture Conference, Fort Leavenworth, MO.

Hammer, M.R., Gudykunst, W.B., and Wiseman, R.L. (1978) "Dimensions of intercultural effectiveness: An exploratory study." *International Journal of Intercultural Relations*, 2(4): 382–393.

Hammer, M.R., Bennett, M.J., and Wiseman, R. (2003) "Measuring intercultural sensitivity: The Intercultural Development Inventory." *International Journal of Intercultural Relations*, 27(4): 421–443.

Hampden-Turner, C. (1994) "The structure of entrapment: Dilemmas standing in the way of women managers and strategies to resolve these." *Deeper News*, 5(1): 1–43.

Hampden-Turner, C. and Trompenaars, F. (2000) *Building Cross-cultural Competence: How to Create Wealth from Conflicting Values*. Chichester, UK: John Wiley.

Handy, C. (2001) *The Elephant and the Flea: Looking Backwards to the Future*. London: Hutchinson.

Harris, J.G. (1973) "A science of the South Pacific: Analysis of the character structure of the Peace Corps volunteer." *American Psychologist*, 28: 232–247.

Harris, J.G. (1975) "Identification of cross-cultural talent: The empirical approach of the Peace Corps." *Topics in Culture Learning*, 3: 66–78.

Harrison, D.A. and Shaffer, M.A. (2005) "Mapping the criterion space for expatriate success: task- and relationship-based performance, effort and adaptation." *International Journal of Human Resource Management*, 16(8): 1454–1474.

Harrison, D.A., Price, K.H., and Bell, M.P. (1998) "Beyond relational demography: Time and the effects of surface- and deep-level diversity on work group cohesion." *Academy of Management Journal*, 41: 96–107.

Harrison, D.A., Shaffer, M.A., and Bhaskar-Shrinivas, P. (2004) "Going places: Roads more or less traveled in research on expatriate experiences." In J.J. Martocchio (ed.) *Research in Personnel and Human Resources Management*. Greenwich, CT: JAI Press, Volume 22: 203–252.

Hart, S. and Milstein, M. (2003) "Creating sustainable value." *Academy of Management Executive*, 17(2): 56–69.

Harvey, M. (1989) "Repatriation of corporate executives: An empirical study." *Journal of International Business Studies*, 20(1): 131–144.

Harvey, M. and Novicevic, M.M. (2004) "The development of political skill and political capital by global leaders through global assignments." *International Journal of Human Resource Management*, 15(7): 1173–1188.

Harzing, A.W. (2001) "Of bears, bumble-bees and spiders: The role of expatriates in controlling foreign subsidiaries." *Journal of World Business*, 36: 366–379.

Haslberger, A. (2010) "Gender differences in expatriate adjustment." *European Journal of International Management*, 4(1/2): 163–183.

Hayashi, K. and Jolley, G. (2002) "Two thoughts on analog and digital language." *Aoyama Journal of International Politics, Economics and Business*, 158: 179–196.

Hedlund, G. (1986) "The hypermodern MNC: A heterarchy?" *Human Resource Management*, Spring: 9–35.

Helfat, C., Harris, D., and Wolfson, P. (2006) "The pipeline to the top: Women and men in the top executive ranks of U.S. corporations." *Academy of Management Perspectives*, 20(4): 42–64.

Hiatt, J. (2006) *ADKAR: A model for Change in Business, Government and Our Community*. Loveland, CO: Prosci Research.

Higgs, M.J. and Rowland, D. (2005) "All changes great and small: Exploring approaches to change and its leadership." *Journal of Change Management*, 5(2): 121–151.

Higgs, M.J. and Rowland, D. (2009) "Change leadership: Case study of a global energy company." *Strategic Change*, 18: 45–58.

Hofstede, G. (1980a) "Motivation, leadership and organization: Do American theories apply?" *Organizational Dynamics*, (9)1: 42–63.

Hofstede, G. (1980b) *Culture's Consequences*. Thousand Oaks, CA: Sage.

Hofstede, G. (2001) *Culture's Consequences: Comparing Values, Behaviors, Institutions and Organizations Across Nations*, 2nd edition. London: Sage Publications.

Hollenbeck, G.P. (2001) "A serendipitous sojourn through the global leadership literature." In W. Mobley and M.W. McCall (eds) *Advances in Global Leadership, vol. 2*. Stamford, CT: JAI Press.

Hoopes, D.S. (1979) "Intercultural communication concepts and the psychology of intercultural experience." In M. Pusch (ed.) *Multicultural Education: A Cross-Cultural Training Approach*. Yarmouth, ME: Intercultural Press: 9–38.

Hosking, D.M. and Morley, I.E. (1988) "The skills of leadership." In J.G. Hunt, B.R. Baliga, H.P. Dachler, and C.A. Schriesheim (eds) *Emerging Leadership Vistas*. Lexington, MA: Lexington Books: 89–106.

House, R.J., Hanges, P.J., Javidan, M., Dorfman, P.W., and Gupta, V. (eds) (2004) *Culture, Leadership and Organizations: The GLOBE Study of 62 Societies*. Thousand Oaks, CA: Sage.

Howell, W.C. and Fleishman, E.A. (eds) (1982) *Human Performance and Productivity. Vol 2: Information Processing and Decision Making*. Hillsdale, NJ: Erlbaum.

Hu, M. (2009) "Knowledge sharing and innovative service behavior relationship: Guanxi as mediator." *Social Behavior and Personality*, 37(7): 977–992.

Hulsheger, U.R., Anderson, N., and Salgado, J.F. (2009) "Team-level predictors of innovation at work: A comprehensive meta-analysis spanning three decades of research." *Journal of Applied Psychology*, 44: 1128–1145.

Hunter, B., White, G., and Godbey, G. (2006) "What does it mean to be globally competent?" *Journal of Studies in International Education*, 10(3): 267–285.

Hunter, W.D. (2004) *Knowledge, Skills, Attitudes, and Experiences Necessary to Become Globally Competent*. Unpublished Dissertation. Lehigh University, Bethlehem, PA.

Husted, B.W. and Allen, D.B. (2006) "Corporate social responsibility in the multinational enterprise: Strategic and institutional approaches." *Journal of International Business Studies*, 37(6): 838–849.

Husted, B.W. and Allen, D.B. (2008) "Toward a model of cross-cultural business ethics: The impact of individualism and collectivism on the ethical decision-making process." *Journal of Business Ethics*, 82: 293–305.

Huxley, A. (1926) *Jesting Pilate*. New York: George H. Doran Company.

IBM (2008) "From project manager to global citizen in one month." IBM Corporate website. http:// www.ibm.com/ibm/ideasfromibm/us/ corporateservice/20081112/index. shtml (accessed January 30, 2012).

Illies, R., Wagner, D.T., and Moregson, F.P. (2007) 'Explaining affective linkages in teams: individual differences in susceptibility to contagion and individualism-collectivism.' *Journal of Applied Psychology*, 92: 1140–1148.

Inkpen, A.C. and Dinur, A. (1998) "Knowledge management processes and international joint ventures." *Organization Science*, 9: 454–468.

Inkson, K., Arthur, M.B., Pringle, J., and Barry, S. (1997) "Expatriate assignment versus overseas experience: Contrasting models of international human resource development." *Journal of World Business*, 32(4): 351–368.

Insch, G.S., McIntyre, N., and Napier, N.K. (2008) "The expatriate glass ceiling: The second layer of glass." *Journal of Business Ethics*, 83(1): 19–28.

Ireland, R.D. and Hitt, M.A. (2005) "Achieving and maintaining strategic competitiveness in the 21st century: the role of strategic Leadership." *Academy of Management Executive,* 19(4):63–77.

Jackson, S.E. and Joshi, A. (2011) "Work team diversity." In S. Zedeck (ed.) *APA Handbook of Industrial and Organizational Psychology*, Vol 1. Washington, DC: American Psychological Association: 651–686.

Jacques, P.H., Garger, J., Brown, C.A., and Deale, C. (2009) "Personality and virtual reality team candidates: The roles of personality traits, technology, anxiety and trust as predictors of perceptions of virtual reality teams." *Journal of Business and Management*, 15: 143–155.

Javidan, M. and House, R.J. (2001) "Cultural acumen for the global manager: Lessons from Project Globe." *Organizational Dynamics*, 29(4): 289–305.

Javidan, M., Dorfman, P., Sully de Luque, M., and House, R. (2006) "In the eye of the beholder: Cross cultural lessons in leadership from Project GLOBE," *Academy of Management Perspectives*, February Issue: 67–90.

Javidan, M., Hough, L., and Bullough, A. (2010a) *Conceptualizing and Measuring Global Mindset: Development of the Global Mindset Inventory.* Glendale, AZ: Thunderbird School of Global Management.

Javidan, M., Teagarden, M., and Bowen, D. (2010b) "Making it overseas." *Harvard Business Review*, 88(4): 109–113.

Jehn, K.A. (1994) "Enhancing effectiveness: An investigation of advantages and disadvantages of value-based intragroup conflict." *International Journal of Conflict Management*, 5: 223–238.

Jehn, K.A. (1995)."A multimethod examination of the benefits and detriments of intragroup conflict." *Administrative Science Quarterly*, 40: 256–282.

Jehn, K.A. and Mannix, E.A. (2001) "The dynamic nature of conflict: A longitudinal study of intragroup conflict and group performance." *The Academy of Management Journal*, 44: 238–251.

Jick, T. and Peiperl, M. (2003) *Managing Change: Cases and Concepts*. Boston, MA: Irwin.

Johnson, M. (1993) *Moral Imagination: Implications of Cognitive Science for Ethics.* Chicago, IL and London: The University of Chicago.

Johnson, S. K., Bettenhausen, K., and Gibbons, E. (2009) "Realities of working in virtual teams: Affective and attitudinal outcomes of using computer-mediated communication." *Small Group Research*, 40: 623–649.

Jokinen, T. (2005) "Global leadership competencies: A review and discussion." *Journal of European Industrial Training*, 29(2/3): 199–216.

Jones, T.M. (1991) "Ethical decision making by individuals in organizations: An issue-contingent model." *Academy of Management Review*, 16(2): 366–395.

Jonsen, K., Maznevski, M.L., and Schneider, S.C. (2011) "Diversity and its not so diverse literature: An international perspective." *International Journal of Cross-Cultural Management*, 11(1): 35–62.

Jonsen, K., Maznevski, M.L., and Canney Davison, S. (2012) "Global virtual team dynamics and effectiveness." In G. Stahl, I. Bjorkman, and S. Morris (eds) *Handbook of Research in International Human Resource Management.* London: Edward Elgar Publishing.

Judge, T.A., Bono, J.E., Ilies, R., and Gerhardt, M.W. (2002) "Personality and leadership: A qualitative and quantitative review." *Journal of Applied Psychology*, 92: 269–277.

Kang, J., Mooweon, R., and Kang, Ki (2010) "Revisiting knowledge transfer: effects of knowledge characteristics on organizational effort for knowledge transfer." *Expert Systems with Applications,* 37 (12): 8155–8160.

Kanter, R.M. (1997) *World Class: Thriving Locally in the Global Economy.* New York: Simon and Schuster.

Kashima, T. (2006) *Phenomenological Research on the Intercultural Sensitivity of Returned Peace Corps Volunteers in the Athens Community.* Unpublished masters thesis. Ohio University.

Katzenbach, J. R. (1997) "The myth of the top management team." *Harvard Business Review*, 75(6): 83–91.

Kaushal, R. and Kwantes, C.T. (2006) "The role of culture and personality in choice of conflict management strategy." *International Journal of Intercultural Relations,* 30: 579–603.

Kayworth, T.R. and Leidner, D.L. (2001/2002) "Leadership effectiveness in global virtual teams." *Journal of Management Information Systems*, 18(3): 7–40.

Kealey, D.J. (2003) "The intercultural living and working inventory: History and research." http://www.dfait–maeci.gc.ca/cfsa–icse/cil–cai/ilwi–ici–background–en.as (accessed December 12, 2003).

Keller, R.T. (2001) "Cross-functional project groups in research and new product development: Diversity, communications, job stress and outcomes." *Academy of Management Journal*, 44: 547–555.

Kelley, C. and Meyers, J. (1995a) *The Cross-cultural Adaptability Inventory*. Minneapolis, MN: National Computer Systems.

Kelley, C. and Meyers, J. (1995b) *The Cross-cultural Adaptability Inventory manual.* Minneapolis, MN: National Computer Systems.

Kelley, T., Littman, J., and Peters, T. (2001). *The Art of Innovation: Lessons in Creativity from Ideo, America's Leading Design Firm.* New York: Doubleday.

Kelly, G. (1963) *A Theory of Personality: The Psychology of Personal Constructs.* New York: W.W. Norton.

Kemper, C. (2003) "Edgewalking: The emerging new century leadership paradigm." http://www.leader–values.com/Content/detail.asp?ContentDetailID=80 (accessed January 30, 2012).

Kets de Vries, M. (2005) *Global Executive Leadership Inventory: Facilitator's Guide.* San Francisco, CA: Pfeiffer.

Kets de Vries, M.F.R. and Mead, C. (1992) "The development of the global leader within the multinational corporation." In V. Pucik, N.M. Tichy, and C.K. Barnett (eds) *Globalizing Management, Creating and Leading the Competitive Organization.* New York: John Wiley and Sons.

Kets De Vries, M.F.R. with Florent-Treacy, E. (1999) *The New Global Leaders.* San Francisco, CA: Jossey-Bass.

Kets De Vries, M. and Florent-Treacy, E. (2002) "Global leadership from A to Z: Creating high commitment organizations." *Organizational Dynamics*, 30(4): 295–309.

Kets de Vries, M.F.R., Vrignaud, P., and Florent-Treacy, E. (2004) "The global leadership life inventory: Development and psychometric properties of a 360-degree feedback instrument." *International Journal of Human Resource Management*, (15) 3: 475–492.

Kezsbom, D. (2000) "Creating teamwork in virtual teams." *Cost Engineering*, 42: 33–36.

Khilji, S., Davis, E.B., and Cseh, M. (2010) "Building competitive advantage in a global environment: Leadership and the mindset." In T. Devinney, T. Pedersen, and T. Tihanyi (eds) *The Past, Present and Future of International Business and Management. Advances in International Management*, Volume 23, Emerald Group Publishing Limited: 353–373.

Kidd, J.B. and Teramoto, Y. (1995) "The learning organization: The case of the Japanese RHQs in Europe." *Management International Review*, 35(2): 39–56.

Kish-Gephart, J.J., Harrison, D.A., and Treviño, L.K. (2010) "Bad apples, bad cases, and bad barrels: Meta-analytic evidence about sources of unethical decisions at work." *Journal of Applied Psychology*, 95(1): 1–31.

Kluckhohn, F. and Strodtbeck, F.L. (1961) *Variations in Value Orientations*. Evanston, IL: Row, Peterson.

Knapp, M. and Hall, J. (2005) *Nonverbal Communication in Human Interaction*. New York: Wadsworth Publishing.

Kochan, T., Batt, R., and Dyer, R. (1992) "International human resource studies: A framework for future research." In D. Lewin, O.S. Mitchell, and P.D. Sherer (eds) *Research Frontiers in Industrial Relations and Human Resources*. Madison, WI: Industrial Relations Research Association.

Kodama, M. (2005a) "How two Japanese high-tech companies achieved rapid innovation via strategic community networks." *Strategy and Leadership*, 33(6): 39–47.

Kodama, M. (2005b) "Technological innovation through networked strategic communities: A study on a high tech company in Japan." *SAM Advanced Management Journal*, 70(Winter Issue): 21–35.

Kohonen, E. (2005) "Developing global leaders through international assignments: An identity construction perspective." *Personnel Review*, 35(4): 22–36.

Konopaske, R., Mendenhall, M., and Thomason, S. (2009) "Toward a typology of the expatriate construct." Paper presented at the Academy of Management meetings. August 10. Chicago, IL.

Kostopoulos, K. and Bozionelos, N. (2011) "Team Exploratory and exploitative learning: Psychological safety, task conflict, and team performance." *Group & Organization Management*, 36: 385–415.

Kotter, J.P. (1990a) "A force for change: How leadership differs from management." *CA Magazine*, 123(10): 22.

Kotter, J.P. (1990b) "What leaders really do?" *Harvard Business Review*, 68(3): 103.

Kotter, J. (1990c) *A Force for Change: How Leadership Differs from Management*. New York: Free Press.

Kotter, J. and Cohen, D. (2002) *The Heart of Change: Real-Life Stories About How People Change Their Organizations*. Cambridge, MA: Harvard Business School Press.

Koudal, P. and Coleman, G.C. (2005) "Coordinating operations to enhance innovation in the global corporation." *Strategy and Leadership*, 33(4): 20–32.

Kozai Group (2008). *The Kozai Learning Model. Global Competencies Inventory Qualified Administrator Training Resources*. Portland, OR: Intercultural Communication Institute.

Kraimer, M.L., Shaffer, M.A., Harrison, D.A., and Ren, H. (2012) "No place like home? An identity strain perspective on repatriate turnover." *Academy of Management Journal,* 55(2), 399–420.

Lane, H.W., Maznevski, M.L., Mendenhall, M.E., and McNett, J. (2004) *The Blackwell Handbook of Global Management: A Guide to Managing Complexity*. London: Blackwell.

Lane, H.W., Maznevski, M.L., DiStefano, J.J. and Dietz, J. (2009) *International Management Behavior: Leading with a Global Mindset*. Chichester: Wiley.

La Tribune (2006) "Des conseils d'administration peu féminisées." June 14. http://www.egonzehnderknowledge.com/knowledge/content/misc/news/index.php?month=JUNE+2006 (accessed December 26, 2006).

Lau, D.C. and Murnighan, J.K. (1998) "Demographic diversity and faultlines: The compositional dynamics of organizational groups." *Academy of Management Review*, 23: 325–340.

Lawson, E. and Price, C. (2003) "The psychology of change management." *The McKinsey Quarterly*, June Issue: 31–41.

Lazarova, M. and Tarique, I. (2005) "Knowledge transfer upon repatriation." *Journal of World Business*, 40(4): 361–373.

Leatherwood, M.L. and Spector, L.C. (1991) "Enforcements, inducements, expected utility and employee misconduct." *Journal of Management*, 17(3): 553–569.

Leavitt, H.J. (2003) "Why hierarchies thrive." *Harvard Business Review*, March: 96–102.

Leiba-O'Sullivan, S. (1999) "The distinction between stable and dynamic cross-cultural competencies: Implications for expatriate trainability." *Journal of International Business Studies*, 30 (4): 709–725.

Leslie, J.B., Dalton, M., Ernst, C., and Deal, J. (2002) *Managerial Effectiveness in a Global Context. A Center for Creative Leadership Report.* Greensboro, NC: CCL Press.

Levy, O., Beechler, S., Taylor, S., and Boyacigiller, N. (2007) "What do we talk about when we talk about global mindset? Managerial cognition in multinational corporations." *Journal of International Business Studies*, 38: 231–258.

Lewin, K. (1947) "Frontiers in group dynamics." *Human Relations*, 1: 5–41.

Liu, W. (2010) "The effect of different motivation factors on knowledge-sharing willingness and behavior." *Social Behavior and Personality*, 38(6), 753–758.

Livermore, D. (2010) *Leading with Cultural Intelligence: The New Secret to Success.* New York: American Management Association.

Lloyd, S.L., Hartel, C., and Youngsamart, D. (2004) "Working abroad: Competencies expatriates need to successfully cope with the intercultural experience." *Journal of Doing Business Across Borders*, 3(1): 54–66.

Lobel, S.A. (1990) "Global leadership competencies: Managing to a different drumbeat." *Human Resource Management*, 29(1): 39–47.

Loewe, P. and Dominiquini, J. (2006) "Overcoming the barriers to effective innovation." *Strategy and Leadership*, 34(1): 24–30.

Logan, G. (2008) "Global leadership talent shortage forecast." Personneltoday.com, May 21. http://www.personneltoday.com/articles/2008/05/21/45938/global-leadership-talent-shortage-forecast.html (accessed May 22, 2012).

Logsdon, J.M. and Wood, D.J. (2005) "Global business citizenship and voluntary codes of ethical conduct." *Journal of Business Ethics,* 59 (1–2): 55–67.

Louis, M.R. (1980a) "Career transitions: Varieties and commonalities." *Academy of Management Review*, 5(3): 329–340.

Louis, M.R. (1980b) "Surprise and sense making: What newcomers experience in entering unfamiliar organizational settings." *Administrative Science Quarterly*, 25: 226–251.

Lubatkin, M., Ndiaye, M., and Vengroff, R. (1997a) "The nature of managerial work in developing countries: A limited test of the universalist hypothesis." *Journal of International Business Studies*, 28(4): 711–733.

Lubatkin, M., Ndiaye, M., and Vengroff, R. (1997b) "Assessing managerial work in Senegal: Do western models apply?" *Gestion Internacional*, 1(1): 67–76.

Lustig, M.W. and Koester, J. (2003) *Intercultural Competence: Interpersonal Communication across Cultures 4th edition.* Boston, MA: Allyn and Bacon.

Maak, T. (2009) "The cosmopolitical corporation." *The Journal of Business Ethics*, 84: 361–372.

Maak, T. and Pless, N.M. (2006) "Responsible leadership in a stakeholder society—a relational perspective." *Journal of Business Ethics*, 66: 99–115.

Maak. T. and Pless, N.M. (2008) "The leader as responsible change agent: Promoting humanism in and beyond business." In H. Spitzeck, M. Pirson, W. Amann, S. Khan and W. von Kimakowitz (eds) *Humanism in Business: Perspectives on the Development of a Responsible Business World.* Cambridge: Cambridge University Press.

Machiavelli, N. (1515; 1992 translation) *The Prince.* Translated by N. H. Thomson. New York: Dover Publications, Inc.

Madsen, S.R. and Hammond, S. (2005) "Where have all the leaders gone? An interview with Margaret J. Wheatley about life-affirming leadership." *Journal of Management Inquiry*, 14(1): 71–77.

Malhotra, A., Majchrzak, A., and Rosen, B. (2007) "Leading virtual teams." *Academy of Management Perspectives*, 21: 60–70.

Management Issue News. (2006) "Women still rare in Europe's boardrooms." June 20. http://www.management–issues.com/2006/8/24/research/women-still-rare-in-europes-boardrooms.asp (accessed December 26, 2006).

Manakkalathil, J. and Rudolf, E. (1995) "Corporate social responsibility in a globalizing market." *SAM Advanced Management Journal* (Winter): 29–32, 47.

Marquardt, M.J. and Berger, N.O. (2000) *Global Leaders for the 21st Century.* Albany, NY: State University of New York Press.

Marquis, C. and Kanter, R.M. (2010) "IBM: The Corporate Service Corps." Harvard Business School Case: 9-409-106. Boston: Harvard Business School Press.

Maruca, R.F. (1994) "The right way to go global: An interview with Whirlpool CEO David Whitwam." *Harvard Business Review*, 72(2): 134.

Masuda, T. and Nisbett, R.E. (2006) "Culture and change blindness." *Cognitive Science*, 30: 381–399.

Matveev, A.V. and Nelson, P.E. (2004) "Cross cultural communication competence and multicultural team performance perceptions of American and Russian managers." *International Journal of Cross Cultural Management,* 4(2): 253–270.

Mayer, R.C., Davis, J.H., and Schoorman, D.F. (1995) "An integrative model of organizational trust." *The Academy of Management Review,* 20: 709–734.

Maznevski, M.L. (1994) "Understanding our differences: Performance in decision-making groups with diverse members." *Human Relations*, 47: 531–552.

Maznevski, M.L. and Athanassiou, N.A. (2006) "Bringing the outside in: Learning and knowledge management through external networks." In I. Nonaka and K. Ichijo (eds) *Knowledge Creation and Management: New Challenges for Managers.* Oxford: Oxford University Press.

Maznevski, M.L. and Chudoba, K.M. (2000) "Bridging space over time: Global virtual team dynamics and effectiveness." *Organization Science*, 11(5): 473–492.

Maznevski, M.L. and DiStefano, J.J. (1995) "Measuring culture in international management: The cultural perspectives questionnaire." The University of Western Ontario Working Paper Series, 95–39.

Maznevski, M.L. and Jonsen, K. (2006) "The value of different perspectives." *Financial Times Mastering Management: Managing Uncertainty,* March 24. Last accessed on June 12, 2012 at http://www.ft.com/intl/cms/s/2/fd159dfe-ba87-11da-980d-0000779e2340.html#axzz1xbJmwxG0

Maznevski, M.L., Canney Davidson, S., and Jonsen, K. (2006) "Global virtual teams dynamics and effectiveness." In G.K. Stahl and I. Björkman (eds) *Handbook of Research in International Human Resource Management,* Cheltenham: Edward Elgar Publishing.

McBer and Company (1995) *Mastering Global Leadership: Hay/McBer International CEO Leadership Study.* Boston, MA: Hay/McBer Worldwide Resource Center.

McCall, M.W. Jr. (1998) *High Flyers: Developing the Next Generation of Leaders.* Boston, MA: Harvard Business School Press.

McCall, M.W. Jr. (2010) "Recasting leadership development." *Industrial and Organizational Psychology*, 3: 3–19.

McCall, M.W. Jr. and Hollenbeck, G.P. (2002) *Developing Global Executives: The Lessons of International Experience.* Boston, MA: Harvard Business School Press.

McClelland, D.C. (1973) "Testing for competence rather than for intelligence." *American Psychologist,* 28: 1–14.

McCloskey, D. (1998) *The Rhetoric of Economics.* Madison, WI: University of Wisconsin Press.

McCrae, R.R. and Costa, P.T. (1990) *Personality in Adulthood.* New York: The Guilford Press.

McFarland, L.J., Senn, L.E., and Childress, J.R. (1993) *21st Century Leadership: Dialogues with 100 Top Leaders.* New York: Leadership Press.

McGarvey, R.J. (2006) "Assembling the leader: Meet the new breed CEOs." In *Global Talent: An Anthology of Human Capital Strategies for Today's Borderless Enterprise.* Washington, DC: Human Capital Institute.

McKibben, G. (1997) *Cutting Edge: Gillette's Journey to Global Leadership.* Cambridge, MA: Harvard Business School Press.

McKinsey and Company. (1998) "The war for talent." *McKinsey Quarterly,* 3: 44–58.

McKinsey and Company. (2006) "The McKinsey global survey of business executives: Business and society." *McKinsey Quarterly,* 2: 33–39.

McKinsey and Company. (2010) "McKinsey global survey results: Rethinking how companies address social issues." *McKinsey Quarterly,* January Issue: 1–8.

McLeod, P.L., Lobel, S.A., and Cox, T.H. (1996) "Ethnic Diversity and creativity in small groups." *Small Group Research,* 27: 248–264.

Mendenhall, M.E. (1999) "On the need for paradigmatic integration in international human resource management." *Management International Review,* 39(3): 65–87.

Mendenhall, M.E. (2001a) "New perspectives on expatriate adjustment and its relationship to global leadership development." In M. Mendenhall, T. Kühlmann, and G. Stahl (eds) *Developing Global Business Leaders: Policies, Processes and Innovations.* Westport, CT: Quorum Books: 1–16.

Mendenhall, M.E. (2001b) "Global assignments, global leaders: Leveraging global assignments as leadership development programs." Paper presented at the Research Colloquium on Expatriate Management, Cranfield Business School, Cranfield, U.K.: March 15.

Mendenhall, M.E. (2006) "The elusive, yet critical challenge of developing global leaders." *European Management Journal,* 24(6): 422–429.

Mendenhall, M.E. (2008) "Leadership and the birth of global leadership." In M.E. Mendenhall, J.S. Osland, A. Bird, G.R. Oddou, and M.L. Maznevski (eds) *Global Leadership: Research, Practice, and Development.* London, New York: Routledge: 1–17.

Mendenhall, M. and Oddou, G. (1985) "The dimensions of expatriate acculturation: A review." *Academy of Management Review,* 10(1): 39–47.

Mendenhall, M. and Osland, J.S. (2002) "Mapping the Terrain of the Global Leadership Construct." Paper presented at the Academy of International Business, Puerto Rico, June 29.

Mendenhall, M.E. and Stahl, G.K. (2000) "Expatriate training and development: Where do we go from here?" *Human Resource Management,* 39(2/3): 251–265.

Mendenhall, M., Kühlmann, T., and Stahl, G. (2001) *Developing Global Business Leaders: Policies, Processes and Innovations.* Westport, CT: Quorum Books.

Mendenhall, M., Kühlmann, T., Stahl, G., and Osland, J.S. (2002) "Employee development and expatriate assignments." In M.J. Gannon and K.L. Newman (eds) *The Blackwell Handbook of Cross-Cultural Management.* Malden, MA: Blackwell: 155–183.

Mendenhall, M., Jensen, R., Gregersen, H., and Black, J.S. (2003) "Seeing the Elephant: HRM challenges in the age of globalization." *Organizational Dynamics,* 32 (3): 261–274.

Mendenhall, M., Ehnert, T., Oddou, G., Osland, J.S., and Stahl, G. (2004) "Evaluation studies of cross-cultural training programs: A review of the literature from 1988–2000." In D. Landis, J. Bennett, and M. Bennet (eds) *Handbook of Intercultural Training, 3rd edition.* Thousand Oaks, CA: Sage: 129–143.

Mendenhall, M.E, Osland, J.S., Bird, A., Oddou, G.R., and Maznevski, M.L. (2008) *Global Leadership: Research, Practice and Development.* London: Routledge.

Mendenhall, M., Reiche, B.S., Bird, A., and Osland, J.S. (2012) "Defining the 'global' in global leadership." *Journal of World Business* 47(4). http://dx.doi.org/10.1016/j.jwb.2012.01.003

Mercer Delta. (2006) "The global leadership imperative." Presentation to the Human Resource Planning Society, March 8.

Meyer, J.P. and Allen, N.J. (1997) *Commitment in the Workplace: Theory, Research and Application.* Thousand Oaks, CA: Sage Publications.

Meyer, S.E. and Kelly, J.E. (1992) *The Cross-cultural Adaptability Inventory Workbook.* Yarmouth, ME: Intercultural Press.

Mezirow, J. (1978) "Perspective transformation." *Adult Education,* XXVIII(2): 100–110.

Miller, E.L. (1973) "The international selection decision: A study of some dimensions of managerial behavior in the selection decision process." *Academy of Management Journal,* 16: 239–252.

Millikin, J.P. and Fu, D. (2005) "The global leadership of Carlos Ghosn at Nissan." *Thunderbird International Business Review,* 47(1): 121–137.

Minbaeva, D.B. (2005) "HRM practices and MNC knowledge transfer." *Personnel Review,* 34(1): 125–144.

Mintzberg, H. (1973) *The Nature of Managerial Work.* New York: Harper and Row.

Mintzberg, H. (2004) *Managers not MBAs: A hard Look at the Soft Practice of Management and Management Development.* San Francisco, CA: Berrett-Koehler.

Mintzberg, H. and Gosling, J. (2002) "Educating managers beyond borders." *Academy of Management Learning and Education,* 1: 64–76.

Mirvis, P. (2008) "Executive development through consciousness-raising experiences." *Academy of Management Learning and Education,* 7: 173–188.

Mobley, W.H., Gessner, M.J., and Arnold, V. (1999) *Advances in Global Leadership, vol. 1.* Stamford, CT: JAI Press.

Mobley, W.H. and McCall, M.W. (2001) *Advances in Global Leadership, vol. 2.* Stamford, CT: JAI Press.

Mobley, W.H. and Dorfman, P.W. (2003) *Advances in Global Leadership, vol. 3.* Stamford, CT: JAI Press.

Mobley, W.H. and Weldon, E. (2006) *Advances in Global Leadership, vol. 4.* Stamford, CT: JAI Press.

Mobley, W.H., Wang, Y., and Li, M. (eds) (2009) *Advances in Global Leadership, vol. 5.* Oxford: Elsevier.

Mobley, W.H., Wang, Y., and Li, M. (eds) (2011) *Advances in Global Leadership, vol. 6.* Bingley, UK: Emerald.

Mobley, W.H., Wang, Y., and Li, M. (eds) (2012) *Advances in Global Leadership, vol. 7.* Bingley, UK: Emerald.

Mogotsi, I., Boon, J., and Fletcher, L. (2011) "Knowledge sharing behaviour and demographic variables among secondary teachers in and around Gaborone, Botswana." *South African Journal of Information Management,* 13, 1: 1–6.

Mol, S.T., Van Oudenhoven, J.P. and Van der Zee, K.I. (2001) "Validation of the Multicultural Personality Questionnaire among an internationally oriented student population in Taiwan." In F. Salili and R. Hoosain (eds) *Multicultural Education Issues, Policies and Practices.* Greenwich, CT: IAP Press: 167–186.

Mol, S.T., Born, M.P., Willemsen, M.E., and Van Der Molen, H.T. (2005) "Predicting expatriate job performance for selection purposes: A quantitative review." *Journal of Cross-Cultural Psychology*, 36(5): 590–620.

Monge, P. and Fulk, J. (1999) "Communication technology for global network organizations." In G. DeSanctis and J. Fulk (eds) *Shaping Organization Form: Communication, Connection and Community.* Thousand Oaks, CA: Sage: 71–100.

Moran, R.T. and Riesenberger, J.R. (1994) *The Global Challenge: Building the New Worldwide Enterprise.* London, McGraw-Hill.

Moro Bueno, C. and Tubbs, S. (2004) "Identifying global leadership competencies: An exploratory study." *Journal of American Academy of Business*, 5(1/2): 80–87.

Morrison, A. (2001) "Integrity and global leadership." *Journal of Business Ethics*, 31(1): 65–76.

Morrison, A. (2006) "Ethical standards and global leadership." In W.H. Mobley and E. Weldon (eds) *Advances in Global Leadership, vol. 4.* Stamford, CT: JAI Press: 165–179.

Morrison, A.J. (2000) "Developing a global leadership model." *Human Resource Management*, 39: 117–127.

Mount, M.K. and Barrick, M.R. (1998) "Five reasons why the 'Big Five' article has been frequently cited." *Personnel Psychology*, 51: 849–857.

Mudrack, P.E. (1989) "Group cohesiveness and productivity: A closer look." *Human Relations*, 42: 771–785.

Mullen, B. and Copper, C. (1994) "The relation between group cohesiveness and performance: An integration." *Psychological Bulletin*, 115: 210–227.

Munchus, G. (1989) "Testing as a selection tool: Another old and sticky managerial human rights issue." *Journal of Business Ethics*, 8(10): 817–820.

Nair, K. (1994) *A Higher Standard of Leadership: Lessons from the Life of Gandhi.* San Francisco, CA: Berrett-Koehler Publishers.

Naor, J. (1982) "A new approach to multinational social responsibility." *Journal of Business Ethics*, 1: 219–25.

Naumann, E. (1992) "A conceptual model of expatriate turnover." *Journal of International Business Studies*, 23(3): 499–531.

Newman, K.L. and Nollen, S.D. (1996) "Culture and congruence: The fit between management practices and national culture." *Journal of International Business Studies*, 27: 753–779.

Ng, K., Van Dyke, L., and Ang, S. (2009) "From experience to experiential learning: Cultural intelligence as a learning capability for global leader development." *Academy of Learning and Education*, 8(4): 51–526.

Nirenberg, J. (2002) *Global Leadership.* Oxford, UK: Capstone.

Nisbett, R.E. (2003) *The Geography of Thought: How Asians and Westerners Think Differently...and Why.* New York: The Free Press.

Nohria, N. (2009) "From regional star to global leader." *Harvard Business Review*, January: 33–39.

Nonaka, I. (1990) "Managing innovation as a knowledge-creation process: A new model for a knowledge-creating organization." Paper presented at New York University, Stern School of Business, International Business Colloquium.

Nonaka, I. (1991a) "Managing the firm as an information creation process." *Advances in Information Processing in Organizations*, 4: 239–275. Greenwich, CT: JAI Press.

Nonaka, I. (1991b) "The knowledge-creating company." *Harvard Business Review*, 69(6): 96–104.

Nonaka, I. (1994) "A dynamic theory of organizational knowledge creation." *Organization Science*, 5: 14–37.

Nonaka, I. and Kenney, M. (1991) "Towards a new theory of innovation management: A case study comparing Canon, Inc. and Apple Computer, Inc." *Journal of Engineering and Technology Management*, 8(1): 67–83.

Nurasimha, S. (2000) "Organizational knowledge, human resource management and sustained competitive advantage: Toward a framework." *Competitiveness Review*, 10: 123–135.

Oddou, G.R. (2002) "Repatriate assets and firm performance: Toward a model." Paper presented at the annual meeting of the Academy of Management, Denver.

Oddou, G. and Mendenhall, M. (1988) "The overseas assignment: A practical look." *Business Horizons*, 31(5): 78–84.

Oddou, G. and Mendenhall, M. (1991) "Succession planning in the 21st century: How well are we grooming our future business leaders?" *Business Horizons*, January –February, 34(1): 26–34.

Oddou, G. and Osland, J.S. (2003) "The transfer of repatriate assets: Variables influencing the knowledge transfer." 7th International Human Resource Management Congress, Limerick, Ireland, June.

Oddou, G., Gregersen, H., Derr, B., and Black, J.S. (1998) "Internationalizing human resources: Strategy differences among European, Japanese and U.S. multinationals." In M. Mendenhall, T. Kühlmann, and G. Stahl (eds) *Developing Global Business Leaders: Policies, Processes, and Innovations*, Westport, CT: Quorum Books: 99–116,

Oddou, G., Mendenhall, M.E., and Ritchie, J.B. (2000) "Leveraging travel as a tool for global leadership development." *Human Resource Management*, 39(2/3): 159–172.

Oddou, G., Osland, J.S., and Blakeney, R. (2009) "Repatriate knowledge transfer: Variables in the transfer process." *Journal of International Business Studies*, 40(2): 188–199.

O'Fallon, M.J. and Butterfield, K.D. (2005) "A review of the empirical ethical decision-making literature: 1996–2003." *Journal of Business Ethics*, 59: 375–413.

Olsen, J.E. and Martins, L.L. (2009) "The effects of expatriate demographic characteristics on adjustment: A social identity approach." *Human Resource Management*, 48(2): 311–328.

Ones, D. S. and Viswesvaran, C. (1998) "The effects of social desirability and faking on personality and integrity assessment for personnel selection." *Human Performance, 11,* 245–271.

Ones, D.S. and Viswesvaran, C. (1999) "Relative importance of personality dimensions for expatriate selection: A policy capturing study." *Human Performance*, 12(3/4): 275–294.

O'Reilly, C.A., Williams, K.Y., and Barsade, S. (1998) "Group demography and innovation: Does diversity help?" *Research on Managing Groups and Teams*, 1: 183–207.

Osland, A. (1996) "The role of leadership and cultural contingencies in TQM in Central America." *Journal of Business and Management*, 3: 64–80.

Osland, J.S. (1991) "A replication of Mintzberg"s managerial roles study." Unpublished working paper. Alajuela, Costa Rica: INCAE.

Osland, J.S. (1995) *The Adventure of Working Abroad: Hero Tales from the Global Frontier.* San Francisco, CA: Jossey-Bass.

Osland, J.S. (2000) "The journey inward: Expatriate hero tales and paradoxes." *Human Resource Management*, 39(2/3): 227–238.

Osland, J.S. (2001) "The quest for transformation: The process of global leadership development." In M. Mendenhall, T. Kühlmann, and G. Stahl (eds) *Developing Global Business Leaders: Policies, Processes and Innovations.* Westport, CT: Quorum Books: 137–156.

Osland, J.S. (2004) "Building community through change." In H.W. Lane, M.L. Maznevski, M.E. Mendenhall, and J. McNett (eds) *The Blackwell Handbook of Global Management: A Guide to Managing Complexity*. Malden, MA: Blackwell Publishing: 134–151.

Osland, J.S. (2008) "An overview of the global leadership literature." In M.E. Mendenhall, J.S. Osland, A. Bird, G.R. Oddou, and M.L. Maznevski (2008) *Global Leadership: Research, Practice and Development*. London: Routledge: 34–63.

Osland, J.S. (2010). "Expert cognition and sense-making in the global organization leadership context: A case study." In U. Fisher and K. Moser (eds) *Informed by Knowledge: Expert Performance in Complex Situations*. New York: Taylor and Francis: 23–40.

Osland, J.S. and Bird, A. (2000) "Beyond sophisticated stereotyping: cultural sensemaking in context." *Academy of Management Executive*, 14(1): 65–76.

Osland, J.S. and Bird, A. (2006) "Global leaders as experts." In W. Mobley and E. Weldon (eds) *Advances in Global Leadership, Volume 4*. Stamford, CT: JAI Press: 123–142.

Osland, A. and Osland, J.S. (2007) "Aracruz Celulose: Best practices icon but still at risk." *International Journal of Manpower*, 28(5), 435–450.

Osland J.S., Adler N.J., and Brody L.W. (2002) "Developing global leadership in women: Lessons and sense making from an organizational change effort." In R. Burke and D. Nelson (eds) *Advancing Women's Careers*. Oxford: Blackwell: 15–36.

Osland, J.S., Oddou, G., and Blakeley, R. (2005) "Getting the 'goods' back home: Variables influencing repatriate knowledge transfer." Paper presented at the Western Academy of Management. Las Vegas, Nevada, April.

Osland, J.S., Bird, A., Mendenhall, M.E., and Osland, A. (2006) "Developing global leadership capabilities and global mindset: A review." In G.K. Stahl and I. Björkman (eds) *Handbook of Research in International Human Resource Management*. Cheltenham, UK: Edward Elgar Publishing: 197–222.

Osland, J.S., Bird, A., Osland, A., and Oddou, G. (2007) "Expert cognition in high technology global leaders." Paper presented at NDM8, 8th Naturalistic Decision Making Conference, Monterey, CA, June.

Osland, J.S., Taylor, S., and Mendenhall, M. (2009) "Global leadership: Challenges and lessons." In R. Steers and R. Bhagat (eds) *Handbook of Cultural Variations in Work*. Oxford: Blackwell Publishing Ltd.: 245–271.

Osland, J.S., Oddou, G., Bird, A., and Osland, A. (2011) "Exceptional global leadership as cognitive expertise." Unpublished manuscript. San José State University.

Osland, J.S., Bird, A., and Oddou, G. (2012a) "The context of expert global leadership." In W.H. Mobley, Y. Wang, and M. Li (eds) *Advances in Global Leadership, vol. 7*. Oxford: Elsevier.

Osland, J.S., Bird, A., and Mendenhall, M.E. (2012b) "Global leadership and global mindset: An updated look. In G. Stahl and I. Bjorkman (eds) *International Human Resources Handbook*. 2nd edition. London: Edward Elgar: 227–259.

O'Sullivan, A. and O'Sullivan, S.L. (2008) "The performance challenges of expatriate supplier teams: a multi-firm case study." *The International Journal of Human Resource Management*, 19: 999–1017.

Paige, R.M. (ed.) (1993) *Education for the Intercultural Experience*. Yarmouth, ME: Intercultural Press.

Paige, R.M., Jacobs-Cassuto, M., Yershova, Y.A., and DeJaeghere, J. (2003) "Assessing intercultural sensitivity: An empirical analysis of the Hammer and Bennett Intercultural Development Inventory." *International Journal of Intercultural Relations*, 27: 467–187.

Palmisano, S. (2007) "The globally integrated enterprise: A new model." Speech given at the Global Leadership Forum, Washington, D.C. July 25. In White, K. and Rosamilia,

T. "Developing global leadership: How IBM engages the workforce of a globally integrated enterprise." White paper. IBM Global Business Services. 2010: 2.

Pan, L. and Wang, Z. (2010) "Knowledge transfer via personnel mobility: The effect of knowledge about the distribution of information." *Social Behavior and Personality*, 38(10): 1391–1400.

Pandya, M. and Shell, R. (2005) *Lasting Leadership*. Upper Saddle River, NJ: Pearson Education /Wharton School Publishing.

Parsons, T. and Shils, E. (1951) *Toward a General Theory of Action*. Cambridge, MA: Harvard University Press.

Pascale, R. (1998) "Grassroots Leadership—Royal Dutch/Shell." *Fast Company* 14: 110. http://www.fastcompany.com/online/14/grassroots.html (accessed February 4, 2007).

Pascale, R.T. (1999) "Surfing the Edge of Chaos." *Sloan Management Review*, 40: 83–94.

Pascale, R.T. and Athos, A.G. (1981) *Art of Japanese Management*. New York: Simon and Schuster.

Payne, R. (1990) "The effectiveness of research teams: A review." In M.A. West and J.L. Farr (eds) *Innovation and Creativity at Work: Psychological and Organizational Strategies*. Oxford, England: John Wiley and Sons: 101–122.

Pedersen, P. (1994) *A Handbook for Developing Multicultural Awareness, 2nd edition*. Alexandria, VA: American Counseling Association.

Pedersen, P. (1995) *The Five Stages of Culture Shock*. London: Greenwood.

Petrick, J.A., Scherer, R.F., Brodzinski, J.D., Quinn, J.F., and Fall Ainina, M. (1999) "Global leadership skills and reputational capital: Intangible resources for sustainable competitive advantage." *Academy of Management Executive*, 13(1): 58–69.

Pettigrew, A. (2000) "Linking change processes to outcomes: A commentary on Ghoshal, Bartlett and Weick." In M. Beer and N. Nohria (eds) *Breaking the Code of Change*. Boston, MA: Harvard Business School Press.

Pettigrew, A. and Tropp, L. (2006) "A meta-analytic test of intergroup contact theory." *Journal of Personality and Social Psychology*, 90(5): 751–783.

Pfeffer, J. (1995) "Producing sustainable competitive advantage through the effective management of people." *Academy of Management Executive*, 9(1): 55–72.

Pfeffer, J. (2005) "Why do bad management theories persist?" *Academy of Management Learning and Education*, 4: 96–100.

Pierce, C.A., Broberg, B.J., McClure, J.R., and Aguinis, H. (2004) "Responding to sexual harassment complaints: Effects of a dissolved workplace romance on decision-making standards." *Organizational Behavior and Human Decision Processes*, 95: 66–82.

Pless, N.M. and Maak, T. (2005) "Relational intelligence for leading responsibly in a connected world." In K.M. Weaver (ed.) *Best Paper Proceedings of the Sixty-fifth Annual Meeting of the Academy of Management*, Honolulu.

Pless, N.M. and Maak, T. (2009) "Responsible leaders as agents of world benefit: Learnings from 'Project Ulysses.'" *Journal of Business Ethics*, 85: 59–71.

Pless, N.M. and Maak, T. (2012) "Levi Strauss and Company: Addressing child labour in Bangladesh." In M.E. Mendenhall, G.R. Oddou, and G.K. Stahl (eds) *Readings and Cases in International Human Resource Management and Organizational Behavior. 5th edition*. London/New York: Routledge.

Pless, N.M., Maak, T., and Stahl, G.K. (2011) "Developing responsible global leaders through International Service Learning Programs: The Ulysses experience." *Academy of Management Learning and Education*, 10(2): 237–260.

Polanyi, M. (1966) *The Tacit Dimension*. London: Routledge.

Politis, J. (2001) "The relationship of various leadership styles to knowledge management." *Leadership and Organization Development Journal*, 22(8): 354–364.

Prahalad, C.K. (1990) "Globalization: The intellectual and managerial challenges." *Human Resource Management*, 29(1): 27–37.

Prahalad, C.K. and Doz, Y. (1987) *The Multinational Mission.* New York: The Free Press and London: Collier-Macmillan.

Prahalad, C.K. and Hamel, G. (1994) "Strategy as a field of study: Why search for a new paradigm?" *Strategic Management Journal*, 15: 5–16.

Price Waterhouse. (1997) *International Assignments: Europeans Policy and Practice.* Price Waterhouse International Assignment Services Europe.

PRNewswire. (2011) "Thomson Reuters names world's 100 most innovative companies." http://www.prnewswire.com/news-releases/thomson-reuters-names-worlds-100-most-innovative-companies-133865218.html (accessed February 5, 2012).

Prokesch S.E. (2000) "Unleashing the power of learning: An interview with British Petroleum's John Browne." In J.E. Garten (ed.) *World View: Global Strategies for the New Economy.* Cambridge, MA: Harvard Business School Press: 302–303.

Pruzan, P. and Miller, W. (2006) 'Spirituality as the basis of responsible leaders and companies.' In T. Maak and N.M. Pless (eds.) *Responsible Leadership.* London, New York: Routledge: 68–92.

Puffer, S.M. and McCarthy, D.J. (2008) "Ethical turnarounds and transformational leadership: A global imperative for corporate social responsibility." *Thunderbird International Business Review*, 50: 303–314.

Pusch, M. (1994) "The chameleon capacity." In R.D. Lambert (ed.) *Educational Exchange and Global Competence.* New York: Council on International Educational Exchange: 205–210.

PwC. (2008) "About the programme." http://www.pwc.com/extweb/manissue.nsf/docid/8A A7ED2A5C07C6FA8525738B00776B78) (accessed January 22, 2008).

Quinn, R. and Cameron, K. (1988) *Paradox and Transformation.* Cambridge, MA: Ballinger.

Redding, S.G. (1997) "The comparative management theory zoo: Getting the elephants and ostriches and even dinosaurs from the jungle into the iron cages." In B. Toyne and D. Nigh (eds) International Business: An Emerging Vision. Columbia, SC: University of South Carolina Press: 416–439.

Reiche, B.S., Kraimer, M.L., and Harzing, A.-W. (2011) "Why do international assignees stay? An organizational embeddedness perspective." *Journal of International Business Studies*, 42: 521–544.

Reiche, S., Harzing, A.-W., and Kraimer, M.L. (2009a) "The role of international assignees' social capital in creating inter-unit intellectual capital: A cross-level model." *Journal of International Business Studies*, 40: 509–526.

Reiche, S., Kraimer, M.L., and Harzing, A.-W. (2009b) "Inpatriates as agents of cross-unit knowledge flows in multinational corporations." In P. Sparrow (ed.) *Handbook of International Human Resource Management: Integrating People, Process and Context.* Oxford: Wiley–Blackwell: 151–170.

Rhinesmith, S. (1993) *A Manager's Guide to Globalization: Six Skills for Success in a Changing World,* 1st edition. New York: McGraw-Hill.

Rhinesmith, S. (1996) *A Manager's Guide to Globalization: Six Skills for Success in a Changing World,* 2nd edition New York: McGraw-Hill.

Rhinesmith, S. (2003) "Basic components of a global mindset." In M. Goldsmith, V. Govindarajan, B. Kaye, and A. Vicere (eds) *The Many Facets of Leadership.* Upper Saddle River, NJ: Financial Times/Prentice Hall.

Richard, O.C. and Johnson, N.B. (2001) "Understanding the impact of human resource diversity practices on firm performance." *Journal of Managerial Issues*, 13: 177–195.

Riding, R. and Rayner, S. (2000) *International Perspectives on Individual Differences*, vol. 1. Stamford, CT: Ablex Publishing Corporation.

Robert C., Probst, T.M., Martocchio, J.J., Drasgow, F., and Lawler, J.J. (2000) "Empowerment and continuous improvement in the United States, Mexico, Poland and India: Predicting fit on the basis of the dimensions of power distance and individualism." *Journal of Applied Psychology*, 85: 643–58.

Roddick, A. (1991) *Body and Soul.* New York: Crown.

Rosen, R., Digh, P., Singer, M., and Phillips, C. (2000) *Global Literacies: Lessons on Business Leadership and National Cultures.* New York: Simon and Schuster.

Rost, J.C. (1993) Leadership for the Twenty-first Century. Westport, CT: Praeger.

Rothman, H. and Scott, M. (2003) *Companies with a Conscience.* Denver, CO: The Publishing Cooperative.

Rotter, J.B. (1966) "Generalized expectancies for internal vs. external control of eeinforcement." *Psychological Monograph*, 80: 1–28.

Ruben, B.D. (1989) "The study of cross-cultural competence: Traditions and contemporary issues." *International Journal of Intercultural Relations*, 13: 229–239.

Saphiere, D.H., Mikk, B.K., and Devries B.I. (2005) *Communication Highwire: Leveraging the Power of Diverse Communication Styles.* Yarmouth, ME: Intercultural Press.

Saulsman, L.M. and Page, A.C. (2004) "The five-factor model and personality disorder empirical literature: A meta-analytic review." *Clinical Psychology Review*, 23: 1055–1085.

Saxe, J.G. (1878) "The blind men and the elephant." In W.J. Linton (ed.) *Poetry of America: Selections from One Hundred American Poets from 1776–1876.* London: George Bell and Sons: 150–152.

Schein, E.H. (1996) "Career anchors revisited: Implications for career development in the 21st century." *Academy of Management Executive*, 10(4): 80–88.

Scherer, A.G., Palazzo, G., and Baumann, D. (2006) "Global rules and private actors: Toward a new role of the transnational corporation in global governance." *Business Ethics Quarterly*, 16: 505–532.

Schneider, S.C. and Barsoux, J.L. (2003) *Managing Across Cultures, 2nd edition.* Harlow: Financial Times Prentice Hall.

Schoenenberger, K. (2000) *Levi's Children: Coming to Terms with Human Rights in the Global Marketplace.* New York: Atlantic Monthly Press.

Schollhammer, H. (1969) "The comparative management theory jungle." *Academy of Management Journal*, 12: 81–97.

Schwartz, M.S. and Carroll, A.B. (2003) "Corporate social responsibility: A three-domain approach." *Business Ethics Quarterly*, 13(4): 503–530.

Schwartz, S.H. (1994) "Beyond individualism/collectivism: New cultural dimensions of values." In U. Kim, H.C. Triandis, C. Katgitcibasi, S. Choi, and G. Yoon (eds) *Individualism and Collectivism: Theory, Method and Applications.* Thousand Oaks, CA: Sage: 85–119.

Schwer S. (2004) "Salsa cultures." Unpublished master's thesis, Vienna University of Economics and Business Administration.

Senge, P. (1990) *The Fifth Discipline.* New York: Currency/Doubleday.

Shaffer, M.A., Harrison, D.A., and Gilley, K.M. (1999) "Dimensions, determinants and differences in the expatriate adjustment process." *Journal of International Business Studies*, 30: 557–581.

Shaffer, M.A., Harrison, D.A., Gregersen, H., Black, J.S., and Ferzandi, L.A. (2006) "You can take it with you: Individual differences and expatriate effectiveness." *Journal of Applied Psychology*, 9(1): 109–125.

Shalley, C.E. and Gilson, L.L. (2004) "What leaders need to know: A review of social and contextual factors that can foster or hinder creativity." *Leadership Quarterly*, 15: 33–53.

Shannon, C.E. and Weaver, W. (1949) *The Mathematical Theory of Communication.* Urbana, IL: University of Illinois Press.

Shih, S., Wang, J.T., and Yeung, A. (2006) "Building global competitiveness in a turbulent environment: Acer's journey of transformation." In W. Mobley and E. Weldon (eds) *Advances in Global Leadership, vol. 4.* Stamford: CT: JAI Press: 201–217.

Shu, W. and Chuang, Y. (2011) "Why people share knowledge in virtual communities." *Social Behavior and Personality*, 39 (5): 67–690.

Simons, J. (2003) "Is it too late to save Schering?" CNNMoney.Com. http://money.cnn.com/magazines/fortune/fortune_archive/2003/09/15/349150/index.htm (accessed January 20, 2007).

Sinangil, H.K. and Ones, D.S. (1995) "Turkiye'de calisan yabanci yoneticilerin kisilik ozellikleri ve bunlarin kriter gecerligi." ("Personality characteristics of expatriates working in Turkey and the criterion-related validities of these constructs.") Unpublished paper, Marmara University, Istanbul, Turkey.

Sinangil, H.K. and Ones, D.S. (1997) "Empirical investigations of the host country perspective in expatriate management." In D.M. Saunders and Z. Aycan (eds) *New Approaches to Employee Management: Vol. 4. Expatriate Management Theory and Research.* Greenwich, CT: JAI.

Smith, P.B. and Peterson, M.F. (1988) *Leadership, Organizations and Culture: An Event Management Model.* London: Sage.

Solomon, C.M. (1996) "Put your ethics to a global test: Prepare to walk a moral tighttope." *Personnel Journal*, January: 66–68, 70, 73–74.

Somech, A. and Drach-Zahavy, A. (2011) "Translating team creativity to innovation implementation: The role of team composition and climate for innovation." *Journal of Management*, 37: 1–25.

Spar, D.L. and La Mure, L.T. (2003) "The power of activism: Assessing the impact of NGOs on global business." *California Management Review*, 45(3): 78–101.

Spencer, R. and Foster, P. (2008) "China milk scandal threatens giant dairy firm." *The Daily Telegraph*, September 24.

Spreitzer, G.M., McCall, M.W. Jr., and Mahoney, J.D. (1997) "Early identification of international executive potential." *Journal of Applied Psychology*, 82(1): 6–29.

Stahl, G.K. (1998) *Internationaler einsatz von Führungskräften.* München: Oldenbourg.

Stahl, G.K. (2001) "Using assessment centers as tools for global leadership development: An exploratory study." In M.E. Mendenhall, T.M. Kühlmann, and G.K. Stahl (eds) *Developing Global Business Leaders: Policies, Processes, and Innovations* Westport: Quorum: 197–210.

Stahl, G.K. (2011) "What drives and hinders responsible managerial behavior?" Paper presented at the Academy of Management 2011 Annual Meeting, San Antonio, United States.

Stahl, G K., Björkman, I., Stiles, P., Paauwe, J., and Wright, P. (2008) "Global talent management: How leading multinationals build and sustain their talent pipeline." *INSEAD Working Paper.*

Stahl, G.K., Pless, N., and Maak, T. (2009) "Approaches to corporate social responsibility in global organizations and their implications for international assignees: Towards a model of transnational responsible leadership." Paper presented at the 25th EGOS Colloquium 2009, Barcelona, Spain.

Staples, S.D. and Zhao, L. (2006) "The effects of cultural diversity in virtual teams versus face-to-face teams." *Group Decision and Negotiation*, 15: 389–406.

Stephens, G.K., Bird, A., and Mendenhall, M.E. (2002) "International careers as repositories of knowledge: A new look at expatriation." In D.C. Feldman (ed.) *Work Careers: A Developmental Perspective.* San Francisco, CA: Jossey-Bass: 294–320.

Stern, N. (2007) "The economics of climate change." *The Stern Review*, Cambridge: University Press.

Stevens, M., Furuya, N., Oddou, G., Bird, A., and Mendenhall, M. (2006) "HR factors affecting repatriate job satisfaction and job attachment for Japanese managers." *International Journal of Human Resource Management*, 17: 831–841.

Stogdill, R.M. (1974) *Handbook of Leadership: A Survey of the Literature.* New York: Free Press.

Straffon, D.A. (2003) "Assessing the intercultural sensitivity of high school students attending an international school." *International Journal of Intercultural Relations*, 27: 421–445.

Stroh, L., Black, J.S., Mendenhall, M.E., and Gregersen, H. (2005) *Global Leaders, Global Assignments: An Integration of Research and Practice.* London: Lawrence Erlbaum and Associates.

Stroh, L.K. (1995) "Predicting turnover among repatriates: Can organizations affect retention rates?" *International Journal of Human Resource Management*, 6: 443–56.

Stroh, L.K. and Caligiuri, P.M. (1997) *Increasing Global Competitiveness Through Effective People Management.* San Diego, CA: Global Leadership Institute.

Stroh, L., Gregersen, H., and Black, J.S. (1998) "Closing the gap: Expectations versus reality among repatriates." *Journal of World Business*, 33(2): 111–124.

Stuart, D. (2007) *Assessment Instruments for the Global Workforce.* White paper. Alexandria, VA: Society for Human Resource Management.

Sundaram, A.K. and Inkpen, A.C. (2004) "The corporate objective revisited." *Organization Science*, 15(3): 350–363.

Sutton, R.I. (2001) "The weird rules of creativity." *Harvard Business Review*, 79(8): 8.

Suutari, V. (2002) "Global leadership development: An emerging research agenda." *Career Development International*, 7(4): 218–233.

Suutari, V. and Taka, M. (2004) "Career anchors of managers with global careers." *Journal of Management Development*, 23(9): 833–847.

Tahvanainen, M. and Suutari, V. (2005) "Expatriate performance management in MNCs." In H. Scullion and M. Linehan (eds) *International Human Resource Management: A Critical Text.* New York: Palgrave Macmillan: 91–113.

Takeuchi R., Yun S., and Tesluk, P.E. (2002) "An examination of crossover and spillover effects of spousal and expatriate cross-cultural adjustment on expatriate outcomes." *Journal of Applied Psychology*, 87(4): 655–666.

Tallman, S. and Fladmoe-Lindquist, K. (2002) "Internationalization, globalization and capability-based strategy." *California Management Review*, 45(1): 116–135.

Tannen, D. (1994) *Gender and Discourse.* New York: Oxford University Press.

Taylor, E.W. (1994) "Intercultural competency: A transformative learning process." *Adult Education Quarterly*, 44(3): 154–174.

Taylor, W. (1991) "The logic of global business: An interview with ABB's Percy Barnevik." *Harvard Business Review*, 69 (2), 91–105.

Taras, V. (2006a) "Instruments for measuring acculturation." Unpublished manuscript. University of Calgary.

Taras, V. (2006b) "Instruments for measuring cultural values and behaviors." Unpublished manuscript. University of Calgary.

Templer, K., Tay, C., and Chandrashekar, N.A. (2006) "Motivational cultural intelligence, realistic job preview, realistic living conditions preview and cross-cultural adjustment." *Group and Organization Management*, 3: 154–171.

Tenbrunsel, A.E. and Smith-Crowe, K. (2008) "Ethical decision making: Where we've been and where we're going." *Academy of Management Annals*, 2: 545–607.

Tenkasi R.V. and Mohrman S.A. (1999) "Global change as contextual collaborative knowledge creation." In D. Cooperrider and J.E. Dutton (eds) *Organizational Dimensions of Global Change: No Limits to Cooperation.* Thousand Oaks, CA: Sage: 114–136.

Tetlock, P.E. (1983) "Accountability and complexity in thought." *Journal of Personality and Social Psychology*, 45: 74–83.

Thaler-Carter, R. (2000) "Whither global leaders?" *HRMagazine*, 45(5): 82–88.

Tharenou, P. and Caulfield, N. (2010) "Will I stay or will I go? Explaining repatriation by self-initiated expatriates." *Academy of Management Journal*, 53(5): 1009–1028.

Thich, N.H. (1991) *Peace is Every Step: The Path of Mindfulness in Everyday Life.* New York: Bantam Books.

Thomas, D.C. (1999) "Cultural diversity and work group effectiveness." *Journal of Cross-Cultural Psychology*, 30: 242–263.

Thomas, D.C. (2006) "Domain and development of cultural intelligence: The importance of mindfulness." *Group and Organization Management*, 31: 78–99.

Thomas, D.C. and Lazarova, M.B. (2006) "Expatriate adjustment and performance: a critical review." In G. K. Stahl and I. Bjorkman (eds) *Handbook of Research in International Human Resource Management.* Cheltenham: Edward Elgar 247–264.

Thomas, D.C., Ravlin, E.C., and Wallace, A.W. (1996) "Effect of cultural diversity in work groups." *Research in the Sociology of Organizations*, 14: 1–33.

Tichy, N. and Charan, R. (1995) "The CEO as coach: An interview with Allied Signal's Lawrence A. Bossidy." *Harvard Business Review,* March Issue: 68–78.

Tichy, N.M. and DeVanna, M.A. (1986) *The Transformational Leader.* New York: John Wiley and Sons.

Tichy, N., Brimm, M., Charan, R., and Takeuchi, H. (1992) "Leadership development as a lever for global transformation." In V. Pucik, N. Tichy, and C.K. Barnett (eds) *Globalizing Management, Creating and Leading the Competitive Organization.* New York: John Wiley and Sons: 47–60.

Ting-Toomey, S. (ed) (1999) *Communicating Across Cultures.* New York: The Guilford Press.

Ting-Toomey, S. and Oetzel, J.G. (2001) *Managing Intercultural Conflict Effectively.* Thousand Oaks, CA: Sage.

Tjosvold, D. (1986) *Working Together to Get Things Done: Managing for Organizational Productivity.* Lexington, MA: Lexington Books.

Tjosvold, D. and Yu, Z. (2007) "Group risk taking. The constructive role of controversy in China." *Group & Organization Management,* 32: 653–674.

Toh, S.M. and DeNisi, A.S. (2005) "A local perspective to expatriate success." *Academy of Management Executive*, 19(1): 132–146.

Toyne, B. and Nigh, D. (1997) "Foundations of an emerging paradigm." In B. Toyne and D. Nigh (eds) *International Business: An Emerging Vision.* Columbia, SC: University of South Carolina Press: 3–26.

Treviño, L.K., Brown, M., and Hartman, L.P. (2003) "A qualitative investigation of perceived executive ethical leadership: Perceptions from inside and outside the executive suite." *Human Relations*, 56(1): 5–37.

Triandis, H.C. (1995) *Individual and Collectivism.* San Francisco, CA: Westview Press.

Trompenaars, F. and Hampden-Turner, C. (1993) *The Seven Cultures of Capitalism.* New York: Doubleday.

Tsang, E. (1999) "Internationalization as a learning process: Singapore MNCs in China." *Academy of Management Executive*, 13(1): 91–101.

Tsui, A.S. and O'Reilly III, C.A. (1989) "Beyond simple demographic effects: The importance of relational demography in superior-subordinate dyads." *Academy of Management Journal*, 32: 402–424.

Tucker, R. (2002) *Driving Growth Through Innovation: How Leading Firms are Transforming Their Futures*. San Francisco, CA: Berrett–Koehler.

Tuckman, B.W. (1965) "Developmental sequence in small groups." *Psychological Bulletin*, 63(6): 384–399.

Tung, R.L. (1981) "Selection and training of personnel for overseas assignments." *Columbia Journal of World Business*, 16(1): 68–78.

Tung, R.L. and Varma, A. (2008) "Expatriate selection and evaluation." In P.B. Smith, M.F. Peterson, and D.C. Thomas (eds) *Handbook of Cross-cultural Management Research*. Thousand Oaks, CA: Sage: 367–378.

Turel, O. and Zhang, Y. (2010) "Does virtual team composition matter? Trait and problem-solving configuration effects on team performance." *Behavior and Information Technology*, 29: 363–375.

Tushman, M.L. and O'Reilly, C.A. (1996) "Ambidextrous organizations: Managing evolutionary and revolutionary change." *California Management Review*, 38(4): 11.

Tye, K. (1990) *Global Education: School-based Strategies*. Orange, CA: Interdependence Press.

Tye M.G., and Chen P.Y. (2005) "Selection of expatriates: Decision-making models used by HR professionals, *Human Resource Planning*, 28(4): 15–20.

Van der Zee, K. and Brinkmann, U. (2004) "Construct validity evidence for the Intercultural Readiness Check against the Multicultural Personality Questionnaire." *International Journal of Selection and Assessment*, 12(3): 285–290.

Van der Zee, K. and Van Oudenhoven, J.-P. (2000) "The multicultural personality questionnaire: A multidimensional instrument of multicultural effectiveness." *European Journal of Personality*, 14: 291–309.

Van der Zee, K. and Van Oudenhoven, J.-P. (2001) "The multicultural personality questionnaire: Reliability and validity of self- and other ratings of multicultural effectiveness." *Journal of Research in Personality*, 35(3): 278–288.

Van Oudenhoven, J.-P. and Van der Zee, K. (2002) "Predicting multicultural effectiveness of international students: The multicultural personality questionnaire." *International Journal of Intercultural Relations*, 26(6): 679–694.

Van Oudenhoven, J.-P., Mol, S., and Van der Zee, K. (2003) "Study of the adjustment of western expatriates in Taiwan ROC with the multicultural personality questionnaire." *Asian Journal of Social Psychology*, 6: 159–170.

Varma, A., Stroh, L.K., and Schmitt, L.B. (2001) "Women and international assignments: The impact of supervisor-subordinate relationships." *Journal of World Business*, 36(4): 380–388.

Varma, A., Toh, S.M., and Budhwar, P. (2006) "A new perspective on the female expatriate experience: The role of host country national categorization." *Journal of World Business*, 41(2): 112–120.

Vickers, M.R. (2005) "Business ethics and the HR role: Past, present, and future." *Human Resource Planning*, 28(1): 26–32.

Vogel, D. (2005) *The Market for Virtue: The Potential and Limits of Corporate Social Responsibility*. Washington, DC: Brookings Institution Press.

Von Glinow, M.A. (2001) "Future issues in global leadership development." In M.E. Mendenhall, T.M. Kühlmann, and G.K. Stahl (eds) *Developing Global Leaders: Policies, Processes and Innovations*. Westport, CT: Quorum Books: 264–271.

Waldman, D.A. and Galvin, B.M. (2008) "Alternative perspectives of responsible leadership." *Organizational Dynamics*, 37(4): 327–341.

Waldman, D.A. and Siegel, D. (2008) "Defining the socially responsible leader." *The Leadership Quarterly*, 19: 117–131.

Wang, C. and Yang, Y. (2007) "Personality and intention to share knowledge: An empirical study of scientists in an R&D laboratory." *Social Behavior and Personality*, 35 (10): 1427–1436.

Ward, C., Fischer, R., Lam, F.S.Z., and Hall, L. (2009) "The convergent, discriminant and incremental validity of scores on a self-report measure of cultural intelligence." *Educational and Psychological Measurement*, 69(1): 85–105.

Warkentin, M.E., Sayeed, L., and Hightower, R. (1997) "Virtual teams versus face to face teams: An exploratory study of web based conference system." *Decision Sciences,* 14: 29–64.

Weber, M. (1946) *From Max Weber: Essays in Sociology.* New York: Oxford University Press.

Weber, M. (1947) *The Theory of Social and Economic Organization.* Glencoe, IL: Free Press.

Weber, W., Festing, M., Dowling, P.J., and Schuler, R.S. (1998) *Internationales personalmanagement.* Wiesbaden: Gabler Verlag.

Weeks, D. (1992) *Recruiting and Selecting International Managers.* Report number R–998. New York: The Conference Board.

Weick, K. (1996) *Sensemaking in Organizations.* Beverly Hills, CA: Sage.

Weick, K.E. and Quinn R.E. (1999) "Organizational change and development." *Annual Review of Psychology*, 50: 361–386.

Welch, D. (1994) "Determinants of international human resource management approaches and activities: A suggested framework." *Journal of Management Studies*, 31(2): 139–163.

Wellsfry, L.W. (1993) *Global Leadership: A Hermeneutic Perspective on the Transnationalizing of Organizations.* Unpublished dissertation. University of San Francisco.

Welsh, D.H.B., Luthans, F., and Sommer, S.M. (1993) "Managing Russian factory workers: The impact of U.S.-based behavioral and participative techniques." *Academy of Management Journal*, 36(1): 58–80.

Werhane, P.H. (1999) *Moral Imagination and Management Decision Making.* New York/ Oxford: Oxford University Press.

Werhane, P.H. (2008) "Mental models, moral imagination and system thinking in the age of globalization." *Journal of Business Ethics*, 78: 463–474.

Wheatley, M. (2006) *Leadership and the New Science: Discovering Order in a Chaotic World, 3rd edition.* San Francisco, CA: Berrett-Koehler Publishers.

White, K. and Rosamilia, T. (2010) "Developing global leadership: How IBM engages the workforce of a globally integrated enterprise." White paper. IBM Global Business Services.

Whittington, R., Pettigrew, A., Peck, S., Fenton, E., and Conyon, M. (1998) "Change and complementarities in the new competitive landscape: A European panel study, 1992–1996." *Organization Science*, 10(5): 583–600.

Wibbeke, E.S. (2009) *Global Business Leader.* Oxford, UK: Elsevier.

Wilbur, K. (1983) *A Sociable God.* New York: McGraw-Hill.

Wills, S. and Barham, K. (1994) "Being an international manager." *European Management Journal*, 12(1): 49–58.

Wilson, M. (2008) *Developing Future Leaders for High-Growth Indian Companies.* Research report. Greensboro, NC: Center for Creative Leadership.

Wilson, M.S. and Yip, J. (2010) "Grounding leader development: Cultural perspectives." *Industrial and Organizational Psychology*, 3 (2010): 52–55.

Winograd, T. and Flores, F. (1986) *Understanding Computers and Cognition.* Reading, MA: Addison-Wesley.

Wiseman, R.L. and Abe, H. (1984) "Finding and explaining differences: A reply to Gudykunst and Hammer." *International Journal of Intercultural Relations*, 8(1): 11–16.

Wolfensohn, J., O'Reilly, D., Campbell, K., Shui-Bian, C., and Arbour, L. (2003) "In their own words: Leaders speak out." *Harvard International Review*, 25(3): 50–67.

Wood, J.T. (1997) *Communication in Our Lives*, Wadsworth: New York.

Woolley, A.W., Gerbasi, M.E., Chabris, C.F., Kosslyn, S.M., and Hackman, J.R. (2007) "Bringing in the experts: How team composition and work strategy jointly shape analytic effectiveness." *Small Group Research*, 39: 352–371.

World Trade Organization (2011) "Trade liberalization statistics." Last accessed on May 20, 2012. http://www.gatt.org/trastat_e.html.

Xuan, Zhaoguo, Haoxiang Xia, and Yanyan Du (2011) "Adjustment of knowledge-connection structure affects the performance of knowledge transfer." *Expert Systems with Applications*, 38(12): 14935–14944.

Yamazaki, Y. and Kayes, D.C. (2004) "An experiential approach to cross-cultural learning: A review and integration of competencies of successful expatriate adaptation." *Academy of Management Learning and Education*, 3(4): 362–379.

Yeung, A.K. and Ready, D.A. (1995) "Developing leadership capabilities of global corporations: A comparative study in eight nations." *Human Resource Management*, 34(4): 529–547.

Yip, J. and Wilson, M. (2008) *Developing Public Service Leaders in Singapore.* Research report. Greensboro, NC: Center for Creative Leadership

Yip, J. and Wilson, M. (2010) "Learning from experience." In E. Van Velsor, C.D. McCauley, and M.N. Ruderman (eds) *The Center for Creative Leadership Handbook of Leadership Development*, 3rd edition. San Francisco, CA: Jossey-Bass.

Yukl, G. (2002) *Leadership in Organizations*, 5th edition. Upper Saddle River, NJ: Pearson Prentice-Hall.

Yukl, G. (2006) *Leadership in Organizations*, 6th edition. Upper Saddle River, NJ: Pearson Prentice-Hall.

Zaccaro, S.J. (2007) "Trait-based perspectives of leadership." *American Psychologist,* 62: 6–16.

Zaccaro, S.J., Rittman, A.L., and Marks, M.A. (2001). "Team leadership." *The Leadership Quarterly,* 12: 451–483.

Zaccaro, S.J., Wood, G., and Herman, J. (2006) "Developing global and adaptive leaders: HRM strategies within a career-long perspective." In R.J. Burke and C.L. Cooper (eds) *The Human Resources Revolution: Why Putting People First Matters.* London: Routledge.

Zadek, S. (2004) "Path to corporate responsibility." *Harvard Business Review*, 82(12): 36–44.

Zahra, S. and George, G. (2002) "Absorptive capacity: A review and extension." *Academy of Management Review*, 27(2): 185–203.

Zander, U. and Kogut, B. (1995) "Knowledge and the speed of the transfer and imitation of organizational capabilities." *Organization Science*, 6(1): 76–92.

Zhou, W. and Shi, X. (2011) "Culture in groups and teams: A review of three decades of research." *International Journal of Cross-Cultural Management*, 11(1): 5–34.

Zolkos, R. (2002) "Unethical behavior tarnishes image of insurance industry." *Business Insurance*, 36(46): 20E–21E.

Index